Abbreviations

AE	amerikan. Englisch	*American English*
Akk.	Akkusativ	*accusative*
Adj.	Adjektiv	*adjective*
Adv.	Adverb	*adverb*
BE	brit. Englisch	*British English*
dem.	demonstrativ	*demonstrative*
f	feminin	*feminin*
Gen.	Genitiv	*genitive*
indekl.	indeklinabel	*indeclinable*
Komp.	Komparation	*comparition*
Konj.	Konjunktion	*conjunction*
Mod.v.	Modalverb	*modal verb*
m	maskulin	*masculine*
n (german column)	neutrum	*neuter*
n (engl. column)	Nomen	*noun*
P.	Person	*person*
Pl.	Plural	*plural*
Pron.	Pronomen	*pronoun*
Präp.	Präposition	*preposition*
Sg.	Singular	*singular*
v	Verb	*verb*
V/i.	intransitives Verb	*intransitive verb*
V/refl.	reflexives Verb	*reflexive Verb*
V/t.	transitives Verb	*transitive verb*
rzp.	reziprok	*reciprocal*

Pronunciation see p. 419

LANGENSCHEIDT

Basic
German Vocabulary

A Learner's Dictionary

divided into subject categories

with example sentences

Edited by the German as a Foreign Language Department

LANGENSCHEIDT

BERLIN · MUNICH · VIENNA · ZURICH · NEW YORK

Translation: Carol L. & Charles J. James

www.langenscheidt.de

The spelling in **Basic German Vocabulary** corresponds to the
Orthography Reform of 2006.

© 1991 Langenscheidt KG, Berlin and Munich

Contents

Topical Concepts

Who needs a "Basic Vocabulary"?

Any student learning a foreign language must master a certain vocabulary base before he or she can communicate or read in that language. Acquisition of that base vocabulary requires study, often outside of the classroom setting.

Langenscheidt's Basic German Vocabulary is designed to facilitate the acquisition of that core vocabulary in the easiest and most efficient manner possible. It is meant for use by beginning learners with no previous knowledge of the German language, by more advanced students as a review and for test preparation, and by anyone as preparation for pleasure or business travel into a German-speaking country.

Those who have successfully worked through Langenscheidt's Basic German Vocabulary will have the necessary knowledge to function and communicate in all everyday situations in German.

Why a "Basic Vocabulary"?

The German Language, like any other language, is comprised of millions of words, yet 50 % of normal spoken and written texts are comprised of only 66 words. Students rightfully ask, which words do I have to learn in order to carry on an everyday conversation or read a text written for the average German speaker?

The magic answer is usually 2,000 words, i.e., a student who has mastered the basic 2,000 core vocabulary words has learned the most important words used in 80 % of all written and oral communication.

Langenscheidt's "Basic German Vocabulary" contains two times 2,000 words. The core 2,000 words are followed by a second group of the 2,000 next most frequently used words which comprise a further 5 %–10 % of all written and oral communication.

The division of the thematically-organized entries into two groups, "1–2,000" and "2,001–4,000", identifies for the learner those words which should be learned immediately and those which can be reserved for second level learning. Once they have mastered the first 2,000 words, students have the option of increasing their vocabulary over a wide subject range, or concentrating on specific areas of interest, such as law, economics, etc.

Why a bilingual "Basic Vocabulary"?

The use of the target language to teach the language is the norm in most programs today. Usually a new word is explained in simple German and illustrated with practical examples.

The practical teaching situation, however, requires flexibility in using the native language, especially when difficult concepts need to be clarified.

Therefore, many monolingual textbooks have bilingual vocabulary lists or glossaries.

Because it is meant to be used independently by the learner to study and review outside class, a text like the Basic Vocabulary must be 100 % bilingual. It is not meant to, and should not, replace a regular German-English/English-German dictionary where a learner can find many more words and definitions, nor a comprehensive grammar text. The Basic Vocabulary is only meant to serve as a supplement for study and learning.

Why these words?

Langenscheidt's Basic Vocabulary selects the most important words for a student to learn and use. The Basic Vocabulary is based on evaluation of numerous lists of basic German vocabulary published in Germany, Austria, Switzerland and other countries. All the important sources of information on word frequency in written and spoken German were considered. An exact source list would go beyond the purpose of this introduction. For those interested, we mention here the vocabulary statistics of Kaeding, Meier, Ortmann, the Mannheimer Korpus 1 and 2, the Bonner Zeitungskorpus and the minimum vocabulary lists prepared by the Council of Europe, vocabulary for the "Zertifikat Deutsch als Fremdsprache" (Certificate of German as a Foreign Language), the "Deutscher Volkshochschulverband" (German Adult Education Association) and the Goethe Institute. The choice of words was not based only on frequency. Factors such as how familiar and useful a word is in everyday conversation were also considered. Langenscheidt's experience in producing dictionaries and teaching materials also helped. The critical choice of example sentences was made by native speakers on an outside of our regular staff.

How is the "Basic Vocabulary" arranged?

Words and expressions in Langenscheidt's Basic Vocabulary German are arranged by topic, not simply in alphabetical order. Educational research indicates that trying to learn words alphabetically is not effective. Similarities in orthography lead to confusion and spelling errors. Most importantly, words are very difficult to learn without context and topic. Alphabetical arrangement can become an obstacle to correct use in a specific thematic situation. Learning basic words in subject areas is easier and more effective. The contextual relationships among words and the physical proximity of words on the page encourage the development of associations in memory. For all these reasons, we emphasize learning in subject areas.

In addition to the thematic presentation, all entries are presented contextually, i.e., sample sentences accompany each basic word and its pronunciation. The presentation of the basic word in sentences is important because the learner sees the word used correctly. The danger of using the word later in the wrong context will disappear. Example sentences often can be used word-for-word because they are taken from common everyday speech an represent frequently used idiomatic expressions.

In the Workbook to the Basic Vocabulary there are further examples of usage. In each of the sample sentences, care has been taken so that the vocabulary used, as far as possible, does not include any words beyond those found in the basic vocabulary.

"Langenscheidt's Basic German Vocabulary" and "Workbook"

The Workbook accompanies the Basic Vocabulary. It is left up to the learner whether to study only with the Basic Vocabulary or to do further exercices for vocabulary building. For a quick and certain expansion of the vocabulary, we recommend the use of the workbook as well as the text. Systematic work with the two volumes creates a certain confidence in vocabulary building which helps the acquisition of new words.

Although gender information and irregular verb forms are given next to the basic word, the text and Workbook are not meant to replace, but rather supplement, the use of a dictionary and grammar book.

In some cases a word has various meanings which are clarified in the sample sentences.

For example:

Fußball ['fuːsbal] *m, -(e)s, kein Pl.* Fußball ist bei uns die beliebteste Sportart.	**football, soccer** *n* Football is the most popular sport in our country. *(football as a game)*

but

Fußball *m, -(e)s, Fußbälle* Die Fußbälle sind aus Leder.	**football, soccer ball** *n* Footballs are made of leather. *(football as an object)*

Naturally a vocabulary list cannot present all the meanings and uses of a word in all circumstances. For example, there are seldom-used forms of verbs that learners will not find here because they are not necessary for acquiring a basic knowledge of the language. There are also very few technical words included; only the common meanings of words are given.

Frequency of use and usefulness of the word determined inclusion into the Basic Vocabulary.

Likewise, the Basic Vocabulary includes only a handful of the many compound words so common in German. But a solid knowledge of basic vocabulary should enable a learner to understand and build a wider vocabulary of compound words.

How to Work with the "Basic Vocabulary"?

Here are nine suggestions for working with the material:

1. Learn the words in the "1–2,000" group first. Do those in the "2,001–4,000" group later.

2. Take advantage of the arrangement by subject area. Don't work on a page-by-page basis, but try to cover one topic at a time (e.g., "Money"). The words of a subject area contain associations which aid memorization. Use the designations of subject areas as learning aids.

3. Work through the individual categories one by one, first covering those whose topics most appeal to you. Always review each category already covered after working on a new category.

4. Set up your own learning system. Learn the amount of material that best suits you. Read an item (the main word in bold print with its example sentences) and memorize the category the word belongs in. Go through eight to ten words this way. Then cover the left column and repeat aloud the covered words. If you wish, also read aloud the sample sentence. Check your progress by uncovering the left column. Work through your "set" this way. Make a mark in the left margin next to the words you haven't memorized yet and work on just those words. For the final check of each "set", speak and write every word again.

5. Vary your study habits: Cover the right column instead of the left, and work as described in suggestion 4 above. Only learn the example sentences that help fix the meaning of the words in your memory.

6. You can also take an individual word that you have had to look up in an alphabetical list, put it in a category, and learn it in a meaningful context.

7. Every day learn a specific amount, taking breaks in between each session. In a few weeks you will have systematically learned a core vocabulary; the actual amount of vocabulary items depends on you. Don't forget to repeat and test yourself at regular intervals.

8. Langenscheidt's Basic Vocabulary German is independent of specific textbooks. It is suitable, however, for reviewing the vocabulary learned in a course, in order to: a) prepare the appropriate vocabulary before free communication exercises or going through certain reading texts; b) work on vocabulary areas after working through a specific text whose various parts include this word field; c) develop and expand from a single word to a complete vocabulary category.

You can also arrange the topics and word families according to the material you have just learned in the chapters of the textbook.

9. Langenscheidt's Basic Vocabulary German and its Workbook have a very practical format. You can learn anywhere, whenever you have time. For example, why not review the chapter "Traffic" in the bus going to or from work? Good luck and have fun!

Notes:

For regular nouns, the pronunciation, the gender, the genitive and nominative plural forms are provided after the basic word. Only irregular forms of the plural are spelled out.
For example:
Ball [bal] m, -s, Bälle

For verbs, three forms: present infinitive, first person singular of the imperfect, and third person singular with **haben** or **sein,** are presented. After that come the various possibilities for using it in transitive or reflexive forms. There are also examples of common prepositions used with it.
For example:

anmelden [ˈanmɛld(ə)n] *V/t., refl., + Präp.* (für) meldete an, hat angemeldet	**register, sign up for** *v*
Das Auto wird morgen angemeldet.	The car will be registered tomorrow.
Ich habe mich für die Prüfung angemeldet.	I've signed up for the test.

Not all the possibilities of using a verb are included, just the most frequent.
( ) in the phonetic script indicate that particular pronunciation is optional.
For adjectives, the comparative forms are given only if they vary from
normal formation.
For example:

gut [guːt] *Adj.*, besser, am besten	**good, well**
Er ist ein guter Handwerker.	He is good with his hands.
Es geht mir gut.	I'm doing well.

If a main word appears twice, the example meanings and/or the grammatical differences will clarify matters.
For example:

abgeben [ˈapgeːb(ə)n] *V/t., + Präp.* (an, bei, in) gab ab, hat abgegeben	**turn in, hand in** *v*
Bitte geben Sie den Brief an der Rezeption ab.	Please hand in the letter at the reception desk.
abgeben *V/t., + Präp.* (von)	**give** *v*
Kannst du mir von den Broten eines abgeben?	Can you give me one of the sandwiches/loaves of bread?

Since most adjectives in German can be used as adverbs, no distinction is
made in English between adjectives and adverbs, even for those words
that are "pure" adverbs.

wirklich [ˈvirklɪç] *Adj., keine Komp.*	**real, true**
Ein wirklicher Freund hätte dir in dieser Situation geholfen.	A real friend would have helped you in this situation.
Hast du wirklich geglaubt, dass sie dir alles erzählt hat?	Did you really believe that she told you everything?

1 Der Mensch

1 The Human Being

1.1 Körper

1-2000

1.1 The Body

Arm [arm] *m*, -(e)s, -e
Ich habe beim Sport meinen rechten Arm verletzt.

arm *n*
I hurt my right arm while exercising.

Auge ['augə] *n*, -s, -n
Meine Schwester und ich haben braune Augen.

eye *n*
My sister and I have brown eyes.

Bauch [baux] *m*, -(e)s, Bäuche
Er schläft am liebsten auf dem Bauch.

stomach *n*
He prefers to sleep on his stomach.

Bein [bain] *n*, -(e)s, -e
Kannst du lange auf einem Bein stehen?

leg *n*
Can you stand on one leg for a long time?

Blut [blu:t] *n*, -(e)s, *kein Pl.*
Ich mag kein Blut sehen.

blood *n*
I can't stand the sight of blood.

Brust [brust] *f*, -, *kein Pl.*
Reiben Sie Brust und Rücken mit dieser Salbe ein!

chest *n*
Rub this salve on your chest and back.

Brust *f*, -, Brüste
Das Baby trinkt Milch an der Brust der Mutter.

breast *n*
The baby drinks milk from its mother's breast.

Finger ['fiŋə*] *m*, -s, -
Sie trägt an jedem Finger einen Ring.

finger *n*
She wears a ring on each finger.

Fuß [fu:s] *m*, -es, Füße
Nach dem Spaziergang hatte sie kalte Füße.

foot *n*
After the walk her feet were cold.

Gesicht [gə'ziçt] *n*, -(e)s, -er
Es war dunkel. Ich konnte ihr Gesicht nicht sehen.

face *n*
It was dark. I couldn't see her face.

Haar [haːˀ] *n*, -(e)s, -e
Bald hat er keine Haare mehr auf dem Kopf.

hair *n*
Soon he won't have any more hair on his head.

Hals [hals] *m*, -es, Hälse
Sie hat einen langen Hals.

neck *n*
She has a long neck.

Hand [hant] *f*, -, Hände
Sie gingen Hand in Hand spazieren.

hand *n*
They were walking hand in hand.

Haut [haut] *f*, -, *kein Pl.*
Seine Haut ist immer ganz rot.

skin *n*
His skin is always very red.

Herz [hɛrts] *n*, -ens, -en
Mein Herz schlägt manchmal unregelmäßig.

heart *n*
Sometimes my heartbeat is irregular.

Knie [kniː] *n*, -s, -
Ich habe den ganzen Tag auf den Knien am Boden gearbeitet.

knee *n*
I spent all day on my knees working on the floor.

Kopf [kɔpf] *m*, -(e)s, Köpfe
Hatte er einen Hut auf dem Kopf?

head *n*
Did he have a hat on his head?

Körper [ˈkœrpəˀ] *m*, -s, -
Sie hat einen durchtrainierten Körper.

body *n*
Her body is in good shape.

Mund [munt] *m*, -es, Münder
Bitte halte den Mund und sei still!

mouth *n*
Please shut your mouth and keep quiet!

Nase [ˈnaːzə] *f*, -, -n
Deine Nase ist rot. Hast du Schnupfen?

nose *n*
Your nose is red. Do you have a cold?

Ohr [oːˀ] *n*, -(e)s, -en
Sie hält sich die Ohren zu.

ear *n*
She covers her ears (so she doesn't have to listen).

Rücken [ˈryk(ə)n] *m*, -s, -
Er hat einen schiefen Rücken.

back *n*
He has a crooked back.

schwach [ʃvax] *Adj.*, schwächer, am schwächsten
Nach der Krankheit fühlte sie sich noch lange schwach.

weak

After the illness she felt weak for a long time.

stark [ʃtark] *Adj.,* stärker, am stärksten
Für diese Arbeit bist du nicht stark genug.

strong
You're not strong enough for this work.

Zahn [tsaːn] *m,* -(e)s, Zähne
Meine Zähne sind alle gesund.

tooth *n*
All my teeth are healthy.

Zunge [ˈtsuŋə] *f,* -, -n
Der Arzt sagt: „Zeigen Sie mir bitte Ihre Zunge!"

tongue *n*
The doctor says, "Please show me your tongue!"

Atem [ˈaːtəm] *m,* -s, *kein Pl.*
Sein Atem geht schwer und unregelmäßig.

breathing, breath *n*
His breathing is difficult and irregular.

atmen [ˈaːtmən] *V/i.,* atmete, hat geatmet
Sie atmet ganz leise. Sicher ist sie eingeschlafen.

breathe *v*
She's breathing very softly. She must have fallen asleep.

Backe [ˈbakə] *f,* -, -n
Unser Kind hat dicke, rote Backen.

cheek *n*
Our child has chubby red cheeks.

Ellbogen [ˈɛlboːg(ə)n] *m,* -s, -
Weil er keine Hand frei hatte, öffnete er die Tür mit dem Ellbogen.

elbow *n*
He didn't have a free hand so he opened the door with his elbow.

Faust [faust] *f,* -, Fäuste
Sie schlug mit der Faust auf den Tisch.

fist *n*
She banged on the table with her fist.

Gehirn [gəˈhirn] *n,* -s, -e
Hoffentlich ist das Gehirn nicht verletzt.

brain *n*
We hope the brain is not injured.

Gelenk [gəˈlɛŋk] *n,* -(e)s, -e
Ich kann mein Handgelenk nicht bewegen.

joint *n*
I can't move my wrist.

Handgelenk

wrist *n*

Fußgelenk [Fußknöchel]

ankle *n*

Kinn [kin] *n,* -(e)s-s, *kein Pl.*
Sie hat ein spitzes Kinn.

chin *n*
She has a pointed chin.

Knochen [ˈknɔx(ə)n] *m,* -s, -
Der Knochen ist gebrochen.

bone *n*
The bone is broken.

Leib [laip] *m*, -(e)s, -er
Sie hat am ganzen Leib rote Flecken.

body *n*
She has red spots all over her body.

(Augen-)Lid [li:t] *n*, -(e)s, -er
Das rechte Augenlid tut weh.

(eye)lid *n*
The right eyelid is sore.

Lippe ['lipə] *f*, -, -n
Komm aus dem Wasser! Du hast schon ganz blaue Lippen.

lip *n*
Get out of the water! Your lips are all blue.

Lunge ['luŋə] *f*, -, -n
Hör auf mit dem Rauchen! Deine Lunge ist bestimmt schon ganz schwarz.

lung *n*
Stop smoking! Your lungs must be all black by now.

Magen ['ma:g(ə)n] *m*, -s, Mägen
Ich kann nicht viel essen. Mein Magen ist nicht in Ordnung.

stomach *n*
I can't eat much. I'm having problems with my stomach.

Muskel ['musk(ə)l] *m*, -s, -n
Er hat starke Muskeln.

muscle *n*
He has strong muscles.

Nerv [nɛrf] *m*, -s, -en
Gott sei Dank hat der Zahnarzt beim Bohren keinen Nerv getroffen.

nerve *n*
Thank God the dentist didn't hit a nerve while he was drilling!

Schulter ['ʃultə*] *f*, -, -n
Das Kind saß auf ihren Schultern.

shoulder *n*
The child sat on her shoulders.

Schweiß [ʃvais] *m*, -es, *kein Pl.*
Der Schweiß lief ihr von der Stirn.

sweat *n*
Her face was dripping with sweat.

Stirn [ʃtirn] *f*, -, -en
Das Kind hat kein Fieber. Die Stirn ist ganz kalt.

forehead *n*
The child doesn't have a fever. His forehead is cool.

Zeh [tse:] *m*, -s, -en

toe *n*

Zehe ['tse:ə] *f*, -, -n
Ich bin mit den Zehen gegen ein Tischbein gestoßen.

toe *n*
I stubbed my toes on a table leg.

1.2 Aussehen 1-2000

1.2 Appearance

aussehen ['ausze:(ə)n] *V/i.*, +
Präp. (wie), sah aus, hat ausge-
sehen
Sie ist erst 17, aber sie sieht aus
wie 20.

appear, look (like) *v*

She is only 17, but she looks (like)
20.

dick [dik] *Adj.*
Findest du mich zu dick?

fat, thick
Do you think I'm too fat?

dünn [dyn] *Adj.*
Warum bist du denn so dünn?

thin
Why are you so thin anyway?

groß [gro:s] *Adj.*, größer, am
größten
Ich bin größer als mein Mann.

big, large, great, tall

I am taller than my husband.

hübsch [hypʃ] *Adj.*, -er, am -esten
Das Kleid sieht hübsch aus.

pretty
The dress looks pretty.

klein [klain] *Adj.*
Ich habe sehr kleine Füße.

small, little
I have very small feet.

schlank [ʃlaŋk] *Adj.*
Er ist groß und schlank.

slender
He is tall and slender.

schön [ʃø:n] *Adj.*
Sie hat schöne Augen.

beautiful
She has beautiful eyes.

2001-4000

abnehmen ['apne:mən] *V/i.*,
nahm ab, hat abgenommen
Er hat über 10 Pfund abgenommen.

take off, lose weight *v*

He lost over 10 pounds.

Bart [ba:ə*t] *m*, -(e)s, Bärte
Dein Bart muss geschnitten
werden.

beard *n*
Your beard has to be trimmed.

blass [blas] *Adj.,* -er, am -esten
Er erschrak sich und wurde blass.

pale
He was frightened and turned pale.

blond [blɔnt] *Adj.,* -er, am -esten
Als Kind war ich blond.

blond
When I was a child I was blond.

Brille [ˈbrilə] *f,* -, -n
Die Brille brauche ich nur zum Lesen.

(pair of) glasses *n*
I only need my glasses for reading.

elegant [eleˈgant] *Adj.,* -er, am -esten
Das Kleid ist zu elegant für diese Party. Zieh lieber eine Jeans an!

elegant
The dress is too elegant for this party. Put jeans on instead.

Figur [fiˈguːɐ*] *f,* -, *kein Pl.*
Sie hat eine tolle Figur.

figure *n*
She has a great figure.

Frisur [friˈzuːɐ*] *f,* -, -en
Die neue Frisur steht dir gut.

hair style *n*
Your new hair style looks good.

hässlich [ˈhɛslɪç] *Adj.*
Er hat ein hässliches Gesicht.

ugly
He has an ugly face.

Locke [ˈlɔkə] *f,* -, -n
○ Hat er Locken?
□ Nein, seine Haare sind ganz glatt.

curl *n*
○ Does he have curly hair [curls]?
□ No, his hair is straight.

mager [ˈmaːgɐ*] *Adj.*
Seit ihrer schweren Krankheit ist sie sehr mager.

thin, gaunt, skinny
Since her severe illness she has become very thin.

zart [tsaːɐ*t] *Adj.,* -er, am -esten
Sie ist ein zartes Kind.
Sie hat eine zarte Haut.

delicate, tender
She is a delicate child.
She has soft skin.

zunehmen [ˈtsuːneːmən] *V/i.,*
nahm zu, hat zugenommen
○ Hast du zugenommen?
□ Ja, drei Kilo.

put on, gain weight *v*
○ "Have you put on weight?"
□ Yes, three kilos.

1.3 Geist und Verstand   1-2000

1.3 Mind and Reason

aufpassen ['aufpas(ə)n] *V/i., + Präp.* (auf), passte auf, hat aufgepasst
Pass auf! Von links kommt ein Auto.

look out (for) *v*

Look out! A car is coming from the left.

bewusst [bə'vust] *Adj.,* -er, am -esten
Es ist ihm bewusst, dass er für seinen Fehler die Verantwortung übernehmen muss.

aware

He is aware of the fact that he has to take responsibility for his mistake.

denken ['dɛŋk(ə)n] *V/i., + Präp.* (über, von, an), dachte, hat gedacht
Bei dieser Arbeit muss man nicht viel denken.
Denken Sie an den Termin um 20.00 Uhr?
Was denkst du über den Vorschlag?

think *v*

For this work you don't have to think much.
You will think of the appointment at 8:00 p.m., won't you?
What do you think of the suggestion?

erfahren [ɛə*'fa:r(ə)n] *V/i., + Präp.* (von, über), erfuhr, hat erfahren
Hast du von Eva etwas Neues erfahren?

hear *v*

Have you heard anything new from Eva?

Erfahrung [ɛə*'fa:ruŋ] *f,* -, -en
Er ist ein guter Arzt. Er hat viel Erfahrung.

experience *n*
He is a good physician. He has a lot of experience.

erinnern [ɛə*'inə*n] *V/t., refl., + Präp.* (an), erinnerte, hat erinnert
Erinnere Eva bitte an ihr Versprechen!
Kannst du dich an ihn erinnern?

remind, remember *v*

Please remind Eva of her promise.
Do you remember him?

Erinnerung [ɛə*'inərʊŋ] *f,* -, -en
Sie hatte gute Erinnerungen an ihre Kindheit.

memory *n*
She had good memories of her childhood.

---

erkennen [ɛə*'kɛnən] *V/t.,* + *Präp.* (an), erkannte, hat erkannt
Er trägt jetzt einen Bart, deshalb habe ich ihn nicht sofort erkannt.

recognize *v*
He has a beard now; that's why I didn't recognize him immediately.

Gedächtnis [gə'dɛçtnis] *n,* -ses, *kein Pl.*
Ich habe ein schlechtes Gedächtnis.

memory *n*
I have a poor memory.

Gedanke [gə'daŋkə] *m,* -ns, -n
Dieser Gedanke gefällt mir.

thought, idea *n*
I like this idea.

Geist [gaist] *m,* -es, *kein Pl.*
Sie ist schon über 90 Jahre alt, aber ihr Geist ist noch jung.

mind, spirit, soul *n*
She is over 90 years old, but her mind is still young.

---

intelligent [intɛli'gɛnt] *Adj.,* -er, am -esten
Sie ist intelligent, aber leider nicht zuverlässig.

intelligent

She is intelligent, but unfortunately not reliable.

Interesse [intə'rɛsə] *n,* -s, -n
An Sport habe ich kein Interesse.

interest *n*
I have no interest in sports.

---

interessieren [intərɛ'siːr(ə)n] *V/t., i., refl.,* + *Präp.* (für, an), interessierte, hat interessiert
Kunst interessiert ihn nicht.
Er ist an Kunst nicht interessiert.
Ich habe ihn für Kunst nicht interessieren können.
Er interessiert sich nicht für alte Bilder.

interest *v*

Art does not interest him.
He is not interested in art.
I have not been able to interest him in art.
He is not interested in old pictures.

---

kennen ['kɛnən] *V/t.,* kannte, hat gekannt
Die Straße kenne ich gut.
Ich kenne ihn nicht gut.

know *v*

I know the street well.
I do not know him well.

Kenntnis ['kɛntnis] *f,* -, -se
Er hat sehr gute Kenntnisse in Mathematik und Physik.

knowledge *n*
His knowledge of mathematics and physics is excellent.

klug [klu:k] *Adj.*, klüger, am klügsten
Wir haben alle viel getrunken. Es ist klüger, ein Taxi zu nehmen.

smart clever, intelligent, wise, sensible
We all had a lot to drink. It would be wiser to take a taxi.

können ['kœnən] *V/t., Mod. V.*
Er kann kein Französisch.
Das kann er auch nicht erklären, bitte frage jemand anderen.

can, could, be able *vm* **know** *v*
He doesn't know French.
He cannot explain that either; please ask someone else.

merken ['mɛrk(ə)n] *V/t., + Präp.* (an, von), *refl.*, merkte, hat gemerkt
Ich merke schon, dass sich die Zeiten ändern.
Sie kann sich keine Zahlen merken.

note, remember, retain, notice *v*
I have noticed that the times are changing.
She cannot retain numbers.

missverstehen ['misfɛə*ʃte:(ə)n] *V/t.* missverstand, hat missverstanden
Das habe ich nicht gesagt, da bin ich missverstanden worden.

misunderstand *v*
I didn't say that; I must have been misunderstood.

Missverständnis ['misfɛə*ʃtentnis] *n*, -ses, -se
So habe ich das nicht gesagt, das ist ein Missverständnis.

misunderstanding *n*
I didn't say it like that; that is a misunderstanding.

nachdenken ['naːxdɛŋk(ə)n] *V/i.*, + *Präp.* (über), dachte nach, hat nachgedacht
Hast du über meinen Vorschlag nachgedacht?

think about *v*

Have you thought about my suggestion?

vergessen [fɛə*'gɛs(ə)n] *V/t.*, vergaß, hat vergessen
Ich habe meinen Schirm im Hotel vergessen.
Entschuldigung, ich habe Ihren Namen vergessen.

forget *v*
I forgot my umbrella at the hotel.

Excuse me, I've forgotten your name.

Vernunft [fɛə*'nunft] *f*, -, *kein Pl.*
Das ist gegen jede Vernunft.

reason, common sense *n*
That violates common sense.

vernünftig [fɛə*'nynftiç°] *Adj.* | **reasonable, sensible**
Man kann gut mit ihr reden. Sie ist sehr vernünftig. | She is good to talk to. She is a very sensible person.

Verstand [fɛə*'ʃtant] *m, -es, kein Pl.* | **mind** *n*
Hast du den Verstand verloren? | Have you lost your mind?

verstehen [fɛə*'ʃteː(ə)n] *V/t., i., + Präp.* (von), *refl.* verstand, hat verstanden | **understand** *v*
Am Telefon konnte ich ihn nicht richtig verstehen. | I could not understand him very well on the telephone.
Ich verstehe nicht, warum sie das macht. | I don't understand why she does that.
Verstehst du diesen Satz? | Do you understand this sentence?
Er versteht etwas vom Kochen. | He knows something about cooking.
Wir verstehen uns gut. | We get along well.

vorstellen ['foːə*ʃtɛl(ə)n] *V/i., refl.,* stellte vor, hat vorgestellt | **imagine, picture** *v*
Ich kann mir vorstellen, dass das klappt. | I can imagine that it will work out.

2001-4000

begreifen [bə'graif(ə)n] *V/t.,* begriff, hat begriffen | **understand, comprehend,** *v*
Diese Frage begreife ich nicht. | I don't understand this question.
Jetzt kann ich begreifen, warum er keine Lust hatte. | Now I can understand why he wasn't interested.

dumm [dum] *Adj.,* dümmer, am dümmsten | **dumb, stupid**
Erzähl nicht so dumme Witze! | Don't tell such stupid jokes.

Einfall ['ainfal] *m, -s,* Einfälle | **notion, idea** *n*
Nachts schwimmen gehen – was für ein verrückter Einfall. | Going swimming at night? What a crazy idea!

einsehen ['ainzeː(ə)n] *V/t.,* sah ein, hat eingesehen | **see, realize** *v*
Ich glaube, er hat seinen Fehler jetzt eingesehen. | I think he realized his mistake.

erfassen [εə*'fas(ə)n] *V/t.*, erfasste, hat erfasst
Bevor jemand die Situation erfasste, brannte das ganze Haus.

realize *v*
Before anyone realized what was going on, the whole house was on fire.

erfinden [εə*'find(ə)n] *V/t.*, erfand, hat erfunden
Die Geschichte hat sie erfunden.
Diese technische Lösung habe ich selbst erfunden.

invent, make up *v*

She made up the story.
I invented this technical solution myself.

Erfindung [εə*'finduŋ] *f*, -, -en
Die Erfindung war gut, aber kein Industriebetrieb hatte daran Interesse.

invention *n*
It was a good invention, but industry wasn't interested in it.

Erkenntnis [εə*'kεntnis] *f*, -, -se
Es wurden neue Erkenntnisse über die Ursache der Krankheit gewonnen.

information, *(research)* **data** *n*
New data on the cause of the disease have been collected.

gescheit [gə'ʃait] *Adj.*, -er, am -esten
Bevor wir anfangen, müssen wir einen gescheiten Plan machen.

intelligent, clever

Before we begin, we have to formulate an intelligent plan.

geschickt [gə'ʃikt] *Adj.*, -er, am -esten
Sie arbeitet sehr geschickt.

skillful, deft

She works very skillfully.

gewandt [gə'vant] *Adj.*, -er, am -esten
Sie ist sprachlich sehr gewandt.

nimble, skillful, skilled

She is very articulate.

Idee [i'de:] *f*, -, -n
Hast du eine Idee, was wir ihr schenken können?

idea *n*
Do you have any idea what gift we could give her?

Phantasie [fanta'zi:] *f*, -, *kein Pl.*
Den Architekten fehlt manchmal ein bisschen praktische Phantasie.

fantasy, imagination *n*
Sometimes architects have little practical imagination.

überlegen [y:bə*'leg(ə)n] *V/t.*, *refl.*, überlegte, hat überlegt
Hast du dir überlegt, ob du das Angebot annimmst?

consider *v*

Have you considered whether you are going to accept the offer?

verrückt [fɛə*'rykt] *Adj.*, -er, am -esten
Er ist ein verrückter Junge, aber ich mag ihn.

crazy
He is a crazy boy, but I like him.

Vorstellung ['foːə*ʃtɛluŋ] *f,* -, -en
Ich habe noch keine klare Vorstellung, wie man das Problem lösen könnte.

idea *n*
I still don't have a clear idea how we can solve the problem.

---

wahnsinnig ['vaːnziniçº] *Adj.*
Dieser Lärm macht mich wahnsinnig.

insane, crazy
This noise is driving me crazy.

---

weise ['vaizə] *Adj.*, -er, am -esten
Das war eine weise Entscheidung.

wise
That was a wise decision.

1.4 Charakter | 1-2000

1.4 Character

---

anständig ['anʃtɛndiçº] *Adj.*
Bitte benimm dich anständig!

respectable, well behaved
Please behave yourself!

---

bescheiden [bə'ʃaid(ə)n] *Adj.*
Obwohl sie reich sind, leben sie sehr bescheiden.

modest
Although they are rich, they live very modestly.

Charakter [ka'raktə*] *m,* -s, -e
Sei vorsichtig, er hat einen schlechten Charakter.

character, personality *n*
Be careful; he has poor character.

---

ehrlich ['eːə*liç] *Adj.*
Ich sage es Ihnen ganz ehrlich: Ihr Kind ist sehr krank.

honest
I'll be quite honest with you; your child is very ill.

---

fleißig ['flaisiçº] *Adj.*
Er ist ein fleißiger Arbeiter.

hard-working
He is a hard-working employee.

Geduld [gə'dult] *f,* -, *kein Pl.*
Herr Kurz kommt gleich. Bitte haben Sie etwas Geduld!

patience *n*
Mr. Kurz is coming right away. Please be patient.

geduldig [gə'duldiç] *Adj.*
Sie wartete geduldig auf die nächste Straßenbahn.

patient
She waited patiently for the next street car/tram.

gerecht [gə'rɛçt] *Adj.*, -er, am -esten
Sie ist eine gerechte Lehrerin.

fair
She is a fair teacher.

nett [nɛt] *Adj.*, -er, am -esten
Sie ist nett und freundlich.

nice
She is nice and friendly.

neugierig ['nɔigiːriç] *Adj.*
Unser Nachbar ist sehr neugierig.

curious, nosy
Our neighbor is very curious.

sparsam ['ʃpaː*zaːm] *Adj.*
Sie leben sehr sparsam und sind bescheiden.

frugal, economical
They live very frugally and are modest.

streng [ʃtrɛŋ] *Adj.*
Sie ist eine ziemlich strenge Chefin.

exacting, demanding
She is a rather demanding boss.

zuverlässig ['tsuːfɛə*lɛsiç] *Adj.*
Sie ist zuverlässig und immer pünktlich.

reliable
She is reliable and always on time.

2001-4000

Eigenschaft ['aig(ə)nʃaft] *f,* -, -en
○ Sie ist faul, dumm und unfreundlich.
□ Hat sie denn gar keine guten Eigenschaften?

quality, feature *n*
○ She is lazy, dumb, and unfriendly.
□ Doesn't she have any good qualities?

Einbildung ['ainbilduŋ] *f,* -, -en
Das gibt es nur in deiner Einbildung.

imagination *n*
That's only in your imagination.

eingebildet ['aingəbildət] *Adj.*
Sie ist eingebildet und auch noch dumm.

conceited
She is conceited and dumb, too.

ernst [ɛrnst] *Adj.*, -er, am -esten
Du bist in letzter Zeit so ernst. Hast du Probleme?

serious
You've been so serious lately. Do you have problems?

fair [fɛ:ə*] *Adj.*
Das war ein faires Spiel.

fair, honest
That was a fair game.

faul [faul] *Adj.*
Wenn du nicht so faul wärst, könntest du mehr Geld verdienen.

lazy
If you weren't so lazy, you could make more money.

großzügig ['gro:stsy:giç°] *Adj.*
Sie hat zum Geburtstag ein Auto bekommen. Ihre Eltern sind sehr großzügig.

generous
She got a car for her birthday. Her parents are very generous.

humorvoll [hu'mo:ə*fɔl] *Adj.*

Er ist ein humorvoller Mensch.

with a sense of humor, humorous
He is somebody with a good sense of humor.

Laune ['launə] *f, -, -n*
Morgens hat sie immer schlechte Laune.

mood *n*
In the morning she is always in a bad mood.

leichtsinnig ['laiçtziniç°] *Adj.*
Ich finde, dass du sehr leichtsinnig fährst.

careless
I think you drive very carelessly.

Mut [mu:t] *m, -(e)s, kein Pl.*
Sie hat dem Chef ihre Meinung gesagt. Sie hat wirklich Mut.

courage *n*
She told the boss off. She is really brave.

nervös [nɛr'vø:s] *Adj., -er, am -esten*
Dieser Lärm hier macht mich ganz nervös.

nervous

The noise here really makes me nervous.

Neugier ['nɔigi:ə*] *f, -, kein Pl.*
Warum willst du das wissen? Deine Neugier ist wirklich schlimm.

curiosity *n*
Why do you want to know about that? Your curiosity is really a problem.

ordentlich ['ɔrd(ə)ntliç] *Adj.*
Petras Büro ist immer aufgeräumt. Sie ist sehr ordentlich.

neat, orderly
Petra's office is always neat. She is very orderly.

schüchtern ['ʃyçtə*n] *Adj.*
○ Hat dein Bruder immer noch keine Freundin?
□ Nein, er ist sehr schüchtern.

shy, timid
○ Doesn't your brother have a girlfriend yet?
□ No. He is very shy.

selbstständig [ˈzɛlpʃtɛndiç] *Adj.*
Ich muss seine Arbeit nicht kontrollieren. Er ist absolut selbstständig.

independent
I don't have to check his work. He is absolutely independent.

Sorgfalt [ˈzɔrkfalt] *f, -, kein Pl.*

Bei dieser Arbeit ist Sorgfalt sehr wichtig.

attentiveness, care, attention to detail *n*
This job requires great care.

sorgfältig [ˈzɔrkfɛltiçº] *Adj.*
Korrigieren erfordert sehr sorgfältiges Lesen.

careful, thorough
Correcting requires very careful reading.

stolz [ʃtɔlts] *Adj., -er, am -esten*
Er ist stolz auf seine Erfolge.

proud
He is very proud of his success.

verlegen [fɛəˈleːg(ə)n] *Adj.*
Dein Lob macht mich verlegen.

embarrassed
Your praise embarrasses me.

1.5 Positive und neutrale Gefühle | 1-2000

1.5 Pleasant and Neutral Emotions

angenehm [ˈangəneːm] *Adj.*
Ist die Wassertemperatur angenehm?

pleasant, comfortable
Is the water temperature comfortable?

dankbar [ˈdaŋkbaː*] *Adj.*
Wir sind Ihnen für die Hilfe sehr dankbar.

grateful
We're very grateful for your help.

empfinden [ɛmˈpfind(ə)n] *V/t.,*
empfand, hat empfunden
Wie empfindest du diese starke Kälte?

react, feel about *v*

How do you feel about this extreme cold?

erleichtert [ɛəˈlaiçtə*t] *Adj.*
Ich bin erleichtert, dass es ihr besser geht.

relieved
I'm relieved that she is feeling better.

Freude [ˈfrɔidə] *f, -, -n*
Mit deinem Geschenk hast du ihm eine große Freude gemacht.

happiness, pleasure *n*
Your gift gave him great pleasure.

freuen [ˈfrɔi(ə)n] *V/refl. + Präp.* (an, auf, über, wegen, mit), freute, hat gefreut.
Ich freue mich auf das Wochenende.

look forward to, be happy about v
I'm looking forward to the weekend.

---

froh [froː] *Adj.*
Ich bin froh, dass es dir gut geht.

happy, glad
I'm happy that you're doing well.

---

fühlen [ˈfyːl(ə)n] *V/t., refl.,* fühlte, hat gefühlt
Im Bein fühle ich keinen Schmerz.
Ich fühle mich ausgezeichnet.

feel v
I feel no pain in my leg.
I feel excellent.

---

gemütlich [gəˈmyːtliç] *Adj.*
Kennen Sie hier im Ort einen gemütlichen Gasthof?

nice, pleasant, cozy
Do you know a nice place to eat around here?

---

genießen [gəˈniːs(ə)n] *V/t.,* genoss, hat genossen
Ich habe meinen Urlaub genossen.

enjoy v

I enjoyed my vacation.

---

gern(e) [ˈgɛə*n(ə)] *Adj.,* lieber, am liebsten
Stehst du gern(e) früh auf?

gladly; like to v

Do you like to get up early?

---

glücklich [ˈglykliç] *Adj.*
Er hatte eine glückliche Kindheit.

happy
He had a happy childhood.

---

hoffen [ˈhɔf(ə)n] *V/i., + Präp.* (auf), hoffte, hat gehofft
Wir hoffen seit Tagen auf besseres Wetter.

hope (for) v

For days we've been hoping for better weather.

Hoffnung [ˈhɔfnuŋ] *f,* -, en
Ich habe große Hoffnung, dass ich nächste Woche aus dem Krankenhaus entlassen werde.

hope n
I have great hopes that I'll be discharged from the hospital next week.

---

lachen [ˈlax(ə)n] *V/i., + Präp.* (über), lachte, hat gelacht
Über Witze kann ich nicht lachen.

laugh (at) v

I can't laugh at jokes.

---

lächeln [ˈlɛçəln] *V/i., + Präp.* (über), lächelte, hat gelächelt
Sie gab ihm die Hand und lächelte freundlich.

smile v

She shook his hand and smiled.

lieb [li:p] *Adj.*
Sie hat mir einen lieben Brief geschrieben.
Der Hund ist lieb, er beißt nicht.
Liebe Frau Kurz, ... (*Anrede in einem Brief*).

dear, nice, lovely
She wrote me a nice letter.
The dog is nice; he won't bite.
Dear Ms. Kurz, ... (*greeting in a letter*)

Liebe ['li:bə] *f, -, kein Pl.*
Sie haben aus Liebe geheiratet.

love *n*
They married for love.

---

lieben ['li:b(ə)n] *V/t.,* liebte, hat geliebt
Ich liebe dich!

love *v*

I love you!

Lust [lust] *f, -, kein Pl.*
Ich habe Lust auf Eis.

interest, desire, inclination *n*
I want some ice cream.

Stimmung ['ʃtimuŋ] *f, -, -en*
Die Stimmung auf der Feier war prima.

mood, atmosphere *n*
The atmosphere at the celebration was great.

2001-4000

erfreut [ɛə*'frɔit] *Adj.,* -er, am -esten
Ich bin erfreut, Sie wieder zu sehen.

pleased

I'm pleased to see you again.

Erleichterung [ɛə*'laiçtəruŋ] *f, -, -en*
Die gute Nachricht hörten wir mit großer Erleichterung.

relief *n*

We heard the good news with great relief.

---

erstaunt [ɛə*'ʃtaunt] *Adj.,* -er, am -esten
Ich bin erstaunt, dass das Restaurant so voll ist.

amazed, astonished

I'm amazed that the restaurant is so crowded.

---

fröhlich ['frø:liç] *Adj.*
Sven ist meistens fröhlich und hat gute Laune.

happy, cheerful
Sven is happy and in a good mood most of the time.

Gefühl [gə'fy:l] *n, -(e)s -e*
Hoffentlich ist nichts passiert. Ich habe so ein komisches Gefühl.

feeling *n*
I hope nothing happened. I have a funny feeling.

Glück [glyk] *n, -(e)s, kein Pl.*
Sie hat in ihrem Leben viel Glück gehabt.

luck, good fortune *n*
She has had a lot of good luck in her life.

---

heiter ['haitə*] *Adj.*
Dieser Film ist mir zu traurig. Wollen wir nicht lieber einen heiteren sehen?

light-hearted
This movie is too sad. Wouldn't we rather see something more light-hearted?

---

sehnen ['ze:nən] *V/refl., + Präp.* (nach), sehnte, hat gesehnt
Ich sehne mich danach, euch endlich wieder zu sehen.

long for, look forward to (very much) *v*
I'm really looking forward to seeing you again.

Spaß [ʃpa:s] *m, -es, Späße*
Diese Arbeit macht mir keinen Spaß.

fun *n*
This work is no fun for me.

---

staunen ['ʃtaunən] *V/i., + Präp.* (über), staunte, hat gestaunt
Alle staunen über den niedrigen Benzinverbrauch meines Autos.

be astonished, be surprised *v*

Everyone is surprised how little gas (*BE:* petrol) my car needs.

---

verliebt [fɛə*'li:pt] *Adj., -er, am -esten*
Er ist in Susi verliebt.

in love with

He is in love with Susi.

---

zärtlich ['tsɛːrtliç] *Adj.*
Sie streichelte zärtlich ihre Katze.

tender
She petted her cat tenderly.

---

zufrieden [tsu'fri:d(ə)n] *Adj.*
Ich bin mit Ihrer Arbeit sehr zufrieden.

satisfied
I'm very satisfied with your work.

1.6 Negative Gefühle | 1-2000

1.6 Negative Emotions

Angst [aŋst] *f, -, Ängste*
Hast du Angst vor der Prüfung?

fear, anxiety *n*
Are you afraid of the test?

ängstlich ['ɛŋstliç] *Adj.*
Sie will nachts nicht alleine im Haus bleiben. Sie ist sehr ängstlich.

anxious, fearful
She does not like to stay home alone at night. She is very fearful.

Ärger ['ɛrgə*] *m, -s, kein Pl.*
Tu bitte, was er will, und mach' keinen Ärger!

anger, irritation, trouble *n*
Please do what he wants, and don't make any trouble!

ärgerlich ['ɛrgə*liç] *Adj.*
Der letzte Bus ist weg. Das ist wirklich ärgerlich.

irritating, maddening, annoying
The last bus is gone. That is really annoying.

---

bedauern [bə'dauə*n] *V/t.*, bedauerte, hat bedauert
Ich bedauere sehr, dass ich Ihre Einladung nicht annehmen kann.

be sorry, regret *v*

I am very sorry that I cannot accept your invitation.

---

befürchten [bə'fyrçt(ə)n] *V/t.*, befürchtete, hat befürchtet
Ich befürchte, es ist etwas Schlimmes passiert.

fear *v*

I fear that something terrible has happened.

---

böse ['bø:zə] *Adj.*, böser, am bösesten
Sie wurde böse, als ich ihr die Geschichte erzählte.

angry

She got angry when I told her the story.

---

fürchten ['fyrçt(ə)n] *V/t., i., refl., + Präp.* (vor), fürchtete, hat gefürchtet
Ich fürchte, dass wir zu spät kommen.
Ich fürchte mich vor dem Hund.
Der Hund wird von allen gefürchtet.

fear, be afraid (of) *v*

I am afraid that we will be late.

I am afraid of the dog.
The dog is feared by everyone.

---

leider ['laidə*] *Adv.*
Morgen können wir leider nicht kommen.

unfortunately
Unfortunately, we cannot come tomorrow.

Schrecken ['ʃrɛk(ə)n] *m, -s, -*
Als er die Polizei sah, bekam er einen großen Schrecken.

shock, fright, panic *n*
When he saw the police, he was frightened.

Sorge ['zɔrgə] *f, -, -n*
Warum hast du nicht früher angerufen? Ich habe mir Sorgen gemacht.

worry, trouble, sorrow *n*
Why didn't you call earlier? I was worried.

sorgen [ˈzɔrg(ə)n] *V/i., + Präp.*
(für), *refl.*, sorgen, hat gesorgt
Wer sorgt für den Hund, wenn ihr
im Urlaub seid?

Sorg dich nicht um mich! Ich werde vorsichtig sein.

worry (about), **be concerned**
(about), **care for** *v*
Who is going to care for the dog
while you are on vacation (*BE:* on
holiday)?

Don't worry about me! I'll be
careful.

Trauer [ˈtrauə*] *f, -, kein Pl.*
Er zeigte keine Trauer über den
Tod seiner Frau.

sorrow, grief *n*
He showed no sorrow at the
death of his wife.

---

traurig [ˈtrauriç°] *Adj.*
Sie ist traurig, weil ihre Katze gestorben ist.

sad, sorrowful
She is sad about the death of her
cat.

---

unangenehm [ˈunangəneːm]
Adj.
Ich habe ihm unangenehme Fra-
gen gestellt.

unpleasant

I asked him unpleasant questions.

---

unglücklich [ˈunglykliç] *Adj.*
Er ist unglücklich, weil seine
Freundin ihn verlassen hat.

unhappy *n*
He is unhappy because his girlfriend has left him.

---

verzweifelt [fɛə*ˈtsvaifəlt] *Adj.*
Sie war so verzweifelt, dass sie
nicht mehr leben wollte.

desperate
She was so desperate that she
didn't want to live any more.

Wut [vuːt] *f, -, kein Pl.*
Sie wurde rot vor Wut.

rage, anger *n*
She turned red with anger.

---

wütend [ˈvyːtənt] *Adj.*
„Lass mich in Ruhe!", schrie er
wütend.

(violently) **angry, furious**
"Leave me alone!" he screamed
angrily.

2001-4000

aufregen [ˈaufreːg(ə)n] *V/t., refl.,*
+ Präp. (über, wegen), regte auf,
hat aufgeregt
Er hat ein schwaches Herz.
Deshalb dürfen wir ihn nicht aufregen. (Deshalb darf er sich nicht
aufregen.)

excite, get excited, upset *v*

He has a weak heart.
That's why we must not upset
him. (That's why he must not get
excited.)

Aufregung [ˈaufrɛːgʊŋ] *f, -, -en*
Sie hatte vor Aufregung vergessen, was sie sagen wollte.

excitement *n*
She was so nervous she forgot what she wanted to say.

besorgt [bəˈzɔrkt] *Adj., -er, am -esten*
Jens hat sich seit Wochen nicht gemeldet. Seine Eltern sind deshalb sehr besorgt.

concerned, worried (about)
Jens has not called in weeks. His parents are therefore very concerned.

beunruhigen [bəˈunruːig(ə)n] *V/t., refl.,* beunruhigte, hat beunruhigt
Du bist so nervös. Beunruhigt dich etwas? (Warum beunruhigst du dich?)

upset, bother, disturb, worry *v*
You are so nervous. Is something bothering you (Why are you so worried)?

Eifersucht [ˈaifə*zuxt] *f, -, kein Pl.*
Die Eifersucht meines Mannes wird immer schlimmer.

jealousy *n*
My husband's jealousy is getting worse.

eifersüchtig [ˈaifə*zyçtiçˈ] *Adj.*
Sie darf keinen anderen Mann ansehen. Ihr Freund ist schrecklich eifersüchtig.

jealous
She cannot look at another man. Her boyfriend is terribly jealous.

einsam [ˈainzaːm] *Adj.*
Ohne dich fühle ich mich einsam.

lonely
Without you I feel lonely.

erregt [ɛə*ˈreːkt] *Adj.* -er, am -esten
Eine erregte Menschenmenge demonstrierte vor dem Parlament.

excited
An excited crowd demonstrated before the parliament building.

erschrecken [ɛə*ˈʃrek(ə)n] *V/i.,* erschrak, ist erschrocken
Er erschrak, als er die hohe Rechnung sah.

be startled, be shocked
He was startled when he saw the high bill.

erschüttert [ɛə*ˈʃytə*t] *Adj.*
Alle waren von seinem frühen Tod erschüttert.

shocked
Everyone was shocked by his untimely death.

Furcht [furçt] *f, -, kein Pl.*
Unsere Katze hat keine Furcht vor Hunden.

fear *n*
Our cat has no fear of dogs.

hassen ['has(ə)n] *V/t.*, hasste, hat gehasst
Jens brauchst du nicht einzuladen. Er hasst Partys.

hate *v*
You don't need to invite Jens. He hates parties.

Hass [has] *m*, -es, *kein Pl.*
Er hat ihn aus Hass erschossen.

hate *n*
He shot him out of hate.

hoffnungslos ['hɔfnuŋslo:s] *Adj.*, -er, am -esten
Die Situation ist ernst, aber nicht hoffnungslos.

hopeless
The situation is serious but not hopeless.

leidtun [laittun:]
Es tut mir leid, dass ich Sie stören muss.

be sorry, regret
I'm sorry I have to disturb you.

schämen ['ʃɛ:mən] *V/refl.*, + Präp. (vor, wegen, für), schämte, hat geschämt
Er schämt sich vor den Leuten wegen seiner großen Ohren.

be or feel ashamed *v*

He is ashamed because of his big ears.

Schock [ʃɔk] *m*, -(e)s, -s
Der Tod seines Sohnes war ein großer Schock für ihn.

shock *n*
The death of his son was a great shock for him.

schockieren [ʃɔ'ki:rən] *V/t.*, schockierte, hat schockiert
Er schockierte seine Eltern, als er mit grünen Haaren nach Hause kam.

shock *v*

He shocked his parents when he came home with green hair.

Unruhe ['unru:ə] *f*, -, -n
Der Regierungswechsel führte zu starken Unruhen.

disturbance, unrest *n*
The change in government led to serious unrest.

Unruhe *f*, -, *nur Sg.*
Er zeigte seine innere Unruhe nicht, obwohl er Angst hatte.

restlessness, inner turmoil *n*
He did not show his inner turmoil, although he was afraid.

vermissen [fɛə*'mis(ə)n] *V/t.*, vermisste, hat vermisst
Ich habe dich sehr vermisst.

miss (someone) *v*

I missed you very much.

Verzweiflung [fɛə*'tsvaifluŋ] *f*, -, *kein Pl.*
Trotz unserer Verzweiflung haben wir noch immer Hoffnung.

despair *n*

In spite of our despair we still have hope.

Zorn [tsɔrn] *m, -(e)s, kein Pl.*
Als wir über ihn lachten, geriet er in Zorn.

anger, rage *n*
When we laughed at him, he flew into a rage.

zornig [ˈtsɔrniçˀ] *Adj.*
Er sprach mit lauter und zorniger Stimme.

angry, enraged
He spoke in a loud and angry voice.

1.7 Gesundheit und Krankheit | 1-2000
1.7 Health and Illness

bluten [ˈbluːt(ə)n] *V/i.,* blutete, hat geblutet
Die Wunde hat nur kurz geblutet.

bleed *v*
The wound only bled a little.

erkälten [ɛəˀˈkɛlt(ə)n] *V/refl.,* erkältete, hat erkältet
Ich habe mich erkältet.

catch a cold *v*
I caught a cold.

Erkältung [ɛəˀˈkɛltuŋ] *f, -, -en*
Sie hat eine starke Erkältung.

cold *n*
She has a bad cold.

Fieber [ˈfiːbəˀ] *n, -s, kein Pl.*
Sie hat hohes Fieber.

fever *n*
She has a high fever.

gesund [gəˈzunt] *Adj.,* gesünder, am gesündesten
Es ist ein sehr gesundes Kind.

healthy
He/She's a very healthy child.

Gesundheit [gəˈzunthait] *f, -, kein Pl.*
Zum Geburtstag wünschen wir dir Glück und Gesundheit.

health *n*
For your birthday we wish you good luck and health.

Grippe [ˈgripə] *f, -, kein Pl.*
Ich möchte ein Medikament gegen Grippe.

influenza, flu *n*
I would like some medicine for the flu.

Husten [ˈhuːst(e)n] *m, -s, kein Pl.*
Haben Sie noch Husten?

cough *n*
Do you still have a cough?

husten ['huːst(ə)n] *V/i.*, hustete, hat gehustet
Wenn jemand raucht, muss ich husten.

cough *v*
When someone smokes, I have to cough.

kräftig ['krɛftiç°] *Adj.*
Vor seiner Krankheit war er ein kräftiger Mann.

powerful, strong
Before his illness he was a strong man.

krank [kraŋk] *Adj.*, kränker, am kränkesten
Wie lange ist Uwe schon krank?

sick, ill *(BE)*
How long has Uwe been sick?

Krankheit ['kraŋkhait] *f*, -, -en
Gegen diese Krankheit gibt es noch kein Medikament.

disease, sickness, illness *n*
There is still no medicine for this disease.

leiden ['laid(ə)n] *V/i.*, + *Präp.* (an, unter) litt, hat gelitten
Er leidet an einer tödlichen Krankheit.
Ich leide unter diesem ständigen Krach.

suffer *v*

He is suffering from a fatal disease.
I'm bothered by this constant noise.

Pille ['pilə] *f*, -, -n
Vergessen Sie nicht, die Pille zu nehmen.

pill *n*
Don't forget to take the pill.

Schmerz [ʃmɛrts] *m*, -es, -en
Ich habe häufig Magenschmerzen.

pain *n*
I frequently have stomach pains.

Verband [fɛə*ˈbant] *m*, -es, Verbände
Der Verband muss täglich gewechselt werden.

bandage, dressing *n*

The bandage must be changed daily.

verletzen [fɛə*ˈlɛts(ə)n] *V/t.*, *refl.*, verletzte, hat verletzt
Sie hat sich am Finger verletzt.

injure *v*

She injured her finger.

Verletzung [fɛə*ˈlɛtsuŋ] *f*, -, -en
Wegen dieser Verletzung musst du nicht zum Arzt gehen.

injury *n*
You don't have to go to the doctor for this injury.

wehtun ['veːtuːn] *V/i.*, tat weh, hat wehgetan
Mit tun die Füße weh.

hurt, be sore *v*

My feet hurt.

wohl [vo:l] *Adv.*
Du siehst schlecht aus.
Fühlst du dich nicht wohl?

good, well
You look bad. Don't you feel good?

Wunde ['vundə] *f, -, -n*
Die Wunde blutet immer noch.

wound *n*
The wound is still bleeding.

2001-4000

---

blind [blint] *Adj., keine Komp.*
Der alte Mann ist fast blind.

blind
The old man is nearly blind.

giftig ['giftiçª] *Adj.*
Diese Pilze kann man nicht essen, die sind giftig.

poisonous
One can't eat these mushrooms; they're poisonous.

Halsschmerzen
['halsʃmɛrts(ə)n] *nur Pl.* (**Halsweh**, *n, -s, kein Pl.*)
Ich habe Halsschmerzen (Halsweh).

sore throat *n*

I have a sore throat.

klagen ['kla:g(ə)n] *V/i., + Präp.* (über), klagte, hat geklagt
Der Patient klagt über große Schmerzen.

complain (about) *v*

The patient is complaining about great pain.

Kopfschmerzen
['kɔpfʃmɛrts(ə)n] *nur Pl.* (**Kopfweh**, *n, -s, kein Pl.*)
Seit Tagen habe ich Kopfschmerzen (Kopfweh).

headache *n*

I've had a headache for days.

Lebensgefahr ['le:b(ə)nsgəfa:ª] *f, -, kein Pl.*
Bei dem Unfall gab es acht Verletzte. Zwei sind noch in Lebensgefahr.

critical condition, mortal danger *n*
Eight were injured in the accident and two are still in critical condition.

Ohnmacht ['o:nmaxt] *f, -, kein Pl.*
Als er das viele Blut sah, fiel er in Ohnmacht.

unconsciousness *n*
When he saw so much blood, he fainted.

ohnmächtig ['o:nmɛçtiçª] *Adj.*
Der Verletzte lag ohnmächtig am Boden.

unconscious
The injured man lay unconscious on the ground.

schmerzhaft [ˈʃmɛrtshaft] *Adj.,*
-er, am -esten
Die Wunde ist nicht gefährlich,
aber schmerzhaft.

painful

The wound is not dangerous, but
painful.

taub [taup] *Adj., keine Komp.*
Mein Vater ist auf einem Ohr taub.

deaf
My father is deaf in one ear.

verbinden [fɛɐˈbɪnd(ə)n] *V/t.,*
verband, hat verbunden
Die Wunde muss sofort verbunden werden.

bandage, dress *v*

The wound must be bandaged
right away.

Zahnschmerzen
[ˈtsaːnʃmɛrts(ə)n] *nur Pl.* (Zahn-
weh, *n, -s, kein Pl.*)
Hast du eine Tablette gegen
Zahnschmerzen?

toothache *n*

Do you have something for
toothache?

zittern [ˈtsɪtə*n] *V/i., + Präp.* (vor,
wegen)
Der Junge zittert vor Kälte.

shiver *v*

The boy is shivering from the
cold.

Übelkeit [ˈyːb(ə)lkait] *f, -, kein Pl.*
Nach dem Unfall klagte sie über
Kopfschmerzen und Übelkeit.

nausea *n*
After the accident she complained of headache and nausea.

übel [ˈyːb(ə)l] *Adj.,* übler, am
übelsten
Mir ist übel, weil ich zu viel gegessen habe.

nauseous

I feel nauseous because I ate too
much.

1.8 Leben und Tod | 1-2000

1.8 Life and Death

alt [alt] *Adj.,* älter, am ältesten
Wie alt sind Sie?
Der alte Herr ist 92 Jahre, aber
noch immer gesund.

old
How old are you?
The old gentleman is 92 years old
but still healthy.

geboren (sein, werden) [gə'bo:r(ə)n]
Unsere Tochter wurde zu Hause geboren.
Wann bist (wurdest) du geboren?

born

Our daughter was born at home.

When were you born?

Geburt [gə'bu:ɐ*t] *f, -, -en*
Herzlichen Glückwunsch zur Geburt Ihres Kindes!

birth *n*
Congratulations on the birth of your child!

Geburtstag [gə'bu:ɐ*tsta:k] *m, -(e)s, -e*
Mein Vater hat morgen Geburtstag.

birthday *n*

My father's birthday is tomorrow.

Jugend ['ju:g(ə)nt] *f, -, kein Pl.*
In ihrer Jugend war sie eine gute Sportlerin.

youth *n*
In her youth she was a good athlete.

jung [juŋ] *Adj.,* jünger, am jüngsten
Sie waren beide sehr jung, als sie heirateten.

young

They were both very young when they got married.

Kindheit ['kinthait] *f, -, kein Pl.*
Meine Geschwister und ich hatten eine glückliche Kindheit.

childhood *n*
My siblings and I had a happy childhood.

leben ['le:b(ə)n] *V/i.,* lebte, hat gelebt
Weißt du, wann dieser Maler gelebt hat?

live *v*

Do you know when that painter lived?

Leben ['le:b(ə)n] *n, -s, kein Pl.*
Er ist unzufrieden mit seinem Leben.

life *n*
He is unhappy with his life.

Leiche ['laiçə] *f, -, -n*
Am Seeufer wurde gestern die Leiche eines jungen Mannes gefunden.

corpse *n*
Yesterday the corpse of a young man was found on the lakeshore.

sterben ['ʃtɛrb(ə)n] *V/i., + Präp.* (an, durch, vor), starb, ist gestorben
Wissen Sie, woran er gestorben ist?

die *v*

Do you know of what he died?

28

Tod [toːt] *m, -es, -e*
Ihr plötzlicher Tod hat alle überrascht.

death *n*
Her sudden death surprised everyone.

tödlich [ˈtøːtlɪç] *Adj.*
Seine Krankheit ist tödlich.

fatal, deadly
His illness is fatal.

tot [toːt] *Adj., keine Komp.*
Vor unserer Haustür liegt ein toter Vogel.

dead
A dead bird is lying outside our door.

2001-4000

Alter [ˈaltə*] *n, -s, kein Pl.*
Trotz ihres hohen Alters macht sie noch weite Reisen.
Erst jetzt im Alter ist er ruhiger geworden.

age *n*
In spite of her advanced age she still does a lot of traveling.
Only now in old age has he become calmer.

aufwachsen [ˈaufvaks(ə)n] *V/i.,*
wuchs auf, ist aufgewachsen
In diesem Dorf bin ich aufgewachsen.

grow up *v*
I grew up in this small town.

beerdigen [bəˈeːrdɪg(ə)n] *V/t.,*
beerdigte, hat beerdigt
Unser Opa wird morgen um 10.00 Uhr beerdigt.

bury *v*
Our grandfather will be buried tomorrow at 10 o'clock.

Begräbnis [bəˈgrɛːpnɪs] *n, -ses, -se*
Zu dem Begräbnis kamen viele Leute.

burial, funeral *n*
Many came to the funeral.

Erbe [ˈɛrbə] *n, -s, kein Pl.*
Gleich nach seinem Tod begann der Streit um das Erbe.

inheritance *n*
Arguing about the inheritance began right after his death.

Friedhof [ˈfriːthoːf] *m, -es, Friedhöfe*
Der Friedhof liegt direkt bei der Kirche.

cemetery *n*
The cemetery is right by the church.

Grab [graːp] *n, -(e)s, Gräber*
In diesem Grab liegen meine Großeltern.

grave *n*
My grandparents are buried in this grave.

jugendlich [ˈjuːg(ə)ntliç] *Adj.*
Am Telefon hat sie eine jugendliche Stimme.

young, youthful
On the telephone her voice sounds young.

Selbstmord [ˈzɛlpstmɔrt] *m,* -es, -e
Man weiß nicht, ob es ein Unfall oder ein Selbstmord war.

suicide *n*

We don't know if it was an accident or suicide.

Testament [tɛstaˈmɛnt] *n,* -(e)s, -e
Das Testament hat sie kurz vor ihrem Tode gemacht.

will (and **testament**) *n*

She made her will shortly before her death.

Tote [ˈtoːtə] *m/f,* -n, -n
Bei dem Unglück gab es über 20 Tote.

fatalities, casualties, dead *n*
In the accident there were over 20 fatalities.

2.1 Sinne und Körperfunktionen | 1-2000

2.1 The Senses and Body Functions

anfassen ['anfas(ə)n] *V/t.,* fasste an, hat angefasst	**touch** *v*
Fass den Hund nicht an, er beißt!	Don't touch the dog; he bites!
ansehen ['anse:(ə)n] *V/t.,* sah an, hat angesehen	**look at, watch, see** *v*
Ich habe mir gestern einen Kriminalfilm angesehen.	Yesterday I watched a detective film.
Ich sah sie die ganze Zeit an.	I looked at her the whole time.
bemerken [bə'mɛrk(ə)n] *V/t.,* bemerkte, hat bemerkt	**notice** *v*
Wann hast du bemerkt, dass du deine Handtasche verloren hast?	When did you notice that you had lost your purse/handbag *(BE)*?
beobachten [bə'o:baxt(ə)n] *V/t.,* beobachtete, hat beobachtet	**watch, observe** *v*
Sie wurde von der Polizei beobachtet.	She was observed by the police.
betrachten [bə'traxt(ə)n] *V/t.,* betrachtete, hat betrachtet	**look at, study, examine** *v*
Sie betrachtete die Bilder ganz genau.	She looked at the pictures very closely.
blicken ['blik(ə)n] *V/i., + Präp.* (aus, auf), blickte, hat geblickt	**view, look** *v*
Er blickte aus dem Fenster, als ich ins Haus ging.	He looked out (of) the window just as I was entering the house.
Blick [blik] *m,* -(e)s, -e	**view** *n*
Von diesem Punkt hat man einen schönen Blick auf die Berge.	From this point you have a wonderful view of the mountains.
frieren ['fri:r(ə)n] *V/i.,* fror, hat gefroren	**be cold, be freezing, freeze** *v*
Wenn du frierst, kannst du meine Jacke haben.	If you are cold, you can have my jacket.

Geruch [gə'rux] *m*, -s, Gerüche Viele Leute mögen den Geruch von Knoblauch nicht.	**odor, smell, aroma** *n* Many people do not like the smell of garlic.
Geschmack [gə'ʃmak] *m*, -s, *kein Pl.* Der Geschmack jedes einzelnen Menschen ist verschieden.	**(sense of) taste** *n* Everyone's sense of taste is different.
hören ['hø:r(ə)n] *V/t., i.*, hörte, hat gehört Hast du das Geräusch gehört? Hast du etwas Neues gehört?	**hear** *v* Did you hear the sound? Have you heard anything new?
müde ['my:də] *Adj.*, müder, am müdesten Ich gehe ins Bett, ich bin müde.	**tired, exhausted** I'm going to bed; I am tired.
riechen ['ri:ç(ə)n] *V/t., i.*, + *Präp.* (nach), roch, hat gerochen Der Hund hat das Fleisch gerochen. In der Küche riecht es nach Kuchen.	**smell** *v* The dog smelled the meat. In the kitchen you can smell cake baking.
schauen ['ʃau(ə)n] *V/i.*, schaute, hat geschaut Er schaute aus dem Fenster, weil er auf den Besuch wartete.	**look** (at) *v* He looked out (of) the window, because he was waiting for company.
Schlaf [ʃla:f] *m*, -(e)s, *kein Pl.* Sie hat einen festen Schlaf.	**sleep** *n* Her sleep is sound.
schlafen ['ʃla:f(ə)n] *V/i.*, schlief, hat geschlafen Haben Sie gut geschlafen?	**sleep** *v* Did you sleep well?
schwitzen ['ʃvits(ə)n] *V/i.*, + *Präp.* (vor, wegen), schwitzte, hat geschwitzt Schwitzt du nicht in dem dicken Pullover?	**sweat** *v* Aren't you sweating in that thick sweater?
sehen ['ze:(ə)n] *V/t., i.*, sah, hat gesehen Ich habe Thomas in der Stadt gesehen. Ich sehe schon, du bist beschäftigt.	**see** *v* I saw Thomas in town. I see you are busy.

spüren ['ʃpy:r(ə)n] *V/t.*, spürte, hat
gespürt
Spürst du Schmerzen im Arm?

feel *v*

Do you feel pain in your arm?

Träne ['trɛ:nə] *f*, -, -n
Ich sah Tränen in seinen Augen.

tear *n*

I saw tears in his eyes.

Traum [traum] *m*, -(e)s, Träume
Heute Nacht hatte ich einen
schrecklichen Traum.

dream *n*

Last night I had a terrible dream.

träumen ['trɔimən] *V/i.*, + *Präp.*
(von), träumte, hat geträumt
Ich träume oft vom Fliegen.

dream *v*

I often dream of flying.

wach [vax] *Adj.*, -er, am -esten
Ich bin morgens immer sehr früh
wach.

awake

I always wake up very early in the
morning.

weinen ['vainən] *V/i.*, + *Präp.*
(über, vor, um), weinte, hat ge-
weint
Er weinte vor Freude.

cry *v*

He cried for joy.

2001-4000

aufwachen ['aufvax(ə)n] *V/i.*,
wachte auf, ist aufgewacht
Er braucht keinen Wecker, er
wacht jeden Morgen vor 6.00 Uhr
auf.

wake up *v*

He doesn't need an alarm clock;
he wakes up every morning before 6 o'clock.

aufwecken ['aufvɛk(ə)n] *V/t.*,
weckte auf, hat aufgeweckt
Sprich leise, du weckst sonst das
Baby auf!

wake (up) *v*

Speak softly; otherwise you'll
wake up the baby!

Beobachtung [bə'o:baxtuŋ] *f*, -,
-en
Die Beobachtungen der Zeugin
waren sehr genau.

observation *n*

The observations of the witness
were very exact.

Duft [duft] *m*, -(e)s, Düfte
Ich mag den Duft von Rosen.

aroma, pleasant smell, scent *n*

I like the scent of roses.

einschlafen [ˈainʃlaːf(ə)n] *V/i.,*   **go to sleep, fall asleep** *v*
schlief ein, ist eingeschlafen
Meine Frau schläft immer vor dem   My wife always falls asleep in
Fernseher ein.   front of the television.

---

ermüden [ɛəˈmyːd(ə)n] *V/t., i.,*   **tire, exhaust** *v*
ermüdete, hat (ist) ermüdet
Der lange Spaziergang hat ihn er-   The long walk tired him.
müdet.
Durch das schnelle Tempo waren   The horses were exhausted be-
die Pferde schnell ermüdet.   cause of the fast pace.

---

erschöpft [ɛəˈʃœpft] *Adj.,* -er, am   **exhausted**
-esten
Du siehst erschöpft aus. Mach   You look exhausted. Take a vaca-
doch mal Urlaub!   tion (*BE:* holiday).

---

schläfrig [ˈʃlɛːfriçˊ] *Adj.*   **sleepy**
Der Hund lag schläfrig in der   The dog lay sleepy in the sun.
Sonne.

---

sichtbar [ˈziçtbaː*] *Adj.*   **visible**
Das Haus ist von der Straße aus   The house is not visible from the
nicht sichtbar.   street.

---

starren [ˈʃtarən] *V/i., + Präp.* (auf),   **stare at** *v*
starrte, hat gestarrt
Er starrte auf das Bild, ohne etwas   He stared at the picture without
zu sagen.   saying anything.

---

wahrnehmen [ˈvaː*neːmən] *V/t.,*   **perceive, notice** *v*
nahm wahr, hat wahrgenommen
Niemand nahm ihn wahr, als er   Nobody noticed him when he left
aus dem Haus ging.   the house.

---

wecken [ˈvɛk(ə)n] *V/t.,* weckte,   **awaken, wake up** *v*
hat geweckt
Wir wurden um 7.30 Uhr geweckt.   We were awakened at 7:30.

---

zusehen [ˈtsuːzeː(ə)n] *V/i., +*   **watch** *v*
Präp. (bei), sah zu, hat zugesehen
Ich habe ihm bei der Arbeit zuge-   I watched him working.
sehen.

2.2 Körperpflege und Sauberkeit | 1-2000

abtrocknen ['aptrɔknən] *V/t., refl.,* trocknete ab, hat abgetrocknet
○ Trocknest du das Kind ab?

□ Ich glaube, es kann sich selbst abtrocknen.

dry (off) *v*

○ Are you going to dry (off) the child?

□ I think the child can dry himself/herself (off).

Bad [ba:t] *n,* -(e)s, Bäder
Das Bad ist rechts neben der Küche.

bath(room) *n*
The bath(room) is to the right of the kitchen.

Bürste ['byrstə] *f,* -, -n
Ich brauche eine neue Haarbürste.

brush *n*
I need a new hairbrush.

Creme [kre:m] *f.* -, -s
Diese Hautcreme ist sehr gut.

cream *n*
This skin cream is very good.

Dusche ['du:ʃə] *f,* -, -n
Ich möchte ein Zimmer mit Dusche.

shower *n*
I would like a room with a shower.

duschen ['du:ʃ(ə)n] *V/t., i., refl.,* duschte, hat geduscht
Er duschte das Kind und sich jeden Abend.

take a shower, give a shower, shower *v*
He gave the child a shower and took one himself every evening.

Fleck [flɛk] *m,* -(e)s, -en
Du hast einen Fleck auf dem Hemd.

spot *n*
You have a spot on your shirt.

Handtuch ['hantu:x] *n,* -(e)s, Handtücher
Gibst du mir bitte ein Handtuch?

towel *n*
Will you hand me a towel?

Kamm [kam] *m,* -(e)s, Kämme
Ich möchte mir die Haare kämmen. Hast du vielleicht einen Kamm?

comb *n*
I would like to comb my hair. Do you have a comb?

kämmen [ˈkɛmən] *V/t., refl.,*
kämmte, hat gekämmt
Du musst dir die Haare kämmen!

comb *v*

You must comb your hair!

---

putzen [ˈputs(ə)n] *V/t.,* putzte, hat
geputzt
Zieh dir die Schuhe aus! Ich will
sie putzen.

clean *v*

Take off your shoes. I want to
clean them.

---

reinigen [ˈrainig(ə)n] *V/t.,* reinigte,
hat gereinigt
Hast du meinen Anzug reinigen
lassen?

(dry) clean *v*

Did you have my suit (dry)-
cleaned?

---

sauber [ˈzaubə*] *Adj.*
Die Tasse ist nicht sauber.

clean
The cup is not clean.

Schmutz [ʃmuts] *m, -es, kein Pl.*
Warum ist so viel Schmutz im
Hausflur?

dirt *n*
Why is there so much dirt in the
entrance hall?

---

schmutzig [ˈʃmutsiçº] *Adj.*
Die Schuhe sind schmutzig.

dirty
The shoes are dirty.

Seife [ˈzaifə] *f, -, -n*
Es fehlt Seife zum Händewa-
schen.

soap *n*
There is no soap to wash your
hands.

---

spülen [ˈʃpyːl(ə)n] *V/t.,* spülte, hat
gespült
Kannst du bitte heute einmal das
Geschirr spülen?

wash (dishes), rinse *v*

Could you please wash the
dishes today?

Staub [ʃtaup] *m, -(e)s, kein Pl.*
Unter dem Schrank liegt viel
Staub.

dust *n*
Under the cabinet there is a lot of
dust.

---

waschen [ˈvaʃ(ə)n] *V/t., refl.,*
wusch, hat gewaschen
Diesen Pullover muss man mit der
Hand waschen.

wash *v*

This sweater has to be washed by
hand.

---

wischen [ˈviʃ(ə)n] *V/t.,* wischte,
hat gewischt
Der Boden in der Küche muss
gewischt werden.

wipe, wash, clean *v*

The floor in the kitchen has to be
washed.

baden ['baːd(ə)n] *V/t., i., refl.*, badete, hat gebadet
Die Mutter badet das Kind.
Ich bade mich jeden Tag.

bathe, take a bath *v*
The mother bathes the child.
I take a bath every day.

fegen ['feːg(ə)n] *V/t.*, fegte, hat gefegt
Die Straße muss gefegt werden.

sweep *v*
The street has to be swept.

glänzen ['glɛnts(ə)n] *V/i.*, glänzte, hat geglänzt
Der Boden glänzt nach dem Wischen wie neu.

shine, sparkle *v*
The floor shines like new after being washed.

kehren ['keːrən] *V/t.*, kehrte, hat gekehrt
Der Hof ist diese Woche nicht gekehrt worden.

sweep *v*
The courtyard has not been swept this week.

Rasierapparat [raˈziːə*apaˈraːt] *m*, -s, -e
Der Rasierapparat rasiert sehr gründlich.

razor *n*
The razor shaves very thoroughly.

rasieren [raˈziːrən] *V/t., refl.*, rasierte, hat rasiert
Er rasiert sich (ihn) nass.

shave *v*
He shaves with soap.

Rasierklinge [raˈziːə*kliŋə] *f*, -, -n
Hast du noch eine scharfe Rasierklinge für mich?

razor blade *n*
Do you have a sharp razor blade for me?

Schwamm [ʃvam] *m*, -(e)s, Schwämme
Ich wasche mich am liebsten mit einem Schwamm.

sponge *n*
I prefer to wash with a sponge.

Tube ['tuːbə] *f*, -, -n
Diese Creme gibt es in einer Dose oder in einer Tube.

tube *n*
This cream comes either in a can or in a tube.

Waschmaschine ['vaʃmaʃiːnə] *f*, -, -n
Unsere Waschmaschine steht im Bad.

washing machine, washer *n*
Our washing machine is in the bathroom.

Wäscherei [vɛʃə'rai] *f,* -, -en
Ich bin mit meiner Wäscherei sehr zufrieden.

laundry *n*
I am quite satisfied with my (neighborhood) laundry.

Zahnbürste ['tsa:nbyrstə] *f,* -, -n
Welche Zahnbürste gehört dir? Die gelbe oder die rote?

toothbrush *n*
Which toothbrush belongs to you? The yellow one or the red one?

Zahnpasta(-e) ['tsa:npasta] *f,* -, Zahnpasten
Welche Zahnpaste nimmst du?

toothpaste *n*

Which toothpaste do you use?

2.3 Tun (allgemein)   1-2000

2.3 Doing

Absicht ['apziçt] *f,* -, -en
Ich hatte nicht die Absicht, dich zu beleidigen.

intention *n*
I did not intend to insult you.

absichtlich ['apziçtliç] *Adj., keine Komp.*
Er macht das absichtlich, um mich zu ärgern.

intentional, deliberate

He does that deliberately, just to make me angry.

Arbeit ['arbait] *f,* -, en, *kein Pl.*
Die Arbeit ist ziemlich langweilig.
Sie wurde vor fünf Monaten entlassen und hat immer noch keine neue Arbeit gefunden.

work, job *n*
The work is rather boring.
She was laid off five months ago and has not yet found a new job.

arbeiten ['arbait(ə)n] *V/i., + Präp.* (an, bei, für), arbeitete, hat gearbeitet
Er arbeitet sehr sorgfältig.

work *v*

He works very carefully.

bemühen [bə'my:(ə)n] *V/refl.,* bemühte, hat bemüht
Wir werden uns bemühen, die Arbeit bis Freitag fertig zu machen.

work (hard), try (hard), do one's best *v*
We will do our best to finish the work by Friday.

beschließen [bə'ʃliːs(ə)n] *V/t.,*
beschloss, hat beschlossen
Sie hat beschlossen, mit dem
Rauchen aufzuhören.

decide *v*

She decided to give up smoking.

beschäftigen [bə'ʃɛftig(ə)n] *V/t.,*
refl., + Präp. (mit) beschäftigte,
hat beschäftigt
Die Firma beschäftigt 200 Mitarbeiter.
Dieses Thema beschäftigt ihn
schon lange.
Sie beschäftigt sich seit Jahren
mit deutscher Literatur.

**occupy, employ, deal with, work
with** *v*

The company employs 200
people.
This topic has been occupying
him (his time) for a long time.
She has been dealing with German literature for years.

Beschäftigung [bə'ʃɛftiguŋ] *f, -,*
-en
Er kann nicht ohne Arbeit sein.
Er sucht immer eine Beschäftigung.

work, employment *n*

He cannot live without work. He is
constantly looking for something
to do.

besorgen [bə'zɔrg(ə)n] *V/t.,* be-
sorgte, hat besorgt
Ich fahre einkaufen. Soll ich für
dich etwas besorgen?

get, pick up *v*

I'm going shopping. Do you want
me to pick up anything for you?

beteiligen [bə'tailig(ə)n] *V/refl., +*
Präp. (an), beteiligte, hat beteiligt
Möchtest du dich an dem Spiel
beteiligen?

take part in, participate in *v*

Would you like to join the game?

gelingen [gə'liŋən] *V/i.,* gelang,
ist gelungen
Es ist mir nicht gelungen, den
Fehler zu finden.

succeed *v*

I did not succeed in finding the
mistake.

gewöhnen [gə'vøːnən] *V/refl., +*
Präp. (an), gewöhnte, hat gewöhnt
An meine neue Brille habe ich
mich schnell gewöhnt.

get used to *v*

I got used to my new glasses very
fast.

Handlung ['handluŋ] *f, -,* -en
War Ihnen nicht klar, welche
Folgen Ihre Handlung haben
könnte?

action, plot *(of a story, play) n*
Wasn't it clear to you what consequences your actions would
have?

können ['kœnən] *V/t., Mod. V.,* konnte, hat gekonnt
Er kann einfach alles.
Wenn Sie Zeit haben, können Sie mich morgen besuchen.
Kann ich Ihnen einen Kaffee anbieten?

be able to, be capable *v*
He can do simply everything.
If you have time, can you come see me tomorrow?
Can I offer you a cup of coffee?

machen ['max(ə)n] *V/t.,* machte, hat gemacht
Wer macht heute das Abendessen?
Diese Arbeit kann ich selbst machen.
Mit dem Geschenk hast du mir eine große Freude gemacht.
Den Schrank habe ich machen lassen.
Wissen Sie, wie das gemacht wird?
Mach schnell!
Das macht 12,40 Euro.

do, make *v*
Who's going to make dinner today?
I can do this work myself.
Your gift has made me very happy.
I had this cabinet made.
Do you know how that is done?
Hurry up!
That makes 12 euros 40.

Mühe ['myːə] *f, -, -n*
Gib dir Mühe, dann klappt es auch.

effort, hard work *n*
Make an effort, and everything will go well.

Plan [plaːn] *m, -(e)s, Pläne*
Der neue Finanzplan muss vom Chef noch genehmigt werden.
Hast du einen Plan des Grundstücks?

plan *n*
The new finance plan still has to be approved by the boss.
Do you have a plan of the lot?

planen ['plaːnən] *V/t., i.,* plante, hat geplant
Die Arbeit ist gut geplant worden.

plan *v*
The work was planned well.

probieren [proˈbiːrən] *V/i.,* probierte, hat probiert
Probier du mal! Ich kann die Tür nicht öffnen.

try (out) *v*
You try it! I can't open the door.

Tätigkeit ['tɛːtiçkait] *f, -, -en*
Für mich ist Putzen die unangenehmste Tätigkeit.

activity *n*
For me cleaning the house is the most unpleasant of activities.

teilnehmen ['tailne:mən] *V/i., +
Präp.* (an), nahm teil, hat teilgenommen
Diesen Winter nehme ich wieder
an einem Skikurs teil.

participate in, take part in *v*

This winter I'm going to take part
in a ski course again.

tun [tu:n] *V/t., i.,* tat, hat getan
Im Geschäft war viel zu tun.

Was tust du in deiner Freizeit?

Ich habe mir wehgetan.
Er ist gar nicht müde. Er tut nur so.

do, pretend, act *v*
In the office there was much to
do.
What do you do in your leisure
time?
I hurt myself.
He is not tired at all. He is just
pretending.

üben ['y:b(ə)n] *V/t.,* übte, hat
geübt
Sie muss noch ein bisschen üben.
Dann kann sie bald gut
schwimmen.

exercise, practice *v*
She has to exercise a bit. Then
she will be able to swim well soon.

vermeiden [fɛə*'maid(ə)n] *V/t.,*
vermied, hat vermieden
Der Unfall hätte vermieden werden können.

avoid *v*

The accident could have been
avoided.

versuchen [fɛə*'zu:x(ə)n] *V/t.,*
versuchte, hat versucht
Ich habe es versucht, aber ich
kann die Kiste nicht alleine
tragen.

try, attempt *v*

I tried, but I cannot carry the box
alone.

verwechseln [fɛə*'vɛks(ə)ln] *V/t.,*
verwechselte, hat verwechselt
Du hast die beiden Flaschen verwechselt.

mix up, confuse *v*

You mixed up the two bottles.

vorhaben ['fo:ə*ha:b(ə)n] *V/i.,*
hatte vor, hat vorgehabt
Was habt ihr am Wochenende
vor?

intend, plan *v*

What are you planning to do on
the weekend?

Werk [vɛrk] *n,* -(e)s, -e
Die bekanntesten Werke der Malerin sind in diesem Museum zu
sehen.

work *n*
The best known works of the
artist can be seen in this museum.

winken ['viŋk(ə)n] *V/i.*, winkte, hat gewunken
Er winkte, als der Zug abfuhr.

wave (good–bye) *v*

He waved as the train departed.

2001-4000

---

aktiv [ak'ti:f] *Adj.*
Trotz ihres hohen Alters ist sie noch sehr aktiv.

active
In spite of her advanced age she is still very active. ?

Aktivität [aktivi'tɛ:t] *f*, -, -en
Wenn Sie Karriere machen wollen, müssen Sie mehr Aktivität zeigen.

activity *n*
If you want to move up the career ladder, you have to show more activity.

Angewohnheit ['angəvo:nhait] *f*, -, -en
Sie hat die Angewohnheit, während des Essens zu lesen.

habit *n*

She has the habit of reading while she eats.

---

anstrengen ['anʃtrɛŋən] *V/t., refl.*, strengte an, hat angestrengt
Der Nachtdienst strengt ihn sehr an.
Du musst dich mehr anstrengen, sonst schaffst du es nicht.

exert, stress, exhaust, make an effort *v*
The night shift really exhausts him.
You have to make more of an effort; otherwise you won't succeed.

Anstrengung ['anʃtrɛŋuŋ] *f*, -, -en
Die Anstrengung hat sich gelohnt.

effort, exertion, exhaustion *n*

The effort was worth it.

---

aushalten ['aushalt(ə)n] *V/t.*, hielt aus, hat ausgehalten
Was für eine Hitze heute! Das kann man ja kaum aushalten.

(with)stand *v*

It is really hot today! You can hardly stand it!

---

beabsichtigen [bə'apziçtig(ə)n] *V/t.*, beabsichtigte, hat beabsichtigt
Klaus und Bernd beabsichtigen, gemeinsam eine Wohnung zu mieten.

intend *v*

Klaus and Bernd intend to rent an apartment (*BE:* flat) together.

beachten [bə'axt(ə)n] *V/t.*, beachtete, hat beachtet
Sein Befehl wurde nicht beachtet.

pay attention (to), regard, obey, respect *v*
His order was not respected.

befassen [bə'fas(ə)n] *V/refl.*, + *Präp.* (mit), befasste, hat befasst
Mit diesem Thema befasse ich mich schon seit Jahren.

deal with *v*
I have been dealing with this topic for years.

Bemühung [bə'my:uŋ] *f*, -, -en
Vielen Dank für Ihre Bemühungen!

effort *n*
Many thanks for your efforts!

Durchführung ['durçfy:ruŋ] *f*, -, *kein Pl.*
Die Durchführung des Plans war schwieriger als alle gedacht hatten.

carrying out, execution *n*

The execution of the plan was more difficult than expected.

durchsetzen ['durçzɛts(ə)n] *V/t.*, setzte durch, hat durchgesetzt
Ich habe meinen Vorschlag durchsetzen können.

push through, enforce, assert *v*
I was able to push through my suggestion.

mühsam ['my:za:m] *Adj.*
Die Arbeit war mühsam, aber sie hat sich gelohnt.

arduous
The work was arduous, but it was worth it.

organisieren [ɔrgani'zi:rən] *V/t.*, organisierte, hat organisiert
Die Feier war gut organisiert worden.

organize *v*

The celebration was well organized.

Planung ['pla:nuŋ] *f*, -, -en
Der Bau ist noch in der Planung.
Die Arbeiten beginnen erst nächstes Jahr.

planning *n*
The building is still in the planning stages. Construction won't begin until next year.

realisieren [reali'zi:rən] *V/t.*, realisierte, hat realisiert
Dieser Plan lässt sich nicht realisieren.

realize, carry out *v*

This plan cannot be realized.

schaffen ['ʃaf(ə)n] *V/t.*, schaffte, hat geschafft
Es tut mir leid, aber wir haben den Termin nicht mehr geschafft.

do, make, accomplish *v*

I'm sorry, but we didn't make the appointment/deadline.

Teilnehmer ['tailne:mə*] *m*, -s,- **Teilnehmerin** ['tailne:mərin] *f*, -, -nen	**participant** *n*
Der Kurs hat 18 Teilnehmer.	The course has 18 participants.
Überwindung [y:bə*'vinduŋ] *f.*, -, *kein Pl.*	**overcoming, surmounting** *n*
Es kostet mich große Überwindung, zu ihm freundlich zu sein.	It's very difficult for me to be friendly to him.
unternehmen [untə*'ne:mən] *V/* *t.*, unternahm, hat unternommen	**undertake,** *v*
Was wollen wir morgen unternehmen?	What do we want to do tomorrow?
Versuch [fɛə*'zu:x] *m*, -(e)s, -e	**attempt, try** *n*
Lass uns noch einen Versuch machen. Vielleicht schaffen wir es doch allein.	Let's make another attempt. Maybe we can do it alone.
vornehmen ['fo:ə*'ne:mən] *V/* *refl.*, nahm vor, hat vorgenommen	**intend, plan, be determined, resolve to do** *v*
Sie hat sich vorgenommen, in Zukunft langsamer zu fahren.	She resolved to drive slower in the future.
zustande (zu Stande) kommen (bringen) [tsu'ʃtandə kɔmən]	**achieve, manage** *v*
Bei dem Gespräch ist keine Einigung zustande gekommen.	In the discussion no agreement could be achieved.
Sie will selbst ein Regal bauen, aber ich glaube nicht, dass sie das zustande bringt.	She wants to build the bookcase herself, but I do not believe that she can manage it.

2.4 Bewegung und Ruhe 1-2000
2.4 Movement and Rest

abwesend ['apve:zənt] *Adj.*, keine Komp.	**absent, away, gone**
Hat jemand angerufen, während ich abwesend war?	Did anyone call while I was gone?

anwesend [ˈanveːzənt] *Adj., keine Komp.* | **present, (t)here**

Ist Frau Sommer anwesend? | Is Ms. Sommer there?

Aufenthalt [ˈaufənthalt] *m, -(e)s, -e* | **stay** *n*

Unser Aufenthalt in London war leider viel zu kurz. | Our stay in London was unfortunately much too short.

ausruhen [ˈausruː(ə)n] *V/refl.,* ruhte aus, hat ausgeruht | **relax, rest** *v*

Ruh dich nach dieser langen Fahrt erst einmal aus! | Sit down and relax after your long trip!

beeilen [bəˈail(ə)n] *V/refl.,* beeilte, hat beeilt | **hurry (up)** *v*

Bitte beeil dich! Wir haben keine Zeit. | Please hurry (up)! We have no time.

befinden [bəˈfind(ə)n] *V/refl.,* befand, hat befunden | **be (located)** *v*

Wo befindet sich hier im Haus die Toilette? | Where is the restroom/lavatory here in the house?

bleiben [ˈblaib(ə)n] *V/i.,* blieb, ist geblieben | **stay, remain** *v*

Bleib doch noch zum Essen! | Come on and stay for dinner!
Bleiben Sie ruhig! Es ist nichts passiert. | Remain calm! Nothing has happened.
Dafür bleibt mir keine Zeit. | I don't have any time remaining.

da sein [ˈdaː zain] *V/i.,* war da, ist da gewesen | **be here/there** *v*

Es ist niemand da. | There's nobody here/there.

Eile [ˈailə] *f, -, kein Pl.* | **hurry** *n*

Ich muss jetzt gehen, ich bin in Eile. | I have to go now; I'm in a hurry.
Sie können den Brief später schicken. Das hat keine Eile. | You can send the letter later. There is no hurry.

eilig [ˈailiçʰ] *Adj.* | **hurried, urgent, in a hurry**

Dieser Auftrag ist eilig. | The task is urgent.
Hast du es eilig, oder können wir noch einen Kaffee trinken? | Are you in a hurry, or can we get another cup of coffee?

fahren ['faːrən] *V/i.*, fuhr, ist gefahren
Sie ist mit dem Fahrrad in die Stadt gefahren.

go, travel, ride *v*
She went to town by bicycle.

---

gehen ['geː(ə)n] *V/i.*, ging, ist gegangen
Wir sind zu Fuß nach Hause gegangen.
Ich gehe heute Nachmittag Tennis spielen.
Die Klingel geht nicht.
Das geht nicht, das ist zu kompliziert.
Es geht ihm ganz gut.
Worum geht es?

go, walk, work, function, be *v*
We walked home.
I'm going to play tennis this afternoon.
The doorbell doesn't work.
That won't work; it's too complicated.
He's quite well.
What's it (all) about?

---

hinsetzen ['hinzɛts(ə)n] *V/refl.*, setzte hin, hat hingesetzt
Dort ist eine Bank, dort können wir uns hinsetzen.

sit (down) *v*
There is a bench where we can sit down.

---

kommen ['kɔmən] *V/i.*, kam, ist gekommen
Wann bist du gekommen?
Es ist Wasser im Keller. Woher kommt das?

come *v*
When did you come?
There is water in the basement. Where does it come from?

---

laufen ['lauf(ə)n] *V/i.*, lief, ist gelaufen
Er lief so schnell er konnte.
Lass uns laufen! Es sind nur ein bis zwei Kilometer.
Wie läuft das Geschäft?

run, walk, go *v*
He ran as fast as he could.
Let's walk! It's only one or two kilometers.
How's business going?

---

liegen ['liːg(ə)n] *V/i.*, lag, hat gelegen
Sie liegt im Bett, weil sie krank ist.

Wo liegt die Tageszeitung?

lie, be *v*
She is lying in bed because she's sick/ill *(BE)*.
Where is the newspaper?

---

rennen ['rɛnən] *V/i.*, rannte, ist gerannt
Warum rennst du so schnell?

run *v*
Why are you running so fast?

Schritt [ʃrit] *m*, -(e)s, -e
Wir waren ein paar Schritte gegangen, da fing es an zu regnen.

step *n*
We had just gone a few steps
when it began to rain.

setzen [ˈzɛts(ə)n] *V/t., refl.*, setzte,
hat gesetzt
Bitte setz das Kind auf seinen
Stuhl!
Bitte setzen Sie sich doch!

set, put *v*

Please put the child on the chair!

Do sit down, please!

sitzen [ˈzits(ə)n] *V/i.*, saß, hat gesessen
Wir saßen draußen auf der Ter-
rasse.

sit *v*

We sat outside on the terrace.

springen [ˈʃpriŋən] *V/i.*, sprang,
ist gesprungen
Wir mussten über einen Bach
springen.

jump, spring *v*

We had to jump over a stream.

Sprung [ʃpruŋ] *m*, -(e)s, Sprünge
Beim Sprung über den Zaun hat
er sich verletzt.

jump *n*
He injured himself in a jump over
the fence.

stehen [ˈʃteː(ə)n] *V/i.*, stand, hat
gestanden
Die Leute standen vor der Tür und
warteten.
Wo stehen die Weingläser?
In der Zeitung steht, dass das
Wetter besser wird.

stand, be located, say *(in print) v*

The people stood outside and
waited.
Where are the wine glasses?
It says in the newspaper that the
weather is going to get better.

Sturz [ʃturts] *m*, -es, Stürze
Beim Sturz hat er sich den Arm
gebrochen.

fall *n*
He broke his arm when he fell.

stürzen [ˈʃtyrts(ə)n] *V/i.*, stürzte,
ist gestürzt
Sie ist von der Leiter gestürzt.

fall *(suddenly, abruptly) v*

She fell from the ladder.

treten [ˈtreː(ə)n] *V/t., i.*, tritt, hat/
ist getreten
Sie hat den Hund getreten.
Er ist mir auf den Fuß getreten.

step, kick *v*

She kicked the dog.
He stepped on my foot.

warten [ˈvart(ə)n] *V/i.*, + *Präp.*
(auf), wartete, hat gewartet
Hast du lange auf mich gewartet?

wait (for) *v*

Have you been waiting for me
long?

$$2001\text{-}4000$$

Abwesenheit [ˈapveːz(ə)nhait] *f,* -, *kein Pl.*   **absence** *n*

Ich weiß während nichts. Die Sache wurde während meiner Abwesenheit beschlossen.   I don't know anything about it. The matter was decided in my absence.

anlehnen [ˈanleːnən] *V/t., refl.,* lehnte an, hat angelehnt   **lean** (on) *v*

Lehn dich nicht an die Wand an! Sie ist schmutzig.   Don't lean against the wall. It is dirty.

Anwesenheit [ˈanveːz(ə)nhait] *f,* -, *kein Pl.*   **presence** *n*

Bitte gehen Sie! Ihre Anwesenheit wird nicht gewünscht.   Please leave! Your presence is not wanted.

aufstehen [ˈaufʃteː(ə)n] *V/i.,* stand auf, ist aufgestanden   **stand up, get up** *v*

Wann bist du heute aufgestanden?   When did you get up this morning?

ausrutschen [ˈausrutʃ(ə)n] *V/i.,* rutschte aus, ist ausgerutscht   **slip** *v*

Vorsicht, rutschen Sie nicht aus! Der Boden ist glatt.   Watch out, don 't slip. The floor is slippery.

fallen [ˈfal(ə)n] *V/i.,* fiel, ist gefallen   **fall** *v*

Die Tasse ist vom Tisch gefallen.   The cup fell from the table.

klettern [ˈklɛtɐn] *V/i.,* kletterte, ist geklettert   **climb** *v*

Er kann wie ein Affe klettern.   He can climb like a monkey.

kriechen [ˈkriːç(ə)n] *V/i.,* kroch, ist gekrochen   **crawl** *v*

Er kroch unter die Bank, um das Geldstück zu suchen.   He crawled under the bench to look for the coin.

nähern [ˈnɛːɐn] *V/refl.,* näherte, hat genähert   **approach, reach** *v*

Wir nähern uns langsam dem Ziel.   We are slowly reaching our goal.

schleichen [ˈʃlaiç(ə)n] *V/i.,* schlich, ist geschlichen   **sneak** *v*

Sie schlich leise in ihr Zimmer.   She sneaked into her room quietly.

überqueren [y:bə*'kve:rən] *V/t.,*
überquerte, hat überquert
Pass auf, wenn du die Straße
überquerst!

cross, go across *v*

Be careful when you cross the
street.

---

umdrehen ['umdre:(ə)n] *V/t.,*
refl., drehte um, hat umgedreht
Das Fleisch muss beim Braten
öfters umgedreht werden.
Als sie sich umdrehte, sah sie ihn.

turn around, turn over *v*

The meat has to be turned over
several times while cooking.
As she turned around, she saw
him.

---

verschwinden [fɛə*'ʃvind(ə)n] *V/*
i., verschwand, ist verschwunden
Unsere Katze ist seit Tagen verschwunden.

disappear *v*

Our cat disappeared several days
ago.

---

vorbeigehen [fo:ə*'baige:(ə)n] *V/*
i., + Präp. (an, bei) ging vorbei, ist
vorbeigegangen
Er ist gerade an mir vorbeigegangen.
Geh bitte nach der Arbeit beim
Bäcker vorbei und bring Kuchen
mit.

pass, go past *v*

He just went past me.

Go to the bakery after work and
get some cake.

---

weggehen ['vɛkge:(ə)n] *V/i.,* ging
weg, ist weggegangen
Sie ist schon früh weggegangen.

leave, go away *v*

She left early this morning.

---

weitergehen ['vaitə*ge:(ə)n] *V/i.,*
ging weiter, ist weitergegangen
Dann wurde der Weg so schlecht,
dass wir nicht weitergehen
konnten.

go on *v*

Then the road got so bad that we
could not go on.

---

zurückgehen [tsu'rykge:(ə)n]
V/i., ging zurück, ist zurückge-
gangen
Ich bin müde, lass uns zum Hotel
zurückgehen.

go back, return *v*

I am tired; let's go back to the
hotel.

---

zurückkehren [tsu'rykke:rən] *V/*
i., kehrte zurück, ist zurückge-
kehrt.
Wann kehrt ihr von der Reise zurück?

return, come back *v*

When are you coming back from
your trip?

2.5 Bewegen von Dingen und Lebewesen

1-2000

2.5 Moving of Objects and Beings

bewegen [bə'veːg(ə)n] *V/t., refl.,* bewegte, hat bewegt	**move** *v*
Mir tut der Arm weh, wenn ich ihn bewege.	My arm hurts when I move it.
Die Hose ist viel zu eng. Ich kann mich kaum bewegen.	The trousers are much too tight. I can hardly move in them.
bringen ['brɪŋən] *V/t.,* brachte, hat gebracht	**bring, take** *v*
Bring bitte das Geschirr in die Küche!	Take the dishes into the kitchen!
Bringst du mich morgen zum Flughafen?	Can you take me to the airport tomorrow?
Was bringt das Fernsehen heute?	What's on television today?
drehen ['dreː(ə)n] *V/t.,* drehte, hat gedreht	**turn** (around) *v*
Wenn man den Schalter nach rechts dreht, wird das Licht stärker.	If you turn the switch to the right, the light gets brighter.
holen ['hoːl(ə)n] *V/t.,* holte, hat geholt	**get, fetch, pick up** *v*
Wenn du Hunger hast, hol dir etwas aus dem Kühlschrank.	If you are hungry, get something from the refrigerator.
hängen ['hɛŋən] *V/t.,* hängte, hat gehängt	**hang** (up) *v*
Häng bitte die Kleider in den Schrank!	Please hang the clothes in the closet/wardrobe *(BE)*.
hängen *V/i.,* hing, hat gehangen	**hang** *v*
Gestern hing der Mantel noch da.	Yesterday the coat was still hanging there.

rollen [ˈrɔl(ə)n] *V/t., i.,* rollte, hat ge-
rollt
Der Stein ist zu schwer zum Tra-
gen, aber man kann ihn rollen.
Vorsicht, der Ball rollt auf die
Straße.

roll v

The stone is too heavy to carry,
but you can roll it.
Watch out, the ball is rolling into
the street!

schicken [ˈʃik(ə)n] *V/t.,* schickte,
hat geschickt
Ich habe dir ein Paket geschickt.

send v

I sent you a package/parcel *(BE).*

schieben [ˈʃiːb(ə)n] *V/t.,* schob,
hat geschoben
Ich musste das Fahrrad nach
Hause schieben, weil ein Reifen
kaputt war.

push v

I had to push the bicycle home
because a tire was flat.

stellen [ˈʃtɛl(ə)n] *V/t.,* stellte, hat
gestellt
Stell bitte noch Weingläser auf
den Tisch.

put v

Please put more wine glasses on
the table.

tragen [ˈtraːg(ə)n] *V/t.,* trug, hat
getragen
Kannst du bitte die Tasche
tragen?

carry, wear *(clothing)* v

Could you please carry the bag.

wenden [ˈvɛnd(ə)n] *V/t.,* wendete,
hat gewendet
Ich kann den Wagen hier nicht
wenden. Die Straße ist zu eng.

turn *(in a circle)* v

I can't turn the car around here.
The street is too narrow.

werfen [ˈvɛrf(ə)n] *V/t.,* warf, hat
geworfen
Sie warf Steine ins Wasser.

throw v

She threw stones into the water.

2001-4000

schleppen [ˈʃlɛp(ə)n] *V/t.,*
schleppte, hat geschleppt
Diesen Sack kann ich alleine
schleppen.

drag, carry *(with effort)* v

I can carry this bag by myself.

schütteln [ˈʃyt(ə)ln] *V/t.,* schüttelte, hat geschüttelt
„Nein", sagte er und schüttelte
den Kopf.

shake v

"No," he said, and shook his
head.

Transport [trans'pɔrt] *m,* -(e)s, -e
Der Transport mit der Bahn ist am
sichersten.

transport(ation) *n*
Transport(ation) by train is the
safest.

treiben ['traib(ə)n] *V/t., i.,* trieb, hat
getrieben
Sie treibt die Kühe in den Stall.
Das Boot trieb ohne Besatzung
auf dem Meer.

drive *v,* **drift** *v*

She drives the cows into the barn.
The boat drifted on the sea
without a crew.

2.6 Geben und Nehmen | 1-2000
2.6 Giving and Taking

anbieten ['anbiːt(ə)n] *V/t.,* bot an,
hat angeboten
Sie hat mir einen Kaffee angeboten.

offer *v*

She offered me a cup of coffee.

annehmen ['anneːmən] *V/t.,*
nahm an, hat angenommen
Würden Sie bitte meine Post annehmen, wenn ich nicht da bin?

accept, take in *v*

Would you take in my mail (*BE:*
post) while I'm gone?

behalten [bə'halt(ə)n] *V/t.,* be-
hielt, hat behalten
Du kannst die Zeitschrift behalten, ich habe sie schon gelesen.

keep *v*

You can keep the magazine; I've
already read it.

bekommen [bə'kɔmən] *V/t.,* bekam, hat bekommen
Heute habe ich Ihren Brief bekommen.

get, receive *v*

I got your letter today.

bieten ['biːt(ə)n] *V/t.,* bot, hat geboten
Er hat mir viel Geld geboten, aber
ich will das Bild nicht verkaufen.

offer *v*

He offered me a lot of money, but I
don't want to sell the picture.

brauchen ['braux(ə)n] *V/t.,*
brauchte, hat gebraucht
Brauchst du das Auto morgen?

need *v*

Do you need the car tomorrow?

52

danken ['daŋk(ə)n] *V/t.,* dankte, hat gedankt | **thank** *v*
Ich danke Ihnen für Ihre Hilfe. | I thank you for your assistance.

empfangen [ɛm'pfaŋən] *V/t.,* empfing, hat empfangen | **receive** *v*
Das Telegramm haben wir empfangen. | We received the telegram.

erhalten [ɛə*'halt(ə)n] *V/t.,* erhielt, hat erhalten | **receive** *v*
Das Geld haben wir erhalten. | We received the money.

geben ['ge:b(ə)n] *V/t.,* gab, hat gegeben | **give** *v*
Gib mir bitte meine Tasche! | Please give me my bag.

Geschenk [gə'ʃɛŋk] *n,* -s,-e | **gift, present** *n*
Du musst das Geschenk noch schön einpacken! | You still have to wrap up the gift nicely.

haben ['ha:b(ə)n] *V/i.,* hatte, hat gehabt | **have** *v*
Sie haben eine Tochter und einen Sohn. | They have a daughter and a son.
Hast du Angst? | Are you afraid?

nehmen ['ne:mən] *V/t.,* nahm, hat genommen | **take** *v*
Er nahm die Teller aus dem Schrank. | He took the plates from the cupboard.
Ich nehme das Menü Nr. 3. | I'll take meal number three.
Nehmen Sie doch noch etwas Fleisch! | Have some more meat!

schenken ['ʃɛŋk(ə)n] *V/t.,* schenkte, hat geschenkt | **give** *(as a gift)* *v*
Was schenkst du deiner Schwester zum Geburtstag? | What are you giving your sister for her birthday?

tauschen ['tauʃ(ə)n] *V/t., + Präp.* (gegen), tauschte, hat getauscht | **exchange, trade, swap** *v*
Ich tausche meine Kleider mit einer Freundin. | I swap my clothes with a friend.

teilen ['tail(ə)n] *V/t., + Präp.* (mit), teilte, hat geteilt | **divide, cut up, share** *v*
Wir haben den Kuchen in 12 Stücke geteilt. | We cut up the cake in twelve pieces.

verteilen [fɛə*'tail(ə)n] *V/t.,* verteilte, hat veteilt	**distribute** *v*
Das Geld wurde gerecht verteilt.	The money was distributed fairly.

verzichten [fɛə*'tsiçt(ə)n] *V/i. + Präp.* (auf), verzichtete, hat verzichtet	**give up, do without** *v*
Wenn wir das Auto kaufen, müssen wir auf die Reise verzichten.	If we buy the car, we'll have to do without the holiday trip.

2001-4000

abgeben ['apge:b(ə)n] *V/t., + Präp.* (an, bei, in), gab ab, hat abgegeben	**turn in, hand in** *v*
Bitte geben Sie den Brief an der Rezeption ab.	Please hand in the letter at the reception desk.

abgeben *V/t., + Präp.* (von)	**give** *v*
Kannst du mir von den Broten eines abgeben?	Can you give me one of the sandwiches/loaves of bread?

aufteilen ['auftail(ə)n] *V/t., + Präp.* (unter, auf), teilte auf, hat aufgeteilt	**divide** (up) *v*
Das Geld wurde aufgeteilt.	The money was divided.

benötigen [bə'nø:tig(ə)n] *V/t.,* benötigte, hat benötigt	**need** *v*
Der Kranke benötigt Ruhe.	The sick person needs quiet.

kriegen ['kri:g(ə)n] *V/t.,* kriegte, hat gekriegt	**get** *v*
Das Gehalt kriegen Sie am Monatsende.	You'll get your salary at the end of the month.

reichen ['raiç(ə)n] *V/t., i.,* reichte, hat gereicht	**be enough, give, hand, pass** *v*
Kannst du mir bitte die Butter reichen?	Could you please give me the butter?
Das Brot reicht nicht.	There is not enough bread.

übergeben [y:bə*'ge:b(ə)n] *V/t.,* übergab, hat übergeben	**hand (over), deliver** *v*
Sie übergab ihm die Blumen.	She handed him the flowers.

54

überlassen [yːbə*'las(ə)n] *V/t.*,
überließ, hat überlassen
Sie hat mir das Radio für 50,–
Euro überlassen.

turn over, give, leave *v*

She gave me the radio for fifty
euros.

übernehmen [yːbə*'neːmən]
V/t., übernahm, hat übernommen
Kannst du meine Arbeit übernehmen? Ich muss heute früher
gehen.

take over *v*

Can you take over my work for me?
I have to leave early today.

überreichen [yːbə*'raiç(ə)n] *V/t.*,
überreichte, hat überreicht
Dem Sieger wurde ein Pokal
überreicht.

hand (over) *v*

A trophy cup was handed (over)
to the winner.

umtauschen ['umtauʃ(ə)n] *V/t.*,
tauschte um, hat umgetauscht
Kann ich die Ware umtauschen?

exchange *v*

Can I exchange the product?

verleihen [fɛə*'lai(ə)n] *V/t.*, +
Präp. (an), verlieh, hat verliehen
Mein Auto verleihe ich an nie-
manden.

lend, award *v*

I don't lend my car to anyone.

verweigern [fɛə*'vaigə*n] *V/t.*,
verweigerte, hat verweigert
Sie verweigerte die Antwort.

refuse *v*

She refused to give an answer.

wegnehmen ['vɛkneːmən] *V/t.*,
nahm weg, hat weggenommen
Hast du meinen Kugelschreiber
weggenommen?

take (away) *v*

Did you take my ball-point pen?

zurückgeben [tsu'rykgeːb(ə)n]
V/t., gab zurück, hat zurückge-
geben
Du kannst mein Fahrrad haben,
aber du musst es mir morgen zurückgeben.

give back, return *v*

You can have my bicycle, but you
have to give it back to me tomorrow.

2.7 Umgang mit Dingen und Lebewesen

1-2000

2.7 Handling Objects and Beings

abmachen ['apmax(ə)n] *V/t.,* machte ab, hat abgemacht	**take off** *v*
Bitte machen Sie das Preisschild ab!	Please take off the price tag.
ändern ['ɛndə*n] *V/t., refl.,* änderte, hat geändert	**change** *v*
Das Gesetz wurde geändert.	The law was changed.
Meine Adresse hat sich geändert.	My address has changed.
Änderung ['ɛndəruŋ] *f, -, -en*	**change** *n*
Mit der Änderung des Vertrags war sie einverstanden.	She agreed to the change in the contract.
anwenden ['anvɛnd(ən)] *V/t.,* wendete an, hat angewendet	**use** *v*
Weißt du, wie man dieses Mittel anwendet?	Do you know how to use this material?
aufhalten ['aufhalt(ə)n] *V/t.,* hielt auf, hat aufgehalten	**hold open** *v*
Sie hielt der Kundin die Tür auf.	She held the door open for the customer.
aufhören ['aufhøːrən] *V/t.,* + *Präp.* (mit), hörte auf, hat aufgehört.	**stop** *(doing something),* **finish** *v*
Wann hörst du mit der Arbeit auf?	When do you finish work?
aufräumen ['aufrɔimən] *V/t.,* räumte auf, hat aufgeräumt	**straighten up, clean up** *v*
Der Keller muss unbedingt aufgeräumt werden.	The cellar has to be cleaned up by all means.
benutzen [bə'nuts(ə)n] *V/t.,* benutzte, hat benutzt	**use** *v*
Darf ich mal Ihr Telefon benutzen?	May I use your telephone?

bereit (sein) [bə'rait] *Adj., keine Komp.*
Bist du bereit mitzumachen?

ready
Are you ready and willing to join in?

berühren [bə'ry:rən] *V/t.*, berührte, hat berührt
Sie dürfen das Bild ansehen, aber nicht berühren.

touch v
You may look at the picture, but you may not touch it.

biegen ['bi:g(ə)n] *V/t.*, bog, hat gebogen
Wenn du den Ast noch mehr biegst, bricht er ab.

bend v
If you keep bending the branch, it will break (off).

brechen ['brɛç(ə)n] *V/t., i.*, brach, hat/ist gebrochen
Er hat die Schokolade in vier Teile gebrochen.
Das Bein ist gebrochen.

break v
He broke the chocolate bar into four pieces.
The leg is broken.

drücken ['dryk(ə)n] *V/t., i., + Präp.* (auf), drückte, hat gedrückt
Die Maschine stoppt, wenn man (auf) diesen Knopf drückt.

push v
The machine stops when you push this button.

dulden ['duld(ə)n] *V/t.*, duldete, hat geduldet
Er duldet es nicht, dass jemand seinen Schreibtisch aufräumt.

tolerate v
He does not tolerate people cleaning up his desk.

durcheinander [durçai'nandə*] *Adv.*
Warum sind die ganzen Kleider durcheinander?

mixed up, in a mess, chaotic
Why are all these clothes in such a mess?

ersetzen [ɛə*'zɛts(ə)n] *V/t.*, ersetzte, hat ersetzt
Leder ist durch kein anderes Material zu ersetzen.
Die Versicherung wird den Schaden ersetzen.

replace v
Leather cannot be replaced by any other material.
The insurance will pay compensation for the damages.

fangen ['faŋən] *V/t.*, fing, hat gefangen.
Sie hat gestern drei Fische gefangen.
Er fing den Ball mit einer Hand.

catch v
Yesterday she caught three fish.
He caught the ball with one hand.

fassen ['fas(ə)n] *V/t., i.,* fasste, hat gefasst

hold v

Sie fasste das Kind fest an der Hand.

She held the child firmly by the hand.

Der Tank fasst über 80 Liter.

The tank holds over 80 liters.

---

festhalten ['fɛsthalt(ə)n] *V/t., i., + Präp.* (an), *refl.* hielt, hat gehalten

hold firm/on v

Bitte halten Sie Ihren Hund fest!

Please hold on to your dog!

Sie hielt an ihrem Plan fest.

She held firm to her plan.

Bitte halten Sie sich während der Fahrt gut fest.

Please hold on well during the ride.

---

finden ['find(ə)n] *V/t.,* fand, hat gefunden

find v

Ich kann meine Autoschlüssel nicht finden.

I cannot find my car keys.

---

führen ['fy:rən] *V/t.,* führte, hat geführt

direct, lead, take v

Morgen führe ich dich durch die Stadt und zeige dir alles.

Tomorrow I'll take you around town and show you everything.

Seit dem Tode seiner Frau führt er die Firma allein.

Since the death of his wife he has directed the company alone.

Führung ['fy:ruŋ] *f, -, -en*

guided tour, leadership, running n

Um 14.00 Uhr gibt es eine Führung durch das Schloss.

At 2 p.m. there is a tour of the castle.

Er alleine ist für die Führung des Geschäfts verantwortlich.

He alone is responsible for running the business.

---

füllen ['fylən] *V/t.,* füllte, hat gefüllt.

fill v

Er füllte die Gläser mit Saft.

He filled the glasses with juice.

---

gebrauchen [gə'braux(ə)n] *V/t., + Präp.* (für), gebrauchte, hat gebraucht

use v

Wofür gebraucht man das Werkzeug?

What do you use the tool for?

Gebrauch [gə'braux] *m, -s, kein Pl.*

use n

Vor dem Gebrauch muss die Flasche geschüttelt werden.

The bottle has to be shaken before use.

Gewohnheit [gə'vo:nhait] *f, -, -en*
Unsere Katze hat die Gewohnheit, im Bücherregal zu schlafen.

habit *n*
Our cat has the habit of sleeping in the bookcase.

gießen ['gi:s(ə)n] *V/t.,* goss, hat gegossen
Die Blumen müssen dringend gegossen werden.

pour, water *(plants)* v
The flowers have to be watered immediately.

graben ['gra:b(ə)n] *V/t., i.,* grub, hat gegraben
Er ist im Garten und gräbt Löcher für die neuen Bäume.

dig v
He is in the garden digging holes for the new trees.

halten ['halt(ə)n] *V/t.,* hielt, hat gehalten
Kannst du bitte kurz die Tasche halten? Ich möchte meine Jacke ausziehen.

hold v
Can you hold the bag for a moment? I would like to take off my jacket.

heben ['he:b(ə)n] *V/t.,* hob, hat gehoben
Er hob das Kind auf seinen Arm.

lift, raise v
He lifted the child onto his arm.

hindern ['hində*n] *V/t., + Präp.* (an), hinderte, hat gehindert
Ich konnte ihn nicht hindern, den Teppich zu kaufen.

stop, prevent v
I couldn't stop him from buying the carpet.

kaputt [ka'put] *Adj.,* -er, am -esten
Das Türschloss ist kaputt.

broken, busted, damaged, out of order
The door lock is broken.

kleben ['kle:b(ə)n] *V/t., i.,* klebte, hat geklebt
Vergiss nicht, eine Briefmarke auf die Karte zu kleben.
Die Briefmarke klebt nicht richtig.

stick, glue v
Don't forget to stick a stamp on the card.
The stamp doesn't stick right.

Kontrolle [kɔn'trɔlə] *f, -, -n*

Fahr langsamer! Hier gibt es oft Geschwindigkeitskontrollen.

check, inspection, control, checkpoint *n*
Slow down! They often check the speed here.

kratzen ['krats(ə)n] *V/t., i., refl., + Präp.* (an), kratzte, hat gekratzt
Au, die Katze hat mich gekratzt.
Ich habe mich an einem alten Nagel gekratzt.

scratch v
Ouch, the cat scratched me.
I scratched myself on an old nail.

kümmern ['kymə*n] *V/refl., + Präp.* (um), kümmerte, hat gekümmert
Ich kümmere mich um die Heizung, damit sie richtig funktioniert.

be concerned about, look after, take care of *v*
I'll take care of the heat, so that it functions properly.

---

kürzen ['kyrts(ə)n] *V/t.,* kürzte, hat gekürzt
Der Rock muss gekürzt werden

shorten *v*
The skirt has to be shortened.

---

lassen ['las(ə)n] *V/t., i., Mod. V., refl.,* ließ, hat gelassen
Lass das! Ich mag das nicht.
Er wurde nicht in Ruhe gelassen.
Lass mir das Bild, dann gebe ich dir das andere.
Ich habe die Maschine reparieren lassen.
Die Sachen lassen sich verbrennen.

leave, stop, have (done) *v*
Stop that! I don't like that.
He was not left alone.
Give me that picture, then I'll give you the other one.
I had the machine repaired.

The materials can be burned.

---

legen ['le:g(ə)n] *V/t., refl.,* legte, hat gelegt
Ich habe die Post auf den Schreibtisch gelegt.
Der Hund legte sich unter den Tisch.

lay (down), **put** *v*
I put the mail (*BE:* post) on the desk.
The dog lay down under the table.

---

leihen ['lai(ə)n] *V/t., i.,* lieh, hat geliehen
Ich habe dem Nachbarn die Bohrmaschine geliehen.
Ich habe mir eine Bohrmaschine (aus)geliehen.

lend, loan, borrow *v*
I lent my neighbor my electric drill.

I borrowed a electric drill.

---

leiten ['lait(ə)n] *V/t.,* leitete, hat geleitet
Frau Jensch leitet diese Abteilung.
Die Autos wurden über eine Hilfsbrücke geleitet.

direct, be director/head/boss/ chief/foreman of *v*
Ms. Jensch is the director of this department.
The cars were directed over a temporary bridge.

---

mahlen ['ma:l(ə)n] *V/t.,* mahlte, hat gemahlt
Du musst erst Kaffee mahlen.

grind *v*
You have to grind the coffee first.

mischen ['mɪʃ(ə)n] *V/t.,* mischte, hat gemischt
Ich mische den Saft immer mit etwas Wasser.

mix *v*
I always mix the juice with some water.

öffnen ['œfnən] *V/t. i., refl.,* öffnete, hat geöffnet
Öffne bitte die Dose!
Wann öffnet die Post?
Die Tür öffnet sich automatisch.

open *v*
Please open the can (*BE:* tin).
When does the post office open?
The door opens automatically.

---

pflegen ['pfle:g(ə)n] *V/t.,* pflegte, hat gepflegt
Wer pflegt euren kranken Vater?

Den Garten pflegt meine Frau.

take care of *v*
Who is taking care of your sick father?
My wife takes care of the garden.

Pflege ['pfle:gə] *f, -, kein Pl.*
Die Pflege des Gartens kostet viel Zeit.

care *n*
Taking care of the garden takes a lot of time.

---

prüfen ['pry:f(ə)n] *V/t.,* prüfte, hat geprüft
Hast du die Rechnung geprüft?

check (over) *v*
Have you checked the invoice?

---

reiben ['raib(ə)n] *V/t., refl.,* rieb, hat gerieben
Die Kartoffeln müssen gerieben werden.
Der Hund reibt sich sein Fell am Baum.

rub, grate *v*
The potatoes have to be grated.
The dog is rubbing his fur on the tree.

---

sammeln ['zam(ə)ln] *V/t.,* sammelte, hat gesammelt
Die Pilze habe ich im Wald gesammelt.
Er sammelt Briefmarken.

collect, gather *v*
I gathered the mushrooms in the forest.
He collects stamps.

Sammlung ['zamluŋ] *f, -, -en*
Er besitzt eine wertvolle Bildersammlung.

collection *n*
He owns a valuable collection of pictures.

---

schaffen ['ʃaf(ə)n] *V/t.,* schaffte, hat geschafft
Heute haben wir fast alles geschafft.

accomplish, manage, get done *v*
We accomplished almost everything today.

schlagen ['ʃlaːg(ə)n] *V/t., i., refl.,*
schlug, hat geschlagen
Sie schlug die Tür zu und ging.
Er schlug mit der Faust gegen die
Tür.
Die Kinder schlagen sich.

hit, slam *v*

She slammed the door and left.
He slammed his fist against the
door.
The children hit each other.

---

schließen ['ʃliːs(ə)n] *V/t., i., refl.,*
schloss, hat geschlossen
Bitte schließen Sie die Tür!
Die Tür schließt schlecht.
Die Geschäfte schließen um
18.30 Uhr.
Abends schließen sich die Blüten
dieser Blume.

close, shut *v*

Please close the door!
The door closes poorly.
The stores close at 6:30 p.m.

In the evening the blossoms of
this flower close up.

---

schneiden ['ʃnaid(ə)n] *V/t., i., refl.,*
schnitt, hat geschnitten
Soll ich den Käse schneiden?
Die Schere schneidet gut.
Ich habe mich (mir) in den Finger
geschnitten.

cut, slice *v*

Shall I slice the cheese?
The scissors cut well.
I cut my finger.

---

schützen ['ʃyts(ə)n] *V/t., i., refl.,*
+ Präp. (vor, gegen)
Du musst dich besser vor Erkäl-
tung schützen.
Die Jacke schützt (mich) gut vor
Wind.

protect, guard *v*

You have to do a better job to
protect yourself from colds.
The jacket is good protection
against the wind.

Schwierigkeit ['ʃviːriçkait] *f, -,*
-en
Es gibt noch Schwierigkeiten,
aber wir schaffen es trotzdem.

difficulty *n*

There are still difficulties, but we'll
make it just the same.

---

stechen ['ʃtɛç(ə)n] *V/t., i.,* stach,
hat gestochen
Ich bin von einer Biene gestochen
worden.
Vorsicht, die Pflanze sticht!

sting, scratch, prick, bite *v*

I was stung by a bee.

Careful, the plant is thorny and
will scratch you!

---

stecken ['ʃtɛk(ə)n] *V/t., + Präp.* (in,
an, auf) steckte, hat gesteckt
Den Ausweis habe ich in deine
Handtasche gesteckt.

stick, place *v*

I put the I.D. card in your
handbag.

stören [ˈʃtøːrən] *V/t.,* störte, hat gestört
Sie wurde dauernd durch das Telefon gestört.

disturb, interrupt *v*
She was constantly interrupted by the telephone.

stoßen [ˈʃtoːs(ə)n] *V/t., i., refl.,* stieß, hat gestoßen
Sie stieß ihn in den Rücken.
Ich bin mit dem Kopf gegen eine Glastür gestoßen.
Ich habe mich am Knie gestoßen.

hit, bang, push, bump *v*
She bumped him in the back.
I banged my head on a glass door.
I banged my knee.

suchen [ˈzuːx(ə)n] *V/t.,* suchte, hat gesucht
Sie sucht eine neue Stelle.
Ich suche meine Brille. Hast du sie gesehen?

look for, search *v*
She's looking for a new job.
I'm looking for my glasses. Have you seen them?

Suche [ˈzuːxə] *f, -, kein Pl.*
Die Suche nach einem Hotelzimmer kostete uns zwei Stunden.

search, hunt *n*
The hunt for a hotel room took us two hours.

treffen [ˈtrɛf(ə)n] *V/t., i., rzp.,* traf, hat getroffen
Er wurde von einem Schlag ins Gesicht getroffen.
Ich treffe Uwe morgen.
Wir treffen uns jeden Tag.

hit, meet *v*
He was hit by a punch in the face.
I'm meeting Uwe tomorrow.
We meet every day.

trennen [ˈtrɛnən] *V/t., refl., rzp.,* trennte, hat getrennt
Der Fluss trennt die beiden Länder.
Es ist besser, wenn wir uns trennen.
Sie haben sich vor kurzem getrennt.

divide, separate *v,* **part** *v*
The two countries are divided by the river.
It would be better if we parted ways.
They separated recently.

verändern [fɛəˈʔɛndəˈn] *V/t., refl.,*
Sie haben die ganze Wohnung verändert und neu eingeräumt.
Er hat sich stark verändert.

change, rearrange *v*
They rearranged the entire apartment/flat (*BE*).
He's changed a lot.

Verantwortung [fɛəˈʔantvɔrtuŋ] *f, -, kein Pl.*
Sie allein(e) haben die Verantwortung für die Entscheidung.

responsibility *n*
You have to bear the responsibility for the decision yourself.

verhindern [fɛə*'hɪndə*n] *V/t.,* verhinderte, hat verhindert
prevent, hinder *v*

Den Streit konnte ich nicht verhindern.
I couldn't prevent the fight.

---

verlieren [fɛə*'liːrən] *V/t.,* verlor, hat verloren
lose *v*

Er hat seine Kreditkarte verloren.
He lost his credit card.

---

versorgen [fɛə*'zɔrg(ə)n] *V/t.,* versorgte, hat versorgt
take care of/for *v*

Mein Mann ist im Stall und versorgt die Tiere.
My husband is in the barn/stable caring for the animals.

---

versprechen [fɛə*'ʃprɛç(ə)n] *V/t.,* versprach, hat versprochen
promise *v*

Mir wurde ein höherer Lohn versprochen.
I was promised a higher wage.

Versprechen [fɛə*'ʃprɛç(ə)n] *n,* -s, -
promise *n*

Er gab mir das Versprechen, niemandem etwas zu erzählen.
He gave me the promise not to tell anyone.

---

verstecken [fɛə*'ʃtɛk(ə)n] *V/t., i., refl., + Präp.* (vor, bei, in, u.a.), versteckte, hat versteckt
hide *v*

Die Schokolade habe ich vor den Kindern versteckt.
I hid the chocolate from the children.

Die Katze hat sich auf dem Dachboden versteckt.
The cat hid in the attic.

---

verwenden [fɛə*'vɛnd(ə)n] *V/t.,* verwendete, hat verwendet
use *v*

Den Rest des Fleisches verwende ich für das Abendessen.
I'm going to use the rest of the meat for dinner.

Verwendung [fɛə*'vɛnduŋ] *f,* -, -en
use *n*

Möchtest du das alte Geschirr haben? Ich habe keine Verwendung mehr dafür.
Would you like to have the old dishes? I have no more use for them.

---

vorbereiten ['foːə*bərait(ə)n] *V/t., refl., + Präp.* (auf), bereitete vor, hat vorbereitet
prepare *v*

Die Arbeiten müssen gut vorbereitet werden.
The work has to be well prepared.

Er hat sich gut auf die Prüfung vorbereitet.
He prepared well for the test.

Vorbereitung [ˈfoːəˈbəraituŋ] *f,* -, -en
Die Vorbereitung für das Fest dauerte drei Tage.

preparation *n*
The preparation for the festival lasted three days.

Vorsicht [ˈfoːəˈziçt] *f,* -, *kein Pl.*
Vorsicht! Die Leiter steht nicht fest.

care, warning, caution *n*
Be careful! The ladder is not steady.

vorsichtig [ˈfoːəˈziçtiçˀ] *Adj.*
Wenn Sie vorsichtig sind, kann Ihnen nichts passieren.

careful, cautious
If you are careful, nothing will happen to you.

warnen [ˈvarnən] *V/t.,* warnte, hat gewarnt
Ich habe ihn vor Dieben gewarnt, aber er war trotzdem unvorsichtig.

warn *v*
I warned him about thieves, but he was careless just the same.

Warnung [ˈvarnuŋ] *f,* -, -en
Im Radio habe ich eine Sturmwarnung gehört.

warning *n*
I heard a storm warning on the radio.

wechseln [ˈvɛks(ə)ln] *V/t., i.,* wechselte, hat gewechselt
Bei dieser Lampe muss die Glühbirne gewechselt werden.
Das Wetter wechselt ständig.
Könnten Sie mir 100,– Euro wechseln?

change, replace *v*
The bulb in this lamp has to be changed.
The weather changes all the time.
Could you change one hundred euros for me?

wickeln [ˈvik(ə)ln] *V/t., refl.,* wickelte, hat gewickelt
Ich muss das Baby noch wickeln.
Er wickelt sich einen dicken Schal um den Hals.

change (diapers; *BE:* nappies), **wrap** *v*
I have to diaper the baby.
He wraps a thick shawl around his neck.

wiegen [ˈviːg(ə)n] *V/t., i.,* wog, hat gewogen
Hast du den Koffer gewogen?
Ich bin 1,65 m groß und wiege 55 Kilogramm.

weigh *v*
Did you weigh the suitcase?
I am 1.65 meters tall and weigh 55 kilos.

ziehen [ˈtsiː(ə)n] *V/t., i.,* zog, hat (ist) gezogen
Der Wagen wurde von zwei Pferden gezogen.

pull *v*
The wagon was pulled by two horses.

zumachen ['tsu:ma:x(ə)n] *V/t., i.,*
machte zu, hat zugemacht
Mach bitte das Fenster zu!
Beeil dich, die Geschäfte machen
bald zu!

close v

Please close the window!
Hurry up, the stores/shops are
closing soon.

$$2001\text{-}4000$$

abschalten ['apʃalt(ə)n] *V/t.,*
schaltete ab, hat abgeschaltet
Die Elektriker haben den Strom
abgeschaltet.

turn off v

The electricians turned the power
off.

abschneiden ['apʃnaid(ə)n] *V/t.,*
+ *Präp.* (von), schnitt ab, hat ab-
geschnitten
Wenn die Jeans zu lang sind,
kannst du sie unten abschneiden.

cut off, shorten v

If the jeans are too long you can
shorten them.

anschalten ['anʃalt(ə)n] *V/t.,*
schaltete an, hat angeschaltet
Hast du den Backofen schon angeschaltet?

turn in, switch on v

Have you already turned on the
oven?

anzünden ['antsynd(ə)n] *V/t.,*
zündete an, hat angezündet
Die Leute glauben, dass er sein
Haus selbst angezündet hat.

set on fire v

They think he set his house on fire
himself.

aufbauen ['aufbau(ə)n] *V/t.,* bau-
te auf, hat aufgebaut
Das Rathaus wurde nach dem
Krieg neu aufgebaut.

build, rebuild v

After the war the city hall was
rebuilt.

aufgeben ['aufge:b(ə)n] *V/t., i.,*
gab auf, hat aufgegeben
Gib bitte den Brief bei der Post
auf!
Der Läufer gab erschöpft auf.

deliver, give up v

Deliver the letter to the post office.
The runner gave up, exhausted.

aufheben ['aufhe:b(ə)n] *V/t.,* hob
auf, hat aufgehoben
Die Rechnungen müssen 10 Jahre aufgehoben werden.
Er hob seinen Mantel vom Boden
auf.

keep, save, pick up v

The receipts must be kept for 10
years.
He picked his coat up off the floor.

aufmachen ['aufmax(ə)n] *V/t., i.,* | **open** *v*
machte auf, hat aufgemacht |
Machst du bitte die Flasche auf? | Would you please open the bottle?
Wann macht der Supermarkt auf? | When does the supermarket open?

aufstellen ['aufʃtɛl(ə)n] *V/t.,* stellte | **set up, stand/put up, place** *v*
auf, hat aufgestellt |
Die Stühle sollen in einer Reihe aufgestellt werden. | The chairs should be placed in a row.
Wir hatten das Zelt direkt am Strand aufgestellt. | We put the tent up right on the beach.

auseinandernehmen [ausai-'nandə*ne:mən] *V/t.,* nahm auseinander, hat auseinandergenommen | **take apart, dismantle** *v*
Den Schrank kann man ganz auseinandernehmen. | The cabinet can be completely taken apart.

ausschalten ['ausʃalt(ə)n] *V/t.,* schaltete aus, hat ausgeschaltet | **turn off** *v*
Hast du die Heizung ausgeschaltet? | Did you turn off the heat(er)?

beaufsichtigen [bə'aufziçtig(ə)n] *V/t.,* beaufsichtigte, hat beaufsichtigt | **take care of, watch, (baby)sit** *v*
Die Kinder werden morgens von ihrer Oma beaufsichtigt. | In the morning the children are taken care of by their grandmother.

bedecken [bə'dɛk(ə)n] *V/t.,* bedeckte, hat bedeckt | **cover** *v*
Das Tischtuch bedeckt nicht den ganzen Tisch. | The tablecloth doesn't cover the whole table.

befestigen [bə'fɛstig(ə)n] *V/t.,* befestigte, hat befestigt | **attach, fasten** *v*
An dieser Wand lässt sich kein Regal befestigen. | No shelf can be attached to this wall.

beherrschen [bəhɛrʃ(ə)n] *V/t., refl.,* beherrschte, hat beherrscht
control, rule, know well *v*

Das Land wird von einem König beherrscht.
The country is ruled by a king.

Welche Fremdsprachen beherrschen Sie?
Which foreign languages do you know well?

Bitte bleib ruhig und beherrsch dich!
Please be calm and control yourself.

berücksichtigen [bə'rykzɪçtig(ə)n] *V/t.,* berücksichtigte, hat berücksichtigt
consider, remember *v*

Sie braucht noch viel Ruhe. Man muss berücksichtigen, dass sie sehr krank war.
She still needs a lot of rest. You have to consider that she was very ill.

Berührung [bə'ry:ruŋ] *f, -, -en*
touch, physical contact *n*

Er hat seine Hand verbrannt. Jede Berührung tut weh.
He burned his hand. The slightest touch hurts.

beschädigen [bə'ʃɛ:dig(ə)n] *V/t.,* beschädigte, hat beschädigt
damage *v*

Das Hoftor ist beschädigt worden.
The door to the courtyard was damaged.

beseitigen [bə'zaitig(ə)n] *V/t.,* beseitigte, hat beseitigt
throw away, get rid of, clean up *v*

Nach dem Picknick haben wir alle Abfälle beseitigt.
After the picnic we cleaned up all the trash.

betreuen [bə'trɔi(ə)n] *V/t.,* betreute, hat betreut
take care of, watch *v*

Meine Mutter betreut unser Haus, wenn wir längere Zeit nicht da sind.
My mother takes care of our house when we're gone for an extended period of time.

bewähren [bə'vɛ:rən] *V/refl.,* bewährte, hat bewährt
be worth it, prove worthwhile *v*

Unsere Waschmaschine hat sich bewährt, sie ist schon 12 Jahre alt und läuft noch gut.
Our washer was worth it; it is already 12 years old and still runs well.

bilden ['bild(ə)n] *V/t., refl.,* bildete, hat gebildet
form *v*

Die Kinder bildeten einen Kreis.
The children formed a circle.

Auf dem Wasser bildete sich verdächtiger Schaum.
On the water a curious foam formed.

blasen ['blaz(ə)n] *V/t., i.*, blies, hat geblasen
Die Maschine bläst frische Luft in den Tunnel.
Der Wind bläst mir ins Gesicht.

blow *v*
The machine blows fresh air into the tunnel.
Wind is blowing in my face.

einbeziehen ['ainbətsi:(ə)n] *V/t., + Präp.* (in), bezog ein, hat einbezogen
Das Problem lässt sich nur gemeinsam lösen, deshalb müssen alle in die Diskussion einbezogen werden.

include *v*

The problem can only be solved together; so everybody has to be included in the discussion.

einschalten ['ainʃalt(ə)n] *V/t.*, schaltete ein, hat eingeschaltet
Wer hat das Radio eingeschaltet?

turn on *v*

Who turned on the radio?

entfernen [ɛnt'fɛrnən] *V/t.*, entfernte, hat entfernt
Diese Flecken lassen sich nicht entfernen.

remove *v*

These spots cannot be removed.

enthalten [ɛnt'halt(ə)n] *V/t.*, enthielt, hat enthalten
Wie viel Stück enthält die Packung?

contain, hold *v*

How many items are in this package?

erhöhen [ɛə*'hø:(ə)n] *V/t.*, erhöhte, hat erhöht
Die Postgebühren wurden erhöht.

raise *v*

Postal fees were raised.

Erhöhung [ɛə*'hø:uŋ] *f, -, -en*
Die Erhöhung der Benzinpreise wurde zurückgenommen.

increase *n*
The price increase for gasoline was rescinded.

ermöglichen [ɛə*'mø:kliç(ə)n] *V/t.*, ermöglichte, hat ermöglicht
Der neue Motor ermöglicht eine höhere Geschwindigkeit.

make possible, enable *v*

The new motor makes a higher speed possible.

erreichen [ɛə*'raiç(ə)n] *V/t.*, erreichte, hat erreicht

reach, attain, get, get to *v*

Das oberste Fach kann ich mit der Hand nicht erreichen.

I can't reach the top shelf.

Sie können mich unter dieser Nummer erreichen.

You can reach me at this number.

Hast du erreicht, was du wolltest?

Did you get what you wanted?

Beeil dich, sonst erreichst du den Bus nicht mehr!

Hurry, or you won't get to the bus on time!

---

erwischen [ɛə*'viʃ(ə)n] *V/t.*, erwischte, hat erwischt

catch, get *v*

Der Dieb wurde erwischt.

The thief was caught.

Hast du den Zug noch erwischt?

Did you still make your train?

Ich habe noch einen Pullover erwischt. Sonst waren fast alle verkauft.

I managed to still get a sweater. Most of them were already sold.

---

falten ['falt(ə)n] *V/t.*, faltete, hat gefaltet

fold *v*

Er faltete die Zeitung und steckte sie in seine Tasche.

He folded the newspaper and stuck it in his briefcase/bag.

---

festmachen ['fɛstmax(ə)n] *V/t.*, machte fest, hat festgemacht

attach, to fix on *v*

Die Bretter kann man so nicht festmachen.

You can't attach the boards like that.

---

fördern ['fœrdə*n] *V/t.*, förderte, hat gefördert

promote, increase *v*

Durch mehr Werbung soll der Verkauf gefördert werden.

Sales should increase with more advertising.

Förderung ['fœrdəruŋ] *f*, -, *kein Pl.*

assistance, support, help, aid *n*

Es gibt an unserer Schule jetzt Kurse zur Förderung der schlechteren Schüler.

At our school there are courses to help weak students.

Gestaltung [gə'ʃtaltuŋ] *f*, -, -en

arrangement, design *n*

Die Gestaltung des Gartens ist wirklich schön.

The arrangement of the garden is very nice.

---

heimlich ['haimliç] *Adj.*

secret, in secret

Die Schüler rauchen heimlich auf den Toiletten.

Students smoke in secret in the lavatories.

hinzufügen [hin'tsuːfyːg(ə)n] *V/t.*, fügte hinzu, hat hinzugefügt
Die Soße schmeckt gut, vielleicht solltest du noch etwas Sahne hinzufügen.

add *v*
The sauce tastes good; perhaps you should add a little cream.

klopfen ['klɔpf(ə)n] *V/i.*, klopfte, hat geklopft
Hörst du? Jemand klopft an die Tür.

knock *v*
Did you hear that? Someone is knocking at the door.

läuten ['lɔit(ə)n] *V/i.*, läutete, hat geläutet
Es läutet. Machst du bitte die Tür auf?

ring *(bells)* *v*
The doorbell rang. Would you please open the door?

lösen ['løːz(ə)n] *V/t.*, löste, hat gelöst
Der Knoten ist zu fest, ich kann ihn nicht lösen.

loosen *v*
The knot is too tight; I can't loosen it.

nachahmen ['naːxaːmən] *V/t.*,
Klaus kann gut malen. Auf einigen Bildern ahmt er van Gogh nach.

imitate *v*
Klaus can paint well. In a number of pictures he imitates van Gogh.

nachgeben ['naːxgeːb(ə)n] *V/i.*, gab nach, hat nachgegeben
Sie verteidigte ihre Rechte und gab nicht nach.

give in *v*
She defended her rights and did not give in.

nähen ['nɛː(ə)n] *V/t.*, nähte, hat genäht
Sie näht alle ihre Kleider selbst.

sew *v*
She sews all her own clothes.

regeln ['reːg(ə)ln] *V/t.*, regelte, hat geregelt
Diese Sache muss schnell geregelt werden.

regulate, settle *v*
The matter must be settled quickly.

reißen ['rais(ə)n] *V/t., i., + Präp.* (an, um, weg, u.a.), riss, hat (ist) gerissen
Der Sturm riss das Zelt um.

tear, rip *v*
The storm knocked down the tent.

Der Dieb hat ihr die Tasche weggerissen.

The thief ripped off her purse.

Achtung, das Seil reißt!

Look out, the rope is tearing!

rühren ['ry:rən] *V/t.,* rührte, hat gerührt
Vorsicht, die Farbe muss vor dem Gebrauch gut gerührt werden!

stir, mix *v*
Careful, the paint has to be stirred well before using it.

---

sägen ['zɛ:g(ə)n] *V/t.,* sägte, hat gesägt
Er hat das Holz mit der Hand gesägt, nicht mit der Maschine.

saw *v*
He sawed the wood by hand, not with a machine.

---

schimpfen ['ʃimpf(ə)n] *V/i., +* *Präp.* (auf, über), schimpfte, hat geschimpft
Der Gast schimpfte über den schlechten Service im Restaurant.

complain (about), **tell off** *v*

The guest complained about the poor service in the restaurant.

---

senken ['zɛŋk(ə)n] *V/t.,* senkte, hat gesenkt
Der Kran senkte das Boot ins Wasser.

lower *v*
The crane lowered the boat into the water.

---

steigern ['ʃtaigə*n] *V/t.,* steigerte, hat gesteigert
Der Zug steigerte seine Geschwindigkeit immer mehr.

increase *v*
The train increased its speed more and more.

Störung ['ʃtø:ruŋ] *f,* -, -en
Entschuldigen Sie bitte die Störung.
Wegen einer Störung konnte er kein Fernsehbild empfangen.

disturbance *n*
Please excuse the disturbance.
Because of an interference he could not get the television picture.

---

streichen ['ʃtraiç(ə)n] *V/t.,* strich, hat gestrichen
Die Fenster müssen gestrichen werden.

paint *v*
The windows have to be painted.

---

stützen ['ʃtyts(ə)n] *V/t., refl., +* *Präp.* (auf), stützte, hat gestützt
Die Äste des Apfelbaumes müssen gestützt werden.
Er stützt sich auf einen Stock.

support *v*

The branches of the apple tree have to be supported.
He supports himself with a cane.

Trennung ['trɛnuŋ] *f,* -, -en
Die Trennung von seiner Familie machte ihn sehr traurig.

separation *n*
The separation from his family made him very sad.

trocknen ['trɔknən] *V/t., i.,* trocknete, hat getrocknet

dry *v*

Du musst noch deine Haare
trocknen.

You still have to dry your hair.

Die Farbe trocknet schnell.

The paint dries quickly.

überprüfen [y:bə*'pry:f(ə)n] *V/t.,*
überprüfte, hat überprüft

check (over) *v*

Das kann nicht stimmen. Bitte
überprüfen Sie die Rechnung
noch einmal!

That can't be right. Please check
the bill again!

Überprüfung [y:bə*'pry:fuŋ] *f, -,*
-en

check(ing) *n*

Bei der Überprüfung der Rechnung wurden einige Fehler festgestellt.

Checking the bill they found a
number of errors.

überraschen [y:bə*'raʃ(ə)n] *V/t.,*
überraschte, hat überrascht

surprise *v*

Wir waren überrascht, dass wir
nicht kontrolliert wurden.

We were surprised that we were
not checked.

Ich überraschte meine Tochter,
als sie heimlich eine Zigarette
rauchte.

I surprised my daughter smoking
a cigarette secretly.

Überraschung [y:bə*'raʃuŋ] *f, -,*
-en

surprise *n*

Ich habe eine große Überraschung für dich.

I have a big surprise for you.

übersehen [y:bə*'ze:(ə)n] *V/t.,*
übersah, hat übersehen

overlook, neglect *v*

Du hast übersehen, dass die Ampel rot war.

You overlooked the red (traffic)
light.

umgehen [um'ge:(ə)n] *V/t.,* um-
ging, hat umgangen

bypass, disregard *v*

Diese Vorschrift kann man nicht
ohne weiteres umgehen.

You cannot disregard the regulation without consequences.

umgehen ['umge:(ə)n] *V/i., +*
Präp. (mit), ging um, ist umge-
gangen

work, handle, deal with *v*

Sie kann sehr gut mit Pferden umgehen.

She can work well with horses.

umrühren [ˈumryːrən] *V./t.*, rührte um, hat umgerührt

stir *v*

Die Suppe muss ständig umgerührt werden.

The soup has to be stirred constantly.

---

unterbrechen [untə*ˈbrɛç(ə)n] *V/t.*, unterbrach, hat (ist) unterbrochen)

interrupt *v*

Plötzlich war das Telefongespräch unterbrochen.

Suddenly the phone call was interrupted.

---

unterlassen [untə*ˈlas(ə)n] *V/t.*, unterließ, hat unterlassen

stop *v*

Unterlassen Sie die laute Musik, sonst werde ich mich beschweren!

Stop (playing) the loud music, or I'll complain!

---

unterstützen [untə*ˈʃtyts(ə)n] *V/t.*, unterstützte, hat unterstützt

support *v*

Gerd muss seine Eltern unterstützen, weil sie zu wenig Rente bekommen.

Gerd has to support his parents because their pension is too small.

Unterstützung [untə*ˈʃtytsuŋ] *f,* -, -en

support *n*

Er bat um Unterstützung für seinen Plan.

He asked for support for his plan.

---

unvorsichtig [ˈunfoːə*ziçtiçˀ] *Adj.*

careless

Er ist ein unvorsichtiger Fahrer, er fährt so wild.

He is a careless driver; he drives wildly.

---

verbergen [fɛə*ˈbɛrg(ə)n] *V/t., refl.*, verbarg, hat verborgen

hide *v*

Verbirgst du ein Geheimnis vor mir?

Are you hiding a secret from me?

Die Tiere verbargen sich bis zum Abend im Wald.

The animals hid in the forest until evening.

---

verbessern [fɛə*ˈbɛsə*n] *V/t., refl.*, verbesserte, hat verbessert

improve, make better, correct *(mistakes) v*

Die Fehler habe ich alle verbessert.

I have corrected all the mistakes.

Die Qualität der Produkte hat sich im letzten Jahr verbessert.

The quality of the products improved last year.

verbinden [fɛə*'bind(ə)n] *V/t.,*
verband, hat verbunden
Der Kanal verbindet zwei Flüsse.
Dieser Plan ist mit sehr viel Arbeit
verbunden.

join, connect v

The canal connects two rivers.
This plan requires (*lit.:* is connected with) a lot of work.

verbrennen [fɛə*'brɛnən] *V/t., i.,*
verbrannte, hat (ist) verbrannt
Nach einem Streit hat sie alle
Briefe von ihm verbrannt.

burn v

After an argument she burned all
his letters.

vergießen [fɛə*'giːs(ə)n] *V/t.,* ver-
goß, hat vergossen
○ Woher kommt der Fleck auf
dem Tisch?
□ Monika hat Kaffee vergossen.

spill v

○ What caused the stain on the
table?
□ Monika spilled coffee.

vermitteln [fɛə*'mit(ə)ln] *V/t.,* ver-
mittelte, hat vermittelt
Sie hat ihm eine Stelle vermittelt.

provide, help to get, mediate v

She helped him get a job.

vernachlässigen
[fɛə*'naːxlɛsig(ə)n] *V/t.,* vernach-
lässigte, hat vernachlässigt
Ich finde, dass du deinen Hund
vernachlässigst.

neglect v

I think you're neglecting your dog.

versäumen [fɛə*'zɔimən] *V/t.,* ver-
säumte, hat versäumt
Diese Chance hast du leider versäumt.

pass up, miss v

You have unfortunately passed
up this chance.

verstärken [fɛə*'ʃtɛrk(ə)n] *V/t.,*
refl., verstärkte, hat verstärkt
Die Wand muss verstärkt werden,
sonst stürzt das Haus ein.
Die Fußballmannschaft verstärkte sich mit einem neuen Spieler.

strengthen, reinforce v

The wall has to be strengthened;
otherwise the house will cave in.
The soccer (*BE:* football)team
was reinforced with a new player.

verwandeln [fɛə*'vand(ə)ln] *V/t.,*
refl., verwandelte, hat verwandelt
Das alte Haus wurde fast in einen
Neubau verwandelt.
Seit ihrer Krankheit hat sie sich
vollkommen verwandelt.

transform, change v

The old house was almost trans-
formed into a new building.
Since her illness she has changed
completely.

verwirklichen [fɛə*'virkliç(ə)n] *V/t.*, verwirklichte, hat verwirklicht
Er hat gute Ideen, aber er kann sie nicht verwirklichen.

realize, accomplish *v*
He has good ideas, but he cannot realize them.

Verwirklichung [fɛə'virkliçuŋ] *f*, -, -en
Die Reise war für ihn die Verwirklichung eines Traums.

realization, accomplishment *n*
The trip was the realization of a dream for him.

---

verwöhnen [fɛə'vø:nən] *V/t.*, verwöhnte, hat verwöhnt
Sie verwöhnt ihre Katze.

spoil *(a personality) v*
She spoils her cat.

---

wagen ['va:g(ə)n] *V/t., refl.*, wagte, hat gewagt
Er wagt nicht, ihr zu widersprechen.

Sie wagt sich nachts nicht allein durch den Park.

dare *v*
He doesn't dare to contradict her.

She does not dare to walk through the park alone at night.

---

wehren ['ve:rən] *V/refl., + Präp.* (gegen), wehrte, hat gewehrt
Er wehrte sich gegen die Vorwürfe.

defend *v*
He defended himself against the accusations.

---

zerbrechen [tsɛə*'brɛç(ə)n] *V/t., i.*, zerbrach, hat (ist) zerbrochen
○ Wer hat das Glas zerbrochen?
□ Niemand, es ist in der Spülmaschine von selbst zerbrochen.

break, shatter *v*
○ Who broke the glass?
□ Nobody; it shattered by itself in the dishwasher.

---

zerreißen [tsɛə*'rais(ə)n] *V/t.*, zerriss, hat zerrissen
Die unscharfen Fotos kannst du zerreißen und wegwerfen.

tear up *v*
You can tear up and throw away the photos that are out-of-focus.

---

zudecken ['tsu:dɛk(ə)n] *V/t.*, deckte zu, hat zugedeckt
Er deckte das schlafende Kind zu.

cover (up) *v*
He covered the sleeping child.

---

zulassen ['tsu:las(ə)n] *V/t.*, ließ zu, hat zugelassen
Ausnahmen werden nicht zugelassen!

permit *v*
Exceptions are not permitted!

zusammenlegen [tsu'zamən-
le:g(ə)n] *V/t.,* legte zusammen,
hat zusammengelegt
Leg den Pullover zusammen und
dann in den Schrank!

fold, put together *v*

Fold up the sweater and put it in
the dresser.

2.8 Lernen und Wissen | 1-2000

aufschreiben ['aufʃraib(ə)n] *V/t.,*
schrieb auf, hat aufgeschrieben
Das muss ich (mir) aufschreiben,
damit ich es nicht vergesse.

**write down, write someone a
note** *v*
I have to write this down so that I
won't forget it.

bedeuten [bə'dɔit(ə)n] *V/i.,* bedeu-
tete, hat bedeutet
Was bedeutet dieses Wort?

mean, signify *v*

What does this word mean?

Bedeutung [bə'dɔituŋ] *f, -,* -en
Dieses Wort hat mehrere Bedeu-
tungen.

meaning, significance *n*
This word has several meanings.

Begabung [bə'ga:buŋ] *f, -,* -en
Sie malt gerne, aber ich finde, sie
hat keine besondere Begabung
dafür.

talent *n*
She likes to paint, but I don't think
she has any special talent for it.

Begriff [bə'grif] *m, -(e)s,* -e
Mein Arzt verwendet oft medizinische Begriffe, die ich nicht verstehe.

concept, term, idea *n*
My doctor often uses medical
terms that I do not understand.

Beispiel ['baiʃpi:l] *n, -s,* -e
Er erklärte das Problem anhand
eines Beispiels.

example *n*
He explained the problem using
an example.

Bibliothek [biblio'te:k] *f, -,* -en
Das Buch habe ich in der Bibliothek ausgeliehen.

library *n*
I borrowed the book from the library.

Bildung ['bilduŋ] *f, -, kein Pl.*
Er ist nicht dumm, aber ihm fehlt
eine allgemeine Bildung.

education *n*
He is not stupid, but he lacks a
general education.

Buch [buːx] *n, -(e)s, Bücher*
Ich lese gerade ein interessantes Buch.

book *n*
I'm reading an interesting book.

Buchstabe ['buːxʃtaːbə] *m, -n, -n*
Das Wort hat neun Buchstaben.

letter *(of the alphabet) n*
The word has nine letters.

Fach [fax] *n, -(e)s, Fächer*
Sie weiß noch nicht, welches Fach sie studieren möchte.

subject *(academic) n*
She does not yet know which subject she would like to study.

Forschung ['fɔrʃuŋ] *f, -, -en*
Die medizinische Forschung hat noch kein Mittel gegen Krebs gefunden.

research *n*
Medical research has yet to find a cure for cancer.

Fortschritt ['fɔrtʃrit] *m, -(e)s, -e*
Sie macht beim Lernen gute Fortschritte.

progress *n*
She is making good progress in her studies.

fähig ['fɛːiçᵒ] *Adj.*
Mit 80 Jahren ist er noch fähig, Gartenarbeit zu machen.

capable, able
At age 80 he is still capable of working in the garden.

Fähigkeit ['fɛːiçkait] *f, -, -en*
Sie hat angeblich die Fähigkeit, die Zukunft vorauszusagen.

capability, ability *n*
She supposedly has the ability to predict the future.

Germanistik [gɛrmaˈnistik] *f, -, kein Pl.*
In Japan und Korea hat die Germanistik eine lange Tradition.

German language and literature, Germanistics, German *n*
In Japan and Korea the study of German language and literature enjoys a long tradition.

Geschichte [gəˈʃiçtə] *f, -, kein Pl.*
Er studierte Deutsch und Geschichte.

history, story *n*
He is studying German and history.

geschichtlich [gəˈʃiçtliç] *Adj.*
Unser geschichtliches Wissen über die Steinzeit ist sehr gering.

historical
Our historical knowledge about the Stone Age is very limited.

Korrektur [kɔrɛkˈtuːə*] *f, -, -en*
Bei der Korrektur des Briefes habe ich keine Fehler entdeckt.

correction *n*
When I corrected the letter, I found no mistakes.

korrigieren [kɔri'giːrən] *V/t.,* korrigierte, hat korrigiert
Bitte korrigieren Sie den Brief und bringen Sie ihn dann zur Post.

correct *v*
Please correct the letter and then take it to the post office.

---

lehren ['leːrən] *V/t.,* lehrte, hat gelehrt
Sie lehrt Physik an der Universität.

teach *(at a university or college) v*
She teaches physics at the university.

Lehrer ['leːrə*] *m,* -s, -
Lehrerin ['leːrərin] *f,* -, nen
Er ist ein sehr guter Lehrer. Die Schüler mögen ihn.

teacher, instructor *n*
He is a very good teacher. The students like him.

---

lernen ['lɛrnən] *V/t.,* lernte, hat gelernt
Sie hat in der Schule Spanisch gelernt.

learn *v*
She learned Spanish in school.

---

lesen ['leːz(ə)n] *V/t.,* las, hat gelesen
Er liest gerade Zeitung.

read *v*
He is reading the newspaper.

Methode [me'toːdə] *f,* -, -n
Es gibt verschiedene Methoden, eine Sprache zu lernen.

method *n*
There are different methods for learning a language.

Naturwissenschaft
[na'tuːə*vis(ə)nʃaft] *f,* -, -en
Mein Bruder interessiert sich für Naturwissenschaft.

(natural) science *n*
My brother is interested in science.

Probe ['proːbə] *f,* -, -n
Nach der Probezeit wurde er fest angestellt.

trial, probation, sample *n*
After the probationary period he was hired full time.

---

rechnen ['rɛçnən] *V/t., i.,* rechnete, hat gerechnet
Diese Aufgabe kann ich nicht im Kopf rechnen.
Sie kann schnell rechnen.

calculate, figure *v*
I cannot figure the problem in my head.
She can calculate quickly.

Rechnung ['rɛçnuŋ] *f,* -, en
Komplizierte Rechnungen mache ich mit dem Taschenrechner.

invoice, bill, check, calculation *n*
Complicated calculations I do with a calculator.

schwer [ʃveːɐ*] *Adj.*

Deutsch gilt als schwere Sprache.

heavy, difficult, complicated, hard

German is considered to be a difficult language.

---

schwierig [ˈʃviːrɪç°] *Adj.*

Die meisten Prüfungsfragen waren nicht schwierig.

difficult, complicated, hard

Most of the examination questions were not difficult.

Seite [ˈzaitə] *f, -, -n*

Das Buch hat 251 Seiten.

page, side *n*

The book has 251 pages.

Theorie [teoˈriː] *f, -, -n*

Über die Entstehung der Erde gibt es verschiedene Theorien.

theory *n*

There are various theories about the origin of the earth.

---

wissen [ˈvɪs(ə)n] *V/i., + Präp. (von, über), wusste, hat gewusst*

Ich weiß nicht, wo er wohnt.

know *v*

I do not know where he lives.

Wissen [ˈvɪs(ə)n] *n, -s, kein Pl.*

Sie hat auf diesem Gebiet ein großes Wissen.

knowledge *n*

She has considerable knowledge in this area.

Wissenschaft [ˈvɪs(ə)nʃaft] *f, -, -en*

Philosophie ist die älteste Wissenschaft.

(branch of) knowledge, academic subject, science *n*

Philosophy is the oldest branch of knowledge.

Wissenschaftler [ˈvɪs(ə)nʃaftlɐ*] *m, -s, -*, **Wissenschaftlerin** [ˈvɪs(ə)nʃaftlərɪn] *f, -, -nen*

An unserem Institut arbeiten sechs Wissenschaftler und Wissenschaftlerinnen.

scientist, researcher *n*

There are six researchers working at our institute.

---

wissenschaftlich [ˈvɪs(ə)nʃaftlɪç] *Adj.*

Über die Ursachen von Krebs gibt es viele wissenschaftliche Untersuchungen.

scientific

There have been many scientific studies on the causes of cancer.

Zeichen [ˈtsaiç(ə)n] *n, -s, -*

'$' ist das Zeichen für Dollar.

sign, symbol *n*

"$" is the symbol for dollar.

Zeile [ˈtsailə] *f, -, -n*

Das Gedicht hat sieben Zeilen.

line *(in a text) n*

The poem has seven lines.

Überlegung [yːbə*ˈleːɡuŋ] *f, -, -en*
Er hat ohne Überlegung gehandelt.

thinking, planning, forethought, consideration *n*
He acted without thinking.

2001-4000

Band [bant] *m, -(e)s, Bände*
Dieses Lexikon besteht aus fünf Bänden.

volume *n*
This encyclopedia consists of five volumes.

besichtigen [bəˈziçtig(ə)n] *V/t.,* besichtigte, hat besichtigt
Das Museum kann man nur vormittags besichtigen.

view, visit *(museums, ruins, etc.) v*
You can visit the museum only in the morning.

Biologie [bioloˈgiː] *f, -, kein Pl.*
Sie studiert im 3. Semester Biologie.

biology *n*
She is in her third semester in biology.

Blatt [blat] *n, -(e)s, die Blätter*
Kannst du mir bitte ein Blatt Papier geben?

piece, sheet *(of paper) n*
Could you please give me a piece of paper?

Block [blɔk] *m, -s, die Blöcke*
Bringe mir bitte einen Block Papier aus dem Schreibwarengeschäft mit.

pad *(of paper),* **block** *n*
Please bring me a pad of paper from the stationery store.

Buchhandlung [ˈbuːxhandluŋ] *f, -, -en*
In dieser Buchhandlung kann man auch Zeitschriften kaufen.

bookstore, bookshop *n*
You can also buy magazines in this bookstore.

Bücherei [byːçəˈrai] *f, -, -en*
Das Buch habe ich in der Stadtbücherei ausgeliehen.

library *n*
I borrowed the book from the municipal library.

Chemie [çeˈmiː] *f, -, kein Pl.*
In der Schule war Chemie mein Lieblingsfach.

chemistry *n*
Chemistry was my favorite subject in school.

chemisch [ˈçeːmiʃ] *Adj.*
H_2O ist die chemische Formel für Wasser.

chemical
H_2O is the chemical formula for water.

entdecken [ɛnt'dɛk(ə)n] *V/t.*, entdeckte, hat entdeckt
1492 hat Kolumbus Amerika entdeckt.

discover v
Columbus discovered America in 1492.

Entdeckung [ɛnt'dɛkuŋ] *f,* -, -en
Das 15. Jahrhundert war das Zeitalter der großen Entdeckungsreisen.

discovery n
The fifteenth century was the age of the great journeys of discovery.

Erdkunde ['eːə*tkundə] *f,* -, *kein Pl.*
Er ist Lehrer für Deutsch und Erdkunde.

geography *(as an academic subject)* n
He is a teacher of German and geography.

Erforschung [ɛə*'fɔrʃuŋ] *f,* -, -en
Bei der Erforschung der Höhle wurden Zeichnungen aus der Steinzeit entdeckt.

research(ing) n
While researching the cave they discovered drawings from the Stone Age.

Fachmann ['faxman] *m,* -(e)s, Fachmänner, meist: **Fachleute**
Fachfrau *f,* -, en
Diese Arbeit muss von einem Fachmann gemacht werden.

expert n
This work has to be done by an expert.

Formel ['fɔrm(ə)l] *f,* -, -n
Die chemische Formel für Wasser ist H_2O.

formula n
The chemical formula for water is H_2O.

Forscher ['fɔrʃə*] *m,* -s, -
Forscherin ['fɔrʃərin] *f,* -, -nen
Die beiden Forscher bekamen für ihre Arbeiten einen Preis.

researcher n
Both researchers received a prize for their work.

fortschrittlich ['fɔrtʃritliç] *Adj.*
Die Kinder an dieser Schule werden sehr fortschrittlich erzogen.

progressive
The children at this school are given a progressive education.

Geographie [geogra'fiː] *f,* -, *kein Pl.*
Geographie ist ein interessantes Fach.

geography *(as academic subject)* n
Geography is an interesting subject.

historisch [his'toːriʃ] *Adj.*
Bei den Bauarbeiten wurden historische Gräber entdeckt.

historical
During construction a number of historical graves were discovered.

imstande sein [im'ʃtandə], *auch* **(im Stande)** war imstande, ist imstande gewesen
Die Forscher waren imstande, alle chemischen Elemente genau zu bestimmen.

be able, be capable v

The researchers were able to identify all the chemical elements.

konkret [kɔn'kreːt] *Adj.*, *-er, am -esten*
Sie hat noch keine konkreten Vorschläge gemacht.

concrete

She has yet to make any concrete suggestions.

Konzentration [kɔntsɛntra'tsjoːn] *f, -, kein Pl.*
Der Text ist schwierig. Das Lesen erfordert hohe Konzentration.

concentration n

The text is difficult. Reading it requires considerable concentration.

konzentrieren [kɔntsɛn'triːrən] *V/t., refl.,* konzentrierte, hat konzentriert
Stör mich nicht! Ich muss mich konzentrieren.

concentrate v

Don't disturb me! I have to concentrate.

Notiz [no'tiːts] *f, -, -en*
Ich habe mir während des Gesprächs einige Notizen gemacht.

note *(written)* n
I took notes during the conversation.

Philosophie [filozo'fiː] *f, -, kein Pl.*
Herr Dr. Kranz ist kein Arzt, er ist Doktor der Philosophie.

philosophy n

Dr. Kranz is not a physician; he is a doctor of philosophy (Ph.D).

Physik [fy'zik] *f, -, kein Pl.*
Mein Bruder studiert Physik und Mathematik.

physics n
My brother is studying physics and mathematics.

Praxis ['praksis] *f, -, kein Pl.*
Sie hat in ihrem Beruf noch wenig Praxis.

practice, experience n
She doesn't yet have a lot of experience in her profession.

Symbol [zym'boːl] *n, -s, -e*
Das x ist das Symbol für Multiplikation in der Mathematik.

symbol n
"x" is the symbol for multiplication in mathematics.

Tabelle [ta'bɛlə] *f, -, -en*
Die genauen Daten finden Sie in der Tabelle.

table *(of information)*, **chart** n
You can find the exact data in the table.

These [ˈteːzə] *f, -, -n*

thesis, *(philosophical)* **concept, hypothesis** *n*

Die Thesen von Prof. Fuchs wurden ausführlich diskutiert.

The concepts of Prof. Fuchs were thoroughly discussed.

Überblick [ˈyːbə*blɪk] *m, -s, kein Pl.*

overview *n*

Das Buch beginnt mit einem allgemeinen Überblick über die Geschichte des 19. Jahrhunderts.

The book begins with a general overview of the history of the nineteenth century.

übersetzen [yːbə*ˈzɛts(ə)n] *V/t., übersetzte, hat übersetzt*

translate *v*

Ich kann leider kein Englisch. Könnten Sie mir den Brief übersetzen?

I do not know English. Could you translate the letter for me?

Übersetzung [yːbə*ˈzɛtsuŋ] *f, -, -en*

translation *n*

Für das Buch gibt es leider noch keine deutsche Übersetzung.

Unfortunately, there is not yet a German translation for the book.

---

unbekannt [ˈunbəkant] *Adj., -er, am -esten*

unknown

Sein Vorname ist Horst, sein Nachname ist mir unbekannt.

His first name is Horst; I do not know his last name.

---

untersuchen [untə*ˈzuːx(ə)n] *V/t., untersuchte, hat untersucht*

examine, investigate *v*

Die Ursache des Unglücks wurde nicht sorgfältig untersucht.

The cause of the accident was not thoroughly investigated.

Untersuchung [untə*ˈzuːxuŋ] *f, -, -en*

examination, test, investigation *n*

Das Ergebnis der Untersuchung war negativ.

The results of the test investigation were negative.

Verfasser [fɛə*ˈfasə*] *m, -s, -*
Verfasserin [fɛə*ˈfasərin] *f, -, -nen*

author *n*

Ich kenne nur den Titel des Buches, den Namen der Verfasserin habe ich vergessen.

I know only the title of the book, I've forgotten the name of the author.

Verständnis [fɛə*ˈʃtɛntnɪs] *n, -ses, kein Pl.*

understanding *n*

Er zeigte viel Verständnis für meine schwierige Situation.

He showed considerable understanding for my difficult situation.

vorlesen ['foːə*leːz(ə)n] *V/t.,* las vor, hat vorgelesen
Ich lese den Kindern jeden Abend eine Geschichte vor.

read aloud, lecture *v*

Every evening I read the children a story.

3.1 Allgemeines | 1-2000

3.1 General

Antwort ['antvɔrt] *f,* -, -en
Auf diese Frage weiß ich keine Antwort.

answer *n*
I don't have an answer to this question.

---

antworten ['antvɔrt(ə)n] *V/i.,*
+ Präp. (auf), antwortete, hat geantwortet
Ich werde Ihnen schriftlich antworten.

answer *v*

I'll answer you in writing.

---

laut [laut] *Adj.,* -er, am -esten
Jens hat eine sehr laute Stimme.

loud
Jens has a very loud voice.

---

leise ['laizə] *adj.* -r, am -sten
Er spricht so leise, dass wir ihn kaum verstehen können.

quiet, soft *(sound)*
He speaks so softly that we can hardly understand him.

---

ruhig ['ruːiç°] *Adj.*
Obwohl sie sehr ärgerlich war, blieb sie ruhig.

quiet, peaceful
Although she was very angry, she kept very quiet.

---

schweigen ['ʃvaig(ə)n] *V/i.,*
schwieg, hat geschwiegen
Der Angeklagte schwieg, als der Richter ihn fragte.

be silent, be quiet

The defendant was silent when the judge questioned him.

Sprache ['ʃpraːxə] *f,* -, -n
Sie spricht drei verschiedene Sprachen.

language *n*
She speaks three different languages.

---

still [ʃtil] *Adj.*
Warum bist du heute so still?

quiet, still
Why are you so quiet today?

Wort [vɔrt] *n,* -es, -e (Wörter)
Dieser Satz hat fünf Wörter.
Sie kann komplizierte Dinge mit einfachen Worten erklären.

word *n*
This sentence has five words.
She is able to explain complicated things in simple words.

wörtlich [ˈvœrtliç] *Adj.*
Diesen Text habe ich wörtlich übersetzt.

literal
I translated this text literally.

zuhören [ˈtsuːhøːrən] *V/i.*, hörte zu, hat zugehört
Was hat sie gesagt? Ich habe nicht zugehört.

listen *v*

What did she say? I was not listening.

$$2001\text{-}4000$$

Anfrage [ˈanfraːgə] *f*, -, -n
Auf meine Anfrage bei der Botschaft habe ich noch keine Antwort bekommen.

inquiry, enquiry, question *n*
I have yet to receive an answer to my question from the embassy.

anhören [ˈanhøːrən] *V/i.*, *refl.*, hörte an, hat angehört
Er hört sich ein Konzert im Radio an.

listen to *v*

He is listening to a concert on the radio.

Aussprache [ˈausʃpraːxə] *f*, -, *kein Pl.*
Die französische Aussprache ist für Deutsche sehr schwer.

pronunciation *n*

The pronunciation of French is very difficult for Germans.

aussprechen [ˈausʃprɛç(ə)n] *V/t.*, sprach aus, hat ausgesprochen
Wie wird Ihr Name ausgesprochen?

pronounce *v*

How is your name pronounced.

buchstabieren [buːxʃtaˈbiːrən] *V/t.*, buchstabierte, hat buchstabiert
Wie schreibt man das? Bitte buchstabieren Sie!

spell *v*

How do you spell that? Please spell it.

Kommentar [kɔmɛnˈtaːʳ] *m*, -s, -e
Der Kommentar in der Zeitung entspricht meiner Meinung.

commentary, editorial *n*
The editorial in the newspaper expresses my opinion.

Laut [laut] *m*, -es, -e
Es war völlig still. Man hörte keinen Laut.

sound *(in words)* *n*
It was completely quiet. You couldn't hear a single sound.

schweigsam [ˈʃvaikzaːm] *Adj.*
Er war den ganzen Abend sehr schweigsam.

silent, taciturn, still
He didn't say much all evening.

Verständigung [fɛɐˈʃtɛndiguŋ] *f, -, kein Pl.*
Die Verständigung am Telefon war sehr schlecht.

understanding, comprehension *n*
You could not understand anything on the telephone.

verständlich [fɛɐˈʃtɛntlɪç] *Adj.*

Ihre Aussprache ist schwer verständlich.

understandable, comprehensible
Your/Her/Their pronunciation is difficult to understand.

Witz [vɪts] *m, -es, -e*
Mein Kollege erzählt gerne Witze.

joke *n*
My colleague likes to tell jokes.

3.2 Sprechen   1-2000

3.2 Speech

Ausdruck [ˈausdruk] *m, -s, Ausdrücke*
Dieser Ausdruck ist sehr passend.

expression *n*

This expression is quite appropriate.

Aussage [ˈauszaːgə] *f, -, -en*
Vor Gericht machten die Zeugen verschiedene Aussagen.

statement *n*
Before the court the witnesses made different statements.

bemerken [bəˈmɛrk(ə)n] *V/t.,* bemerkte, hat bemerkt
„Dieses Bild gefällt mir gut", bemerkte sie.

comment, note *v*

"I like this picture a lot," she commented.

Bemerkung [bəˈmɛrkuŋ] *f, -, -en*
Deine Bemerkung hat ihn beleidigt.

comment *n*
Your comment insulted him.

erzählen [ɛɐˈtsɛːl(ə)n] *V/t.,* erzählte, hat erzählt
Was hat sie dir über Frank erzählt?

tell, say *v*

What did she tell you about Frank?

Gespräch [gəˈʃprɛːç] *n, -s, -e*
Ich hatte heute ein langes Gespräch mit unserem Chef.

conversation *n*
Today I had a long conversation with our boss.

---

mitteilen [ˈmittail(ə)n] *V/t.,* teilte mit, hat mitgeteilt
Den Angestellten wurde mitgeteilt, dass die Firma verkauft wird.

communicate, inform *v*

The employees were informed that the firm would be sold.

Mitteilung [ˈmittailuŋ] *f, -, -en*
Wir bekamen die Mitteilung, dass Irene schwer verletzt ist.

communication, report *n*
We received the report that Irene has been badly injured.

Muttersprache [ˈmutə*ʃpraːxə] *f, -, -en*
Ihre Muttersprache ist Deutsch, aber sie ist Italienerin.

native language *n*

Her native language is German, but she is Italian.

---

reden [ˈreːd(ə)n] *V/i., + Präp.* (über, von, mit), redete, hat geredet
Über diese Sache kann man mit ihr nicht reden.

talk, speak *v*

You cannot talk to her about this matter.

---

rufen [ˈruːf(ə)n] *V/t., i., + Präp.* (nach, zu), rief, hat gerufen
Wir müssen einen Arzt rufen.
Sie rief laut nach ihrem Hund.

call, shout *v*

We have to call a doctor.
She called her dog loudly.

---

sagen [ˈzaːg(ə)n] *V/t.,* sagte, hat gesagt
Er sagt niemandem, wie alt er ist.

say, tell *v*

He tells nobody how old he is.

Satz [zats] *m, -es,* Sätze
Das Buch ist in einfachen und kurzen Sätzen geschrieben.

sentence *n*
The book is written in simple and short sentences.

---

sprechen [ˈʃprɛç(ə)n] *V/t., i., + Präp.* (von, über), sprach, hat gesprochen
Sie spricht drei Fremdsprachen.

Er spricht sehr undeutlich.

speak *v*

She speaks three foreign languages.
He enunciates poorly.

Stimme [ˈʃtimə] *f, -, -n*
Am Telefon klingt deine Stimme ganz anders.

voice *n*
On the telephone your voice sounds quite different.

wiederholen [viːdə*ːhoːl(ə)n] *V/t.,* wiederholte, hat wiederholt
Bitte wiederholen Sie den letzten Satz!

repeat *v*

Please repeat the last sentence!

2001-4000

Äußerung [ˈɔisəruŋ] *f, -, -en*
Diese unvorsichtige Äußerung hat ihm geschadet.

utterance, remark, comment *n*
This imprudent remark did him a lot of damage.

ankündigen [ˈankyndig(ə)n] *V/t.,* kündigte an, hat angekündigt
Herr Schröder hat für morgen seinen Besuch angekündigt.

announce *v*

Mr. Schröder announced his visit for tomorrow.

Anmerkung [ˈanmɛrkuŋ] *f, -, -en*
Zu dem Vertrag habe ich noch einige Anmerkungen.

note, comment *n*
I still have a few notes about/on the contract.

ausdrücken [ˈausdryk(ə)n] *V/t., refl.,* drückte aus, hat ausgedrückt
Das ist ein Missverständnis. Ich habe mich wohl nicht richtig ausgedrückt.

express *v*

That is a misunderstanding. I guess I did not express myself correctly.

bekanntgeben
[bəˈkantgeːb(ə)n] *V/t.,* gab bekannt, hat bekanntgegeben
Das Wahlergebnis wird morgen bekanntgegeben.

announce *v*

The results of the election will be announced tomorrow.

benachrichtigen
[bəˈnaːxriçtig(ə)n] *V/t.,* benachrichtigte, hat benachrichtigt
Herr Weber hatte einen Unfall. Bitte benachrichtigen Sie seine Frau.

inform *v*

Mr. Weber has had an accident. Please inform his wife.

besprechen [bəˈʃprɛç(ə)n] *V/t.,* besprach, hat besprochen
Das müssen Sie mit Frau Bartels besprechen.

discuss *v*

You'll have to discuss that with Ms. Bartels.

Besprechung [bəˈʃprɛçuŋ] *f*, -, -en
Bitte rufen Sie später an. Frau Seel ist in einer Besprechung.

discussion, meeting *n*
Please call later. Ms. Seel is in a meeting.

---

betonen [bəˈtoːnən] *V/t.*, betonte, hat betont
Das Wort wird auf der ersten Silbe betont.

emphasize, stress, *v*
This word is stressed on the first syllable.

---

erwähnen [ɛəˈvɛːnən] *V/t.*, erwähnte, hat erwähnt
Er hat ihren Namen nicht erwähnt.

mention *v*
He did not mention her name.

---

flüstern [ˈflʏstəˈn] *V/t., i.*, flüsterte, hat geflüstert
Sie flüsterte leise seinen Namen.
In der Bibliothek darf man nur flüstern.

whisper *v*
She whispered his name softly.
In the library, you are only allowed to whisper.

---

hinzufügen [hinˈtsuːfyːg(ə)n] *V/t.*, fügte hinzu, hat hinzugefügt
Frau Wirtz hat alles Notwendige gesagt. Es gibt nichts hinzuzufügen.

add *v*
Ms. Wirtz said everything that was necessary. There is nothing to add.

---

murmeln [ˈmʊrm(ə)ln] *V/t.*, murmelte, hat gemurmelt
Er murmelte einige Worte, die ich nicht verstanden habe.

mumble *v*
He mumbled a few words that I did not understand.

---

mündlich [ˈmʏntlɪç] *Adj., keine Komp.*
Die mündliche Prüfung findet in Raum 124 statt.

oral
The oral examination takes place in Room 124.

---

schildern [ˈʃɪldəˈn] *V/t.* schilderte, hat geschildert
Der Zeuge konnte den Unfall genau schildern.

describe *v*
The witness could describe the accident accurately.

Schilderung [ˈʃɪldəruŋ] *f*, -, -en
Bitte geben Sie eine genaue Schilderung des Vorfalls.

description *n*
Please give an exact description of the incident.

Schrei [ʃrai] *m*, -(e)s, -e
Ich hörte Schreie und Hilferufe.

cry, scream *n*
I heard screams and calls for help.

schreien ['ʃrai(ə)n] *V/t., i.,* schrie, hat geschrien | **cry, scream, yell, call out** *v*

Als er Susi sah, schrie er laut ihren Namen. | When he saw Susi, he called out her name loudly.

Er schrie vor Schmerz. | He screamed with pain.

Unterredung [untə*'re:duŋ] *f,* -, -en | **discussion, talk** *n*

Mit dem neuen Kunden hatte ich eine lange Unterredung. | I had a long talk with the new customer.

---

vereinbaren [fɛə*'ainba:rən] *V/t.,* vereinbarte, hat vereinbart | **arrange** *(a date, a time, an appointment)* *v*

Wir haben für Freitag, 16.00 Uhr, einen Termin vereinbart. | We arranged to meet Friday at 4 o'clock.

Vereinbarung [fɛə*'ainba:ruŋ] *f,* -, -en | **arrangement, agreement** *n*

Zwischen Österreich und der Bundesrepublik gibt es neue Vereinbarungen über den Grenzverkehr. | There are new border traffic agreements between Austria and the Federal Republic.

Wiederholung [vi:də*'ho:luŋ] *f,* -, -en | **repetition, repeat** *n*

Eine Wiederholung der Sendung gibt es morgen Vormittag. | There will be a repeat of the broadcast tomorrow morning.

3.3 Schreiben und Lesen | 1-2000

3.3 Writing and Reading

schreiben ['ʃraib(ə)n] *V/t., i.,* schrieb, hat geschrieben | **write** *v*

Ich will heute Abend einen Brief schreiben. | I want to write a letter this evening.

Über dieses Thema wird zzt. viel in den Zeitungen geschrieben. | There is a lot being written about this topic in the newspaper at the moment.

Schrift [ʃrift] *f, -, -en*
Er kennt alle Schriften dieser Autorin.
Deine (Hand-)schrift kann ich nicht lesen.

writing *n*
He knows all the writings of this author.
I cannot read your (hand)writing.

Zettel ['tsɛt(ə)l] *m, -s, -*
Ich habe dir auf einen Zettel geschrieben, was du einkaufen sollst.

note, piece of paper *n*
I wrote you a note about what you should buy.

2001-4000

Bleistift ['blaiʃtift] *m, -(e)s-, -e*
Kannst du mir einen Bleistift oder einen Kugelschreiber geben?

pencil *n*
Could you lend me a pencil or pen?

lauten ['laut(ə)n] *V/i.,* lautete, hat gelautet
Wie lautet ihre Adresse?

be, sound like, read like, *v*

What's your address?

Rechtschreibung ['rɛçtʃraibuŋ] *f, -, kein Pl.*
Er hat Schwierigkeiten mit der Rechtschreibung.

spelling, orthography *n*

He has trouble with spelling.

schriftlich ['ʃriftliç] *Adj., keine Komp.*
Diesen Vertrag müssen Sie schriftlich kündigen.

in writing

You have to cancel this contract in writing.

unlesbar ['unle:sba:*] *Adj.*
Der letzte Teil des Briefes ist unlesbar.

illegible
The last part of this letter is illegible.

3.4 Auskunft | 1-2000

Auskunft [ˈauskunft] *f, -,* Auskünfte
Ich kann Ihnen leider keine genaue Auskunft geben.

information *n*
I cannot give you any specific information.

berichten [bəˈrɪçt(ə)n] *V/t., i., +* *Präp.* (von, über), berichtete, hat berichtet
Er hat mir alle Einzelheiten des Gesprächs berichtet.
Sie hat mir von ihrem Urlaub berichtet.

tell, tell about, inform *v*
He told me all the details of the conversation.
She told me about her vacation.

beschreiben [bəˈʃraib(ə)n] *V/t.,* beschrieb, hat beschrieben
Können Sie mir bitte den Weg zum Bahnhof beschreiben?

describe *v*
Could you describe the way to the train station?

Beschreibung [bəˈʃraibuŋ] *f, -,* -en
Die Zeugin konnte eine genaue Beschreibung des Täters geben.

description *n*
The witness could give an exact description of the culprit.

erklären [ɛəˈklɛːrən] *V/t.,* erklärte, hat erklärt
Der Lehrer hat mir die Bedeutung des Wortes erklärt.

explain *v*
The teacher explained the meaning of the word to me.

Erklärung [ɛəˈklɛːruŋ] *f, -,* -en
Für den Flugzeugabsturz gibt es bis jetzt keine Erklärung.

explanation *n*
There has not yet been an explanation of the plane crash.

Information [ɪnfɔrmaˈtsjoːn] *f, -,* -en
Diese Information ist streng geheim!

information *n*
This information is extremely confidential.

informieren [infor'miːrən] *V/t., refl.,* informierte, hat informiert

inform *v*

Bitte informieren Sie mich über die Ergebnisse des Gesprächs.

Please inform me about the results of the conversation.

Auf der Messe habe ich mich über neue Computer informiert.

At the fair I collected information on new computers.

los (sein) [loːs zain], war los, ist los gewesen

be going on *v*

Abends ist im Stadtzentrum nicht viel los.

In the evening there is not much going on downtown.

melden ['mɛld(ə)n] *V/t., refl.,* meldete, hat gemeldet

report, inform, contact *v*

Das müssen wir dem Chef melden.

We have to report that to the boss.

Nach der Ankunft melde ich mich sofort.

I'll contact you immediately upon arriving.

Nachricht ['naˈxriçt] *f, -, -en*

news, message *n*

Aus dem Unglücksgebiet gibt es keine neuen Nachrichten.

There is no news from the area of the catastrophe.

Neuigkeit ['nɔiiçkait] *f, -, -en*

interesting thing(s) to say, news *n*

Ich habe zwei Stunden mit Bernd telefoniert. Er wusste viele Neuigkeiten.

I spoke to Bernd on the telephone for two hours. He had a lot of news.

Rat [raːt] *m, -(e)s,* **Ratschläge**

advice *n*

Jochen hat mir gute Ratschläge für den Autokauf gegeben.

Jochen gave me good advice about buying a car.

raten ['raːt(ə)n] *V/t.,* riet, hat geraten

advise *v*

Ich rate Ihnen, das Angebot anzunehmen.

I advise you to accept the offer.

zeigen ['tsaig(ə)n] *V/t.,* zeigte, hat gezeigt

show *v*

Maria hat mir ihre neue Wohnung gezeigt.

Maria showed me her new apartment/flat.

Können Sie mir zeigen, wie die Maschine funktioniert?

Can you show me how the machine works?

2001-4000

beantworten [bə'antvɔrt(ə)n] *V/t.,* beantwortete, hat beantwortet
answer *(a question) v*

Die Prüfung war sehr schwer. Viele Fragen konnte ich nicht beantworten.
The exam was very difficult. There were many questions I could not answer.

beraten [bə'ra:t(ə)n] *V/t., i., + Präp.* (über), beriet, hat beraten
advise, discuss, counsel *v*

Der Verkäufer hat mich gut beraten.
The salesman advised me well.

Über die neuen Vorschläge haben wir lange beraten.
We discussed the new suggestions for a long time.

Bescheid (+ geben, bekommen, sagen, wissen, u.a.) [bə'ʃait] *m,* -(e)s, -e
inform *v*

Über unsere Entscheidung geben wir Ihnen bald Bescheid.
We'll inform you of our decision soon.

erkundigen [ɛə*'kundig(ə)n] *V/ refl.,* erkundigte, hat erkundigt
ask *v*

Werner hat sich erkundigt, wie es dir geht.
Werner asked how you are feeling.

Tipp [tip] *m,* -s, -s
tip, hint *n*

Er hat mir einen guten Tipp gegeben.
He gave me a good tip.

unterrichten [untə*'riçt(ə)n] *V/t., refl., + Präp.* (über), unterrichtete, hat unterrichtet
teach, instruct *v*

Wir sind über die neuen Vorschriften unterrichtet worden.
We were instructed about the new regulations.

Ich muss mich über den Sachverhalt noch unterrichten.
I have to learn about the subject.

verraten [fɛə*'ra:t(ə)n] *V/t.,* verriet, hat verraten
betray, reveal *v*

Meine Kollegin hat mir verraten, dass sie kündigen will.
My colleague revealed to me that she plans to quit.

3.5 Meinungsäußerung

3.5 Expressing Opinions

allerdings [ˈaləˈ*dɪŋs] *Adv.*
Ich komme morgen vorbei, allerdings habe ich wenig Zeit.

however
I'll stop by tomorrow; however, I won't have much time.

andererseits [ˈandərəˈ*zaits] *Adv.*
Einerseits ist die Wohnung sehr schön, andererseits finde ich sie sehr laut.

on the other hand

On the one hand the apartment/ flat is very attractive; on the other hand, I find it very noisy.

Ansicht [ˈanziçt] *f, -, -en*
Ich kann ihn nicht leiden, er hat komische Ansichten.

opinion, idea *n*
I don't like him; he has strange ideas.

begründen [bəˈgrynd(ə)n] *V/t.,* begründete, hat begründet
Der Minister hat seinen Rücktritt mit Krankheit begründet.

justify *v*

The Secretary justified his resignation on account of illness.

Begründung [bəˈgryndʊŋ] *f, -, -en*
Für ihre Verspätung gab sie keine Begründung.

justification, reason *n*

She gave no justification for arriving late.

beurteilen [bəˈurtail(ə)n] *V/t.,* beurteilte, hat beurteilt
Den Wert dieses Bildes kann nur ein Fachmann beurteilen.

judge, determine *v*

Only an expert can judge the value of this picture.

Diskussion [diskuˈsjoːn] *f, -, -en*
Über die neuen Steuergesetze gab es lange Diskussionen.

discussion *n*
There were long discussions about the new tax laws.

einerseits [ˈainəˈ*zaits] *Adv.*
Einerseits sind die Nachbarn sehr nett, andererseits möchte ich lieber ganz einsam wohnen.

on the one hand
On the one hand my neighbors are very nice; on the other hand, I would prefer to live all by myself.

---

empfehlen [ɛmˈpfeːl(ə)n] *V/t.,*   **recommend** *v*
empfahl, hat empfohlen
Können Sie mir einen guten Arzt   Can you recommend a good
empfehlen?   doctor?

---

feststellen [ˈfɛstʃtɛl(ə)n] *V/t.,*   **determine, learn, state, realize** *v*
i., stellte fest, hat festgestellt
Erst als es regnete, stellte ich fest,   Only after it was raining did I rea-
dass ich meinen Schirm vergessen   lize that I had forgotten my um-
hatte.   brella.
Ich möchte feststellen, dass ich   I would like to state that I was
von Anfang an gegen den Plan   against the plan from the begin-
war.   ning.

---

meinen [ˈmainən] *V/t., i.,* meinte,   **have an opinion, mean, believe** *v*
hat gemeint
Nicht das linke, sondern das   I do not mean the car on the left,
rechte Auto meine ich.   but the one on the right.
Ich meine, dass unsere Regie-   I believe that our government
rung endlich zurücktreten sollte.   should finally resign.

Meinung [ˈmainuŋ] *f, -, -en*   **opinion** *n*
In dieser Sache habe ich eine an-   My opinion on this matter is dif-
dere Meinung als du.   ferent from yours.

Standpunkt [ˈʃtantpuŋkt] *m,*   **view, opinion, stand** *n*
-(e)s, -e
Ich stehe auf dem Standpunkt,   I hold the view that new elections
dass Neuwahlen die beste Lö-   are the best solution to the go-
sung für die Regierungskrise   vernment crisis.
sind.

überreden [yːbəˈreːd(ə)n] *V/t.,*   **persuade** *v*
überredete, hat überredet
Wir haben sie überredet, am Wo-   We persuaded her to come along
chenende mitzufahren.   for the weekend.

überzeugen [yːbəˈtsɔig(ə)n]   **convince** *v*
V/t., refl., überzeugte, hat über-
zeugt
Ihre Argumente haben mich nicht   Your arguments have not con-
überzeugt.   vinced me.
Ich habe mich überzeugt, dass   I confirmed that Vera is telling the
Vera die Wahrheit sagt.   truth.

wesentlich [ˈveːz(ə)ntliç] *Adj.*
Das neue Programm der Regierung führte zu keiner wesentlichen Verbesserung der wirtschaftlichen Lage.

essential
The new government program led to no essential improvement in the economic situation.

> 2001-4000

Argument [arguˈmɛnt] *n,* -(e)s, -e
Es gibt viele Argumente gegen die neuen Sozialgesetze.

argument *n*
There are many arguments against the new social laws.

Auffassung [ˈauffasuŋ] *f,* -, -en
Sogar in der Regierung gibt es verschiedene Auffassungen über das neue Programm.

opinion *n*
Even in the government there are different opinions about the new program.

bezeichnen [bəˈtsaiçnən] *V/t.,*
bezeichnete, hat bezeichnet
Die Regierungspolitik kann man als unsozial bezeichnen.

characterize, call, designate, label *v*
The government's policies can be characterized as unsocial.

diskutieren [diskuˈtiːrən] *V/t.,*
+ *Präp.* (über), diskutierte, hat diskutiert
Wir haben Ihren Vorschlag ausführlich diskutiert.

discuss *v*

We discussed your suggestion thoroughly.

Einstellung [ˈainʃtɛluŋ] *f,* -, -en
Ihre politische Einstellung kenne ich nicht.

attitude, position *n*
I do not know her political position.

gewissermaßen
[gəvisə*ˈmaːs(ə)n] *Adv.*
Er ist gewissermaßen der heimliche Chef der Partei.

to a certain extent, so to speak

It could be said that he is the secret leader of the party.

ohnehin [oːnəˈhin] *Adv.*
Wir können uns in Hamburg treffen, ich bin nächste Woche ohnehin dort.

anyway, in any event
We can meet in Hamburg since I'll be there next week anyway.

sachlich [ˈzaxliç] *Adj.*
Die Diskussion war sehr sachlich.

factual, objective
The discussion was very objective.

selbstverständlich
['zɛlpstfɛə*'ʃtɛntliç] *Adv.*
Selbstverständlich fahre ich dich nach Hause. Das ist doch klar.

of course, naturally

Of course I'll drive you home. You don't have to ask!

sowieso [zovi'zo:] *Adv.*
Ich nehme deinen Brief mit. Ich muss sowieso zur Post.

anyway
I'll take your letter. I'm going to the post office anyway.

sozusagen [zo:tsu'za:g(ə)n] *Adv.*
Sie ist sozusagen die Mutter unseres Vereins, sie kümmert sich um alles.

so to speak
She is the mother of our club, so to speak; she takes care of everything.

Stellungnahme ['ʃtɛluŋna:mə] *f,*
-, -en
Zu den Vorwürfen der Opposition gibt es immer noch keine Stellungnahme der Regierung.

comment, statement, response
n
The government still has not given a response to the opposition's accusations.

Überzeugung [y:bə*'tsɔiguŋ] *f, -,*
-en
„Ich bin der festen Überzeugung, dass wir auf dem richtigen Weg sind", sagte der Regierungschef.

conviction, firm opinion *n*

"I am of the firm opinion that we are on the right path," said the prime minister.

unerwartet ['unɛə*'vartət] *Adj.*
Der Rücktritt des Ministers kam unerwartet.

unexpected
The resignation of the Secretary came unexpectedly.

ungewöhnlich ['ungəvø:nliç]
Adj.
Die Lösung des Problems ist ungewöhnlich, aber erfolgreich.

unusual

The solution to the problem is unusual but successful.

Urteil ['urtail] *n, -s, -e*

Das Urteil in der Presse über die neuen Steuergesetze war sehr negativ.

opinion, judgement, estimation
n
Press reviews of the new tax laws were very negative.

verurteilen [fɛə*'urtail(ə)n] *V/t.,*
verurteilte, hat verurteilt
Alle Parteien im Parlament haben die politischen Morde verurteilt.

condemn *v*

All parties condemned the assassinations.

3.6 Zustimmung und Ablehnung | 1-2000

ablehnen [ˈapleːnən] *V/t.,* lehnte ab, hat abgelehnt
Ihre Einladung zum Essen muss ich leider ablehnen.
Die Lohnforderungen der Gewerkschaft wurden von den Arbeitgebern abgelehnt.

turn down, refuse *v*

Unfortunately, I have to turn down your dinner invitation.
The union's raise demands were turned down by the employers.

Ablehnung [ˈapleːnuŋ] *f, -, -en*
Die Gründe für die Ablehnung meines Antrags verstehe ich nicht.

refusal, rejection *n*
I don't understand why my application was rejected.

Bedenken [bəˈdɛŋk(ə)n] *n, -s, -*
Ich habe Bedenken, ob Frau Bess für diesen Posten geeignet ist.

doubt *n*
I have my doubts whether Ms. Bess is qualified for this job.

Beschwerde [bəˈʃveːəˀdə] *f, -, -n*
Gegen den Bau der neuen Straße gibt es viele Beschwerden.

complaint, protest *n*
There are many complaints against the construction of the new road.

---

beschweren [bəˈʃveːrən] *V/refl.,* beschwerte, hat beschwert
Ich habe mich bei meinem Wohnungsnachbarn wegen seiner lauten Musik beschwert.

complain *v*

I complained to my neighbor in the next apartment about his loud music.

---

dennoch [ˈdɛnɔx] *Adv.*
Er ist kein Fachmann, dennoch hat er versucht, die Heizung selbst zu reparieren.

however, anyway, in spite of, but
He's no expert, but he tried to repair the heater himself anyway.

---

doch [dɔx] *Adv.*
Sie ist stark erkältet und doch geht sie zur Arbeit.
○ Bist du nicht eingeladen?
□ Doch!

anyway, yet, still; yes
She has a bad cold, and yet she is going to work.
○ Aren't you invited?
□ Oh yes, I am.

egal [e'ga:l] *Adv.*
Mir ist egal, was du anziehst.

all the same
It's all the same to me what you wear.

---

einig sein ['ainiç°] *Adv.*

Wir streiten selten, meistens sind wir uns einig.

in agreement, of the same opinion
We seldom argue; we usually are of the same opinion.

---

einverstanden
['ainfɛə*ʃtand(ə)n] *Adv.*
Ich bin mit deinem Vorschlag einverstanden.

in agreement

I'm in agreement with your suggestion.

---

falsch [falʃ] *Adj., keine Komp.*
Wir sind falsch gefahren, wir hätten links abbiegen müssen.
Sie hat mir eine falsche Adresse gegeben.

wrong, incorrect, false
We took the wrong way; we were supposed to turn left.
She gave me the wrong address.

---

gegen ['ge:g(ə)n] *Präp.*
Ich bin gegen die neuen Arbeitszeiten.

against, not in favor of
I'm not in favor of the new work hours.

---

ja [ja:] *Adv.*
○ Bleibst du zu Hause?
□ Ja.

yes
○ Are you staying home?
□ Yes.

---

lieber ['li:bə*] *Adv.*
Willst du mitgehen oder lieber noch bleiben?

rather, preferably
Are you coming along, or would you rather stay here?

---

meinetwegen ['mainət've:g(ə)n] *Adv.*
○ Kann ich morgen dein Auto haben?
□ Meinetwegen!

I don't care!, It's all the same to me!, Sure!
○ Can I have your car tomorrow?
□ Sure!

---

nein [nain] *Adv.*
○ Sind Sie morgen im Büro?

□ Nein, leider nicht.

no
○ Will you be in the office tomorrow?
□ No, I'm afraid not.

---

nicht [niçt] *Adv.*
Frau Behrens kenne ich nicht.
Ich lache nicht über dich, sondern über den Hund dort.

not
I don't know Ms. Behrens.
I'm not laughing at you but about that dog.

richtig ['riçtiç°] *Adj.*
Die Antwort ist richtig.

right, correct
The answer is correct.

Sinn [zin] *m, -(e)s, kein Pl.*
Es hat keinen Sinn, bei diesem Regen weiterzuarbeiten.
Den Sinn des Textes verstehe ich nicht.

sense, point, meaning *n*
There's no sense in going on working in this rain.
I don't understand the meaning of this text.

unbedingt ['unbədiŋt] *Adj.*
Ein Visum ist eine unbedingte Voraussetzung für eine Reise nach China.
Ich muss unbedingt noch Brot für das Wochenende kaufen.

certain, sure, necessary, definite
A visa is a necessary prerequisite for a trip to China.

I definitely need to buy some bread for the weekend.

Wahl [va:l] *f, -, -en*
Das muss ich tun, ich habe keine andere Wahl.

choice *n*
I have to do that; I have no other choice.

wählen ['vɛ:l(ə)n] *V/t., i.,* wählte, hat gewählt
Wir haben das richtige Restaurant gewählt. Das Essen war gut.
Ich kann zwischen drei Angeboten wählen.

choose *v*

We chose the right restaurant. The food was great.
I can choose among three offers.

widersprechen [vidə*'ʃprɛç(ə)n] *V/i.,* widersprach, hat widersprochen
Das ist falsch, da muss ich widersprechen.

contradict, give another view *v*

That is incorrect; I have to contradict you.

zugeben ['tsu:ge:b(ə)n] *V/t.,* gab zu, hat zugegeben
Ute hat zugegeben, einen Fehler gemacht zu haben.

admit, agree *v*

Ute admitted that she had made a mistake.

Zustimmung ['tsu:ʃtimuŋ] *f, -, kein Pl.*
In der Geschäftsleitung fand sein Plan sofort Zustimmung.

approval, agreement *n*

His plan got approved by the management right away.

2001-4000

anerkennen ['anɛə*kɛnən] *V/t.*, erkannte an, hat anerkannt
Man muss anerkennen, dass sie ihre Arbeit sehr gut macht.

acknowledge, admit, recognize, realize *v*
You have to admit that she does her work very well.

---

ausnahmsweise ['ausna:msvaizə] *Adv.*
Wir haben heute ausnahmsweise früher Feierabend.

exceptionally, as an exception
As an exception we finish work early today.

---

bedenken [bə'dəŋk(ə)n] *V/t.*, bedachte, hat bedacht
Ich habe nicht bedacht, dass es schon so spät ist. Ich muss unbedingt gehen.

realize, consider *v*
I didn't realize it's already so late. I have to leave.

---

bestreiten [bə'ʃtrait(ə)n] *V/t.*, bestritt, hat bestritten
Sie bestreitet, dass sie die Schreibmaschine kaputt gemacht hat.

deny *v*
She denies she broke the typewriter.

Einigung ['ainiguŋ] *f*, -, *kein Pl.*
Über diesen Punkt gibt es noch keine Einigung.

agreement *n*
There's still no agreement on this point.

---

erwidern [ɛə*'vi:də*n] *V/i.*, erwiderte, hat erwidert
Auf meine Frage hat sie nichts erwidert.

answer, respond, react *v*
She didn't answer my question.

---

gleichgültig ['glaiçgyltiç°] *Adj.*
○ Willst du Kaffee oder Tee?
□ Das ist mir gleichgültig.

all the same, indifferent
○ Do you want coffee or tea?
□ It's all the same to me.

---

keinesfalls ['kainəs'fals] *Adv.*

Wir sind keinesfalls vor 17.00 Uhr fertig.

in no case, under no circumstance
Under no circumstances will we be finished before 5 p.m.

Klage ['kla:gə] *f*, -, -en
○ Gefällt Ihnen das Hotel?
□ Ja, wir haben keine Klagen.

complaint *n*
○ Do you like the hotel?
□ Yes. We have no complaints.

klar [kla:*] *Adj.*
Diese Frage verlangt eine klare Entscheidung.
○ Machst du mit?
□ Ja klar.

clear, certain, of course
This question demands a clear decision.
○ Are you coming along?
□ Yes, of course.

Kompromiss [kɔmpro'mis] *m,* -es, -e
Er ist nicht bereit, einen Kompromiss zu machen.

compromise *n*
He is not ready to agree to a compromise.

Protest [pro'tɛst] *m,* -es, -e
Gegen das neue Gesetz gab es heftige Proteste.

protest *n*
There were many protests against the new law.

---

protestieren [protɛs'ti:rən] *V/i.,* protestierte, hat protestiert
Die Studenten protestieren gegen die Kürzungen im Bildungsbereich.

protest *v*
Students are protesting the cutbacks in the educational sector.

Übereinkunft [y:bə*'ainkunft] *f,* -, Übereinkünfte
Im Büro gibt es eine Übereinkunft, nicht zu rauchen.

agreement *n*
In the office there is an agreement not to smoke.

übereinstimmen [y:bə*'ainʃtimən] *V/i.,* stimmte überein, hat übereingestimmt
Wir stimmen in unseren politischen Ansichten überein.

agree *v*
We agree on our political opinions.

---

unrecht ['unrɛçt] *Adj., keine Komp.*
Sie will nicht zugeben, dass sie unrecht hat.

wrong
She won't admit she was wrong.

Vorwurf ['fo:ə*vurf] *m,* -(e)s, Vorwürfe
Er hat mir Vorwürfe gemacht, weil ich zu spät gekommen bin.

accusation, reproach *n*
He reproached me for being late.

3.7 Gewissheit und Zweifel | 1-2000

3.7 Certainty and Doubt

angeblich ['ange:pliç] *Adj., keine Komp.*
Sie ist angeblich krank.

supposed, alleged

She is supposedly ill.

Annahme ['anna:mə] *f, -, -n*
Sicher bin ich nicht, das ist nur eine Annahme.

assumption *n*
I'm not certain; that is only an assumption.

annehmen ['anne:mən] *V/t.,* nahm an, hat angenommen
Ich nehme an, dass es gleich regnet.

assume *v*

I assume it'll rain any minute.

anscheinend ['anʃainənt] *Adv.*
Frank meldet sich nicht am Telefon. Er ist anscheinend nicht zu Hause.

apparent

Frank isn't answering the phone. He's apparently not home.

behaupten [bə'haupt(ə)n] *V/t.,* behauptete, hat behauptet
Er behauptet, dass er davon nichts gewusst hat.

claim *v*

He claims he knew nothing about it.

bestimmt [bə'ʃtimt] *Adv.*
Ich werde bestimmt anrufen.

certain
I will certainly call.

bestätigen [bə'ʃtɛ:tig(ə)n] *V/t.,* bestätigte, hat bestätigt
Die Zeugin hat seine Aussage bestätigt.

acknowledge, confirm *v*

The witness confirmed his testimony.

deutlich ['dɔitliç] *Adj.*
Man kann ihn gut verstehen. Er spricht sehr deutlich.

clear
We can understand him well. He speaks very clearly.

eindeutig ['aindɔitiç°] *Adj.*
Ihre Antwort war eindeutig ‚nein'.

clear, unambiguous
Her answer was clearly "no".

Eindruck ['aindruk] *m, -s, Eindrücke*
Ich habe den Eindruck, dass dir das Essen nicht schmeckt.

impression *n*

I have the impression that you don't like the food.

entscheiden [ɛnt'ʃaid(ə)n] *V/t., refl.,* entschied, hat entschieden
Ich kann selbst entscheiden, wann ich mit der Arbeit beginne.
Sie kann sich nicht entscheiden, welchen Pullover sie kaufen möchte.

decide *v*
I can decide on my own when to start work.
She can't decide which sweater to buy.

Entscheidung [ɛnt'ʃaiduŋ] *f, -, -en*
Die Entscheidung war richtig, den Vertrag zu kündigen.

decision *n*
The decision to cancel the contract was right.

eventuell [evɛntu'ɛl] *Adj., keine Komp.*
Susanne bringt eventuell ihre Schwester mit.

perhaps, maybe
Maybe Susanne is bringing along her sister.

Frage ['fraːgə] *f, -, -n*
Er hat die Frage richtig beantwortet.

question *n*
He answered the question correctly.

fragen ['fraːg(ə)n] *V/t., i., refl.,* fragte, hat gefragt
Er hat mich gefragt, ob ich ihn nach Hause bringen kann.
Der Kunde hat nach dem Liefertermin gefragt.
Ich frage mich, wie wir das schaffen sollen.

question, ask *v*
He asked me if I could take him home.
The customer asked when it would be delivered.
I wonder [*lit.:* ask myself] how we're supposed to manage that.

gelten ['gɛlt(ə)n] *V/t.,* galt, hat gegolten
Der Pass gilt fünf Jahre.

Sie gilt als zuverlässig.

be good for, count, be *v*
The passport is good for five years.
She is considered to be reliable.

gewiss [gə'vis] *Adj.*
Er hat eine gewisse Ähnlichkeit mit seinem Vater.
Der Tod ist jedem Menschen gewiss.
Er ist gewiss noch nicht fertig, er braucht immer viel Zeit.

certain
He has a certain resemblance to his father.
Death is a certain fact for everyone.
He is certainly not finished yet; he always needs a lot of time.

glauben ['glaub(ə)n] *V/t., i.,* glaubte, hat geglaubt | **think, believe** *v*
Ich glaube, ihr Nachname ist Weber. | I think her last name is Weber.
Er glaubt an eine bessere Zukunft. | He believes in a better future.

hoffentlich ['hɔf(ə)ntliç] *Adv.* | **hopefully**
Hoffentlich wird er bald gesund. | Hopefully he will get well soon.

irren ['irən], *V/refl.,* irrte, hat geirrt | **be mistaken, wrong** *v*
Sie irren sich, in Mühldorf gibt es keinen Bahnhof. | You are mistaken; there's no train station in Mühldorf.

Irrtum ['irtu:m] *m,* -s, Irrtümer | **error, mistake** *n*
○ Sie haben mir den falschen Zimmerschlüssel gegeben. | ○ You gave me the wrong key.
□ Verzeihung, das war ein Irrtum. | □ I'm sorry – that was a mistake.

klappen ['klap(ə)n] *V/i.,* klappte, hat geklappt | **work out, turn out successfully** *v*
Es gab keine Schwierigkeiten, alles hat geklappt. | There were no difficulties; everything worked (out).

können ['kœnən] *Mod.V/i.,* konnte, hat gekonnt | **can** *vm*
Sei nicht traurig, das Wetter kann morgen schon besser sein. | Don't be sad; the weather might/could be better tomorrow.

leugnen ['lɔignən] *V/t.,* leugnete, hat geleugnet | **deny** *v*
Der Angeklagte leugnete seine Schuld. | The defendant denied his guilt.

möglich ['mø:kliç] *Adj., keine Komp.* | **possible**
Es ist möglich, dass er gelogen hat. | It is possible that he lied.
○ Ich möchte Frau Simon sprechen. | ○ I'd like to speak to Ms. Simon.
□ Das ist leider nicht möglich, sie ist heute verreist. | □ That is unfortunately not possible; she is out of town today.

möglicherweise [mø:kliçə*'vaizə] *Adv.* | **possibly, maybe**
Möglicherweise komme ich heute später nach Hause. | Maybe I will get home late today.

Möglichkeit ['mø:klɪçkait] *f, -, -en*

possibility *n*

Ich sehe keine Möglichkeit, ihm zu helfen.

I see no possibility of helping him.

müssen ['mys(ə)n] *Mod.V.,* musste, hat gemusst

must, have to *v*

Ingrid und Sven sind ständig zusammen, sie müssen verliebt sein.

Ingrid and Sven are always together; they must be in love.

scheinbar ['ʃainbaː*] *Adj., keine Komp.*

apparent

Sie hat mich gegrüßt. Scheinbar kennt sie mich.

She greeted me. Apparently she knows me.

scheinen ['ʃainən] *(+ zu + Inf.),* schien, *kein Perf.*

appear, seem *v*

Es scheint keine andere Lösung für dieses Problem zu geben.

There seems to be no other solution to this problem.

sicher ['zɪçə*] *Adj.*

certain, sure

Ich bin sicher, dass ich die Prüfung bestehe.

I'm sure I'll pass the exam.

Sie ist immer noch nicht da, sicher hat sie den Termin vergessen.

She's still not here; she certainly forgot the appointment.

Sicherheit ['zɪçə*hait] *f, -, -en*

certainty *n*

Du kannst ihn so spät nicht mehr anrufen, mit Sicherheit schläft er schon.

You can't call him so late; he's surely asleep already.

Tatsache ['taːtzaxə] *f, -, -n*

fact *n*

Das sind Tatsachen, die man nicht leugnen kann.

These are facts we cannot deny.

tatsächlich ['taːtzɛxlɪç] *Adv.*

real

Willst du bei diesem Wetter tatsächlich spazieren gehen?

Do you really want to go for a walk in this weather?

Ich wollte es erst nicht glauben, aber sie haben tatsächlich sieben Töchter.

At first I didn't believe it, but they really do have seven daughters.

vermuten [fɛə*'muːt(ə)n] *V/t.,* vermutete, hat vermutet

suppose, presume, suspect *v*

Die Polizei vermutet, dass der Mann ermordet wurde.

The police suspect the man was murdered.

ielleicht [fi'laiçt] *Adv.*
Fragen Sie Herrn Busch. Vielleicht weiß er Bescheid.

perhaps, maybe
Ask Mr. Busch. Maybe he knows.

'oraussichtlich [fo'rauziçtliç] *Adj., keine Komp.*
Voraussichtlich wird es heute Nacht sehr kalt werden.

probable, likely
It is likely to get very cold tonight.

vahrscheinlich [va:*'ʃainliç] *Adj.*
Es geht mir nicht gut. Wahrscheinlich bekomme ich eine Erkältung.

possible, probable
I don't feel well. I'm probably getting a cold.

vohl [vo:l] *Adv.*
Frau Pelz fährt ein teures Auto. Sie verdient wohl gut.

probably
Ms. Pelz has a very expensive car. I guess she earns a lot.

ögern ['tsø:gə*n] *V/i.,*
Er zögerte einen Moment, bevor er antwortete.

hesitate *v*
He hesitated a moment before he gave an answer.

Zweifel ['tsvaif(ə)l] *m, -s, -*
Es besteht kein Zweifel, dass er an dem Unfall schuld war.

doubt *n*
There's no doubt he was guilty of the accident.

2001-4000

Ahnung ['a:nuŋ] *f, -, -en*
Ich hatte keine Ahnung, dass Kurt verheiratet ist.

idea *n*
I had no idea Kurt was married.

ausschließen ['ausʃli:s(ə)n] *V/t.,*
schloss aus, hat ausgeschlossen
Man kann nicht ausschließen, dass er bei der Operation stirbt.

exclude *v*

The possibility that he may die during the operation cannot be excluded.

Behauptung [bə'hauptuŋ] *f, -, -en*
Kannst du deine Behauptung beweisen?

statement, assertion *n*

Can you prove your assertion?

Beweis [bə'vais] *m, -es, -e*
Vermutlich war er der Täter, aber es gibt keine Beweise.

evidence, proof *n*
He was probably the one who did it, but there is no proof.

beweisen [bə'vaiz(ə)n] *V/t.*, bewies, hat bewiesen
Können Sie beweisen, dass Sie am 3. August den ganzen Tag zu Hause waren?

prove *v*
Can you prove you were at home all day on the third of August?

---

bezweifeln [bə'tsvaif(ə)ln] *V/t.*, bezweifelte, hat bezweifelt
Ich bezweifle, dass er für die Arbeit kräftig genug ist.

doubt, have doubts *v*
I doubt that he is strong enough for this work.

---

entschließen [ɛnt'ʃliːs(ə)n] *V/refl.*, entschloss, hat entschlossen
Ich habe mich entschlossen, mit dem Rauchen aufzuhören.

decide *v*
I have decided to stop smoking.

---

erraten [ɛə*'raːt(ə)n] *V/t.*, erriet, hat erraten
Er hat die Lösung des Tests nicht gewusst, aber erraten.

guess *v*
He didn't know the answer to the test question, but he guessed it.

---

geheim [gə'haim] *Adj.*
Die Papiere sind an einem geheimen Ort versteckt.

secret
The papers are hidden in a secret place.

Geheimnis [gə'haimnis] *n*, -ses, -se
Sie hat Staatsgeheimnisse an eine Zeitung verraten.

secret *n*
She revealed state secrets to a newspaper.

---

klären ['klɛːrən] *V/t.*, klärte, hat geklärt
Ich glaube, diese Fragen lassen sich schnell klären.

clear up, explain *v*
I think these questions can be cleared up quickly.

---

offenbar ['ɔf(ə)nbaː*] *Adv.*
Unter seiner alten Telefonnummer kann man ihn nicht erreichen. Er ist offenbar umgezogen.

apparent
We can't reach him at the number he gave us. Apparently he's moved.

---

offensichtlich ['ɔf(ə)nziçtliç] *Adj.*
Rainer hat schlechte Laune, er hat sich offensichtlich über etwas geärgert.

apparent, obvious
Rainer is in a bad mood; apparently he's angry about something.

---

raten ['raːt(ə)n] *V/t.*, riet, hat geraten
Zu dieser langen Reise kann ich dir nicht raten.

advise, give advice, recommend *v*
I don't recommend that you take this long trip.

sicherlich ['ziçərliç] *Adv.*
○ Warum ruft Rüdiger nicht an?
□ Das hat er sicherlich vergessen.

certainly, surely
○ Why doesn't Rüdiger call?
□ He has certainly forgotten.

---

so genannt ['zo:gənant] *Adj., keine Komp.*
Seine so genannte Cousine ist in Wahrheit seine Freundin.

so-called
His so-called cousin is really his girlfriend.

---

wirklich ['virkliç] *Adj., keine Komp.*
Ein wirklicher Freund hätte dir in dieser Situation geholfen.
Hast du wirklich geglaubt, dass sie dir alles erzählt hat?

real, true
A real friend would have helped you in this situation.
Did you really believe that she told you everything?

Wirklichkeit ['virkliçkait] *f, -, kein Pl.*
Seine Freunde nennen ihn Teddy, in Wirklichkeit heißt er Theodor.

truth, reality *n*
His friends call him Teddy, but in reality his name is Theodor.

Wunder ['vundə*] *n, -s, -*
Du bist viel zu dünn angezogen, kein Wunder, dass du frierst.
Es wäre ein Wunder, wenn er pünktlich nach Hause käme.

surprise, miracle, wonder *n*
You're much too lightly dressed; no wonder you're freezing.
It would be a surprise if he came home on time.

---

zweifellos ['tsvaif(ə)llo:s] *Adv.*

Wien ist zweifellos eine interessante Stadt.

doubtless, indubitable, certain, sure
Vienna is certainly an interesting city.

---

zweifeln ['tsvaif(ə)ln] *V/i., + Präp. (an)*
Ich zweifle daran, dass sich das Auto noch reparieren lässt.

doubt *v*
I doubt that the car can still be repaired.

3.8 Positive Wertung und Neutralität

3.8 Positive Evaluation and Neutrality

bewundern [bə'vundə*n] *V/t.,*
bewunderte, hat bewundert
Er wird von seinen Mitschülern
bewundert, weil er ein guter
Sportler ist.

admire *v*

He's admired by his class mates
because he's good in sports.

echt [ɛçt] *Adj.*
Er hat sich wie ein echter Freund
verhalten.
Der Schmuck ist echt.

real, genuine, true, authentic
He was a real friend in the situa-
tion.
The jewelry is real.

einfach ['ainfax] *Adj.*
Die Erklärung ist sehr einfach.
Das Haus ist einfach toll.

simple
The explanation is very simple.
The house is simply wonderful!

für [fy:ə*] *Präp.*
Die Mehrheit ist für das neue Gesetz.

for, in favor of *prep*
The majority is in favor of the new
law.

gefallen [gə'fal(ə)n] *V/i.,* gefiel,
hat gefallen
Der Film hat mir gut gefallen.

please, like *v*

I liked the movie a lot.

günstig ['gynstiç°] *Adj.*

Ich musste nicht viel bezahlen,
die Schreibmaschine war eine
günstige Gelegenheit.

**low–cost, a good buy, inexpen-
sive**
I didn't have to pay much; the
typewriter was a good buy.

gut [gu:t] *Adj.,* besser, am besten
Er ist ein guter Handwerker.
Es geht mir gut.
Ich bekomme ein gutes Gehalt.

good, well
He is good with his hands.
I'm doing well.
I get a good salary.

halten ['halt(ə)n] *V/t.,* + *Präp.* (für),
hielt, hat gehalten
Ich halte sie für sehr intelligent.

consider *v*

I consider her to be very intelligent.

herrlich [ˈhɛrlıç] *Adj.*

Wir hatten im Urlaub herrliches Wetter.

wonderful, marvelous, splendid, magnificent
We had wonderful weather during our vacation.

---

immerhin [ˌiməˈhin] *Adv.*
Er ist ein schlechter Fahrer, aber immerhin fährt er langsam.

at least
He is a bad driver, but at least he drives slowly.

---

interessant [int(ə)rɛˈsant] *Adj.*, -er, am -esten
Er hat mir eine interessante Geschichte erzählt.

interesting

He told me an interesting story.

Lob [lo:p] *n*, -(e)s, *kein Pl.*
Dieses Lob hat sie wirklich verdient.

praise *n*
She has really earned this praise.

---

loben [ˈlo:b(ə)n] *V/t.*, lobte, hat gelobt
Für seine erfolgreiche Arbeit wurde er von der Chefin gelobt.

praise *v*

The boss praised him for his successful work.

---

lohnen [ˈlo:nən] *V/refl.*, lohnte, hat gelohnt
Das Geschäft hat sich gelohnt.

be worth it *v*

The deal was worth it.

---

lustig [ˈlustiçº] *Adj.*
Der Film war sehr lustig.

funny, humorous
The film was very humorous.

---

mögen [ˈmøːg(ə)n] *Mod.V., V/t., i.*, mochte, hat gemocht
Ich mag heute nicht fernsehen.

Blumen mag ich sehr.
Ich möchte gern ein Kotelett essen.

like, want *v*

I don't want to watch television today.
I like flowers a lot.
I'd like to eat a pork chop.

---

normal [nɔrˈma:l] *Adj.*
Sie fuhr mit normaler Geschwindigkeit.

normal
She drove at a normal speed.

---

nötig [ˈnø:tiçº] *Adj.*
○ Soll ich dich zum Flughafen bringen?
□ Nein danke, das ist nicht nötig.

necessary
○ Should I take you to the airport?
□ No thanks; that's not necessary.

notwendig [ˈnoːtvɛndɪçˀ] *Adj.*
Die Reparatur war sehr teuer, aber leider notwendig.

necessary, obligatory
The repair was very expensive, but unfortunately necessary.

---

nutzen (nützen) [ˈnuts(ə)n] [(ˈnytsən)] *V/t., i.,* nutzte, hat genutzt
Sie hat ihre Chancen genutzt.
Sein gutes Zeugnis hat ihm bei der Stellensuche viel genutzt.

use, be good for, help *v*
She used her opportunities.
His good grades helped him a lot in his job search.

---

nützlich [ˈnytslɪç] *Adj.*
Dieses Werkzeug ist sehr nützlich.

useful, helpful
This equipment is very useful.

---

nutzlos [ˈnutsloːs] *Adj.* -er, am -esten
Er kauft viele nutzlose Dinge.

useless
He buys a lot of useless things.

---

passend [ˈpas(ə)nt] *Adj.*
Seine Kleidung war für die Feier nicht passend.

appropriate
His clothes were not appropriate for the celebration.

---

positiv [ˈpoːzitif] *Adj.*
Die Testergebnisse waren sehr positiv.

positive
The test results were very positive.

---

prima [ˈpriːma] *Adj., indekl.*

Das Essen schmeckte prima.

wonderful, excellent, fantastic, great
The meal was excellent.

---

recht [rɛçt] sein, **Recht** (+ bekommen, haben, geben)
Das ist mir recht.
Du kommst gerade recht, das Essen ist fertig.

right, fair, appropriate

That is all right with me.
You've come at just the right time; dinner is ready.

---

richtig [ˈrɪçtɪçˀ] *Adj.*
Das ist die richtige Wohnung für uns.
Haben Sie bisher alles richtig verstanden?

right, correct
This is the right apartment for us.

Have you understood everything correctly so far?

---

stehen [ˈʃteː(ə)n] *V/i.,* stand, hat gestanden
Das Hemd steht dir gut.

stand *v*

The shirt looks good on you.

---

spannend [ˈʃpanənt] *Adj.*
Der Roman ist recht spannend.

exciting, suspenseful
The novel is quite suspenseful.

sympathisch [zym'pa:tiʃ] *Adj.*
Die meisten Leute finden ihn sympathisch.

friendly, good-natured, pleasant, likeable
Most people think he is nice.

Vorteil ['fo:ə*tail] *m, -s, -e*
Nutzen Sie die Vorteile unserer Sonderangebote.

advantage *n*
Take advantage of our special offers.

vorziehen ['fo:ə*tsi:(ə)n] *V/t.,* zog vor, hat vorgezogen
Dieser Wein ist nicht schlecht, aber ich ziehe einen süßeren vor.

prefer *v*

This wine is not bad, but I prefer a sweeter one.

wahr [va:*] *Adj.*
Ist es wahr, dass du keinen Fernsehapparat hast?
Was ist der wahre Grund für deine Abreise?

true, real
Is it true that you do not have a television?
What is the real reason for your departure?

Wahrheit ['va:*hait] *f, -, -en*
Sie hat nicht die Wahrheit gesagt.

truth *n*
She did not tell the truth.

wichtig ['viçtiçº] *Adj.*
Der Termin ist sehr wichtig.

important
The appointment is very important.

Widerspruch ['vi:də*ʃprux] *m, -s,* Widersprüche
Gegen die Entscheidung gab es keinen Widerspruch.

contradiction, opposition *n*

There was no opposition to the decision.

wundern ['vundə*n] *V/refl.,* wunderte, hat gewundert
Ich wundere mich (es wundert mich), dass sie es geschafft hat.

surprise *v*

It surprises me that she did it.

2001-4000

ausgezeichnet ['ausgə'tsaiçnət] *Adj.*
Die Ausstellung war ausgezeichnet.

excellent

The exhibition was excellent.

außergewöhnlich ['ausə*gəvø:nliç] *Adj.*
Er ist außergewöhnlich groß.

unusual, exceptional

He is unusually big.

befriedigend [bə'fri:dig(ə)nt] *Adj.*
Für das Problem gibt es keine befriedigende Lösung.

satisfactory
There is no satisfactory solution to the problem.

begeistern [bə'gaistə*n] *V/t., refl.,* begeisterte, hat begeistert
Die Vorstellung begeisterte das Publikum.
Ich kann mich für Sport nicht begeistern.

excite *v*

The audience was enthusiastic about the performance.
I cannot get excited about sports.

bevorzugen [bə'fo:ə*tsu:g(ə)n] *V/t.,* bevorzugte, hat bevorzugt
Sie bevorzugt starke Zigaretten.

prefer *v*

She prefers strong cigarettes.

eignen ['aignən] *V/refl.,* eignete, hat geeignet
Diese Schuhe eignen sich nicht zum Tanzen.

be suitable *v*

These shoes are not suitable for dancing.

erstaunlich [εə*'ʃtaunliç] *Adj.*
Seine Eltern sind erstaunlich jung.

amazing, astonishing
His parents are amazingly young.

erstklassig ['ε:rstklasiç°] *Adj.*
Diese sportliche Leistung war erstklassig.

first-class
This athletic accomplishment was first-class.

geeignet [gə'aignət] *Adj.*
Für diese harte Arbeit ist er nicht geeignet.

suitable
He is not suitable for this hard work.

gewohnt [gə'vo:nt] *Adj.*
Ich bin gewohnt, früh aufzustehen.

used, accustomed (to)
I am used to getting up early.

hervorragend
[hεə*'fo:ə*ra:g(ə)nt] *Adj.*
Zum Essen gab es einen hervorragenden Wein.

excellent

There was an excellent wine for dinner.

ideal [ide'a:l] *Adj.*
Das Wetter war ideal zum Schilaufen.

ideal
The weather was ideal for skiing.

jedenfalls ['je:d(ə)nfals] *Adv.*
Ich glaube, Heiner ist wieder gesund, jedenfalls sieht er gut aus.

in any event, anyway
I believe Heiner is well again; in any event he looks good.

komisch ['ko:mɪʃ] *Adj.*

Ich mag ihn nicht. Er ist ein komischer Mensch.
Wir haben sehr gelacht. Die Situation war sehr komisch.

curious, peculiar, funny, odd, weird

I do not like him. He is a curious person.
We laughed a lot. The situation was so peculiar.

---

korrekt [kɔ'rɛkt] *Adj.*, -er, am -esten

Die Kontrolle an der Grenze war lästig, aber korrekt.

correct

The border check was annoying, but done correctly.

---

neutral [nɔi'tra:l] *Adj.*

Viele Zuschauer fanden, dass der Schiedsrichter nicht neutral war.

neutral

Many spectators thought that the referee was not neutral.

---

objektiv [ɔpjɛk'ti:f] *Adj.*

Die Prüfer waren objektiv.

objective

The examiners were objective.

---

perfekt [pɛr'fɛkt] *Adj.*, -er, am -esten

Die Veranstaltung war perfekt organisiert.

perfect

The performance was perfectly organized.

---

praktisch ['praktɪʃ] *Adj.*

Die neue Küchenmaschine ist sehr praktisch.

practical

The new kitchen appliance is very practical.

---

sinnvoll ['zɪnfɔl] *Adj.*

Es ist sinnvoll, noch etwas zu warten.

sensible

It makes sense to wait a while longer.

---

stimmen ['ʃtɪmən] *V/i.*, stimmte, hat gestimmt

Das Datum auf der Quittung stimmt nicht.

be correct, agree *v*

The date on the receipt is not correct.

---

vertraut [fɛə*'traut] *Adj.*, -er, am -esten

Sie ist mit der Bedienung der Maschine vertraut.

familiar

She is familiar with how to use the machine.

Vorbild ['fo:ə*'bɪlt] *n*, -(e)s, -er

Sein erfolgreicher Bruder war immer sein Vorbild.

(role) model *n*

His successful brother was always his model.

---

wunderbar ['vundə*ba:*] *Adj.*

Der Sänger hat eine wunderbare Stimme.

wonderful

The singer has a wonderful voice.

3.9 Negative Wertung

3.9 Negative Evaluation

kompliziert [kɔmpli:'tsi:ə*t] *Adj.*, -er, am -esten
Diese grammatische Regel ist kompliziert.

complicated
This grammar rule is complicated.

Kritik [kri'ti:k] *f,* -, -en
Diese Kritik hat er nicht verdient.

criticism *n*
He doesn't deserve this criticism.

kritisch ['kri:tiʃ] *Adj.*
Der Reporter stellte kritische Fragen.

critical
The reporter asked critical questions.

Mangel ['maŋ(ə)l] *m,* -s, Mängel
Das Kleid war billiger, weil es einige kleine Mängel hatte.

defect, fault *n*
The dress was marked down because it had a number of small defects.

merkwürdig ['mɛrkvyrdiçᵒ] *Adj.*
Ich finde es merkwürdig, wie sie sich benimmt.

strange, odd, curious
I find the way she acts curious.

Nachteil ['na:xtail] *m,* -s, -e
Durch sein Alter hat er Nachteile bei der Stellensuche.

disadvantage *n*
His age is a disadvantage in his job search.

Problem [pro:'ble:m] *n,* -s, -e
Er hat persönliche Probleme.

problem *n*
He has personal problems.

schade ['ʃa:də] *Adv.*
Es ist schade, dass du keine Zeit hast.

too bad, it's a pity
It's too bad (that) you don't have time.

schlecht [ʃlɛçt] *Adj.*, -er, am -esten
Sie ist eine schlechte Schülerin.

poor *(achievement),* **bad**

She is a poor student.

schlimm [ʃlim] *Adj.*
Er hat eine schlimme Krankheit.

bad, serious
He has a serious disease.

unmöglich [unˈmøːklɪç] *Adj.*
Wenn sie Alkohol getrunken hat, hat sie ein unmögliches Benehmen.
Die Idee ist gut, aber unmöglich zu verwirklichen.

impossible
When she's been drinking, her behavior is impossible!

The idea is good but impossible to put into effect.

Unsinn [ˈunzin] *m, -s, kein Pl.*
Red doch nicht so einen Unsinn!

nonsense *n*
Don't talk such nonsense!

vergeblich [fɛəˈgeːplɪç] *Adj.*
Ich habe vergeblich versucht, ihn anzurufen.

in vain
I tried in vain to call him.

$$2001-4000$$

furchtbar [ˈfurçtbaː*] *Adj.*
Ich finde den Mantel furchtbar hässlich.
○ Meine Schwester ist letzte Woche tödlich verunglückt.
□ Das ist ja furchtbar.

terrible, awful
I think the coat is terribly ugly.

○ My sister had a fatal accident last week.
□ That's awful!

gering [gəˈrin] *Adj.*
Meine Englischkenntnisse sind gering.

minimal, limited, poor
My knowledge of English is minimal.

langweilig [ˈlaŋvailɪçᵒ] *Adj.*
Der Film war langweilig.

boring
The film was boring.

mangeln [ˈmaŋ(ə)ln] *V/i.,* mangelte, hat gemangelt
Für diese Aufgabe mangelt es ihm an Erfahrung.

lack, be lacking, be missing, be short on *v*
For this work, he lacks experience.

peinlich [ˈpainlɪç] *Adj.*
Es war ihr peinlich, nach der Toilette zu fragen.

embarrassing
She was embarassed to ask for the restroom.

schrecklich [ˈʃrɛklɪç] *Adj.*
Ich habe einen schrecklichen Durst.
In Mittelamerika gab es ein schreckliches Unwetter.

terrible
I'm terribly thirsty.

There was a terrible storm in Central America.

seltsam ['zɛltza:m] *Adj.*
Sie hat seltsame Freunde.

unusual, strange, odd
She has strange friends.

unnütz ['unnyts] *Adj.*, -er, am
-esten
Mach dir doch keine unnützen
Sorgen.

useless

You don't need to worry so much.

vergebens [fɛə*'ge:b(ə)ns] *Adv.*
Sie haben sich viel Mühe gegeben, aber es war alles vergebens.

in vain, useless
They went to a lot of trouble, but it
was all in vain.

3.10 Wunsch, Bitte, Auftrag | 1-2000

3.10 Wish, Request, Order

auffordern ['auffɔrdə*n] *V/t.*, forderte auf, hat aufgefordert
Sie forderte uns auf, im Wartezimmer Platz zu nehmen.

tell, request, invite v

She told us to have a seat in the
waiting room.

befehlen [bə'fe:l(ə)n] *V/t.*, befahl,
hat befohlen
Ich lasse mir von dir nichts befehlen.

order, command v

I won't take orders from you.

Bitte ['bitə] *f*, -, -en
Ich habe eine Bitte. Könnten Sie
das Fenster schließen?

request n
I have a request. Could you
please close the window?

bitten ['bit(ə)n] *V/t., i., + Präp.* (um)
bat, hat gebeten
Wir müssen jemanden um Hilfe
bitten.

ask for, request v

We must ask someone for help.

dürfen ['dyrf(ə)n] *Mod. V./i.*, durfte, hat gedurft
Darf ich bitte Ihr Telefon benutzen?

be permitted to, may v

May I please use your telephone?

erlauben [ɛə*'laub(ə)n] *V/t.*, er-
laubte, hat erlaubt
Der Arzt hat mir erlaubt, wieder zu
arbeiten.

permit, let, allow v

The doctor has allowed me to
start work again.

Erlaubnis [ɛə*'laupnis] *f, -, kein Pl.*

permission *n*

Dafür brauchen Sie die Erlaubnis des Chefs.

For that I need the boss's permission.

---

fordern ['fɔrdə*n] *V/t.,* forderte, hat gefordert

ask, demand *v*

Der Preis, den sie fordert, ist zu hoch.

The price she's asking is too high.

Forderung ['fɔrdəruŋ] *f, -, -en*

demand, claim *n*

Die Forderungen der Opposition wurden im Parlament abgelehnt.

The opposition's demands were voted down.

---

möglichst ['mø:kliçst] *Adv.*

the most, -est, as …ly as

Bitte schreiben Sie die Briefe möglichst schnell!

Please write the letters as soon as possible!

---

müssen ['mys(ə)n] *Mod. V/i.,* musste, hat gemusst

have to, must *v*

Diese Woche muss ich Samstag arbeiten.

This week I have to work on Saturday.

Du musst nicht so viel rauchen.

You must not smoke so much.

Man müsste mehr Zeit haben.

One should have more time.

---

sollen ['zɔl(ə)n] *Mod. V./i.,* sollte, hat gesollt

ought to, should *v*

Du sollst den Tisch decken, hat sie gesagt.

She said you should set the table.

Hör auf! Das sollst du nicht machen.

Stop it! You shouldn't do that.

---

verlangen [fɛə*'laŋ(ə)n] *V/t.,* verlangte, hat verlangt

demand, ask for, request, want *v*

Ich verlange, dass der Schaden von Ihnen bezahlt wird.

I request that you pay for the damage.

Diese Arbeit verlangt viel Geduld.

The work calls for a lot of patience.

Vorschlag ['fo:ə*ʃla:k] *m, -(e)s, Vorschläge*

suggestion, proposition *n*

Er hat einen interessanten Vorschlag gemacht.

He made an interesting suggestion.

---

vorschlagen ['fo:ə*ʃla:g(ə)n] *V/t.,* schlug vor, hat vorgeschlagen

suggest, propose *v*

Ich schlage vor, dass wir uns in meinem Büro treffen.

I suggest we meet in my office.

weigern [ˈvaigə*n] V/refl., weigerte, hat geweigert
Er weigerte sich, dem Polizisten
seinen Führerschein zu zeigen.

refuse v
He refused to show the police
officer his driver's license.

wollen [ˈvɔl(ə)n] Mod.V., V/t., i.,
wollte, hat gewollt
Ich will gerne mit ihm sprechen,
wenn du das wünschst.

want, be willing v
I'd be willing to speak with him if
that's what you want.

Wunsch [vunʃ] m, -es, Wünsche
Diesen Wunsch kann ich Ihnen
leider nicht erfüllen.

request, wish n
Unfortunately I cannot comply
with your request.

wünschen [ˈvynʃ(ə)n] V/t., refl.,
wünschte, hat gewünscht
Ich wünsche dir viel Glück!

wish v
I wish you good luck!

2001-4000

anordnen [ˈanɔrdnən] V/t., ordnete an, hat angeordnet
Wegen der schlechten Luft wurde
in Hamburg ein Fahrverbot für
Autos angeordnet.

order, decree v
A smog-related stop to all car
traffic was decreed in Hamburg.

Anregung [ˈanreːguŋ] f, -, -en
Haben Sie eine Idee? Wir sind für
jede Anregung dankbar.

suggestion, inspiration n
Do you have an idea? We're grateful for any suggestion.

beauftragen [bəˈauftraːg(ə)n]
V/t., beauftragte, hat beauftragt
○ Willst du die Garage selber
   bauen?
□ Nein, ich habe eine Firma be-
   auftragt.

hire, engage, contract v

○ Do you want to build the garage yourself?
□ No. I've hired a firm.

bestimmen [bəˈʃtimən] V/t., be-
stimmte, hat bestimmt
Das bestimmt der Chef alleine.

determine, decide v
The boss decides that himself.

drängen [ˈdrɛŋən] V/t., i., drängte, hat gedrängt
Er drängte mich, noch zu bleiben.
Die Kinder drängten, einen Spaziergang zu machen.

press (somebody to do something), **insist** v
He urged I stay on.
The children insisted on going out
for a walk.

erfüllen [ɛə*'fyl(ə)n] *V/t.,* erfüllte, hat erfüllt
Leider kann ich Ihre Bitte nicht erfüllen.

fulfill, carry out *v*
Sorry I cannot carry out your wish.

---

freiwillig ['fraivilig°] *Adj.*
Unsere Kinder gehen nie freiwillig ins Bett.

willing, voluntary
Our children never go to bed willingly.

---

gehorchen [gə'hɔrç(ə)n] *V/i.,* gehorchte, hat gehorcht
Der Hund ist lieb, aber er gehorcht nicht.

obey *v*
The dog is good humored, but he doesn't obey.

---

gestatten [gə'ʃtat(ə)n] *V/t.,* gestattete, hat gestattet
Gestatten Sie, dass ich rauche?

permit, allow *v*
Do you mind if I smoke?

---

veranlassen [fɛə*'anlas(ə)n] *V/t.,* veranlasste, hat veranlasst
Ich habe veranlasst, dass die Türen neu gestrichen werden.

see to it that, cause *v*
I have seen to it that the doors will be painted.

---

verbieten [fɛə*'biːt(ə)n] *V/t.,* verbot, hat verboten
Dieser Film ist für Jugendliche unter 18 verboten worden.

forbid *v*
This film is now forbidden for anyone under 18.

---

verpflichten [fɛə*'pfliçt(ə)n] *V/t., refl.,* verpflichtete, hat verpflichtet
Sein Beruf als Arzt verpflichtet ihn, jedem Verletzten zu helfen.
Ich habe mich verpflichtet, darüber zu schweigen.

require, oblige *v*
His profession as doctor requires him to help any injured person.
I promised to keep quiet about that.

3.11 Höflichkeitsformeln, Ausrufe, Floskeln

1-2000

3.11 Courtesy Formulas, Exclamations, Conversational Fillers

auf Wiedersehen
[auf 'vi:də*se:(ə)n]
Auf Wiedersehen bis morgen, Frau Schröder!

good-bye

Good-bye, see you tomorrow, Ms. Schröder!

bitte ['bitə] *Adv.*
○ Danke sehr!
□ Bitte!
○ Darf ich Ihnen helfen?
□ Ja bitte!

please, you're welcome
○ Thank you very much!
□ You're welcome!
○ May I help you?
□ Yes, please.

Dank [daŋk] *m, -(e)s, kein Pl.*
Vielen Dank für Ihren Brief.

thanks
Many thanks for your letter.

danken ['daŋk(ə)n] *V., i., + Präp.*
(für), dankte, hat gedankt
Ich danke Ihnen für Ihre Hilfe.

thank *v*

I thank you for your help.

Frau [frau] *f, -, -en*
Guten Tag, Frau Volkers! Wie geht es Ihnen?

Ms., Mrs.
Good morning, Ms. Volkers! How are you?

Fräulein ['frɔilain] *n, -s, - (veraltet)*
Guten Abend, Fräulein Welz!

Miss
Good afternoon, Miss Welz!

geehrt [gə'e:ə*t]
Sehr geehrte Frau Weber, ...
(Anrede in einem Brief)

dear
Dear Ms. Weber, ...
(greeting in a formal letter)

Glückwunsch ['glykvunʃ] *m, -(e)s, Glückwünsche*
Hérzlichen Glückwunsch zum Geburtstag!

wish, greeting *n*

Happy birthday!

gratulieren [gratu'li:r(ə)n] *V., i., gratulierte, hat gratuliert*
Wir gratulieren dir zur bestandenen Prüfung!

congratulate *v*

We congratulate you for passing your exam!

guten Abend ['gu:t(ə)n 'a:b(ə)nt]
Guten Abend, Herr Pelz!

good evening
Good evening, Mr. Pelz!

guten Morgen
['gu:t(ə)n 'mɔə*g(ə)n]
Guten Morgen!

good morning

Good morning!

---

guten Tag ['gu:t(ə)n 'ta:k]
Guten Tag, Herbert!

Hello, Good morning, Good day
Hello, Herbert!

Herr [hɛə*] m, -n, -en
Guten Morgen, Herr Albers! Wie geht's?

Mr.
Good morning, Mr. Albers. How are you?

---

ich wünsche Ihnen ...
[iç 'vynʃe i:nən]
Ich wünsche Ihnen viel Erfolg bei den Verhandlungen!

I wish you ...

I wish you all the best in the negotiations!

---

willkommen [vil'kɔmən] Adj.
Willkommen in unserem Haus!

welcome
Welcome to our home!

2001-4000

Achtung ['axtuŋ] f, -, kein Pl.

Achtung Stufe! Pass auf!

Watch out! Look out! Attention! Be careful!
Be careful, there is a step! Look out!

Grüß Gott [gry:s'gɔt] (süddt.)
Grüß Gott, Frau Berner!

Good day! Hello!
Hello, Ms. Berner!

---

herzlich ['hɛrtsliç] Adj.
Herzlichen Dank für das schöne Geschenk!

heartfelt, many
Many thanks for the beautiful gift!

Wie geht es Ihnen? / Wie geht's? [vi:'ge:tɛs'i:nən/-:'gets]
○ Wie geht es Ihnen, Frau Simmer?
□ Gut!

How are you?

○ How are you, Ms. Simmer?

□ Fine!

---

leidtun ['laittu:n]
Es tut mir leid, dass ich zu spät komme.

be sorry v
I'm sorry; I've come too late.

Verzeihung [fɛə*'tsaiuŋ] f, -, kein Pl.
Verzeihung! Können Sie mir sagen, wie spät es ist?

Excuse me, Pardon

Excuse me – could you tell me what time it is?

4.1 Identifizierung | 1-2000

4.1 Identification

erwachsen [ɛə*'vaks(ə)n] *Adj.* Er hat zwei erwachsene Kinder.	**grown, grown-up** He has two grown children.
Erwachsene [ɛə*'vaks(ə)nə] *m/f,* -n, -n Der Eintritt kostet für Erwachsene 4,– €, für Kinder die Hälfte.	**adult** *n* Admission is 4.– € for adults and half price for children.
Familienname [fa'mi:ljənna:mə] *m,* -ns, -n Ihr Familienname ist Wenzel.	**family name, last name, sur-** **name** *n* Her last name is Wenzel.
Frau [frau] *f,* -, -en In unserer Abteilung arbeiten vier Männer und drei Frauen.	**woman** *n* Four men and three women work in our department.
heißen ['hais(ə)n] *V/i.,* hieß, hat geheißen Ich heiße Petra, und wie heißt du?	**be named, be called** *v* My name is Petra, and what's your name?
Jugendliche ['ju:g(ə)ntliçə] *m/f,* -n, -n Die Arbeitslosigkeit bei Jugendli- chen ist recht hoch.	**youth, young people** *n* Unemployment among young people is quite high.
Junge ['juŋə] *m,* -n, -n Vera hat letzte Woche ihr Kind bekommen, es ist ein Junge.	**boy** *n* Vera had her baby last week; it's a boy.
Kind [kint] *n,* -es, -er Wir haben zwei Kinder.	**child** *n* We have two children.
Mann [man] *m,* -(e)s, Männer Den Beruf ‚Automechaniker' ler- nen heute nicht nur Männer, son- dern auch einige Frauen.	**man** *n* Today not only men become auto mechanics, but also some women.

Mensch [mɛnʃ] *m*, -en, -en
Auf der Erde leben ca. 6 Milliarden
Menschen.

person, human being *n*
World population is about 5 billion
people.

menschlich [ˈmɛnʃliç] *Adj.*
Fehler zu machen, ist menschlich.

human
Making mistakes is human.

Mädchen [ˈmɛːtçən] *n*, -s, -
In unserer Klasse gibt es nur Mädchen, keine Jungen.

girl *n*
In our class there are only girls, no
boys.

Name [ˈnaːmə] *m*, -ns, -n
Kennst du seinen Namen?

name *n*
Do you know his name?

nennen [ˈnɛnən] *V/t.*, nannte, hat
genannt
Sie heißt Ursula, aber genannt
wird sie Uschi.

name, call *(a name) v*

Her name is Ursula, but she is
called Uschi.

Pass [pas] *m*, -es, Pässe
An der Grenze muss man seinen
Pass zeigen.

passport *n*
You have to show your passport
at the border.

persönlich [pɛrˈzøːnliç] *Adj.*
Wir haben mehrere Male miteinander telefoniert, aber wir kennen uns nicht persönlich.

personal
We have spoken to each other on
the telephone several times, but
we have never met personally.

Vorname [ˈfoːɐ̯*naːmə] *m*, -ns, -n

Sie hat drei Vornamen.

**first name, christian name, given
name** *n*
She has three first names.

Zuname [ˈtsuːnaːmə] *m*, -ns, -n

Wie ist Ihr Zuname? Meyer?

**family name, surname, last
name** *n*
What's your family name?
Meyer?

2001-4000

Baby [ˈbeːbi] *n*, -s, -s
Als Baby war er ziemlich dick.

baby *n*
He was rather fat as a baby.

Dame [ˈdaːmə] *f*, -, -n
Sehr geehrte Damen und Herren,
ich bitte um Ihre Aufmerksamkeit.

lady, woman *n*
Ladies and gentlemen, I ask for
your attention.

128

Geschlecht [gə'ʃlɛçt] *n*, -(e)s, -er
Bei der Berufswahl gibt es auch
heute noch große Unterschiede
zwischen den Geschlechtern.

sex, gender *n*
There are still many differences
between the sexes in selecting a
profession.

Herr [hɛə] *m*, -n, -en
Kennen Sie den Herrn in dem hel-
len Anzug?

gentleman *n*
Do you know the gentleman in the
fair suit?

Lebenslauf ['le:b(ə)nslauf] *m*,
-(e)s, Lebensläufe
Für die Bewerbung muss der
Lebenslauf handschriftlich geschrieben werden.

résumé, curriculum vitae *n*

For the application it is necessary
to write a handwritten résumé.

männlich ['mɛnliç] *Adj.*
Er hat eine sehr männliche
Stimme.

masculine, male, manly
He has a very masculine voice.

Person [pɛr'zo:n] *f*, -, -en
Wie viele Personen kommen zu
deiner Geburtstagsfeier?

person *n*
How many people are coming to
your birthday party?

Rasse ['rasə] *f*, -, -n
Leider gibt es immer wieder Ras-
senkonflikte.

race *n*
Unfortunately racial conflicts
come up over and over again.

Titel ['ti:t(ə)l] *m*, -s, -
Frau Prof. Dr. Scholz möchte
mit ihrem Titel angesprochen
werden.

title *n*
Professor Scholz would like to be
addressed by her title.

weiblich ['vaipliç] *Adj.*
Sie hat eine weibliche Figur.

feminine, female, womanly
She has a feminine figure.

4.2 Familie und Verwandtschaft | 1-2000

4.2 Family and Relationships

Angehörige ['angəhø:rigə] *m/f*,
-n, -n
Der Verstorbene hatte keine An-
gehörigen.

relatives, family members *n*

The deceased had no relatives.

Bruder ['bru:də*] *m, -s, Brüder*
Mein Bruder lebt in Kanada.

brother *n*
My brother lives in Canada.

Ehe ['e:ə] *f, -, -n*
In Deutschland wird zurzeit jede dritte Ehe geschieden.

marriage *n*
Currently in Germany every third marriage will end in divorce.

Ehefrau ['e:əfrau] *f, -, -en*
Seine Ehefrau ist in Italien geboren.

wife *n*
His wife was born in Italy.

Ehemann ['e:əman] *m, -(e)s, Ehemänner*
Ich habe meinen Ehemann schon als Kind gekannt.

husband *n*

I knew my husband already when we were children.

Ehepaar ['e:əpa:*] *n, -(e)s, -e*
Wir sind mit einem dänischen Ehepaar befreundet.

couple *n*
We're acquainted with a Danish couple.

Eltern ['ɛltə*n] *nur Pl.*
Er wohnt mit 30 Jahren immer noch bei seinen Eltern.

parents *n*
He's thirty and still lives with his parents.

Familie [fa'mi:ljə] *f, -, -n*
Sie hat eine große Familie.

family *n*
She has a large family.

Geschwister [gə'ʃvistə*] *nur Pl.*
Ich habe keine Geschwister.

siblings, brothers and sisters
I have no brothers and sisters; I'm an only child.

heiraten ['haira:t(ə)n] *V/t.,* heiratete, hat geheiratet
Er hat seine Jugendfreundin geheiratet.

marry, get married *v*

He married his friend from childhood.

Kuss [kus] *m, -es, Küsse*
Sie gab ihm zum Abschied einen Kuss.

kiss *n*
She gave him a kiss when they parted.

küssen ['kys(ə)n] *V/t.,* küsste, hat geküsst
Das Kind mag nicht gerne geküsst werden.

kiss *v*

The child doesn't like to be kissed.

Mutter ['mutə*] *f, -, Mütter*
Sie telefoniert täglich mit ihrer Mutter.

mother *n*
She calls her mother every day.

Onkel ['ɔŋk(ə)l] *m, , -s, -*
Ich habe meinen Onkel lange nicht gesehen.

uncle *n*
I haven't seen my uncle for a long time.

Paar [pa:*] *n, -(e)s, -e*
Auf der Feier waren fast nur Paare.

couple *n*
There were mostly couples at the celebration.

Schwester ['ʃvɛstə*] *f, -, -n*
Sie sieht ihrer Schwester sehr ähnlich.

sister *n*
She looks a lot like her sister.

Sohn [zo:n] *m, -(e)s, Söhne*
Sie möchte, dass ihr Sohn Ingenieur wird.

son *n*
She would like her son to become an engineer.

Tante ['tantə] *f, -, -n*
Meine Tante ist noch sehr jung.

aunt *n*
My aunt is still very young.

Tochter ['tɔxtə*] *f, -, Töchter*
Ihre Tochter geht noch zur Schule.

daughter *n*
Their daughter is still in school.

Vater ['fa:tə*] *m, -s, Väter*
Er ist mit 60 Jahren noch einmal Vater geworden.

father *n*
He fathered another child at age sixty.

verwandt [fɛə*'vant] *Adj., keine Komp.*
Wir sind miteinander verwandt.

related

We are related to each other.

Verwandte [fɛə*'vantə] *m/f, -n, -n*
Bei der Familienfeier haben sich viele Verwandte getroffen.

relatives, family members *n*

We met a lot of relatives at the family reunion.

2001-4000

Braut [braut] *f, -, Bräute*
Seine Braut ist älter als er.

bride *n*
His bride is older than he is.

Bräutigam ['brɔitigam] *m, -s, -e*
Der Bräutigam war bei der Hochzeit sehr nervös.

groom *n*
The groom was very nervous at the wedding.

Enkel [ˈɛŋk(ə)l] *m*, -s, -
Enkelin [ˈɛŋkəlin] *f*, -, -nen
Der Großvater geht mit seinem
Enkel oft in den Zoo.

**grandson, granddaughter,
grandchild** *n*
The grandfather often takes his
grandson to the zoo.

erziehen [ɛəˈtsiː(ə)n] *V/t.*, erzog,
hat erzogen
Sie erziehen ihr Kind sehr frei.

bring up, educate *v*
They're bringing up their child
very liberally.

Erziehung [ɛəˈtsiːuŋ] *f*, -, *kein Pl.*
Sie hat viele Bücher über Kinder-
erziehung gelesen.

upbringing, education *n*
She has read a lot of books about
bringing up children.

Großeltern [ˈgroːsɛltəˈn] *nur Pl.*
Unsere Tochter verbrachte die
Ferien bei ihren Großeltern.

grandparents *n*
Our daughter spent her vacation
with her grandparents.

Großmutter [ˈgroːsmutəˈ] *f*, -,
Großmütter
Meine Großmutter ist vor fünf
Jahren gestorben.

grandmother *n*
My grandmother died five years
ago.

Großvater [ˈgroːsfaːtəˈ] *m*, -s,
Großväter
Ihr Großvater ist 73 Jahre alt.

grandfather *n*
Their grandfather is 73 years old.

Hochzeit [ˈhɔxtsait] *f*, -, -en
Unsere Hochzeit haben wir in einem Restaurant gefeiert.

wedding, marriage *n*
We celebrated our wedding in a
restaurant.

Kusine [ˈkuziːnə] *f*, -, -n (auch:
Cousine)
Meine Kusine habe ich seit Jah-
ren nicht gesehen.

(female) **cousin** *n*

I haven't seen my cousin for
years.

ledig [ˈleːdɪçᵒ] *Adj., keine Komp.*
Petra ist immer noch ledig.

single, unmarried *n*
Petra is still single.

Neffe [ˈnɛfə] *m*, -n, -n
Mein Neffe und ich verstehen uns
gut.

nephew *n*
My nephew and I get along well.

Nichte [ˈnɪçtə] *f*, -, -n
Meine Nichte lebt in Mailand.

niece *n*
My niece lives in Milan.

scheiden [ˈʃaid(ə)n] *V/refl., rzp.,*
schied, hat geschieden
Wir werden uns scheiden lassen.

divorce, get divorced *v*

We're going to get divorced.

Schwager [ˈʃvaːgə*] *m*, -s, Schwäger

brother-in-law *n*

Schwägerin [ˈʃvɛːgərin] *f*, -, -nen
Mit meinem Schwager bin ich zusammen zur Schule gegangen.

sister-in-law *n*
I went to school with my brother-in-law.

Schwiegereltern [ˈʃviːgə*ɛltə*n] *nur Pl.*
Meine Schwiegereltern finde ich nicht sehr sympathisch.

parents-in-law *n*

I don't like my parents-in-law.

Trauung [ˈtrauuŋ] *f*, -, -en
Die Trauung ist am nächsten Freitag.

wedding, marriage *(ceremony) n*
The wedding is next Friday.

verloben [fɛə*ˈloːb(ə)n] *V/refl.*, verlobte, hat verlobt
Brigitte und Uwe haben sich letzte Woche verlobt.

get engaged *v*

Brigitte and Uwe got engaged last week.

Vetter [ˈfɛtə*] *m*, -s, -n, **Cousin** [kuˈzɛ̃]
Ich bin mit meinem Vetter zusammen aufgewachsen.

(male) **cousin** *n*

I grew up with my cousin.

Witwe [ˈvitvə] *f*, -, -n **Witwer**, *m*, -s, -
Sie ist schon seit vielen Jahren Witwe.

widow *n*

She has already been a widow for many years.

4.3 Soziale Bindungen	1–2000

4.3 Social Ties

Bekannte [bəˈkantə] *m/f*, -n, -n
Frau Renken ist eine alte Bekannte von mir.

acquaintance, friend *n*
Mrs. Renken is an old acquaintance of mine.

fremd [frɛmt] *Adj.*
Ich bin von einer fremden Person gefragt worden, ob in unserem Haus ein Herr Zech wohnt.

unfamiliar, strange, unknown *n*
A stranger asked me if a Mr. Zech lives in our building.

Fremde ['frɛmdə] *m/f,* -n, -n
Unser Hund bellt sofort, wenn ein Fremder auf unser Grundstück kommt.

stranger *n*
Our dog barks right away if a stranger comes onto our property.

Freund [frɔint] *m,* -es, -e
Freundin ['frɔindin] *f,* -, -nen
Elmar spielt draußen mit seinen Freunden.

friend *n*

Elmar is playing outside with his friends.

Freundschaft ['frɔintʃaft] *f,* -, -en
Du musst dich nicht bedanken. Das habe ich aus Freundschaft getan.

friendship *n*
You don't have to thank me. I did it out of friendship.

Gesellschaft [gə'zɛlʃaft] *f,* -, -en
In unserer Gesellschaft gibt es eine sehr kleine und reiche Oberschicht.
Ich fühle mich in seiner Gesellschaft nicht wohl.
Ich bin Mitglied der „Deutsch-Arabischen Gesellschaft".

society, company *n*
In our society there is a very small and rich upper class.

I do not feel comfortable in his company.
I'm a member of the "German-Arabian Society."

Partner ['partnə*] *m,* -s, -
Partnerin ['partnərin] *f,* -, -nen
Frau Janßen ist meine Geschäftspartnerin.
Sie ist ohne ihren Partner zur Feier gekommen.

partner *n*

Ms. Janßen is my business partner.
She came to the celebration without her partner.

Pflicht [pfliçt] *f,* -, -en
Es ist meine Pflicht, Ihnen zu helfen.

duty, obligation *n*
It is my duty to help you.

---

privat [pri'vaːt] *Adj.* -er, am -esten
Privat ist er ein anderer Mensch als im Betrieb.

in private
In private he is a different person than at work.

134

abhängen [ˈaphɛŋən] *V/i.*, + *Präp.* (von), hing ab, hat abgehangen
Es hängt vom Wetter ab, wann wir das Haus streichen.

depend on *v*

It depends on the weather when we'll paint the house.

abhängig [ˈaphɛŋiçº] *Adj.*
Sie ist finanziell von ihren Eltern abhängig.

dependent
She is financially dependent on her parents.

angehören [ˈangəhøːr(ə)n] *V/i.*, gehörte an, hat angehört
Sie gehören beide demselben Sportverein an.

belong to *v*

They both belong to the same sports club.

Feind [faint] *m*, -es, -e
Feindin [ˈfaindin] *f*, -, -nen
Die meisten Leute mögen ihn nicht, aber wirkliche Feinde hat er sicher nicht.

enemy *n*

Most people don't like him, but he doesn't have real enemies.

freundschaftlich [ˈfrɔintʃaftliç] *Adj.*
Zwischen Frankreich und der Bundesrepublik gibt es eine freundschaftliche Beziehung.

friendly

France and Germany have friendly relations.

gesellschaftlich [gəˈzɛlʃaftliç] *Adj., keine Komp.*
Die Arbeitslosigkeit ist ein wichtiges gesellschaftliches Problem.

social

Unemployment is an important social problem.

Kamerad [kaməˈraːt] *m*, -en, -en
Kameradin [kaməˈraːdin] *f*, -, -nen
Georg und ich sind Schulkameraden.

friend, chum, buddy, pal *n*

George and I went to school together.

4.4 Berufe | 1-2000

Angestellte ['angəʃtɛltə] *m/f*, -n, -n
Sie arbeitet als Büroangestellte bei Helmers & Co.

employee *n*
She's an office employee at Helmers & Co.

Arbeiter ['arbaita*] *m*, -s, -
Arbeiterin ['arbaitərin] *f*, -, -nen
Die Arbeiter werden morgens mit einem Kleinbus zur Baustelle gebracht.

worker *n*
In the morning the workers are brought to the construction site in a small bus.

Bäcker ['bɛkə*] *m*, -s, -
Bäckerin ['bɛkərin] *f*, -, -nen
Der Bäcker in der Holzstraße backt die besten Brötchen.

baker *n*
The baker on Holzstraße makes the best rolls.

Bauer ['bauə*] *m*, -n, -n
Bäuerin ['bɔiərin] *f*, -, -nen
Frische Milch kaufe ich direkt beim Bauern.

farmer *n*
I buy fresh milk directly from the farmer.

Beamte [bə'amtə] *m*, -n, -n
Beamtin [bə'amtin] *f*, -, -nen
Er arbeitet als Beamter bei der Post.

public employee, civil servant *n*
He is a civil servant at the Post Office.

Beruf [bə'ru:f] *m*, -(e)s, -e
Was sind Sie von Beruf?

occupation, profession, career, vocation *n*
What is your profession?

beruflich [bə'ru:fliç] *Adj., keine Komp.*
Sie ist beruflich sehr erfolgreich.

on the job, in a career
She is very successful in her career.

berufstätig [bə'ru:fstɛ:tiç°] *Adj., keine Komp.*
Die Eltern von Sven sind beide berufstätig.

working
Sven's parents are both working.

Hausfrau ['hausfrau] *f*, -, -en
Meine Mutter war immer Hausfrau.

housewife *n*
My mother was always a housewife.

Ingenieur [inʒen'jøːə*] *m*, -s, -e
Ingenieurin [inʒen'jøːrin] *f*, -, -nen
Sie studiert an einer Fachhochschule, um Ingenieurin zu werden.

engineer *n*
She is studying at a technical college to become an engineer.

Meister ['maistə*] *m*, -s, -
Meisterin ['maistərin] *f*, -, -nen
Unser Sohn ist Automechaniker. Nächstes Jahr will er seine Meisterprüfung machen.

master (craftsman) *n*
Our son is an auto mechanic. Next year he wants to take his final exam fot the master craftsman's diploma.

Politiker [po'liːtikə*] *m*, -s, -
Politikerin [po'liːtikərin] *f*, -, -nen
Sie ist seit zehn Jahren Politikerin.

politician *n*
She has been a politician for ten years.

Sekretär [zekre'tɛːə*] *m*, -s, -e
Sekretärin [zekre'tɛːrin] *f*, -, nen
Sie sucht eine interessante Stelle als Sekretärin.

secretary *n*
She is seeking an interesting job as secretary.

Techniker ['tɛçnikə*] *m*, -s, -
Technikerin ['tɛçnikərin] *f*, -, -nen
Besprechen Sie dieses Problem bitte mit unserem Techniker. Er kennt die Maschine genau.

technician, *n*
Please speak with our technician about the problem. He knows all about the machine.

Verkäufer [fɛə*'kɔifə*] *m*, -s, -
Verkäuferin [fɛə*'kɔifərin] *f*, -, -nen
Der Verkäufer war freundlich und hat mich gut bedient.

salesperson *n*
The salesperson was friendly and served me well.

2001-4000

Architekt [arçi'tɛkt] *m*, -en, -en
Architektin [arçi'tɛktin] *f*, -, -nen
Wir haben unser Haus von einem Architekten planen lassen.

architect *n*
We had an architect draw up the plans for our house.

Assistent [asisˈtɛnt] *m*, -en, -en
Assistentin [asisˈtɛntin] *f*, -, -nen
Unser Chef hat seit Januar einen neuen Assistenten.

assistant *n*

Our boss has had a new assistant since January.

Dolmetscher [ˈdɔlmɛtʃə*] *m*, -, -s, -
Dolmetscherin [ˈdɔlmɛtʃərin] *f*, -, -nen
Sie ist Dolmetscherin für Spanisch.

interpreter *n*

She is an interpreter for Spanish.

Fleischer [ˈflaiʃə*] *m*, -s, -
Fleischerin [ˈflaiʃərin] *f*, -, -nen
Der Fleischer in der Gaststraße macht ausgezeichnete Wurst.

butcher *n*

The butcher on Gaststraße makes excellent sausage.

Friseur [friˈzøː*] *m*, -s, -e
Friseuse [friˈzøːzə] *f*, -, -n
Ich lasse meine Haare immer bei demselben Friseur schneiden.

hairdresser *n*

I always get the same hairdresser to cut my hair.

Geschäftsmann [gəˈʃɛftsman] *m*, -(e)s, -männer, **Geschäftsfrau** [gəˈʃɛftsfrau] *f*, -, -en
Auch ihre Freunde wundern sich, aber Sabine ist eine erfolgreiche Geschäftsfrau geworden.

businessman
businesswoman *n*

Sabine has become a successful businesswoman; even her friends are astonished.

Handwerker [ˈhantvɛrkə*] *m*, -s, -
Handwerkerin [ˈhantvɛrkərin] *f*, -, -nen
Gute Handwerker sind heutzutage schwer zu bekommen.

craftsman, (skilled) manual worker *n*

Nowadays it is not easy to find good skilled manual workers.

Journalist [ʒurnaˈlist] *m*, -en, -en
Journalistin [ʒurnaˈlistin] *f*, -, -nen
Er ist freier Journalist und arbeitet für verschiedene Zeitungen.

journalist *n*

He is a free-lance journalist and works for various newspapers.

Manager [ˈmɛnɛdʒə*] *m*, -s, -
Managerin [ˈmɛnɛdʒərin] *f*, -, -nen
Er ist Manager in einer Metallwarenfabrik.

manager *n*

He is a manager in a metal-processing factory.

Mechaniker [meˈçaːnikə*]
m, -s, -
Mechanikerin [meˈçaːnikərin]
f, -, -nen
Unsere Firma sucht einen Mechaniker.

mechanic *n*

Our company is looking for an mechanic.

Metzger [ˈmɛtsgə*] *m*, -s, -
Metzgerin [ˈmɛtsgərin] *f*, -, -nen
Der Metzger im Supermarkt verkauft gutes Fleisch.

butcher *n*

The butcher at the supermarket sells good meat.

Rentner [ˈrɛntnə*] *m*, -s, -
Rentnerin [ˈrɛntnərin] *f*, -, -nen
Wegen einer Berufskrankheit ist er schon mit 54 Jahren Rentner geworden.

retired person *n*

He retired at the age 54 because of a work-related health problem.

Schneider [ˈʃnaidə*] *m*, -s, -
Schneiderin [ˈʃnaidərin] *f*, -, -nen
○ Wo hast du diesen Anzug gekauft?
□ Er ist nicht gekauft. Ich habe ihn von einem Schneider machen lassen.

tailor, dressmaker *n*

○ Where did you buy that suit?
□ I didn't buy it ready-made. I had a tailor make it.

Unternehmer [untə*ˈneːmə*] *m*, -s, -, **Unternehmerin**
[untə*ˈneːmərin] *f*, -, -nen
Sie ist Unternehmerin. Ihr gehört die Maschinenfabrik Cordes.

entrepreneur, employer *n*

She is an entrepreneur. The Cordes engine factory belongs to her.

Vertreter [fɛə*ˈtreːtə*] *m*, -s, -
Vertreterin [fɛə*ˈtreːtərin]
f, -, -nen
Als Handelsvertreter ist er sehr viel mit dem Auto unterwegs.

representative *n*

He drives a lot because he is a business representative.

Wirt [virt] *m*, -(e)s, -e
Wirtin [ˈvirtin] *f*, -, -nen
Die Wirtin der neuen Gaststätte ist sehr freundlich.

owner of a restaurant, innkeeper *n*

The owner of the new restaurant is very friendly.

4.5 Soziale Position | 1-2000

4.5 Social Position

Ansehen ['anze:(ə)n] *n,* -s, *kein Pl.*
Der Bürgermeister genießt bei fast allen Bürgern der Stadt ein hohes Ansehen.

reputation *n*
The mayor has an excellent reputation among almost everyone in the city.

---

arm [arm] *Adj.,* ärmer, am ärmsten
Er ist nicht arm geworden, aber er hat durch seine letzten Geschäfte viel Geld verloren.

poor
He didn't get poor, but he lost a lot of money in his most recent transactions.

---

reich [raiç] *Adj.*
Reich kann man in meinem Beruf nicht werden, aber ich verdiene recht gut.

rich
No one can get rich in my profession, but I earn quite a good living.

2001-4000

Abstieg ['apʃtiːk] *m,* -s, -e
Der wirtschaftliche Abstieg der Firma begann eigentlich schon vor fünf Jahren.

decline, descent *n*
The financial decline of the firm probably began more than five years ago.

Aufstieg ['aufʃtiːk] *m,* -s, -e
Ihr steiler beruflicher Aufstieg wurde von vielen bewundert.

ascent, rise *n*
Her fast ascent in the profession astounded many.

Autorität [autoːriˈtɛːt] *f,* -, -en
In seinem Fach ist er eine Autorität, die alle anerkennen.

authority *n*
He's a recognized authority in his field.

Ehre ['eːrə] *f,* -, *kein Pl.*
Es hat seine Ehre verletzt, dass er auf der Feier keine Rede halten durfte.

honor *n*
His feelings were hurt because he was not allowed to give a speech at the celebration.

Elend ['e:lɛnt] *n, -s, kein Pl.*
Soziales Elend ist oft die Folge von langer Arbeitslosigkeit.

misery, distress *n*
Poverty is often the consequence of a long period of unemployment.

individuell [individu'ɛl] *Adj.*
Jeder Antrag wird individuell geprüft.

individual
Every application is tested individually.

Rang [raŋ] *m, -es, Ränge*
Er ist beim Militär und hat dort einen recht hohen Rang.

rank *n*
He is in the military and has quite a high rank.

Status ['ʃta:tus] *m, -, kein Pl.*
Er verdient gut, aber als Vertreter ist sein sozialer Status nicht sehr hoch.

status *n*
He makes a lot of money, but as a salesman his social status isn't very high.

4.6 Positives und neutrales Sozialverhalten

1-2000

4.6 Positive and Neutral Social Behavior

abmachen ['apmax(ə)n] *V/t.,* machte ab, hat abgemacht
Wir haben abgemacht, uns morgen wieder zu treffen.

agree *v*
We agreed to meet again tomorrow.

bedanken [bə'daŋk(ə)n] *V/refl.,* bedankte, hat bedankt
Ich bedanke mich für Ihr Angebot.

thank *v*
Thank you for your offer.

begegnen [bə'ge:gn(ə)n] *V/i.,* begegnete, ist begegnet
Ich bin ihr im Flur begegnet.

meet, encounter *v*
I met her in the corridor.

begrüßen [bə'gry:s(ə)n] *V/t.,* begrüßte, hat begrüßt
Sie begrüßte alle ihre Gäste persönlich.

greet, welcome *v*
She welcomed all her guests personally.

ehandeln [bə'hand(ə)ln] *V/t.,*
behandelte, hat behandelt
Warum behandelst du den Post-
boten so besonders freundlich?

treat, take care of *v*

Why do you treat the mailman/
postman *(BE)* especially kindly?

enehmen [bə'ne:mən] *V/refl.,*
benahm, hat benommen
Obwohl der Kunde sehr freundlich war, benahm sich der Verkäufer sehr unhöflich.

behave *v*

Although the client was very
friendly, the salesperson behaved
very impolitely.

eruhigen [bə'ru:ig(ə)n] *V/t., refl.,*
beruhigte, hat beruhigt
Der Vater versucht das weinende
Kind zu beruhigen.
Nach dem Schreck hat sie sich
sehr schnell beruhigt.

calm *v*

The father tried to calm the crying
child.
She calmed down quickly after
the fright.

influss ['ainflus] *m,* -es, Ein-
flüsse
Sie hat großen Einfluss auf die
Entscheidung.

influence *n*

She has considerable influence
on the decision.

ntschuldigen [ɛnt'ʃuldig(ə)n]
V/t., refl., entschuldigte, hat ent-
schuldigt
Entschuldigen Sie, dass ich Ihnen
erst jetzt schreibe.
Sie hat sich für ihren Irrtum ent-
schuldigt.

excuse *v*

Please excuse me for not writing
you until now.
She excused herself for her mistake.

ntschuldigung [ɛnt'ʃuldiguŋ]
f, -, -en
Für dein Verhalten gibt es keine
Entschuldigung.

excuse *n*

There is no excuse for your be-
haviour.

rwarten [ɛə*'vart(ə)n] *V/t.,* er-
wartete, hat erwartet
Ich erwarte seit Wochen eine Antwort auf mein Schreiben.

wait (for), **await** *v*

I've been waiting for weeks for an
answer to my letter.

eundlich ['frɔintliç] *Adj.*
Sei freundlich zu Horst, auch
wenn du ihn nicht magst.

friendly
Be friendly to Horst even if you
don't like him.

Gruß [gru:s] *m*, -es, Grüße
Bestell Klaus herzliche Grüße von
mir!

greeting *n*
Give Klaus my love!

grüßen ['gry:s(ə)n] *V/t.*, grüßte,
hat gegrüßt
Grüße deinen Bruder von mir!

greet, send greetings *n*

Send my greetings to your brother.

helfen ['hɛlf(ə)n] *V/i.*, half, hat geholfen
Ich helfe dir beim Aufräumen.

help *v*

I'll help you clean up.

Hilfe ['hilfə] *f*, -, *kein Pl.*
Sie hat es ohne fremde Hilfe ge-
schafft.
Brauchst du Hilfe?

help, assistance *n*
She did it without help from
anyone.
Do you need help?

höflich [høːfliç] *Adj.*
In diesem Geschäft wird man sehr
höflich bedient.

polite
In this shop you will be very polite-
ly treated.

Rücksicht ['rykziçt] *f*, -, -en
Die Autofahrer sollten mehr Rücksicht auf die Fußgänger nehmen.

consideration *n*
Drivers should have more consideration for pedestrians.

treu [trɔi] *Adj.*, -er, am -esten
Sie ist eine sehr treue Freundin.

loyal, true
She's a very loyal friend.

verhalten [fɛə*'halt(ə)n] *V/refl.*,
verhielt, hat verhalten
Alle waren aufgeregt, nur Ruth
verhielt sich sehr ruhig.

behave, act *v*

Everyone was excited; only Ruth
behaved very calmly.

Verhalten *n*, -s, *kein Pl.*
Fast alle Kollegen finden sein Verhalten merkwürdig.

behavior, conduct *n*
Nearly all the co-workers think his
behavior is strange.

vertrauen [fɛə*'trau(ə)n] *V/i.*, +
Präp. (auf), vertraute, hat vertraut
Er ist zwar etwas komisch, aber
man kann ihm vertrauen.

trust *v*

He is certainly a bit strange, but
you can trust him.

Vertrauen *n*, -s, *kein Pl.*
Sie hat leider kein Vertrauen zu
mir.

confidence, trust *n*
Unfortunately, she has no confidence in me.

$$2001-4000$$

achten ['axt(ə)n] *V/t., i., + Präp.* (auf) | **respect, pay attention to** *v*

Alle achten ihn wegen seiner langen Berufserfahrung.
Bitte achten Sie genau auf die Spielregeln.

He is respected by everyone because of his long experience.
Please pay attention to the rules of the game.

---

beeindrucken [bə'aindruk(ə)n] *V/t.,* beeindruckte, hat beeindruckt | **impress** *v*

Ihre klugen Augen haben mich beeindruckt.

Her intelligent eyes impressed me.

---

beeinflussen [bə'ainflus(ə)n] *V/t.,* beeinflusste, hat beeinflusst | **influence** *v*

Seine Eltern haben ihn bei der Berufswahl stark beeinflusst.

His parents strongly influenced his career choice.

---

begleiten [bə'glait(ə)n] *V/t.,* begleitete, hat begleitet | **accompany, come along, go along** *v*

Ich gehe noch etwas spazieren. Willst du mich nicht begleiten?

I'm going for a walk. Don't you want to come along?

---

beschützen [bə'ʃyts(ə)n] *V/t.,* beschützte, hat beschützt | **protect, guard** *v*

Die Polizei musste den Politiker vor den Demonstranten beschützen.

The police had to protect the politician from the demonstrators.

Brauch [braux] *m, -(e)s, Bräuche* | **custom, common usage, tradition** *n*

Die Hochzeit wurde nach altem Brauch gefeiert.

The wedding was celebrated according to established tradition.

---

ertragen [ɛə*'tra:g(ə)n] *V/t.,* ertrug, hat ertragen | **bear, endure, stand** *v*

Ihr dummes Gerede ist schwer zu ertragen.

Her silly gossip is hard to bear.

---

gefallen lassen [gə'fal(ə)n] *V/refl.,* ließ gefallen, hat gefallen lassen | **stand for, put up with, bear, tolerate** *v*

Warum lässt du dir gefallen, dass er immer nur Schlechtes über dich erzählt?

Why do you tolerate that he is always saying bad things about you?

Gelächter [gə'lɛçtə*] *n, -s, kein Pl.*
Die Versprechungen des Politikers beantworteten die Zuhörer mit Gelächter.

laughter *n*
The listeners responded to the politician's promises with laughter.

passiv ['pasif] *Adj.*
Seit vielen Jahren ist er nur noch passives Mitglied im Sportverein.

passive, non-active
For years he's only been a non-active member of the sports club.

Respekt [re'spɛkt] *m, -(e)s, kein Pl.*
Die Kinder haben wenig Respekt vor ihrem neuen Lehrer.

respect *n*
The children have little respect for their new teacher.

respektieren [respɛk'tiːr(ə)n] *V/t., respektierte, hat respektiert*
Ich finde deine Entscheidung nicht richtig, aber ich respektiere sie.

respect *v*
I don't think your decision is right, but I respect it.

Scherz [ʃɛə*ts] *m, -es, -e*
Sei doch nicht beleidigt! Das war doch nur ein Scherz.

joke *n*
Don't be hurt. That was only a joke.

vertragen [fɛə*'traːg(ə)n] *V/t., refl., vertrug, hat vertragen*
Er kann keine Kritik vertragen.
Mit seiner Schwester verträgt er sich sehr gut.

bear, stand, tolerate, get along with *v*
He can't bear criticism.
He gets along very well with his sister.

verzeihen [fɛə*'tsai(ə)n] *V/t., verzieh, hat verziehen*
Verzeihen Sie bitte die Störung!

excuse, pardon *v*
Please excuse the disturbance!

4.7 Negatives Sozialverhalten | 1-2000

4.7 Negative Social Behavior

ärgern [ˈɛrgə*n] *V/t., refl., + Präp.*
(über), ärgerte, hat geärgert
Es macht ihr Spaß, ihren kleinen
Bruder zu ärgern.
Es hat keinen Zweck, sich über
das schlechte Wetter zu ärgern.

get angry, annoy, irritate *v*

She likes to annoy her little
brother.
It's useless to get angry about the
bad weather.

---

drohen [ˈdroː(ə)n] *V/i.,* drohte, hat
gedroht
Der Chef drohte, ihm zu kündigen.

threaten *v*

The boss threatened to dismiss
him.

---

enttäuschen [ɛntˈtɔiʃ(ə)n] *V/t.,*
enttäuschte, hat enttäuscht
Sein Verhalten hat mich sehr enttäuscht.

disappoint *v*

His behavior has really disappointed me.

---

erschrecken [ɛə*ˈʃrɛk(ə)n] *V/t.,*
erschreckte, hat erschreckt
Man kann ihn leicht erschrecken.

frighten, shock, scare *v*

He is easy to scare.

---

erschrecken *V/i.,* erschrak, ist
erschrocken
Ich bin sehr erschrocken, wie
krank er aussah.

be shocked, be frightened

I was really shocked to see how ill
he looked.

Lüge [ˈlyːgə] *f, -, -n*
Das ist eine Lüge. Ich weiß, dass
das nicht wahr ist.

lie *n*
That's a lie. I know that it's not
true.

---

lügen [ˈlyːg(ə)n] *V/i.,* log, hat gelogen
Du bist doch gar nicht krank. Warum lügst du?

lie, tell a lie *v*

You're not really sick. Why are
you lying?

Misstrauen [ˈmistrau(ə)n] *n, -s,*
kein Pl.
Das Misstrauen gegen die Regierung wächst ständig.

distrust, mistrust *n*

Distrust of the government is
growing constantly.

Streit [ʃtrait] *m, -(e)s, kein Pl.*
Was ist die Ursache eures Streites?

argument, dispute *n*
What's the cause of your dispute?

streiten [ˈʃtrait(ə)n] *V/refl.,* stritt, hat gestritten
Ich habe keine Lust, mich mit dir zu streiten.

argue, fight *v*
I don't want to fight with you.

2001–4000

aggressiv [agrɛˈsiːf] *Adj.*
Warum bist du so aggressiv? Habe ich dir etwas getan?

aggressive
Why are you so aggressive? Did I do something to you?

Auseinandersetzung [ausaiˈnandəˈzɛtsuŋ] *f, -, -en*
Über das neue Strafrecht gab es starke Auseinandersetzungen zwischen den politischen Parteien.

arguing, argument(s), intense discussion *n*
There was a lot of argument among the political parties over the new criminal laws.

beleidigen [bəˈlaidig(ə)n] *V/t.,* beleidigte, hat beleidigt
Warum bist du so komisch zu mir? Habe ich dich beleidigt?

insult, offend *v*
Why do you treat me so strangely? Did I offend you?

Beleidigung [bəˈlaidiguŋ] *f, -, -en*
Diese Bemerkung ist eine Beleidigung.

insult *n*
This remark is an insult.

fluchen [ˈfluːx(ə)n] *V/i.,* + *Präp.* (über, auf), fluchte, hat geflucht
Sie fluchte über ihr Auto, das nicht starten wollte.

swear, curse *v*
She swore at her car that wouldn't start.

Trick [trik] *m, -s, -s*
Pass auf, er kennt viele Tricks.

trick *n*
Watch out – he knows lots of tricks.

unfreundlich [ˈunfrɔintliç] *Adj.*
Obwohl ich immer höflich war, ist sie unfreundlich zu mir.

unfriendly
Though I've always been polite, she is unfriendly to me.

unhöflich [ˈunhøːfliç] *Adj.*
Der Kellner war sehr unhöflich.

impolite, rude
The waiter was very impolite.

verlassen [fɛə*'las(ə)n] *V/t., refl., + Präp.* (auf), verließ, hat verlassen

Sie verließ den Raum, ohne sich zu verabschieden.

Auf Karin kann man sich verlassen, wenn sie etwas versprochen hat.

leave, abandon, desert, count on *v*

She left without saying good-bye.

You can count on Karin when she's promised something.

Vorurteil ['fo:ə*uə*tail] *n,* -s, -e
Auch in unserem Betrieb gibt es gegen Frauen mit Männerberufen immer noch Vorurteile.

bias, prejudice *n*
There is still bias against women in our profession.

4.8 Kontakte und Veranstaltungen | 1-2000
4.8 Contacts and Events

abholen ['apho:l(ə)n] *V/t.,* holte ab, hat abgeholt
Könntest du mich bitte vom Busbahnhof abholen?

pick up *v*

Could you please pick me up at the bus station?

besuchen [bə'zu:x(ə)n] *V/t.,* besuchte, hat besucht
Ihr habt uns lange nicht besucht. Wann kommt ihr mal?

visit *v*

You haven't visited us for a long time. When will you becoming by?

Besuch [bə'zu:x] *m,* -(e)s, -e
Nächste Woche haben wir Besuch.

visit, visitors, guests *n*
Next week we're having guests.

einladen ['ainla:d(ə)n] *V/t.,* lud ein, hat eingeladen
Wir sind zur Hochzeitsfeier von Gerd und Carola eingeladen.

invite *v*

We're invited to Gerd and Carola's wedding.

feiern ['faiə*n] *V/t.,* feierte, hat gefeiert
Der 60. Geburtstag meiner Mutter wurde kräftig gefeiert.

celebrate *v*

My mother's sixtieth birthday was heartily celebrated.

Fest [fɛst] *n, -(e)s, -e*
Unser Sportverein veranstaltet jedes Jahr ein großes Sommerfest.

celebration, party *n*
Every summer our sports club has a big celebration.

Gast [gast] *m, -es, Gäste*
Weil wir sehr viel Besuch haben, haben wir ein Gästezimmer eingerichtet.

guest *n*
We set up a room for guests because we have lots of visitors.

Leute ['lɔɪtə] *nur Pl.*
Viele Leute blieben stehen und hörten den Straßenmusikern zu.

people *n*
Many people stopped and listened to the street musicians.

Mitglied ['mɪtgliːt] *n, -(e)s, -er*
Der Jahresbeitrag für jedes Vereinsmitglied beträgt 50,– €.

member *n*
Yearly dues for each club member are 50 €.

Nachbar ['naxbaː*] *m, -n, -n*
Nachbarin ['naxbaːrɪn] *f, -, -nen*
Unsere Nachbarn haben ihr Haus verkauft.

neighbor *n*

Our neighbors sold their house.

Party ['paːˑti] *f, -, -s*
Dieses Jahr findet meine Geburtstagsparty im Garten statt.

party *n*
This year I'm having a garden birthday party.

treffen ['trɛf(ə)n] *V/t., rzp.,* traf, hat getroffen
Ich habe ihn zufällig auf der Post getroffen.
Wo wollen wir uns treffen?

meet *v*

I ran across him in the Post Office.

Where shall we meet?

unterhalten [untə*'halt(ə)n] *V/t., refl.,* unterhielt, hat unterhalten
Der Künstler konnte sein Publikum gut unterhalten.
Worüber habt ihr euch unterhalten?

entertain, talk (about) *v*

The artist could entertain his audience well.
What did you talk about?

Verein [fɛə*'ain] *m, -s, -e*
Bist du Mitglied in einem Sportverein?

club, organization *n*
Do you belong to a sports club?

2001-4000

empfangen [ɛmˈpfaŋən] *V/t.,*
empfing, hat empfangen
Sie hat alle ihre Gäste persönlich
empfangen.

welcome, receive, greet *v*

She received all her guests personally.

Gastgeber [ˈgastgeːbɐ*] *m,* -s, -
Gastgeberin [ˈgastgeːbərin] *f,* -,
-nen
Er ist ein guter Gastgeber.

host, hostess *n*

He is a good host.

---

kennen lernen [ˈkɛnən lɛrnən]
V/t., rzp., lernte kennen, hat kennen gelernt
Wo hast du ihn kennen gelernt?
Wir haben uns beim Tanzen kennen gelernt.

meet, get to know *v*

○ Where did you meet him?
□ We met at a dance.

Klub [klup] *m,* -s, -s
Sie ist Mitglied in einem Schachklub.

club, organization *n*
She belongs to a chess club.

Kontakt [kɔnˈtakt] *m,* -(e)s, -e
Wir haben schon seit Jahren keinen Kontakt mehr miteinander.

contact *n*
We haven't been in contact for years.

---

stattfinden [ˈʃtatfind(ə)n] *V/i.,*
fand statt, hat stattgefunden
Die Veranstaltung findet nur bei gutem Wetter statt.

take place *v*

The event only takes place if the weather permits.

Treffen [ˈtrɛf(ə)n] *n,* -s, -
Der Geburtstag meiner Urgroßmutter ist immer ein großes Familientreffen.

meeting, reunion *n*
My great-grandmother's birthday is always a big family reunion.

Verabredung [fɛɐ*ˈapreːduŋ] *f,* -,
-en
○ Wollen wir morgen zusammen essen gehen?
□ Tut mir leid, ich habe schon eine Verabredung.

appointment *n*

○ Shall we go out to eat tomorrow?
□ Sorry, I already have an appointment.

verabschieden [fɛə*'apʃi:d(ə)n]   **say good-bye, depart** *v*
V/t., refl., verabschiedete, hat ver-
abschiedet
Er verabschiedete seinen Besuch   He said good-bye to his guests at
an der Haustür.   the door.
Er verließ den Raum, ohne sich zu   He left without saying good-bye.
verabschieden.

veranstalten [fɛə*'anʃtalt(ə)n]   **organize, arrange** *v*
V/t., veranstaltete, hat veran-
staltet
Sie will zu ihrem 30. Geburtstag   She wants to organize a big cele-
ein großes Fest veranstalten.   bration for her thirtieth birthday.

Veranstaltung [fɛə*'anʃtaltuŋ] *f,*   **event** *n*
-, -en
Die Veranstaltung findet im Les-   The event takes place in the Les-
sing-Saal statt und beginnt um   sing Hall and begins at 8 p.m.
20.00 Uhr.

Versammlung [fɛə*'zamluŋ] *f,* -,   **meeting, assembly** *n*
-en
Der alte Vorsitzende wurde auf   The former chairman was re-
der Versammlung wiedergewählt.   elected at the meeting.

vorbeikommen [fo:ə*'baikɔmən]   **stop by, call in (on)** *v*
V/i., kam vorbei, ist vorbeige-
kommen
Ich will mit ein Buch von dir aus-   I would like to borrow a book from
leihen. Kann ich heute Abend   you. May I stop by this evening?
kurz bei dir vorbeikommen?

vorstellen ['fo:ə*ʃtɛl(ə)n] *V/t.,*   **introduce** *v*
refl., stellte vor, hat vorgestellt
Vera hat uns ihren Mann vorge-   Vera introduced her husband to
stellt.   us.
Darf ich mich vorstellen? Mein   May I introduce myself? My name
Name ist Urban.   is Urban.

4.9 Schicksal und Zufall | 1-2000

4.9 Fate and Coincidence

brennen [ˈbrɛnən] *V./i.,* brannte, hat gebrannt	**burn, be on fire** *v*
Nach dem Unfall brannte das ganze Auto.	After the accident the car was on fire.
Chance [ˈʃ̃ãːsə] *f, -, -n*	**chance** *n*
Trotz vieler Torchancen hat unsere Mannschaft das Spiel verloren.	Our team lost in spite of many chances to make goals.
Ereignis [ɛəˈʔaignis] *n, -ses, -se*	**event, occurrence** *n*
Der Besuch des Präsidenten ist für die Stadt ein großes Ereignis.	The president's visit is a big event for the city.
erleben [ɛəˈleːb(ə)n] *V./t.,* erlebte, hat erlebt	**experience, live to see** *v*
Die Geburt seines ersten Sohnes hat er nicht mehr erlebt.	He didn't live to see the birth of his first son.
Feuer [ˈfɔiəʳ] *n, -s, -*	**fire** *n*
Im Wald ist Feuermachen verboten.	It's forbidden to make a fire in the woods.
Gefahr [gəˈfaːʳ] *f, -, -en*	**danger** *n*
Noch ist das Hochwasser keine Gefahr für die Stadt, aber es steigt ständig.	The flooding is still no danger to the city, but the water level keeps on rising.
gefährlich [gəˈfɛːəʳliç] *Adj.*	**dangerous**
Pass auf, da vorne ist eine gefährliche Kurve.	Be careful; there's a dangerous curve ahead.
Gelegenheit [gəˈleːg(ə)nhait] *f, -, -en*	**opportunity** *n*
Ich hatte noch keine Gelegenheit, mit ihm zu sprechen.	I still haven't had an opportunity to speak with him.
geschehen [gəˈʃeː(ə)n] *V./i.,* geschah, ist geschehen	**happen, occur** *v*
Der Überfall geschah um 12.00 Uhr.	The attack happened around noon.

Not [noːt] *f, -, kein Pl.*
Er behauptet, dass er aus Not gestohlen habe.

need, want, necessity, emergency *n*
He claimed he stole because of need.

Opfer [ˈɔpfə*] *n, -s, -*
Der Flugzeugabsturz forderte 142 Todesopfer.

victim *n*
The air crash claimed 142 victims.

passieren [paˈsiːrən] *V/i., passierte, ist passiert*
Fahr bitte vorsichtiger, sonst passiert noch ein Unfall.

happen, take place *v*

Please drive more carefully or there will be an accident.

Pech [pɛç] *n, -s, kein Pl.*
Es ist nicht ihre Schuld, sie hat nur Pech gehabt.

bad luck *n*
It's not her fault; she just had bad luck.

retten [ˈrɛt(ə)n] *V/t., refl., rettete, hat gerettet*
Das Kind konnte aus dem Wasser gerettet werden.
Alle Personen konnten sich aus dem brennenden Bus retten.

save, escape *v*

The child could be saved from the water.
Everyone was able to escape from the burning bus.

Schaden [ˈʃaːd(ə)n] *m, -s, Schäden*
Durch den Sturm gab es am Dach einige Schäden.

damage *n*

The storm caused some damage to the roof.

Situation [zituaˈtsjoːn] *f, -, -en*
Die wirtschaftliche Situation im Lande ist zur Zeit gut.

situation *n*
The economic situation of the country is very good right now.

Unglück [ˈunglyk] *n, -s, -e*
Bei dem Zugunglück gab es viele Verletzte, aber keine Toten.

accident, misfortune *n*
Many were injured in the train accident, but no one was killed.

Zufall [ˈtsuːfal] *m, -s, Zufälle*
Durch Zufall habe ich meinen Schlüssel wiedergefunden.

accident, chance, coincidence *n*
I found my keys by chance.

zufällig [ˈtsuːfɛliçº] *Adj., keine Komp.*
Meine Freundin ist zufällig am gleichen Tag wie ich geboren.

by chance, coincidental

Coincidental, my girlfriend was born on the same day I was.

2001-4000

Ausweg ['ausve:k] *m,* -s, -e
Er sah keinen anderen Ausweg als den Selbstmord.

way out *n*
He saw no other way out than suicide.

Brand [brant] *m,* -es, Brände
Die Fabrik wurde durch einen Brand zerstört.

fire *n*
The factory was destroyed in a fire.

ereignen [ɛə*'aignən] *V/refl.,* ereignete, hat ereignet
Der Unfall ereignete sich bei Nebel.

take place, happen *v*

The accident took place when it was foggy.

Explosion [ɛksplo'zjo:n] *f,* -, -en
Bei der Explosion wurde niemand getötet.

explosion *n*
No one was killed in the explosion.

Flamme ['flamə] *f,* -, -n
Die Flammen des Waldbrands waren z. T. über 10 Meter hoch.

flame *n*
Some of the flames from the forest fire were over 10 meters high.

Gewinner [gə'vinə*] *m,* -s, -
Gewinnerin [gə'vinərin] *f,* -, -nen
Die Namen der Gewinner wurden in der Zeitung veröffentlicht.

winner *n*

The names of the winners were published in the newspaper.

glücklicherweise
['glyklɪçə*valzə] *Adv.*
Glücklicherweise wurde sie nur leicht verletzt.

luckily, fortunately

Luckily she was only slightly injured.

Lage ['la:gə] *f,* -, -n
Was würdest du in meiner Lage tun?

situation *n*
What would you do in my situation?

Notfall ['no:tfal] *m,* -(e)s, Notfälle
Im Notfall können Sie mich unter dieser Nummer erreichen.

emergency *n*
In an emergency you can reach me at his number.

Rettung ['rɛtuŋ] *f,* -, -en
Die Rettung kam für die vermissten Seeleute in letzter Sekunde.

rescue *n*
Rescue came at the last moment for the missing sailors.

Risiko ['ri:ziko] *n, -s,* Risiken
Dieses Geschäft ist nicht ohne wirtschaftliches Risiko.

risk *n*
This business is not without economic risks.

riskieren [ris'ki:rən] *V/t.,* riskierte, hat riskiert
Wenn du nichts riskierst, kannst du auch nichts gewinnen.

risk, take a chance *v*
If you don't risk anything, you can't gain anything.

scheitern ['ʃaitə*n] *V/i.,* scheiterte, ist gescheitert
Nach vielen vergeblichen Versuchen musste er zugeben, dass sein Plan gescheitert ist.

fail *v*
After a lot of futile tries, he had to admit his plan had failed.

zusammenbrechen [tsu'zamənbrɛç(ə)n] *V/i.,* brach zusammen, ist zusammengebrochen
Der Läufer war so erschöpft, dass er nach dem Lauf zusammenbrach.

break down *v*
The runner was so exhausted that he broke down after his run.

5.1 Haus und Wohnung   1-2000

5.1 House and Apartment

abschließen ['apʃliːs(ə)n] *V/t.,*
schloss ab, hat abgeschlossen
Die Haustür wird jeden Abend um
22.00 Uhr abgeschlossen.

lock, close up *v*

The front door will be locked every night at 10.

Ausgang ['ausgaŋ] *m,* -s, Ausgänge
Der Saal hat drei Ausgänge.

exit *n*

The hall has three exits.

Boden ['boːd(ə)n] *m,* -s, Böden
Die Koffer stehen oben auf dem
Boden (Dachboden).
Die Tasse ist mir auf den Boden
(Fußboden) gefallen.

floor, attic *n*
The suitcases are upstairs on the
attic.
My cup fell on the floor.

Dach [dax] *n,* -(e)s, Dächer
Das Dach muss repariert werden,
es ist nicht dicht.

roof *n*
The roof has to be repaired; it's
leaking.

Eingang ['aingaŋ] *m,* -s, Ein-
gänge
Das Haus hat nur einen Eingang.

entrance, entry door *n*

The house has only one entrance.

Erdgeschoss ['eːə*tgəʃɔs] *n,* -es,
-e
Im Erdgeschoss des Hauses ist
eine Wohnung zu vermieten.

first floor *(BE:* **ground floor)***, n*

There's an apartment (*BE:* flat) for
rent on the first floor.

Fenster ['fɛnstə*] *n,* -s, -
Stell die Pflanzen näher ans Fenster, sie brauchen mehr Licht!

window *n*
Put the plants closer to the window; they need more light!

Fußboden ['fuːsboːd(ə)n] *m,* , -s,
Fußböden
In allen Räumen liegen Teppiche
auf den Fußböden.

floor *n*

There are rugs on the floor in every room.

Garage [ga'raːʒə] *f,* -, -n
Das Auto steht in der Garage.

garage *n*
The car is in the garage.

Garten ['gart(ə)n] *m, -s,* Gärten
Zum Haus gehört ein großer Garten.

garden, yard *n*
The house has a large yard.

Haus [haus] *n, -es,* Häuser
In dieser Gegend dürfen keine neuen Häuser gebaut werden.

house, residential building *n*
No new houses may be built in this area.

Heizung ['haitsuŋ] *f, -, -en*
Es ist so kalt hier. Funktioniert die Heizung nicht?

heat *n*
It's so cold here. Doesn't the heat work?

Keller ['kɛlə*] *m, -s, -*
Unser Keller ist leider sehr feucht.

basement *n*
Our basement is unfortunately very damp.

klingeln ['kliŋ(ə)ln] *V/i.,* klingelte, hat geklingelt
Hast du nicht gehört? Es hat geklingelt.

ring *v*

Didn't you hear the doorbell ring?

Küche ['kyçə] *f, -, -n*
Er ist in der Küche und wäscht ab.

kitchen *n*
He's in the kitchen cleaning up.

Mauer ['mauə*] *f, -, -n*
Die beiden Grundstücke sind durch eine Mauer getrennt.

wall *n*
There's a wall between the two lots.

Miete ['mi:tə] *f, -, -n*
Unsere Wohnung kostet 720,– € Miete pro Monat.

rent *n*
The rent for our apartment is 720 € a month.

mieten ['mi:t(ə)n] *V/t.,* mietete, hat gemietet
Im Urlaub haben wir uns ein Ferienhaus gemietet.

rent *v*

We rented a house for our vacation.

Mieter ['mi:tə*] *m, -s, -*
Mieterin ['mi:tərin] *f, -, -nen*
Alle Mieter müssen abwechselnd den Hausflur reinigen.

tenant *n*

The tenants have to take turns cleaning the hall.

Raum [raum] *m, -(e)s,* Räume
Wie viele Räume hat die Wohnung?

room *n*
How many rooms does the apartment have?

Steckdose ['ʃtɛkdo:zə] *f, -, -n*
Gibt es im Bad keine Steckdose?
Ich habe einen elektrischen Rasierapparat.

electric socket *n*
Isn't there a socket in the bathroom? I have an electric shaver.

Stecker ['ʃtɛkə*] *m, -s, -*
Der Stecker an der Waschmaschine ist kaputt.

electric plug *n*
The plug on the washer is broken.

Stock [ʃtɔk] *m, -(e)s, kein Pl.*
Wir wohnen im dritten Stock.

floor *n*
We live on the third (U.S.: fourth) floor.

Stockwerk ['ʃtɔkvɛrk] *n, -(e)s, -e*
Das Haus hat 34 Stockwerke.

floor, story, storey *(BE) n*
The building has 34 stories/storeys.

Toilette [toa'lɛtə] *f, -, -n*
Die Toilette ist besetzt.

toilet *n*
The toilet is being used.

Treppe ['trɛpə] *f, -, -n*
Unsere Kellertreppe ist sehr steil.

stairs, stairway *n*
Our basement stairs are very steep.

Tür [ty:ə*] *f, -, -en*
Bitte mach die Tür zu! Es wird kalt.

door *n*
Please close the door. It's getting cold!

Wand [vant] *f, -, Wände*
Die Wände im Wohnzimmer sind weiß gestrichen.

wall *n*
The living-room walls are painted white.

WC [ve:'tse:] *-(s), -(s)*
Das WC ist links neben dem Eingang.

toilet *n*
The toilet is to the left, by the entrance.

---

wohnen ['vo:nən] *V/i., wohnte, hat gewohnt*
In diesem Haus wohnen meine Eltern seit über 20 Jahren.

live, reside *v*
My parents have been living in this house for over 20 years.

Wohnung ['vo:nuŋ] *f, -, -en*
Er hat eine Wohnung in der Innenstadt.

apartment *n*
He has an apartment downtown.

Zimmer ['tsimə*] *n, -s, -*
Heike ist im Zimmer nebenan.

room *n*
Heike is in the next room.

Aufzug [ˈauftsuːk] *m*, -(e)s, Aufzüge
Wir müssen die Treppe benutzen. Der Aufzug ist kaputt.

elevator *(AE)*, **lift** *(BE)* n

We'll have to use the stairs; the elevator/lift *(BE)* is out of order.

Balkon [balˈkɔŋ] *m*, -s, -e
Die Wohnung hat leider keinen Balkon.

balcony n
Unfortunately, the apartment has no balcony.

bauen [ˈbau(ə)n] *V/t.*, baute, hat gebaut
Das Haus ist 1952 gebaut worden.

build v

The house was built in 1952.

Decke [ˈdɛkə] *f*, -, -n
Der Raum war völlig leer, nur eine Lampe hing an der Decke.

ceiling n
The room was completely empty except for a ceiling lamp.

Durchgang [ˈdurçɡaŋ] *m*, -s, Durchgänge
Hier können wir nicht weitergehen. Der Durchgang ist versperrt.

way through, passageway n

We can't go any further here; the way through is closed.

einziehen [ˈaintsiː(ə)n] *V/i.*, zog ein, ist eingezogen
Das Haus ist fast fertig. Nächste Woche können wir einziehen.

move in v

The house is almost finished; we can move in next week.

Etage [eˈtaːʒə] *f*, -, -n
In der vierten Etage ist eine Wohnung frei.

floor n
There's an apartment free on the fourth (U.S.: fifth) floor.

Esszimmer [ˈɛstsimə*] *n*, -s, -
Ein Esszimmer brauchen wir nicht, die Küche ist groß genug.

dining room n
We don't need a dining room; the kitchen is big enough.

Fassade [faˈsaːdə] *f*, -, -n
Die Fassade des Hauses sieht nicht mehr schön aus, sie muss gestrichen werden.

outside, exterior, façade n
The outside of the house doesn't look good; it has to be painted.

Haushalt [ˈhaushalt] *m*, -s, -e
Zu unserem Haushalt gehören fünf Personen.

household n
We have a household of five.

heizen ['haits(ə)n] *V/t.*, heizte, hat geheizt
Unser Haus wird mit Gas geheizt.

heat *v*
Our house is heated with gas.

Hof [ho:f] *m*, -(e)s, Höfe
Das Auto kannst du im Hof parken.

yard *n*
You can park the car in the yard.

Lift [lift] *m*, -(e)s, -e
Der Lift ist abends ab 10.00 Uhr außer Betrieb.

elevator, lift *(BE) n*
The elevator doesn't work after 10 at night.

möbliert [mø'bli:ə*t] *Adj., keine Komp.*
Das Zimmer ist komplett möbliert.

furnished

The room is completely furnished.

Neubau ['nɔibau] *m*, -s, Neubauten
Obwohl das Haus ein Neubau ist, sind die Wände in den Wohnungen feucht.

new building *n*
Although the house is newly-built, the walls of the apartments are damp.

Saal [za:l] *m*, -(e)s, Säle
Die Veranstaltung findet im kleinen Saal statt.

hall, auditorium *n*
The event takes place in the small auditorium.

Scheibe ['ʃaibə] *f*, -, -n
Die Scheibe des Küchenfensters muss erneuert werden.

pane *(of glass) n*
The glass in the kitchen window has to be repaired.

Schlafzimmer ['ʃla:ftsimə*] *n*, -s, -
Das Schlafzimmer ist so klein, dass wir keinen Kleiderschrank aufstellen können.

bedroom *n*

The bedroom is so small we can't put a closet/wardrobe *(BE)* in it.

Tor [to:ə*] *n*, -(e)s, -e
Bitte schließen Sie das Hoftor!

gate *n*
Please close the gate to the yard.

Untermieter ['untə*mi:tə*] *m*, -s, -, **Untermieterin** ['untə*mi:tərin] *f*, -, -nen
Unsere Tochter wohnt als Untermieterin bei einer älteren Dame.

roomer *(AE)*/**lodger** *(BE) n*

Our daughter is a roomer at an elderly lady.

vermieten [fɛə*'mi:t(ə)n] *V/t.*, vermietete, hat vermietet
Alle Wohnungen in diesem Haus sind vermietet.

rent *v*

All the apartments in this place are rented.

Vermieter [fɛə*'miːtə*] *m,* -s, -
Vermieterin [fɛə*'miːtərin] *f,* -,
-nen
Unsere Vermieterin verlangt ab
nächsten Monat 5 % mehr Miete.

landlord, landlady *n*

Our landlady is raising the rent
5% next month.

Wohnzimmer ['voːntsimə*] *n,*
-s, -
Euer Wohnzimmer ist sehr gemütlich.

living-room *n*

Your living-room is very comfortable.

| 5.2 Einrichtung | 1-2000 |

Bank [baŋk] *f,* -, Bänke
Die Bank, auf der du sitzt, ist über
80 Jahre alt.

bench *n*
The bench you're sitting on is
over 80 years old.

Bett [bɛt] *n,* -es, -en
Dieser Ferienort ist sehr beliebt.
In der (Hoch-)Saison ist oft kein
Bett mehr frei.

bed *n*
This holiday resort is very popular. During season there's often
not a bed left in the place.

Decke ['dɛkə] *f,* -, -n
Heute Nacht brauchen wir zwei
Decken. Es soll sehr kalt werden.

blanket *n*
Tonight we'll need two blankets.
It's supposed to get very cold.

einrichten ['ainriçt(ə)n] *V/t.,* rich-
tete ein, hat eingerichtet
Ihr Haus wurde von einer Innenar-
chitektin eingerichtet.

furnish *v*

Their house was furnished by an
interior decorator.

Einrichtung ['ainriçtuŋ] *f,* -, -n
Die Einrichtung des Wohnzim-
mers scheint sehr teuer zu sein.

furniture, furnishing(s) *n*
The living-room furniture seems
to be very expensive.

Fach [fax] *n,* -(e)s, Fächer
Der Küchenschrank ist sehr praktisch. Er hat viele Fächer.

compartment *n*
The kitchen cabinet is very practical; there are lots of compart-
ments.

Kühlschrank ['ky:lʃrank] *m*, -(e)s, Kühlschränke
Stell die Milch bitte in den Kühlschrank!

refrigerator *n*
Please put the milk in the refrigerator.

Lampe ['lampə] *f*, -, -n
Es brennt noch Licht im Wohnzimmer. Mach bitte die Lampe aus!

lamp *n*
There's still a light on in the livingroom. Please turn off the lamp.

Möbel ['møːb(ə)l] *n*, -s, -
Seine Möbel sind sehr wertvoll.

furniture *n*
His furniture is worth a lot.

Ofen ['oːf(ə)n] *m*, -s, Öfen
Machst du das Feuer im Ofen an?

oven, stove *n*
Are you going to light the store?

Schrank [ʃrank] *m*, -(e)s, Schränke
Im Schlafzimmer fehlt mir noch ein kleiner Schrank für Wäsche.

cabinet, cupboard *(BE) n*
In the bedroom I still need a small linen cabinet.

Sessel ['zɛs(ə)l] *m*, -s, -
Deine Sessel finde ich sehr bequem.

chair, armchair *n*
I think your chairs are very comfortable.

Sitz [zits] *m*, -es, -e
Die Sitze in diesem Kino sind sehr hart.

seat *n*
The seats at this cinema are very hard.

Sofa ['zoːfa] *n*, -s, -s
Sie machte auf dem Sofa einen kleinen Mittagsschlaf.

sofa *n*
She took a little nap on the sofa.

Stuhl [ʃtuːl] *m*, -(e)s, Stühle
Wenn ich Gäste habe, reichen die Stühle oft nicht.

chair *n*
When I have guests, there often are not enough chairs.

Teppich ['tɛpiç] *m*, -s, -e
Den Teppich finde ich zu bunt.

carpet, rug *n*
I think the carpet is too colorful.

Tisch [tiʃ] *m*, -(e)s, -e
An diesem Tisch können höchstens sechs Personen sitzen.

table *n*
At most, six people can sit at this table.

2001-4000

Badewanne ['ba:dəvanə] *f, -, -n*
In unserem Bad haben wir nur eine Dusche, keine Badewanne.

bathtub *n*
In our bathroom we have a shower, but no bathtub.

bequem [bə'kve:m] *Adj.*
Dieser Sessel sieht nicht nur schön aus, er ist auch bequem.

comfortable *n*
This chair doesn't only look nice; it's comfortable, too.

Couch [kautʃ] *f, -, -es*
Du kannst gerne bei uns übernachten und auf der Couch schlafen.

couch, sofa *n*
You're welcome to spend the night here; you can sleep on the couch.

Garderobe [gard(ə)'ro:bə] *f, -, -n*
Häng deinen Mantel bitte an die Garderobe!

closet, hall-stand *(BE) n*
Please hang your coat in the closet.

Kissen ['kis(ə)n] *n, -s, -*
Beim Schlafen brauche ich mindestens zwei Kopfkissen.

pillow *n*
I need at least two pillows for sleeping.

Kleiderschrank ['klaidə*ʃraŋk] *m, -(e)s*, Kleiderschränke
Der Kleiderschrank ist für den kleinen Raum eigentlich zu groß.

clothes closet, cabinet, wardrobe *n*
The wardrobe is really too big for the small room.

Liege ['li:gə] *f, -, -n*
Wenn sie abends noch arbeiten muss, schläft sie auf einer Liege in ihrem Büro.

couch *n*
When she has to work late, she sleeps on a couch in her office.

Regal [re'ga:l] *n, -s, -e*
Das Buch steht ganz oben im Regal.

shelf, shelves, bookcase *n*
The book is on the top shelf.

Schreibtisch ['ʃraiptiʃ] *m, -(e)s, -e*
Das Briefpapier liegt in der obersten Schublade des Schreibtischs.

desk *n*
The stationery is in the top desk drawer.

Schublade ['ʃu:pla:də] *f, -, -n*
Im Schrank ist kein Platz. Alle Schubladen sind voll.

drawer *n*
There is no room in the cabinet. All the drawers are full.

Tischtuch ['tiʃtuːx] *n,* -(e)s, Tischtücher
Auf dem Tischtuch ist ein großer Kaffeefleck.

tablecloth, table linen *n*
There's a big coffee stain on the tablecloth.

Vorhang ['foːɐ̯ˌhaŋ] *m,* -(e)s, Vorhänge
Die Farbe der Vorhänge passt nicht zu den Möbeln.

curtain *n*
The color of the curtains doesn't go with the furniture.

5.3 Gebrauchsgegenstände | 1-2000

Ding [dɪŋ] *n,* -(e)s, -e
○ Hast du alles eingekauft?
□ Nein, es fehlen noch ein paar Dinge.

thing *n*
○ Did you buy everything?
□ No, we still have to get a few things.

gebraucht [ɡəˈbrauxt] *Adj., keine Komp.*
Die Waschmaschine haben wir gebraucht gekauft.

used, second-hand
We bought a used washing-machine.

Gegenstand [ˈɡeːɡ(ə)nˌʃtant] *m,* -(e)s, Gegenstände
Beim Umzug sind einige Gegenstände kaputtgegangen.

item, object, thing *n*
A few items broke during the move.

Gerät [ɡəˈrɛːt] *n,* -(e)s, -e
Dieses Küchengerät ist sehr praktisch.

appliance, device *n*
This kitchen appliance is very practical.

Geschirr [ɡəˈʃɪr] *n,* -s, *kein Pl.*
Hilfst du mir, das Geschirr zu spülen?

kitchen ware, dishes, crockery (BE) *n*
Will you help me do the dishes?

Griff [ɡrɪf] *m,* -(e)s, -e
Vorsicht, der Griff der Pfanne ist heiß!

handle *n*
Careful, the skillet handle is hot!

Kette ['kɛtə] *f, -, -n*
Das Tor ist mit einer Kette verschlossen.

chain *n*
The gate is locked with a chain.

Kiste ['kistə] *f, -, -n*
Die Werkzeuge liegen alle in dieser Kiste.

chest, box *n*
The tools are all in this chest.

Klingel ['klɪŋ(ə)l] *f, -, -n*
Du musst klopfen, unsere Klingel funktioniert nicht.

doorbell *n*
You'll have to knock; our doorbell doesn't work.

Messer ['mɛsə*] *n, -s, -*
Mit diesem alten Messer kann man nicht mehr richtig schneiden.

knife *n*
This old knife doesn't cut well any more.

Nadel ['na:d(ə)l] *f, -, -n*
Beim Nähen habe ich mir mit einer Nadel in den Finger gestochen.

needle *n*
I stuck a needle in my finger while sewing.

Pfanne ['pfanə] *f, -, -n*
Nimm die dunkle Pfanne, die ist besser zum Braten!

skillet, pan *n*
Use the dark skillet; it's better for frying.

Sache ['zaxə] *f, -, -n*
Deine Sachen habe ich in dein Zimmer gebracht.

thing *n*
I put your things in your room.

Schachtel ['ʃaxt(ə)l] *f, -, -n*
Bring mir bitte eine Schachtel Zigaretten mit.

carton, box, packet, pack *n*
Please bring me a pack of cigarettes.

Schere ['ʃe:rə] *f, -, -n*
Nimm diese Schere! Sie schneidet gut.

scissors *n*
Take these scissors; they cut well.

Schirm [ʃirm] *m, -(e)s, -e*
Es wird bestimmt nicht regnen. Wir müssen keinen Schirm mitnehmen.

umbrella *n*
It certainly won't rain. We don't have to take an umbrella.

Schlüssel ['ʃlys(ə)l] *m, -s, -*
Der Schlüssel steckt im Schloss.

key *n*
The key is in the lock.

Schraube ['ʃraubə] *f, -, -n*
Ich konnte das Rad nicht wechseln. Die Schrauben waren zu fest.

screw *n*
I couldn't change the wheel. The screws were too tight.

Schüssel ['ʃys(ə)l] *f,* -, -n
Nimm die große Schüssel für den
Salat.

bowl *n*
Use the big bowl for the salad.

Spiegel ['ʃpi:g(ə)l] *m,* -s, -
So ein Pech, ich habe den Spiegel
zerbrochen.

mirror *n*
Too bad! I broke the mirror.

Streichholz ['ʃtraiçhɔlts] *n,* -es,
Streichhölzer
Meine Streichhölzer sind nass ge-
worden. Hast du ein Feuerzeug?

match *n*

My matches got wet. Do you have
a lighter?

Tasche ['taʃə] *f,* -, -n
Pass auf, die Tasche ist sehr
schwer.

bag, sack, pocket *n*
Be careful; the bag is very heavy.

Taschentuch ['taʃ(ə)ntu:x] *n,*
-(e)s, Taschentücher
Kannst du mir ein Papiertaschen-
tuch geben?

handkerchief *n*

Could you give me a paper handkerchief?

Tasse ['tasə] *f,* -, -n
Möchtest du eine Tasse Kaffee
trinken?

cup *n*
Would you like to drink a cup of
coffee?

Teller ['tɛlə*] *m,* -s, -
Möchtest du noch einen Teller
Suppe?

plate *n*
Would you like another plate of
soup?

Topf [tɔpf] *m,* -es, Töpfe
Wir haben den Topf ganz leer gegessen.

pot *n*
We ate everything in the pot.

Werkzeug ['vɛrktsɔik] *n,* -s, -e
Ohne Spezialwerkzeuge lässt sich
die Maschine nicht reparieren.

tools, equipment *n*
The machine can't be fixed without special tools.

Wäsche ['vɛʃə] *f,* -, *kein Pl.*
Die Wäsche muss noch gewaschen werden.

laundry *n*
The laundry still has to be done.

2001-4000

Besen ['be:z(ə)n] *m,* -s, -
Der Besen ist zu hart, damit kann
man nicht gut fegen.

broom *n*
The broom is too stiff to sweep
well.

Brieftasche ['bri:ftaʃə] *f, -, -n*
Weißt du, wo mein Führerschein
ist? In der Brieftasche ist er nicht.

briefcase, wallet, portfolio *n*
Do you know where my driver's
license is? It's not in the briefcase.

Eimer ['aimə*] *m, -s, -*
Holst du mir bitte einen Eimer
frisches Wasser?

bucket, pail *n*
Can you please get me a bucket
of fresh water?

Faden ['fa:d(ə)n] *m, -s, Fäden*
Kannst du mir eine Nadel und ei-
nen Faden geben? An meinem
Hemd ist ein Knopf lose.

thread *n*
Could you get me a needle and
thread?
A button on my shirt is loose.

Feuerzeug ['fɔiə*tsɔik] *n, -s, -e*
Dieses Feuerzeug kann man nicht
füllen.

(cigarette) lighter *n*
This lighter can't be refilled.

Glühbirne ['gly:birnə] *f, -, -n*
In der Küchenlampe ist die Glühbirne kaputt.

lightbulb *n*
The lightbulb in the kitchen lamp
has burnt out.

Grill [gril] *m, -s, -s*
Auf dem Grill gebratenes Fleisch
schmeckt besser.

grill *n*
Meat cooked on the grill tastes
better.

Haken ['ha:k(ə)n] *m, -s, -*
Du kannst deine Jacke dort an
den Haken hängen.

hook, peg *n*
You can hang your jacket on the
hook there.

Hammer ['hamə*] *m, -s, Hämmer*
Dieser Hammer ist zu leicht.
Damit kann man diesen dicken
Nagel nicht in die Wand schlagen.

hammer *n*
This hammer is too light; you
can't pound this big nail in the wall
with it.

Kalender [ka'lɛndə*] *m, -s, -*
○ Welchés Datum haben wir
heute?
□ Das weiß ich auch nicht. Schau
doch mal in deinen Kalender!

calendar *n*
○ What's today's date?
□ I don't know either. Why don't
you look at your calendar.

Kanne ['kanə] *f, -, -n*
Ist noch Kaffee in der Kanne?

pot, pitcher *n*
Is there still coffee in the pot?

Kasten ['kast(ə)n] *m, -s, Kästen*
Das ganze Werkzeug ist in dem
braunen Holzkasten.

box, chest *n*
All the tools are in the brown
wooden chest.

Kerze ['kɛrtsə] *f,* -, -n
Ich liebe es, abends bei Kerzen-
licht zu essen.

candle *n*
I like to eat dinner by candlelight.

Kessel ['kɛs(ə)l] *m,* -s, -
Nimm den Kessel vom Herd! Das
Wasser kocht.

kettle *n*
Take the kettle off the stove; the
water is boiling.

Korb [kɔrp] *m,* -(e)s, Körbe
Ein Korb ist zum Einkaufen prakti-
scher als eine Tasche.

basket *n*
A basket is more practical for
shopping than a bag.

Leiter ['laitə*] *f,* -, -n
Um die Gardinen aufzuhängen,
brauche ich die längere Leiter.

ladder *n*
I need the longer ladder to hang
the curtains.

Nagel ['na:g(ə)l] *m,* -s, Nägel
Dieser Nagel ist zu schwach, um
das Bild daran aufzuhängen.

nail *n*
This nail is too weak to hang the
picture on.

Papierkorb [pa'pi:ə*kɔrp] *m,* -(e)s,
Papierkörbe
Die alten Zeitungen kannst du in
den Papierkorb werfen.

wastebasket *n*

You can throw the old newspapers in the wastebasket.

Sack [zak] *m,* -(e)s, Säcke
Pack die alten Kleider in einen
Sack und bringe sie auf den
Dachboden!

sack, bag *n*
Put the old clothes in a sack and
take them up to the attic.

Schlauch [ʃlaux] *m,* -(e)s,
Schläuche
Der Wasserschlauch ist zu kurz.

hose *n*

The water hose is too short.

Spaten ['ʃpa:t(ə)n] *m,* -s, -
Mit diesem Spaten kann man
nicht gut graben. Er ist zu stumpf.

spade *n*
You can't dig well with this spade;
it's too blunt.

Spielzeug ['ʃpi:ltsɔik] *n,* -s, -e
Unsere Tochter mag technisches
Spielzeug sehr gerne.

toy, plaything *n*
Our daughter really likes technical
toys.

Untertasse ['untə*tasə] *f,* -, -n
Die Untertassen und die Tassen
passen nicht zusammen.

saucer *n*
The cups and saucers don't go
together.

Waage ['va:gə] *f,* -, -n
Diese Waage wiegt sehr genau.

scale *n*
This scale gives exact weight.

Waschlappen [ˈvaʃlap(ə)n] *m,*
-s, -
Ich wasche mich lieber mit einem
Waschlappen als mit einem
Schwamm.

washcloth, face flannel *(BE) n*

I prefer a washcloth to a sponge.

Wasserhahn [ˈvasə*haːn] *m,*
-(e)s, Wasserhähne
Der Wasserhahn im Bad lässt
sich nicht mehr aufdrehen.

faucet, tap *n*

The tub faucet can't be turned on
any more.

Wecker [ˈvɛkə*] *m,* -s, -
Ohne Wecker könnte ich morgens nicht pünktlich aufstehen.

alarm clock *n*
I couldn't get up in the morning
without an alarm clock.

5.4 Kleidung und Schmuck   1-2000

5.4 Clothing and Jewelry

anziehen [ˈantsiː(ə)n] *V/t., refl.,*
zog an, hat angezogen
Unser Sohn kann sich jetzt selbst
anziehen.

put on *(clothing),* **dress** *v*

Our son can put his clothes on by
himself now.

ausziehen [ˈaustsiː(ə)n] *V/t., refl.,*
zog aus, hat ausgezogen
Zieh bitte die nassen Schuhe aus!

take off *(clothing),* **undress** *v*

Please take off your wet shoes!

Band [bant] *n,* -(e)s, Bänder
Bei der Arbeit binde ich mir meine
Haare mit einem Band zu-
sammen.

ribbon *n*
At work I tie my hair up with a
ribbon.

Bluse [ˈbluːzə] *f,* -, -n
Diese Bluse passt nicht zu deinem Rock.

blouse *n*
That blouse doesn't go with your
skirt.

Gürtel [ˈgyrt(ə)l] *m,* -s, -
Ohne Gürtel kann ich die Hose
nicht tragen.

belt *n*
I can't wear these pants without a
belt.

Hemd [hɛmt] *n, -es, -en*
Das Hemd ist am Hals zu eng.

shirt *n*
The shirt is too tight around the neck.

Hose ['ho:zə] *f, -, -n*
Die Hose muss kürzer gemacht werden.

pants, trousers *n*
These pants/trousers have to be shortened.

Hut [hu:t] *m, -(e)s, Hüte*
Mit Hut siehst du komisch aus.

hat *n*
You look funny in a hat.

Jacke ['jakə] *f, -, -n*
Für den Winter ist diese Jacke nicht warm genug.

jacket *n*
This jacket isn't warm enough for winter.

Kleid [klait] *n, -(e)s, -er*
Das Kleid passt ausgezeichnet.

dress *n*
The dress fits perfectly.

Kleidung ['klaiduŋ] *f, -, kein Pl.*
Seine Kleidung ist unmodern.

clothing *n*
His clothing is out of date.

Knopf [knɔpf] *m, -(e)s, Knöpfe*
An der Bluse fehlt ein Knopf.

button *n*
A button is missing on the blouse.

Leder ['le:də*] *n, -s, kein Pl.*
Die Jacke ist aus Leder.

leather *n*
This jacket is leather.

Mantel ['mant(ə)l] *m, -s, Mäntel*
Warum trägst du nur schwarze Mäntel?

coat *n*
Why do you wear only black coats?

Mode ['mo:də] *f, -, -n*
Die Mode wechselt heute schneller als früher.

fashion, style *n*
Today styles change faster than they used to.

Mütze ['mytsə] *f, -, -n*
Setz eine Mütze auf! Es ist kalt draußen.

cap *n*
Put on a cap! It's cold outside.

nackt [nakt] *Adj., -er, am -esten*
Ich mag gerne nackt im Meer schwimmen.

nude, naked *n*
I like to swim nude in the ocean.

passen ['pas(ə)n] *V/i., passte, hat gepasst*
Die Hose passt mir nicht.

fit *v*

The trousers don't fit me.

Pullover [pu'lo:və*] *m, -s, -*
Dieser Pullover ist aus reiner Wolle.

sweater *n*
This sweater is pure wool.

Ring [rɪŋ] *m*, -(e)s, -e
Vera trägt an vier Fingern Ringe.

ring *n*
Vera wears rings on four fingers.

Rock [rɔk] *m*, -(e)s, Röcke
Dieses Jahr sind kurze Röcke modern.

skirt *n*
This year short skirts are in style.

Schmuck [ʃmuk] *m*, -(e)s, *kein Pl.*
Sie hat einen guten Geschmack bei der Wahl ihres Schmuckes.

jewelry *n*
She has good taste in choosing her jewelry.

Schuh [ʃuː] *m*, -s, -e
In der Wohnung trage ich keine Schuhe, nur Hausschuhe.

shoe *n*
Inside my apartment I don't wear shoes, only slippers.

Socke ['zɔkə] *f*, -, -n
Diese Schuhe kann ich nur mit dicken Socken tragen.

sock *n*
I can only wear these shoes with thick socks.

Stoff [ʃtɔf] *m*, -(e)s, -e
Ich mag helle Stoffe am liebsten.

material, fabric *n*
I like bright-colored fabrics best.

Strumpf [ʃtrumpf] *m*, -(e)s, Strümpfe
Die Farbe der Strümpfe passt nicht zu deinem Anzug.

socks, stockings *n*
The color of these socks doesn't go with your suit.

Tuch [tuːx] *n*, -(e)s, Tücher
Weil er leicht Halsschmerzen bekommt, trägt er immer ein Halstuch.

scarf *n*
He is prone to get a sore throat, so he always wears a scarf around his neck.

Uhr [uːɐ*] *f*, -, -en
○ Weißt du, wie spät es ist?
□ Nein, ich habe auch keine Uhr.

clock, watch *n*
○ Do you know what time it is?
□ No, I don't have a watch either.

2001-4000

Absatz ['apzats] *m*, -es, Absätze
Die Absätze der Schuhe sind kaputt.

heel *n*
The heels of these shoes are in bad shape.

anprobieren ['anprobiːrən] *V/t.*,
probierte an, hat anprobiert
Sie können das Kleid natürlich anprobieren.

try on *v*

Of course you can try on this dress.

Anzug ['antsu:k] *m*, -s, Anzüge
Er trägt gerne dunkle Anzüge.

suit *n*
He likes to wear dark suits.

Armbanduhr ['armbantu:ə*] *f*, -, -en
Armbanduhren mag ich nicht, ich habe eine Taschenuhr.

wristwatch
I don't like wristwatches; I have a pocket watch.

Ärmel ['ɛrm(ə)l] *m*, -s, -
Im Ärmel deiner Jacke ist ein Loch.

sleeve *n*
There's a hole in your jacket sleeve.

Diamant [dia'mant] *m*, -en, -en
An ihrer Halskette hängt ein kleiner Diamant.

diamond *n*
There's a little diamond on her necklace.

Handschuh ['hantʃu:] *m*, -(e)s, -e
Trotz der Kälte trägt sie nie Handschuhe.

glove *n*
Even in cold weather she never wears gloves.

Handtasche ['hanttaʃə] *f*, -, -en
Das Geld ist in deiner Handtasche.

(hand)bag, purse *n*
The money is in your handbag.

Jackett [ʒa'kɛt] *n*, -s, -s
Das Jackett des Anzugs kannst du noch tragen, aber die Hose sieht wirklich nicht mehr schön aus.

jacket
You can still wear the suit jacket, but the trousers really don't look good any more.

(Hals-) Kette ['kɛtə] *f*, -, -n
Deine Halskette finde ich schön.

necklace
I think your necklace is very nice.

kleiden ['klaid(ə)n] *V/t., refl.*, kleidete, hat gekleidet
Sie kleidet ihre Kinder wie Erwachsene. Sie selbst kleidet sich immer sehr bunt.

dress *v*
She dresses her children like adults. She herself always dresses in bright colors.

Kleiderbügel ['klaidə*by:g(ə)l] *m*, -s, -
Häng bitte deinen Mantel auf den Kleiderbügel!

hanger *n*
Please put your coat on a hanger.

kostbar ['kɔstba:*] *Adj.*
Sie trägt kostbaren Schmuck.

valuable
She wears valuable jewelry.

Kragen ['kra:g(ə)n] *m, -s, -*
Das Hemd kannst du nicht mehr anziehen. Der Kragen ist dreckig.

collar *n*
You can't wear this shirt again. The collar is dirty.

Krawatte [kra'vatə] *f, -, -n*
Warum trägst du immer so unmoderne Krawatten?

(neck)tie *n*
Why do you always wear such old-fashioned ties?

Perle ['pɛrlə] *f, -, -n*
Ich habe keinen Schmuck, nur eine Perlenkette.

pearl *n*
Apart from a pearl necklace I have no jewelry.

Regenmantel ['re:g(ə)nmant(əl)l] *m, -s, Regenmäntel*
Trotz des Regenmantels bin ich ziemlich nass geworden.

raincoat *n*

I got really wet in spite of the raincoat.

Reißverschluss ['raisfɛə*ʃlus] *m, -es, -verschlüsse*
Der Reißverschluss lässt sich nicht aufmachen.

zipper *n*

The zipper won't open.

Stiefel ['ʃti:f(ə)l] *m, -s, -*
Zieh die Winterstiefel an. Es ist kalt.

boots *n*
Put on winter boots. It's cold out

umziehen ['umtsi:(ə)n] *V/refl., zog um, hat umgezogen*
Nach der Arbeit ziehe ich mich immer sofort um.

change *(clothes)* v

After work I always change clothes right away.

Uniform [uni'fɔrm] *f, -, -en*
Unsere Tochter geht in eine Privatschule, in der die Kinder Schuluniformen tragen.

uniform *n*
Our daughter goes to a private school where the children wear school uniforms.

Unterwäsche ['untə*vɛʃə] *f, -, kein Pl.*
Für diese kurze Reise nehme ich nicht viel mit. Nur etwas Unterwäsche, eine Hose und ein Hemd.

underwear *n*

I'm not taking much on this short trip. Only some underwear, a pair of trousers and a shirt.

5.5 Mahlzeiten, Restaurant | 1-2000

5.5 Meals, Restaurant

backen ['bak(ə)n] V/t., backte, hat gebacken	**bake** v
Er kann gute Kuchen backen.	He can bake good cakes.
bedienen [bə'di:nən] V/t., refl., bediente, hat bedient	**serve, help, wait on** v
Bitte bedienen Sie sich selbst!	Please help yourself!
In diesem Restaurant wird man schnell und freundlich bedient.	In this restaurant they wait on you quickly and pleasantly.
Bedienung [bə'di:nuŋ] f, -, -en,	**waiter, waitress** n
Sie arbeitet als Bedienung in einem Restaurant.	She works as a waitress in a restaurant.
Bedienung bitte! Ich warte schon 20 Minuten.	Waiter, please! I've already been waiting twenty minutes.
bestellen [bə'ʃtɛl(ə)n] V/t., bestellte, hat bestellt	**order** v
Zum Nachtisch habe ich mir ein Eis bestellt.	For dessert I ordered ice cream.
braten ['bra:t(ə)n] V/t., briet, hat gebraten	**roast, fry** v
Du hast das Fleisch zu lange gebraten. Es ist ganz trocken.	You roasted the meat too long; it is very dry.
Café [ka'fe:] n, -s, -s	**café** n
○ Wo wollen wir uns treffen?	○ Where shall we meet?
□ Am besten im „Cafe Bauer".	□ The 'Café Bauer' would be best.
Dose ['do:zə] f, -, -n	**can, tin** (BE) n
Das Gemüse schmeckt gut, obwohl es aus der Dose ist.	The vegetable tastes good, even though it is out of a can.
essen ['ɛs(ə)n] V/t., i., aß, hat gegessen	**eat** v
Unsere Kinder essen gerne Nudeln mit Soße.	Our children really like to eat pasta in a sauce.
Was wollen wir zu Mittag essen?	What do we want to eat for lunch?

Essen ['ɛs(ə)n] *n, -s, -*
Ute hat mich heute Abend zum Essen eingeladen.
Das Essen war sehr gut.

dinner, meal, food *n*
Ute has invited me for dinner to night.
The food was very good.

frühstücken ['fryːʃtyk(ə)n] *V/i.,*
frühstückte, hat gefrühstückt
Ich frühstücke immer im Büro.

have, eat breakfast *v*
I always eat breakfast in the of fice.

Gabel ['gaːb(ə)l] *f, -, -n*
Unser Kind kann schon mit Messer und Gabel essen.

fork *n*
Our child can already eat with a knife and fork.

Hunger ['huŋə*] *m, -s, kein Pl.*
Ich habe großen Hunger.

hunger *n*
I am really hungry.

hungrig ['huŋriçᵒ] *Adj.*
Ich bin nicht sehr hungrig.

hungry
I'm not very hungry.

Kellner ['kɛlnə*] *m, -s, -*
Kellnerin ['kɛlnərin] *f, -, -nen*
Die Rechnung stimmt nicht. Der Kellner hat sicher falsch gerechnet.

waiter, waitress *n*

The bill isn't right. The waiter cer tainly figured it wrong.

Koch [kox] *m, -(e)s, Köche*
Köchin ['kœçin] *f, -, -nen*
In diesem Restaurant arbeitet ein ausgezeichneter Koch.

cook *n*

An excellent cook works at this restaurant.

Löffel ['lœf(ə)l] *m, -s, -*
Die Suppe ist gut. Probier doch mal einen Löffel voll!

spoon *n*
The soup is good. So try a spoonful.

Mahlzeit ['maːltsait] *f, -, -en*
In diesem Restaurant gibt es warme Mahlzeiten nur bis 21.00 Uhr.

meal *n*
This restaurant only serves warm meals until 9 p.m.

Portion [pɔrˈtsjoːn] *f, -, -en*
Das kann ich nicht alles essen. Die Portion ist viel zu groß.

portion, serving *n*
I can't eat all of this. The serving is much too big.

probieren [proˈbiːrən] *V/t.,* probierte, hat probiert
Probier doch mal die Milch!
Ich glaube, sie ist sauer.

try *v*

Try the milk!
I think it's sour.

Restaurant [rɛstoˈrãː] *n, -s, -s*
Er geht zum Essen oft ins Restaurant.

restaurant *n*
He often eats in a restaurant.

satt [zat] *Adj.*, -er, am -esten
Ich kann nicht mehr essen. Ich bin satt.

full
I can't eat any more. I'm full.

---

schmecken [ˈʃmɛk(ə)n] *V/i., + Präp.* (nach), schmeckte, hat geschmeckt
Die Suppe schmeckt mir gut.

taste *v*

The soup tastes good.

Speisekarte [ˈʃpaizəkartə] *f,* -, -n
Bitte bringen Sie mir die Speisekarte! Ich möchte etwas essen.

menu *n*
Please bring me the menu! I'd like to get something to eat.

Trinkgeld [ˈtriŋkgɛlt] *n,* -(e)s, -er
Ich habe dem Kellner ein gutes Trinkgeld gegeben. Er war sehr freundlich.

tip *n*
I gave the waiter a good tip. He was very friendly.

2001-4000

Abendessen [ˈaːbəntɛs(ə)n] *n,* -s, -
Bleib doch noch! Ich habe ein Abendessen für uns vorbereitet.

dinner, supper, evening meal *n*

Please stay! I've prepared dinner for us.

Appetit [apəˈtiːt] *m,* -(e)s, *kein Pl.*
Ich habe großen Appetit auf ein Stück Kuchen.

appetite *n*
I really feel like having a piece of cake.

Deckel [ˈdɛk(ə)l] *m,* -s, -
Das Wasser kocht schneller, wenn du den Deckel auf den Topf tust.

lid, cover *n*
The water boils faster if you put a lid on the pot.

Frühstück [ˈfryːʃtyk] *n,* -s, *kein Pl.*
Möchtest du ein Ei zum Frühstück?

breakfast *n*
Would you like an egg for breakfast?

Gasthaus [ˈgasthaus] *n,* -es, Gasthäuser
Im Nachbarort ist ein kleines Gasthaus, in dem man essen und übernachten kann.

inn *n*

There's a little inn nearby where you can eat and spend the night.

Gericht [gəˈriçt] *n,* -(e)s, -e
In der Kantine kann man mittags zwischen drei Gerichten wählen.

dish *n*
In the cafeteria at lunch there is a choice of three dishes.

Imbiss [ˈimbis] *m,* -es, -e
Ich habe Hunger. Lass uns schnell einen kleinen Imbiss nehmen.

snack *n*
I'm hungry. Let's get a quick snack.

Konservendose
[kɔnˈzɛrv(ə)ndoːzə] *f,* -, -n
Wo liegt der Öffner für Konservendosen?

can, tin *(BE) n*
Where's the can-opener?

Mittagessen [ˈmitaːkɛs(ə)n] *n,* -s, -
Zum Mittagessen komme ich nach Hause.

lunch *n*
I come home for lunch.

Ober [ˈoːbə*] *m,* -s, -
Herr Ober, bringen Sie mir bitte noch ein Bier!

waiter *n*
Waiter, please bring me another beer.

zubereiten [ˈtsuːbərait(ə)n] *V/t.,* bereitete zu, hat zubereitet
Dieses Essen ist schwer zuzubereiten.

prepare *v*
This food is hard to prepare.

Zubereitung [ˈtsuːbəraituŋ] *f,* -, -en
Das ist ein schnelles Gericht. Die Zubereitung dauert nur 20 Minuten.

preparation *n*
That is a quick dish. Preparation takes only 20 minutes.

5.6 Lebensmittel und Speisen | 1-2000

5.6 Groceries and Food

bitter [ˈbitə*] *Adj.*
Der Obstsalat schmeckt etwas bitter. Am besten tust du etwas Zucker dazu.

bitter
The fruit salad tastes a little bitter. You should add a little sugar.

Braten ['braːt(ə)n] *m, -s, -*
Der Braten ist noch nicht gar.

roast, roast meat *n*
The roast is not done yet.

Brot [broːt] *n, -(e)s, -e*
Bring bitte frisches Brot vom Bäcker mit!

bread *n*
Bring some fresh bread from the
bakery.

Butter ['butə*] *f, -, kein Pl.*
Ohne Butter schmeckt das Brot
nicht.

butter *n*
This bread doesn't taste good
without butter.

Ei [ai] *n, -s, -er*
Eier esse ich am liebsten hart gekocht.

egg *n*
I prefer to eat hard-boiled eggs.

Eis [ais] *n, -es, kein Pl.*
Schokoladeneis mag ich nicht.

ice cream *n*
I don't like chocolate ice cream.

Fleisch [flaiʃ] *n, -(e)s, kein Pl.*
Ist das Fleisch zart?

meat *n*
Is the meat tender?

frisch [friʃ] *Adj., -er, am -esten*
Im Winter gibt es hier wenig
frisches Gemüse zu kaufen.

fresh
In the winter it's difficult to get
fresh vegetables here.

Gemüse [gə'myːzə] *n, -s, kein Pl.*
Wir haben eigenes Gemüse im
Garten.

vegetables *n*
We have our own vegetables in
the garden.

Gewürz [gə'vyrts] *n, -es, -e*
Pfeffer und die anderen Gewürze
sind in der oberen Schublade.

spice *n*
Pepper and the other spices are
in the top drawer.

haltbar ['haltbaː*] *Adj.*
Die Wurst muss heute gegessen
werden. Sie ist nicht mehr lange
haltbar.

lasting, good
We have to eat this sausage. It
won't keep much langer.

Huhn [huːn] *n, -(e)s, Hühner*
Zum Mittagessen gab es Huhn
mit Reis.

chicken *n*
For lunch there was chicken with
rice.

Käse ['kɛːzə] *m, -s, kein Pl.*
Möchtest du Wurst oder Käse
aufs Brot?

cheese *n*
Would you like sausage or cheese
on the bread?

kochen ['kox(ə)n] *V/t., i.,* kochte,
hat gekocht
○ Ich habe keine Lust zu kochen.
□ Lass uns essen gehen!
Kocht das Wasser schon?

cook, boil *v*

○ I don't want to cook.
□ Let's go out to eat.
Is the water boiling yet?

Kotelett [kot(ə)'lɛt] *n*, -s, -s
Möchten Sie das Kotelett mit Reis oder Kartoffeln?

chop *n*
Would you like rice or potatoes with the chop?

Kuchen ['ku:x(ə)n] *m*, -s, -
Nachmittags esse ich gerne ein Stück Kuchen.

cake *n*
I like to eat a piece of cake in the afternoon.

Lebensmittel ['le:b(ə)nsmit(ə)l] *n*, -s, -
Im Supermarkt sind viele Lebensmittel billiger.

food, groceries *n*
A lot of food is cheaper at the supermarket.

Margarine [marga'ri:nə] *f*, -, *kein Pl.*
Isst du lieber Margarine oder Butter?

margarine *n*
Do you prefer to eat margarine or butter?

Marmelade [marmə'la:də] *f*, -, -n
Morgens esse ich nur ein halbes Brötchen mit Marmelade, sonst nichts.

jam *n*
In the morning all I eat is half a roll with jam, nothing else.

Mehl [me:l] *n*, -(e)s, *kein Pl.*
Ich kann keinen Kuchen backen. Es ist kein Mehl mehr da.

flour *n*
I can't make a cake. There's no flour left.

Pfeffer ['pfɛfə*] *m*, -s, *kein Pl.*
Dieser Pfeffer ist besonders scharf.

pepper *n*
This pepper is especially hot.

Reis [rais] *m*, -es, *kein Pl.*
Koch den Reis bitte nicht zu lange! Er wird sonst zu weich.

rice *n*
Don't cook the rice too long or it will be too soft.

Rezept [re'tsɛpt] *n*, -(e)s, -e
Sie kann auch ohne Rezepte gut kochen.

recipe *n*
She also cooks well without recipes.

Rindfleisch ['rintflaiʃ] *n*, -(e)s, *kein Pl.*
Für dieses Gericht braucht man 1 kg Rindfleisch.

beef *n*
For this dish you need a kilo of beef.

roh [ro:] *Adj.*, -er, am -esten
Steaks schmecken am besten, wenn sie innen noch etwas roh sind.

raw
Steaks taste best when they are still a bit raw inside.

Sahne ['za:nə] *f, -, kein Pl.*
Möchtest du Sahne auf den Kuchen?

cream *n*
Would you like cream on the cake?

Salz [zalts] *n, -es, kein Pl.*
An der Suppe fehlt Salz.

salt *n*
The soup needs salt.

sauer ['zauə*] *Adj.*, sau(e)rer, am -sten
Die Milch kann man nicht mehr trinken. Sie ist sauer.
Ich esse gerne saure Äpfel.

sour
We can't drink this milk. It's sour.
I like to eat sour apples.

scharf [ʃarf] *Adj.*, schärfer, am schärfsten
Sei vorsichtig, die Soße ist ziemlich scharf.

sharp, hot, spicy
Be careful; the sauce is rather hot.

Schnitzel ['ʃnits(ə)l] *n, -s, -*
Wenn du das Schnitzel jetzt nicht magst, kannst du es ja später kalt essen.

cutlet *n*
If you don't want the cutlet now, you can eat it cold later.

Schweinefleisch ['ʃvainəflaiʃ] *n, -(e)s, kein Pl.*
Das Schweinefleisch, das du gekauft hast, ist ziemlich fett.

pork *n*
The pork you bought is rather fat.

Soße ['zo:sə] *f, -, -n*
Ich esse Kartoffeln am liebsten mit Soße.

sauce, gravy *n*
I like potatoes best with gravy.

Suppe ['zupə] *f, -, -n*
Pass auf, die Suppe ist sehr heiß!

soup *n*
Be careful! The soup is very hot.

süß [zy:s] *Adj.*, -er, am -esten
Ich trinke gerne süßen Kaffee.

sweet
I like to drink sweet coffee.

Süßigkeit ['zy:siçkait] *f, -, -en*
Das Kind isst zu viele Süßigkeiten.

sweet, sweet thing, candy *n*
That child eats too much candy.

Wurst [vurst] *f, -, Würste*
Diese Wurst kann man braten oder kochen.

sausage, lunch meat *n*
You can fry or boil this sausage.

Zucker ['tsukə*] *m, -s, kein Pl.*
○ Wie möchtest du deinen Tee?

□ Mit Milch und Zucker.

sugar *n*
○ What would you like in your tea?

□ Milk and sugar.

2001-4000

Brötchen ['brøːtçən] *n, -s, -*
Der Bäcker bringt uns jeden Morgen frische Brötchen.

roll *n*
The baker brings us fresh rolls every morning.

Fett [fɛt] *n, -(e)s, kein Pl.*
Zu viel Fett schadet der Gesundheit.

fat *n*
Too much fat is bad for your health.

fett [fɛt] *Adj., -er, am -esten*
Die Wurst mag ich nicht. Sie ist mir zu fett.

fat, fatty
I don't like the sausage. It's too fatty for me.

gar [gaː*] *Adj. indekl.*
Wir können gleich essen. Die Kartoffeln sind in fünf Minuten gar.

cooked, done
We can eat now. The potatoes will be done in five minutes.

grillen ['grɪl(ə)n] *V/t., grillte, hat gegrillt*
Möchten Sie den Fisch gegrillt oder gebraten?

fry *v*

Would you like the fish roasted or fried?

Honig ['hoːnɪç] *m, -s, kein Pl.*
Abends trinkt er immer ein Glas Milch mit Honig.

honey *n*
In the evening he always drinks a glass of milk with honey.

Kalbfleisch ['kalpflaiʃ] *n, -(e)s, kein Pl.*
Ich esse gerne Kalbfleisch, weil es nicht so fett ist.

veal *n*

I like veal because it's not so fat.

Konfitüre [kɔnfi'tyːrə] *f, -, -n*
Die Erdbeerkonfitüre habe ich selbst gemacht.

jam *n*
I made the strawberry jam myself.

mager ['maːgə*] *Adj.*
Fleisch, das zu mager ist, schmeckt meistens nicht.

lean
Meat that's too lean usually doesn't taste very good.

Scheibe ['ʃaibə] *f, -, -n*
Kannst du mir bitte noch eine Scheibe Wurst abschneiden?

slice *n*
Can you please cut me another slice of sausage?

Schinken ['ʃɪŋk(ə)n] *m, -s, -*
Ich möchte 200 g rohen Schinken.

ham *n*
I'd like 200 grams of smoked ham.

Schnitte ['∫nitə] *f, -, -n*
Für das 2. Frühstück im Büro nehme ich zwei Schnitten Brot mit.

slice *n*
For a morning snack at the office I take two slices of bread.

Schokolade [∫oko'la:də] *f, -, -*
Ich möchte noch ein Stück Schokolade.

chocolate *n*
I'd like another piece of chocolate.

Speck [∫pɛk] *m, -(e)s, kein Pl.*
Gebratene Kartoffeln schmecken mit Speck am besten.

bacon *n*
Fried potatoes taste best with bacon.

Steak [ste:k] *n, -s, -s*
Ich esse Steaks am liebsten, wenn sie noch etwas roh sind.

steak *n*
I prefer to eat steaks medium rare.

Würstchen ['vyrstçən] *n, -s, -*
Ich mache uns schnell ein paar heiße Würstchen als Imbiss.

sausage, wiener, hot dog *n*
I'll make us a couple of hot dogs for a snack.

zäh [tsɛ:] *Adj. -er, am -esten*
Der Braten ist zäh und trocken.

tough
The roast is tough and dry.

zart [tsa:*t] *Adj., -er, am -esten*
Du musst das Gemüse nicht lange kochen, es ist sehr zart.

tender
You don't have to cook the vegetables long; they're very tender.

Zwiebel ['tsvi:b(ə)l] *f, -, -n*
Zwiebeln esse ich nur gekocht oder gebraten.

onion *n*
I like to eat onions only if they are cooked.

5.7 Obst und Gemüse | 1-2000

5.7 Fruits and Vegetables

Apfel ['apf(ə)l] *m, -s, Äpfel*
Aus den Äpfeln in unserem Garten machen wir Apfelsaft.

apple *n*
We make apple juice from the apples in our garden.

Apfelsine [apf(ə)l'zi:ne] *f, -, -n*
Diese Apfelsinen kommen aus Marokko.

orange *n*
These oranges come from Morocco.

Birne ['birnə] *f, -, -n*
Zum Nachtisch gibt es gekochte Birnen.

pear *n*
For dessert there are poached pears.

Kartoffel [kar'tɔf(ə)l] *f, -, -n*
Hilfst du mir, die Kartoffeln zu
schälen?

potato *n*
Will you help me peel the potatoes?

Kirsche ['kirʃə] *f, -, -n*
Alle Kirschen in unserem Garten
haben die Vögel gefressen.

cherry *n*
The birds ate all the cherries in our
garden.

Nuss [nus] *f, -, Nüsse*
Ich habe einen Nusskuchen ge-
backen.

nut *n*
I made some nut bread.

Obst [oːpst] *n, -es, kein Pl.*
Es gibt zurzeit wenig frisches
Obst zu kaufen.

fruit *n*
Right now there's not much fresh
fruit to buy.

Orange [o'rãːʒə] *f, -, -n*
Morgens trinke ich gerne ein Glas
Orangensaft.

orange *n*
In the morning I like to drink a
glass of orange juice.

Salat [zaˈlaːt] *m, -(e)s, -e*
○ Wie machst du die Salatsoße?

□ Mit Sahne und Zitronensaft.

salad *n*
○ How will you make the salad
dressing?
□ With cream and lemon juice.

2001-4000

Banane [baˈnaːne] *f, -, -n*
Die Bananen sind jetzt sehr billig.

banana *n*
Bananas are very cheap at the
moment.

Bohne ['boːnə] *f, -, -n*
Heute gibt es Bohnensuppe zum
Mittagessen.

bean *n*
Today there's bean soup for
lunch.

Erbse ['ɛə*psə] *f, -, -n*
Als Gemüse koche ich Erbsen
und Karotten.

pea *n*
For vegetables I'll cook peas and
carrots.

Erdbeere ['ɛːə*tbeːrə] *f, -, -n*
Wenn die Erdbeeren billig sind,
mache ich Erdbeermarmelade.

strawberry *n*
If the strawberries are cheap, I am
going to make strawberry jam.

Karotte [kaˈrɔtə] *f, -, -n*
Weil der Sommer sehr feucht war,
sind die Karotten nicht besonders
groß geworden.

carrot *n*
The carrots didn't get very big
because we had a very wet summer this year.

Kohl [ko:l] *m, -(e)s, kein Pl.*
In unserer Gegend isst man viel Kohl.

cabbage *n*
In our region people eat a lot of cabbage.

Kopfsalat ['kɔpfzala:t] *m, -(e)s, -*
Der Kopfsalat muss gut gewaschen werden.

(bib) lettuce *n*
The lettuce has to be washed carefully.

Möhre ['mø:rə] *f, -, -n*
Schneidest du bitte die Möhren in Scheiben!

carrot *n*
Would you please slice the carrots.

reif [raif] *Adj.*
Ich habe die Birnen probiert. Sie sind noch nicht reif.

ripe
I tried the pears. They're not ripe yet.

Zitrone [tsi'tro:nə] *f, -, -n*
Tee trinke ich mit Zitrone und Zucker.

lemon *n*
I drink tea with lemon and sugar.

5.8 Trinken und Rauchen | 1-2000

5.8 Drinking and Smoking

Alkohol ['alkoho:l] *m, -s, kein Pl.*
Ich darf keinen Alkohol trinken. Ich muss noch Auto fahren.

alcohol *n*
I can't drink any alcohol. I still have to drive.

Bier [bi:ə*] *n, -s, -e*
Im Kühlschrank ist noch Bier.

beer *n*
There's more beer in the refrigerator.

Durst [durst] *m, -es, kein Pl.*
○ Möchtest du etwas trinken?
□ Nein danke, ich habe keinen Durst.

thirst *n*
○ Would you like something to drink?
□ No thanks. I'm not thirsty.

Flasche ['flaʃə] *f, -, -n*
Wir haben nur noch eine Flasche Wein.

bottle *n*
We only have one bottle of wine left.

Getränk [gə'trɛŋk] *n, -(e)s, -e*
Hast du für die Feier auch alkoholfreie Getränke gekauft?

drink, beverage *n*
Did you also buy non-alcoholic beverages for the celebration?

Glas [gla:s] *n, -es,* Gläser
Möchtest du noch ein Glas Wein?

glass *n*
Would you like another glass of wine?

Kaffee ['kafe] *m, -s kein Pl.*
Wenn ich abends Kaffee trinke, kann ich nicht schlafen.

coffee *n*
If I drink coffee in the evening, I can't sleep.

Milch [milç] *f, -, kein Pl.*
Die Kinder trinken Milch zum Frühstück.

milk *n*
The children drink milk for breakfast.

---

rauchen ['raux(ə)n] *V/t., i.,* rauchte, hat geraucht
Sie raucht 30 Zigaretten am Tag.

smoke *v*

She smokes 30 cigarettes a day.

Saft [zaft] *m, -(e)s,* Säfte
Ich habe frischen Orangensaft. Möchtest du ein Glas?

juice *n*
I have fresh orange juice. Would you like a glass?

Tabak ['ta:bak] *m, -s, -e*
Welche Tabakmarke rauchst du?

tobacco *n*
What brand of tobacco do you smoke?

Tee [te:] *m, -s, kein Pl.*
Wir trinken mehr Tee als Kaffee.

tea *n*
We drink more tea than coffee.

---

trinken ['triŋk(ə)n] *V/t.,* trank, hat getrunken
Was möchten Sie trinken?

drink *v*

What would you like to drink?

Wein [vain] *m, -(e)s, -e*
Der Wein schmeckt gut, aber er ist zu warm.

wine *n*
The wine tastes good, but it is too warm.

Zigarette [tsiga'rɛtə] *f, -, -n*
Er hat aufgehört, Zigaretten zu rauchen.

cigarette *n*
He stopped smoking cigarettes.

Zigarre [tsi'garə] *f, -, -n*
Manchmal rauche ich auch Zigarren.

cigar *n*
Sometimes I also smoke cigars.

2001-4000

alkoholfrei [alko'ho:lfrai] *Adj., keine Komp.*
○ Möchtest du auch ein Bier?
□ Nein, lieber ein alkoholfreies Getränk.

non-alcoholic, soft (drink)
○ Would you like a beer, too?
□ No, I'd rather have something non-alcoholic.

Bar [ba:*] *f, -, -s*
Die Bar hat bis 4.00 Uhr morgens geöffnet.

bar *n*
The bar is open until 4 a.m.

betrunken [bə'truŋk(ə)n] *Adj.*
Wenn er betrunken ist, wird er aggressiv.

drunk
When he's drunk, he gets aggressive.

durstig ['durstiç°] *Adj.*
Hast du etwas zu trinken für mich? Ich bin sehr durstig.

thirsty
Do you have something I can drink? I'm very thirsty.

Kakao [ka'ka:o] *m, -s, kein Pl.*
Bernd trinkt gerne warmen Kakao mit Sahne.

cocoa, hot/drinking chocolate *n*
Bernd likes to drink warm cocoa with cream.

Korken ['kɔrk(ə)n] *m, -s, -*
Ich kann die Flasche nicht öffnen, weil der Korken so fest sitzt.

cork *n*
I can't open the bottle because the cork is so tight.

Mineralwasser [minə'ra:lvasə*] *n, -s, kein Pl.*
Zum Essen trinke ich meistens Mineralwasser.

mineral water *n*
I usually drink mineral water with my meals.

Pfeife ['pfaifə] *f, -, -n*
Seit wann rauchst du Pfeife?

pipe *n*
Since when have you smoked a pipe?

Raucher ['rauxə*] *m, -s, -*
Raucherin ['rauxərin] *f, -, -nen*
Sie ist eine starke Raucherin.

smoker *n*

She is a heavy smoker.

5.9 Arzt und Krankenhaus | 1-2000

5.9 Doctor and Hospital

Apotheke [apo'te:kə] *f,* -, -n
Weißt du, welche Apotheke z. Z. Nachtdienst hat?

pharmacy, drugstore *n*
Do you know which pharmacy is open all night today?

Arzt [artst] *m,* -es, Ärzte
Ärztin ['ɛrtstin] *f,* -, -nen
Der Arzt meinte, dass ich mich ins Bett legen sollte.

doctor, physician *n*
The doctor believes I should stay in bed.

Doktor ['dɔktɔr] *m,* -s, -en
Doktorin [dɔk'to:rin] *f,* -, -nen
Der Doktor muss sofort kommen.

doctor *n*
The doctor must come immediately.

Gift [gift] *n,* -(e)s, -e
In unserem Garten verwenden wir keine Pflanzengifte.

poison *n*
We don't use any herbicides in our garden.

heilen ['hail(ə)n] *V/t., i.,* heilte, hat/ (ist) geheilt
Durch ein neues Medikament kann die Krankheit geheilt werden.
Die Verletzung ist schnell geheilt.

heal, cure *v*
This disease can be cured with a new medicine.

The injury healed quickly.

Klinik ['kli:nik] *f,* -, -en
Er liegt in einer Universitätsklinik.

clinic, hospital *n*
He's in a university clinic.

Kranke ['kraŋkə] *m/f,* -n, -n
Der Kranken geht es wieder besser.

sick person, ill person, patient *n*
The patient is doing better.

Krankenhaus ['kraŋk(ə)nhaus] *n,* -es, Krankenhäuser
Nächste Woche darf sie das Krankenhaus verlassen.

hospital *n*
She may leave the hospital next week.

Krankenschwester ['kraŋk(ə)nʃvɛstə*] *f,* -, -n
Auf der Unfallstation fehlen Krankenschwestern.

(female) nurse *n*
There are not enough nurses in the emergency ward.

Medikament [medika'mɛnt] *n*, -(e)s, -e
Nimmst du Medikamente gegen die Erkältung?

medicine *n*
Are you taking medicine for your cold?

Patient [pa'tsjɛnt] *m*, -en, -en
Patientin [pa'tsjɛntin] *f*, -, -nen
Der neue Augenarzt hat sehr viele Patienten.

patient *n*

The new eye specialist has many patients.

Pflaster ['pflastə*] *n*, -s, -
Hast du ein Pflaster? Meine Wunde fängt wieder an zu bluten.

bandaid/adhesive plaster *(BE)* *n*
Do you have a bandaid? The wound is starting to bleed again.

Salbe ['zalbə] *f*, -, -n
Die Salbe, die du mir empfohlen hast, ist wirklich gut.

salve, ointment *n*
The salve you recommended is really good.

Tablette [ta'blɛtə] *f*, -, -n
Ich kann ohne Schlaftabletten nicht einschlafen.

tablet, pill *n*
I can't go to sleep without sleeping pills.

Wartezimmer ['vartətsimə*] *n*, -s, -
Bitte setzen Sie sich kurz ins Wartezimmer!

waiting room *n*

Please have a seat for a short time in the waiting room.

Zahnarzt ['tsa:nartst] *m*, -es, Zahnärzte, **Zahnärztin** ['tsa:nɛrtstin] *f*, -, -nen
Der Zahnarzt meinte, dass er zwei Zähne ziehen muss.

dentist *n*

The dentist said he has to pull two teeth.

2001-4000

Behandlung [bə'handluŋ] *f*, -, -en
Trotz der langen Behandlung habe ich immer noch Rückenschmerzen.

treatment *n*

In spite of the lengthy treatment I still have back pain.

Chirurg [çi'rurk] *m*, -s, -en
Chirurgin [çi'rurgin] *f*, -, -nen
Dr. Christ ist ein bekannter Herzchirurg.

surgeon *n*

Dr. Christ is a famous heart surgeon.

Facharzt ['faxartst] *m*, -es, Fach-
ärzte
In unserer Stadt fehlt ein Facharzt
für Hals, Nasen und Ohren.

(medical) specialist *n*

In our city there is no specialist for
ear, nose, and throat.

Krankenkasse ['kraŋk(ə)nkasə]
f, -, -n
Die Krankenkasse bezahlt die
ganze Behandlung.

medical insurance *n*

The medical insurance will pay
the whole bill.

Krankenwagen
['kraŋk(ə)nva:g(ə)n] *m*, -s, -
Der Krankenwagen war sehr
schnell an der Unfallstelle.

ambulance *n*

The ambulance got to the accident site very quickly.

Kur [ku:ə*] *f*, -, -en

Wohin fährst du zur Kur?

treatment (at a spa), health cure
n
Where do you go for your treatment?

Medizin [medi'tsi:n] *f*, -, *kein Pl.*
Die Medizin, die der Arzt verschrieben hat, hat geholfen.
Die moderne Medizin wird heute
von vielen als ‚Apparatemedizin'
kritisiert.

medicine *n*
The medicine the doctor prescri-
bed helped.
Modern medicine is critized by
many today as too "technical".

Mittel ['mit(ə)l] *n*, -s, -

Gegen Schnupfen gibt es heute
einige Mittel.

**means, treatment, (here) medi-
cine** *n*
There are some treatments for
colds nowadays.

Operation [opəra'tsjo:n] *f*, -, -en
Nach der Operation ging es der
Patientin nicht gut.

operation *n*
The patient didn't do well after the
operation.

operieren [opə'ri:rən] *V/t.*, ope-
rierte, hat operiert
Der Schwerverletzte musste sofort operiert werden.

operate on *v*

The injured had to be operated on
immediately.

Rauschgift ['rauʃgift] *n*, -(e)s, -e
Leider nehmen immer mehr Jugendliche Rauschgift.

drug, drugs *n*
It's a shame that an increasing
number of young people are taking drugs.

Sprechstunde ['ʃprɛçʃtundə] *f*, -, -n
Morgens hat Dr. Behrens von 8.00–12.00 Uhr Sprechstunde.

office hour, surgery hour *(BE) n*
In the morning, Dr. Behrens has office hours from 8 until 12.

Spritze ['ʃpritsə] *f*, -, -n
Im Krankenhaus bekam ich täglich eine Spritze.

shot, injection *n*
In the hospital I got an injection every day.

Thermometer [tɛrmo'meːtə*] *n*, -s, -
Ich möchte Fieber messen. Weißt du, wo das Thermometer ist?

thermometer *n*
I'd like to take my temperature. Do you know where the thermometer is?

verschreiben [fɛə*'ʃraib(ə)n] *V/t.*, verschrieb, hat verschrieben
Was für ein Mittel hat dir der Arzt verschrieben?

prescribe *v*

What kind of medicine did the doctor prescribe for you?

6.1 Allgemeines | 1-2000

6.1 General

Angebot [ˈangəboːt] *n,* -s, -e
Das Angebot der Firma Jung ist am günstigsten.

offer, supply *n*
The offer from the Jung Company is the most attractive.

Auftrag [ˈauftraːk] *m,* -s, Aufträge
Die Firma mit dem günstigsten Angebot bekommt den Auftrag.

order, contract *n*
The firm with the best offer gets the order.

ausrechnen [ˈausrɛçnən] *V/i.,*
rechnete aus, hat ausgerechnet
Können Sie mir ausrechnen, wieviel Quadratmeter Holz ich brauche?

calculate, figure out *v*

Can you calculate for me how many square meters of wood I need?

Betrieb [bəˈtriːp] *m,* -(e)s, -e

Unser Betrieb ist wirtschaftlich sehr gesund.

business, concern, operation, office *n*
Our business is economically very sound.

Buchführung [ˈbuːxfyːruŋ] *f,* -, -en

Wir haben einige Fehler in der Buchführung entdeckt.

bookkeeping, accounting *n*

We discovered a mistake in the bookkeeping.

Fabrik [faˈbriːk] *f,* -, -en
In unserer Fabrik wird die Produktion von Computern gesteuert.

factory *n*
At our factory, production is guided by computers.

Firma [ˈfirma] *f,* -, Firmen
Die Firma Hertz & Sohn gibt es schon seit über 100 Jahren.

firm *n*
Hertz & Son have existed for over 100 years as a firm.

Geschäft [gəˈʃɛft] *n,* -(e)s, -e

Wir müssen uns beeilen. Die Geschäfte schließen bald.
Peter will mein altes Auto kaufen, aber ich mache nicht gerne Geschäfte mit Freunden.

business, store, deal, transaction *n*
We have to hurry. The stores are closing soon.
Peter wants to buy my old car, but I don't like to do business with friends.

Industrie [indus'tri:] *f, -, -n*
Die Industrie klagt über die hohen Lohnkosten.

industry *n*
Industry is complaining about high salary costs.

Konkurrenz [kɔnku'rɛnts] *f, -, kein Pl.*
Trotz starker Konkurrenz hat unsere Firma den Auftrag bekommen.

competition *n*
In spite of strong competition, our firm got the contract.

Kosten ['kɔst(ə)n] *nur Pl.*
Wegen gestiegener Kosten müssen die Preise erhöht werden.

costs *n*
Because of a rise in costs, prices must be increased.

Lager ['la:gə*] *n, -s, -*
Das eine Ersatzteil haben wir auf Lager, das andere bestellen wir.

stock, storage *n*
We have one of the spare parts in stock; we'll order the other one.

liefern ['li:fə*n] *V/t.,* lieferte, hat geliefert
Wir liefern schnell und pünktlich.

deliver *v*
We deliver quickly and on time.

Produkt [pro'dukt] *n, -s, -e*
Unsere Produkte sind zurzeit konkurrenzlos.

product *n*
Right now our products have no competition.

Produktion [produk'tsjo:n] *f, -, kein Pl.*
Wegen der vielen Aufträge musste die Produktion erhöht werden.

production *n*
Production had to be increased because of the many contracts.

Rechnung ['rɛçnuŋ] *f, -, en*
Diese Rechnung muss bis zum 3. 11. bezahlt werden.

bill *n*
This bill must be paid by November 3.

senken ['zɛŋk(ə)n] *V/t.,* senkte, hat gesenkt
Die Preise für die alten Modelle wurden gesenkt.

lower, cut *v*
The prices for the old models were lowered.

steigern ['ʃtaigə*n] *V/t.,* steigerte, hat gesteigert
Die Firma konnte ihren Umsatz um 10 % steigern.

raise, increase *v*
The firm was able to raise its sales by 10%.

Steuer ['ʃtɔiə*] *f, -, -n*
Zu diesem Betrag kommt noch die Umsatzsteuer dazu.

tax *n*
The sales tax must be added to this amount.

Umsatz ['umzats] *m,* -es, Umsätze
Der Umsatz ist um 20% gestiegen.

sales, turnover *n*
Sales have gone up 20%.

Unkosten ['unkɔst(ə)n] *nur Pl.*
Trotz der Unkosten hat sich das Geschäft gelohnt.

costs, expenses *n*
The transaction was worth it, in spite of the expenses.

Unternehmen [untə*'ne:mən] *n,* -s, -
Die Unternehmen der Chemieindustrie haben gegen die neuen Wasserschutzgesetze protestiert.

enterprise, company *n*
The chemical industry companies have protested the new water protection laws.

Versicherung [fɛə*'ziçərun] *f,* -, -en
Eine Krankenversicherung ist in Deutschland für alle Studenten Pflicht.

insurance *n*
Health insurance in Germany is required for all students.

Werbung ['vɛrbun] *f,* -, *kein Pl.*
Für das neue Produkt wird in Presse und Fernsehen Werbung gemacht.

advertising *n*
There is advertising for the new product in the press and on TV.

Wirtschaft ['virtʃaft] *f,* -, *kein Pl.*
Die Regierung hofft auf eine gute Wirtschaftsentwicklung.

economy, business *n*
The government is hoping for good development in the economic sector.

2001-4000

Abmachung ['apmaxun] *f,* -, -en
Trotz unserer Abmachung will Ihre Firma die Waren nicht mehr umtauschen. Warum?

agreement *n*
In spite of our agreement, your firm won't exchange the goods. Why?

Bedarf [bə'darf] *m,* -(e)s, *kein Pl.*
Der Bedarf an Kleinwagen nimmt ab.

need *n*
The need for small cars is going down.

Bilanz [bi'lants] *f*, -, -en
Nach den Verlusten im letzten Jahr ist die Bilanz der Firma jetzt wieder positiv.

balance *n*
After last year's losses the balance of the firm is once again positive.

Einnahme ['ainna:mə] *f*, -, -n
Die Einnahmen sind in den letzten Wochen gesunken.

income, revenue *n*
Revenues have gone down in recent weeks.

Ersatzteil [ɛə*'zatstail] *n*, -(e)s, -e
Die Werkstatt hat ein großes Ersatzteillager.

spare part *n*
The garage has a large supply of spare parts.

Export [ɛks'pɔrt] *m*, -(e)s, -e
Die Firma lebt vor allem von Exportaufträgen.

export, exportation *n*
The firm lives mostly on its export orders.

exportieren [ɛkspɔr'ti:rən] *V/t.*, exportierte, hat exportiert
Diese Maschine wird nach Frankreich exportiert.

export *v*

This machine will be exported to France.

Garantie [garan'ti:] *f*, -, n
Das Radio ist gebraucht. Eine Garantie kann ich Ihnen dafür nicht geben.

guarantee, warranty *n*
The radio is second-hand. I can't give you a guarantee for it.

geschäftlich [gə'ʃɛftliç] *Adj., keine Komp.*
Herr Benz ist geschäftlich verreist.

on/for business

Mr. Benz is away on business.

Geschäftsführer [gə'ʃɛftsfy:rə*] *m*, -s, **Geschäftsführerin** [gə'ʃɛftsfy:rərin] *f*, -, -nen
Ich möchte bitte den Geschäftsführer sprechen.

managing director, manager *n*

I'd like to speak to the manager, please.

Geschäftsleitung [gə'ʃɛftslaituŋ] *f*, -, -en
Die Büros der Geschäftsleitung sind im 3. Stock.

(the) management *n*

The offices of the management are on the third floor.

herstellen ['he:ə*ʃtɛl(ə)n] *V/t.*, stellte her, hat hergestellt
Die Firma stellt seit über 60 Jahren Büromaschinen her.

manufacture, make *v*

The company has been manufacturing office machines for over 60 years.

Hersteller ['heːə*ʃtɛlə*] *m, -s, -*
Wir haben Computer verschiedener Hersteller im Programm.

manufacturer *n*
We have computers from different manufacturers in our catalogue.

Herstellung ['heːə*ʃtɛluŋ] *f, -, kein Pl.*
Die Gefahren bei der Herstellung chemischer Produkte wurden früher wenig beachtet.

manufacturing *n*
The dangers involved in manufacturing chemical products were not previously recognized.

Import [im'pɔrt] *m, -(e)s, -e*
Die Preise der Importwaren sind gesunken.

import *n*
The prices of imported goods have fallen.

importieren [impɔr'tiːrən] *V/t.,*
importierte, hat importiert
Die Bundesrepublik hat dieses Jahr mehr Öl importiert als letztes Jahr.

import *v*

The Federal Republic imported more oil this year than last year.

Investition [invɛsti'tsjoːn] *f, -, -en*
Durch die hohen Investitionen für wirtschaftlichere Maschinen ist die Firma konkurrenzfähiger geworden.

investment *n*
By increasing investment in more economical machines the company became more competitive.

Krise ['kriːzə] *f, -, -n*
Die wirtschaftliche Krise in der Textilindustrie hat viele Leute arbeitslos gemacht.

crisis *n*
The economic crisis in the textile industry has caused unemployment for many people.

Kundendienst ['kund(ə)ndiːnst] *m, -es, -e*
Unsere Waschmaschine war kaputt. Der Kundendienst kam sofort und hat die Maschine repariert.

customer service *n*

Our washing machine was broken. The service (representative) came immediately and repaired the machine.

Lieferung ['liːfəruŋ] *f, -, -en*
Die bestellten Ersatzteile kommen mit der nächsten Lieferung.

delivery *n*
The ordered replacement parts we will arrive with the next delivery.

Markt [markt] *m, -(e)s, Märkte*
Auf dem Markt für Werkzeugmaschinen gibt es zzt. einen harten Preiskampf.

market *n*
At the moment prices are under heavy pressure in the machine tool market.

Muster ['mustə*] *n, -s, -*
Der Vertreter zeigte dem Händler Muster des Teppichprogramms seiner Firma.

sample *n*
The representative showed the dealer samples of the different carpets made by his company.

Nachfrage ['na:xfra:gə] *f, -, kein Pl.*
Die Nachfrage nach Elektro-Kleingeräten ist stark gesunken.

inquiry, demand *n*
The demand for electric appliances has dropped dramatically.

ökonomisch [ø:ko'no:miʃ] *Adj.*
Es wäre ökonomischer gewesen, die alten Maschinen nicht zu reparieren, sondern neue zu kaufen.

economical
It would have been more economical not to repair the old machines, but to buy new ones.

produzieren [produ'tsi:rən] *V/t., produzierte, hat produziert*
Ersatzteile für diese alten Geräte werden nicht mehr produziert.

produce *v*

Replacement parts for these old appliances are no longer being produced.

Profit [pro'fi:t] *m, -(e)s, -e*
Bei dem letzten Geschäft haben wir keinen Profit gemacht.

profit *n*
Our last transaction yielded no profit.

Prospekt [pro'spɛkt] *m, -(e)s, -e*

Könnten Sie mir einen Prospekt für dieses Gerät geben.

prospectus, advertising brochure *n*
Could you give me a prospectus for this device?

ruinieren [rui'ni:rən] *V/t., ruinierte, hat ruiniert*
Die Firma wurde vor allem durch falsche Entscheidungen der Manager ruiniert.

ruin *v*

The company was ruined primarily by poor decisions by the managers.

selbstständig ['zɛlpʃtɛndiç°] *Adj.*
Früher war er angestellt, jetzt ist er selbstständig und hat ein eigenes Geschäft.

independent, self-employed
Previously he was employed, now he is self-employed and has his own business.

Statistik [ʃta'tistik] *f, -, -en*
Die Zahlen der Verkaufsstatistik sind wichtig für die Investitionsplanung.

statistics *n*
The figures for the sales statistics are important for investment planning.

Steigerung [ˈʃtaigəruŋ] *f*, -, -en
Ohne neue Mitarbeiter ist eine Steigerung der Produktion nicht möglich.

increase *n*
Without new workers an increase in production is not possible.

verbrauchen [fɛə*ˈbraux(ə)n] *V/t.*, verbrauchte, hat verbraucht
Die neuen Maschinen verbrauchen weniger Strom als die alten.

consume, use up *v*

The new machines consume less electricity than the old ones.

Verbraucher [fɛə*ˈbrauxə*] *m*, -s, -, **Verbraucherin** [fɛə*ˈbrauxərin] -, -nen
Die Verbraucher sind heute kritischer als früher.

consumer *n*

Consumers are more critical than they used to be.

versichern [fɛə*ˈziçə*n] *V/t.*, versicherte, hat versichert
Das Haus ist gegen Feuer und Sturm versichert.

insure *v*

The house is insured against fire and storm damage.

Versorgung [fɛə*ˈzɔrguŋ] *f*, -, *kein Pl.*
Bei einigen Herstellern gibt es Versorgungsprobleme mit Ersatzteilen.

supply *n*

Several manufacturers have supply problems with replacement parts.

wirtschaftlich [ˈvirtʃaftliç] *Adj.*
Die wirtschaftliche Situation der Metallindustrie ist besser geworden.

economic
The economic situation in the metal industry has improved.

6.2 Geschäfte und Einkauf | 1-2000

6.2 Stores and Shopping

aussuchen [ˈauszu:x(ə)n] *V/t.*, suchte aus, hat ausgesucht
Diesen Pullover gab es in fünf verschiedenen Farben. Ich habe mir einen roten ausgesucht.

select *v*

This sweater was available in five different colors. I selected a red one.

Bäckerei [bɛkəˈrai] *f*, -, -en
- ○ Wo hast du den Kuchen gekauft?
- □ In der Bäckerei neben der Kirche.

bakery *n*
- ○ Where did you buy the cake?
- □ At the bakery next to the church.

---

billig [ˈbiliçˀ] *Adj.*
Auf dem Markt ist das Gemüse billiger.

cheap, inexpensive
Vegetables are cheaper at the (farmer's) market.

---

einkaufen [ˈainkauf(ə)n] *V/t., i.*, kaufte ein, hat eingekauft
Für das Wochenende müssen wir noch ein paar Lebensmittel einkaufen.

Die Geschäfte sind zu. Du kannst nicht mehr einkaufen.

shop, go shopping, buy, purchase *v*
We still have to buy some food for the weekend.

The stores are closed. You can't shop any more.

Handel [ˈhand(ə)l] *m*, -s, *kein Pl.*
Der japanische und der deutsche Wirtschaftsminister besprachen Probleme des Handels zwischen ihren beiden Ländern.

trade *n*
The Japanese and German Secretaries of Commerce discussed trade problems between the two countries.

---

handeln [ˈhand(ə)ln] *V/i.*, handelte, hat gehandelt
- ○ Was macht dein Bruder beruflich?
- □ Er handelt mit Südfrüchten.
Über den Preis müssen wir noch handeln.

do business, (make a) deal, barter *v*
- ○ What does your brother do for a living?
- □ He deals in citrus fruits.
We'll have to barter about the price.

Händler [ˈhɛndlə*] *m*, -s, -
Händlerin [ˈhɛndlərin] *f*, -, -nen
Den Wein kaufe ich immer bei dem gleichen Händler.

dealer *n*

I always buy the wine from the same dealer.

Kasse [ˈkasə] *f*, -, -n
Bitte bezahlen Sie die Sachen an der Kasse Nr. 5!

cash register, checkout *n*
Please pay for these things at checkout 5.

Kauf [kauf] *m*, -s, Käufe
Gestern haben wir den Kaufvertrag für die Wohnung unterschrieben.

purchase *n*
Yesterday we signed the purchase contract for the apartment.

kaufen ['kauf(ə)n] *V/t.*, kaufte, hat gekauft
Diese (Hals-)Kette habe ich im Urlaub gekauft.

buy, purchase *n*
I bought this necklace when I was on vacation.

Kaufhaus ['kaufhaus] *n*, -es, Kaufhäuser
Das neue Kaufhaus ist sehr groß. Man kann dort praktisch alles kaufen.

department store *n*
The new department store is very big. You can buy practically everything there.

Kiosk ['kiːɔsk] *m*, -s, -e
Zeitungen gibt es dort am Kiosk.

newsstand *n*
You can get newspapers there at the newsstand.

kosten ['kɔst(ə)n] *V/i.*, kostete, hat gekostet
Die Eier kosten 23 Cent pro Stück.

cost *v*
The eggs cost 23 cents each.

Kunde ['kundə] *m*, -n, -n
Kundin ['kundin] *f*, -, -nen
Ich bin schon seit vielen Jahren Kundin in diesem Geschäft.

customer, client *n*
I've been a customer for years at this store.

Laden ['laːd(ə)n] *m*, -s, Läden
Die Läden im Hauptbahnhof sind auch sonntags geöffnet.

store *n*
The stores at the main train station are also open on Sunday.

Marke ['markə] *f*, -, -n
○ Möchtest du eine Zigarette?
□ Nein danke, das ist nicht meine Marke.

brand *n*
○ Would you like a cigarette?
□ No, thanks. That's not my brand.

Metzgerei [mɛtsgəˈrai] *f*, -, -en
In dieser Metzgerei bekommt man gutes Fleisch.

butcher's, meat market, *n*
You can get good meat at this butcher's.

Preis [prais] *m*, -es, -e
Ich habe den Tisch für den halben Preis bekommen, weil er ein paar Fehler hat.

price *n*
I got the table for half price because it has some defects.

Quittung ['kvituŋ] *f*, -, -en
Eine Quittung bekommen Sie an der Hauptkasse.

receipt *n*
You can get a receipt at the main desk.

Supermarkt ['zu:pɐ*markt] *m,* -(e)s, Supermärkte
Das Warenangebot des Supermarktes ist gut.

supermarket *n*
The selection at the supermarket is good.

---

teuer ['tɔiɐ*] *Adj.,* teurer, am teuersten
Sie hat sich einen teuren Fotoapparat gekauft.

expensive
She bought herself an expensive camera.

Verkauf [fɛɐ*'kauf] *m,* -(e)s, Verkäufe
Der Verkauf von Alkohol an Jugendliche ist verboten.

sale *n*
The sale of alcohol to youths is forbidden.

---

verkaufen [fɛɐ*'kauf(ə)n] *V/t.,* verkaufte, hat verkauft
Meine alten Möbel habe ich verkauft oder verschenkt.

sell *v*
I sold or gave away my old furniture.

Vorrat ['fo:ɐ*ra:t] *m,* -(e)s, Vorräte
Ich habe noch einen großen Vorrat an Nägeln. Du musst keine neuen kaufen.

supply *n*
I still have a large supply of nails. You don't need to buy any new ones.

Ware ['va:rə] *f,* -, -n
Diese Ware kommt aus dem Ausland.

merchandise, product, wares *n*
This merchandise is imported.

---

zahlen ['tsa:l(ə)n] *V/t., i.,* zahlte, hat gezahlt
Kann ich mit Scheck zahlen?
Die Steuern müssen monatlich gezahlt werden.

pay *v*
Can I pay with a check?
Taxes must be paid monthly.

2000-4000

Artikel [ar'ti:k(ə)l] *m,* -s, -
Dieser Artikel ist heute im Sonderangebot.

article *n*
This article is at a special price today.

Auswahl ['ausva:l] *f,* -, *kein Pl.*
Das Textilgeschäft Schneider hat eine große Auswahl an Röcken und Blusen.

selection *n*
The clothing store "Schneider" has a large selection of skirts and blouses.

Drogerie [drogə'ri:] *f, -, -n*
Bring mir aus der Drogerie bitte
eine Tube Zahnpasta mit!

drugstore, chemist's shop *(BE) n*
Please get me a tube of toothpaste at the drugstore.

Einkauf ['ainkauf] *m, -(e)s, Einkäufe*
Ich muss noch ein paar Einkäufe
machen.

purchase, shopping *n*

I still have to do some shopping.

Inhaber ['inha:bə*] *m, -s, -*
Inhaberin ['inha:bərin] *f, -, -nen*
Der Inhaber des Gemüsege-
schäfts ist immer sehr freundlich.

proprietor, owner *n*

The owner of the produce store is
always very friendly.

kostenlos ['kɔst(ə)nlo:s] *Adj., keine Komp.*
Wenn Sie bei uns 12 Flaschen
Wein kaufen, bekommen Sie eine
kostenlos.

free

If you buy twelve bottles of wine
from us, you get one free.

Käufer ['kɔifə*] *m, -s, -*
Käuferin ['kɔifərin] *f, -, -nen*
Gerd sucht einen Käufer für sein
altes Auto.

customer, buyer *n*

Gerd is looking for a buyer for his
old car.

Markt [markt] *m, -(e)s, Märkte*
In unserer Stadt ist jeden Mitt-
woch Markt.

(open air) market *n*
In our town every Wednesday is
market day.

Reinigung ['rainiguŋ] *f, -, -en*
Diesen Pullover darf man nicht
waschen, ich muss ihn zur Reinigung bringen.

dry cleaning *n*
This sweater can't be washed; I
have to take it in for dry cleaning.

Reklame [re'kla:mə] *f, -, -n*
Ich kenne das Produkt aus der
Reklame im Fernsehen.

advertising *n*
I know that product from advertising on television.

Schaufenster ['ʃaufɛnstə*] *n, -s, -*
Die Mäntel waren schnell ausverkauft. Die Verkäuferin hat mir den
letzten aus dem Schaufenster ge-
holt.

window display *n*
The coats sold out quickly. The
saleslady got me the last one from
the window display.

Schlange ['ʃlaŋə] *f, -, -n*
An der Kasse steht eine lange
Schlange.

line, queue
There's a long line at the box office.

Service ['zøːəˈ*vis] *m, -s, kein Pl.*
Der Service in dieser Autowerkstatt ist ausgezeichnet.

service *n*
The service at this auto repair shop is excellent.

Sonderangebot
['zɔndəˈ*angəboːt] *n, -s, -e*
Die Wurst ist heute im Sonderangebot. 100 g kosten jetzt 1,20 € statt 1,80 €.

special offer, special price *n*

The sausage ist at a special price today. 100 grams now cost 1.20 € instead of 1.80 €.

Zahlung ['tsaːluŋ] *f, -, -en*
Wir liefern nur bei Barzahlung.

payment *n*
We only deliver if the payment is in cash.

6.3 Geld und Besitz | 1-2000

6.3 Money and Property

ausgeben ['ausgeːb(ə)n] *V/t.,*
gab aus, hat ausgegeben
Wir geben jede Woche ca. 400,– € für Lebensmittel aus.

spend *v*

We spend about 400 € a week for food.

Bank [baŋk] *f, -, -en*
Ich muss noch Geld von der Bank holen.

bank *n*
I still have to get money from the bank.

bar [baː*] *Adj., keine Komp.*
Wollen Sie bar oder mit Scheck bezahlen?

cash *n*
Do you want to pay cash or with a check?

Besitz [bəˈzits] *m, -es, kein Pl.*
In der Wirtschaftskrise hat er seinen Besitz verloren.

property *n*
He lost his property in the economic depression.

Besitzer [bəˈzitsə*] *m, -s, -*
Besitzerin [bəˈzitsərin] *f, -, -nen*
Unser Vermieter hat sein Haus verkauft, aber wir kennen den neuen Besitzer noch nicht.

owner *n*

Our landlord sold his house, but we don't know the new owner yet.

besitzen [bə'zits(ə)n] *V/t.,* besaß, hat besessen
Sie besitzt ein eigenes Flugzeug.

own *v*
She owns her own airplane.

bezahlen [bə'tsaːl(ə)n] *V/t.,* bezahlte, hat bezahlt
Die Rechnung muss bis zum 13. 6. bezahlt werden.

pay *v*
The bill must be paid by June 13.

Cent [tsɛnt] *m,* -, -
Das macht zusammen 26 Euro und 62 Cent.

cent *n*
That adds up to 26 euros and 62 cents.

Darleh(e)n ['daːˑleː(ə)n] *n,* -s, -
Die Zinsen für Bankdarlehen sind zzt. sehr günstig.

loan *n*
The interest rates for bank loans are very good right now.

Eigentum ['aig(ə)ntuːm] *n,* -s, *kein Pl.*
Ich habe das Haus nicht gemietet. Es ist mein Eigentum.

property *n*
I didn't rent the house. It's my property.

Euro ['ɔi'ro] *m,* -, -s
Eine Fahrt mit der U-Bahn kostet 2,- Euro.

euro *n*
A trip on the subway/underground *(BE)* costs 2 euros.

Franken ['fraŋk(ə)n] *m,* -s, -
Ich möchte 500,- Euro in Schweizer Franken wechseln.

franc *n*
I'd like to exchange 500 euro for Swiss francs.

Geld [gɛlt] *n,* -(e)s, *kein Pl.*
Wie viel Geld verdienst du im Monat?

money *n*
How much money do you earn in a month?

haben ['haːb(ə)n] *V/t.,* hatte, hat gehabt
Wir haben ein Ferienhaus an der Nordseeküste.

have *v*
We have a vacation house on the North Sea coast.

Konto ['kɔnto] *n,* -s, Konten
Bitte zahlen Sie den Rechnungsbetrag auf eines unserer Konten!

account *n*
Please pay the amount due to one of our accounts.

Kredit [kre'diːt] *m,* -s, -e
Die Kreditzinsen sind bei allen Banken verschieden.

credit *n*
The interest rates are different at all the banks.

Münze ['myntsə] *f,* -, -n
Mein Bruder sammelt ausländische Münzen.

coin *n*
My brother collects foreign coins.

preiswert ['praisve:ə*t] *Adj.*, -er, am -esten
Orangen sind zzt. preiswert.

inexpensive
Oranges are inexpensive right now.

---

reich [raiç] *Adj.*
Durch kluge Exportgeschäfte ist er reich geworden.

rich
He got rich on smart export deals.

Scheck [ʃɛk] *m*, -s, -s
Kann ich mit Scheck bezahlen?

check/cheque *(BE) n*
Can I pay by check?

Schulden ['ʃuld(ə)n] *nur Pl.*
Sie hat Schulden gemacht, um sich die neuen Möbel kaufen zu können.

debt *n*
She went into debt to be able to buy the new furniture.

---

schulden *V/t.*, schuldete, hat geschuldet
Du schuldest mir noch 20,- Euro

owe *v*
You still owe me 20 euros.

---

sparen ['ʃpa:rən] *V/t., i.*, sparte, hat gespart
Mit der neuen Maschine spart man Geld und Zeit.
Sie spart für den Urlaub.

save *v*

You save time and money with the new machine.
She is saving for her vacation.

---

umsonst [um'zɔnst] *Adv.*
Die Reparatur während der Garantiezeit ist umsonst.
Ich bin umsonst gegangen. Die Bank hatte schon geschlossen.

free, in vain
Repair during the guarantee time is free.
I went in vain. The bank had already closed.

---

verdienen [fɛə*'di:nən] *V/t.*, verdiente, hat verdient
Bei der neuen Firma verdient sie mehr.
Bei diesem Geschäft haben wir viel Geld verdient.

earn *v*

She earns more at the new company.
We earned a lot of money in that business.

Verlust [fɛə*'lust] *m*, -es, -e
Am Anfang machte die Firma Verluste, jetzt arbeitet sie mit Gewinn.

loss *n*
At first the firm had losses, but now it's operating at a profit.

Währung ['vɛ:ruŋ] *f, -, -en*
In Österreich kann man in den meisten Hotels auch mit deutscher Währung bezahlen.

currency *n*
In most hotels in Austria you can also pay in German currency.

Wert [ve:ə*t] *m, -s, -e*
Gold hat in letzter Zeit viel an Wert verloren.

value *n*
Gold has lost a lot of its value recently.

---

wert *Adj., keine Komp.*
Wie viel ist dieser Ring wert?

worth
How much is this ring worth?

---

wertvoll ['ve:ə*tfɔl] *Adj.*
Das Haus ist mit wertvollen Möbeln eingerichtet.

valuable
The house is decorated with valuable furniture.

Zins [tsins] *m, -es, -en*
Die Kreditzinsen sind in den letzten Monaten gestiegen.

interest *n*
Interest on purchases has gone up in recent months.

2001-4000

---

abheben ['aphe:b(ə)n] *V/t.,* hob ab, hat abgehoben
Ich möchte 800,- Euro von meinem Konto abheben.

withdraw *v*
I'd like to withdraw 800 euros from my account.

Ausgabe ['ausga:bə] *f, -, -n*
Ich finde, deine Ausgaben für Kleidung und Schuhe sind zu hoch.

expense, expenditure *n*
I think your expenses for clothes and shoes are too high.

Bargeld ['ba:*gɛlt] *n, -(e)s, kein Pl.*
Ich habe nicht genug Bargeld. Kann ich mit Kreditkarte bezahlen?

cash *n*
I don't have enough cash. May I pay with a credit card?

---

bargeldlos ['ba:*gɛltlo:s] *Adj., keine Komp.*
Wir bezahlen alle Rechnungen bargeldlos.

without cash, cashless
We pay all the bills without cash.

Bezahlung [bə'tsa:luŋ] *f, -, -*
Für die Bezahlung haben Sie vier Wochen Zeit.

payment *n*
You have four weeks to make the payment.

Börse ['bœrzə] *f, -, -n*
Die Entwicklung der Börsenkurse war in letzter Zeit positiv.

stock market *n*
Values on the stock market have turned positive in recent times.

Einkommen ['ainkɔmən] *n, -s, -*
Wie hoch ist dein Jahreseinkommen?

income *n*
How high is your yearly income?

einzahlen ['ainzaːl(ə)n] *V/t.*, zahlte ein, hat eingezahlt
Ich möchte 2000,- Euro auf das Konto 32456-876 einzahlen.

deposit *v*
I'd like to deposit EUR 2000 in(to) account 32456-876.

finanziell [finanˈtsjɛl] *Adj., keine Komp.*
Die finanzielle Situation der Firma ist besser geworden.

financial
The financial situation of the firm has gotten better.

finanzieren [finanˈtsiːrən] *V/t.*
Das Haus ist über ein Bankdarlehen finanziert worden.

finance *v*
The house was financed with a loan from the bank.

Geldbeutel ['gɛltbɔit(ə)l] *m, -s, -*
Ich habe 20,- Euro aus deinem Geldbeutel genommen.

purse *n*
I took 20 euros out of your purse.

Gewinn [gəˈvin] *m, -s, -e*
Sie hat bei dem Verkauf ihres Hotels einen guten Gewinn gemacht.

profit *n*
She made a good profit on the sale of her hotel.

Kleingeld ['klaingɛlt] *n, -(e)s, kein Pl.*
Ich kann leider nicht wechseln. Ich habe kein Kleingeld.

coin *n*

Sorry I can't make any change. I don't have any coins.

Rappen ['rap(ə)n] *m, -s, -*
Können Sie mir einen Franken in Rappen wechseln?

Swiss centime *n*
Could you exchange a frank for centimes for me?

Rente ['rɛntə] *f, -, -n*
Meine Eltern bekommen beide eine gute Rente.

pension *n*
My parents both get a good pension.

Scheckkarte ['ʃɛkkartə] *f, -, -n*
Ohne Scheckkarte dürfen wir
Ihren Scheck nicht annehmen.

check (identification) card *n*
We cannot accept your check
without a check (identification)
card.

Schein [ʃain] *m, -(e)s, -e*
Dieser Tankautomat nimmt auch
Zehnmarkscheine an.

bill, banknote *n*
This gasoline dispenser also ac-
cepts 10 mark bills.

Überweisung [y:bə*'vaizuŋ] *f, -,
-en*
Bitte bezahlen Sie bargeldlos
durch Überweisung!

transfer *n*

Please pay without cash through
a transfer.

überweisen [y:bə*'vaiz(ə)n] *V/t.,*
überwies, hat überwiesen
Der Betrag ist letzte Woche überwiesen worden.

transfer (money) *v*

The amount was transfered last
week.

Verdienst [fɛə*'diːnst] *m, -(e)s, -e*
Ich spare regelmäßig einen Teil
meines Verdienstes.

profit, earnings *n*
I regularly save part of my earnings.

Vermögen [fɛə*'møːg(ə)n] *n, -s, -*
Das Vermögen des Betriebs
reicht als Sicherheit für den Bank-
kredit nicht aus.

means, fortune, credit *n*
The fortune of the company is not
high enough for credit at the
bank.

verschwenden [fɛə*'ʃvɛnd(ə)n]
V/t., verschwendete, hat ver-
schwendet
Bei der Produktion wird zu viel
Material verschwendet.

squander, waste *v*

Too much material is wasted
during production.

Wechselgeld ['vɛks(ə)lgɛlt] *n,
-(e)s, kein Pl.*
Es ist kein Wechselgeld in der
Kasse.

change *n*

There's no change at the cash
register.

6.4 Arbeitswelt | 1-2000

6.4 Work

Angelegenheit ['aŋgəle:g(ə)n-hait] *f, -, -en*
Um diese Angelegenheit kümmert sich Frau Rabe.

matter *n*
Ms. Rabe is taking care of this matter.

arbeitslos ['arbaitslo:s] *Adj., keine Komp.*
Sie war nur drei Monate arbeitslos.

out of work, unemployed
She was only out of work for three months.

Aufgabe ['aufga:bə] *f, -, -n*
Herr Weiss hat neue Aufgaben in einer anderen Abteilung übernommen.

job, task *n*
Mr. Weis has taken a new job in another division.

Bedingung [bə'diŋuŋ] *f, -, -en*
Die Arbeitsbedingungen in unserer Firma sind gut.
Ich habe die Bedingung gestellt, dass ich ein eigenes Büro bekomme.

condition *n*
Work conditions are very good at our company.
I made it a condition that I get an office of my own.

beschäftigen [bə'ʃɛftig(ə)n] *V/t.,* beschäftigte, hat beschäftigt
Unsere Firma beschäftigt 130 Angestellte und Arbeiter.

occupy, employ *v*
Our company employs 130 office employees and workers.

bewerben [bə'vɛrb(ə)n] *V/refl.,* bewarb, hat beworben
Ich habe mich bei zwei Firmen beworben.

apply for a job *v*
I've applied to two companies for a job.

Bewerbung [bə'vɛrbuŋ] *f, -, -en*
Auf meine Bewerbung habe ich noch keine Antwort.

application *n*
I still don't have any response to my application.

Büro [by'ro:] *n, -s, -s*
Sonja arbeitet in einem Versicherungsbüro.

office *n*
Sonja works in the office of an insurance company.

Chef [ʃɛf] *m*, -s, -s
Chefin [ˈʃɛfin] *f*, -, -nen
Mit unserem Chef kann man gut zusammenarbeiten.

boss *n*

We can work well with our boss.

Dienst [diːnst] *m*, -es, -e
Nächste Woche habe ich Nachtdienst im Krankenhaus.

service, working hours, shift *n*
Next week I have the night shift at the hospital.

einstellen [ˈainʃtɛl(ə)n] *V/t.*, stellte ein, hat eingestellt
Wir schaffen die Arbeit nicht.
Es müssen unbedingt ein paar neue Leute eingestellt werden.

employ, hire *v*

We can't get the work done. We absolutely have to hire a few new people.

Erfolg [ɛəˈfɔlk] *m*, -(e)s, -e
Mit den neuen Produkten hat die Firma großen Erfolg.

success *n*
The company is having great success with the new products.

erfolgreich [ɛəˈfɔlkraiç] *Adj.*
Sie ist eine erfolgreiche Geschäftsfrau.

successful
She is a successful business woman.

erledigen [ɛəˈleːdig(ə)n] *V/t.*, erledigte, hat erledigt
Diese Sache muss unbedingt bis morgen erledigt werden.

take care of, settle *v*

These things must absolutely be taken care of by tomorrow.

Gehalt [gəˈhalt] *n*, -(e)s, Gehälter
Die Gehälter werden ab nächsten Monat um 2,7 % erhöht.

salary *n*
Salaries will go up 2.7% next month.

Karriere [karˈjɛːrə] *f*, -, -n
Von seinen Kollegen wird er bewundert, weil er sehr schnell Karriere gemacht hat.

career *n*
He is admired by his colleagues for the rapid rise in his career.

Kopie [koˈpiː] *f*, -, -n
Bitte machen Sie drei Kopien von dem Brief. Das Original behalte ich.

copy *n*
Please make three copies of the letter. I'll keep the original.

kündigen [ˈkyndig(ə)n] *V/t.*, kündigte, hat gekündigt
Ich habe meine Stelle zum 1. Mai gekündigt.

resign, quit *v*

I'm resigning as of May 1.

Landwirtschaft ['lantvirtʃaft] *f, -, kein Pl.*

farming, agriculture *n*

Früher hat er in der Landwirtschaft gearbeitet. Jetzt hat er eine Stelle in der Industrie.

He used to work in agriculture. Now he is in industry.

Leistung ['laistuŋ] *f, -, en*

performance *n*

Ihre berufliche Leistung wird von allen Kollegen anerkannt.

Her professional performance is recognized by all her colleagues.

Leitung ['laituŋ] *f, -, kein Pl.*

leadership, management *n*

Die Geschäftsleitung hat die Arbeitszeiten geändert.

The company management has changed the working hours.

Lohn [lo:n] *m, -(e)s, Löhne*

wage *n*

Wie hoch ist dein Stundenlohn?

How high is your hourly wage?

Personal [pɛrzo'na:l] *n, -s, kein Pl.*

personnel, staff *n*

Die Firma ‚Schmidt & Koch' hat sehr gutes Personal.

The 'Schmidt & Koch' firm has a very good staff.

Qualität [kvali'tɛ:t] *f, -, -en*

quality *n*

Mit der Qualität der neuen Möbel bin ich zufrieden.

I'm satisfied with the quality of the new furniture.

Stelle ['ʃtɛlə] *f, -, -n*

position, job, opening *n*

In unserer Firma ist eine Stelle als Fahrer frei.

Our company has an opening for a driver.

Stellung ['ʃtɛluŋ] *f, -, -en*

job, position *n*

Meine Frau hat eine gute Stellung als Verkäuferin in einem Kaufhaus.

My wife has a good job as a salesperson in a department store.

tippen ['tip(ə)n] *V/t., tippte, hat getippt*

type *v*

Haben Sie den Brief an Herrn Behrens schon getippt?

Have you already typed the letter to Mr. Behrens?

Urlaub ['u:ə*laup] *m, -s, kein Pl.*

vacation, holiday's *(BE) n*

Ich mache gerne im Winter Urlaub.

I like to take a vacation in the winter.

verantwortlich [fɛə*'antvɔrtliç] *Adj.*

responsable

Herr Ahrens ist für die Qualitätskontrolle verantwortlich.

Mr. Ahrens is responsible for quality control.

Vertrag [fɛə*'traːk] *m*, -(e)s, Verträge
Heute habe ich den Arbeitsvertrag mit meiner neuen Firma unterschrieben.

contract *n*
Today I signed the contract with my new employer.

vertreten [fɛə*'treːt(ə)n] *V/t.*, vertrat, hat vertreten
Während des Urlaubs vertritt er die Abteilungsleiterin.

stand in for, represent, substitute for *v*
He represents the head of the department during her vacation.

Werk [vɛrk] *n*, -(e)s, -e
Die Firma hat ein Werk in Unna und eins in Hagen.

factory *n*
The company has a factory in Unna and another in Hagen.

Werkstatt ['vɛrkʃtat] *f*, -, Werkstätten
Die Maschine muss in der Werkstatt repariert werden.

workshop, garage *n*
The machine must be repaired in the workshop.

2001-4000

Abteilung [ap'tailuŋ] *f*, -, -en
In unserer Abteilung ist das Betriebsklima sehr gut.

department, division *n*
The work atmosphere is very good in our department.

Aktie ['aktsjə] *f*, -, -n
Die Banken raten, jetzt Aktien zu kaufen.

stock *n*
The banks advise us to buy stock now.

Anforderung ['anfɔrdəruŋ] *f*, -, -en
Die Anforderungen, die unsere Chefin stellt, sind hoch.

demand, requirement *n*
The demands our boss is making are high.

anstellen ['anʃtɛl(ə)n] *V/t.*, stellte an, hat angestellt
Sie ist nach der Probezeit fest angestellt worden.

employ *v*
After a trial period she was permanently employed.

Arbeitgeber ['arbait'geːbə*] *m*, -s, -, **Arbeitgeberin** ['arbait'geːbərin] *f*, -, -nen
Die Gewerkschaft und die Arbeitgeber verhandeln seit zwei Wochen über einen neuen Tarifvertrag.

employer *n*

The union and the employers have been working on a new contract for two weeks.

Arbeitnehmer [ˈarbaitˈneːmə*]
m, -s, -, **Arbeitnehmerin**
[ˈarbaitˈneːmərin] *f*, -, -nen | **employee, worker** *n*

Die Arbeitnehmer haben für den neuen Tarifvertrag gestimmt. | The workers voted for the new contract.

Arbeitslosigkeit [ˈarbaitsloːziçkait] *f*, -, *kein Pl.* | **unemployment** *n*

Die Arbeitslosigkeit ist im letzten Jahr um 2,7 % gestiegen. | Unemployment has increased 2.7% in the past year.

Arbeitsplatz [ˈarbaitsplats] *m*, -es, Arbeitsplätze | **job** *n*

In der Schiffsindustrie gibt es immer weniger Arbeitsplätze. | There are fewer and fewer jobs in the shipbuilding industry.

Arbeitszeit [ˈarbaitstsait] *f*, -, -en | **working hours** *n*

Die Arbeitszeit in unserem Betrieb ist von 7.30 Uhr bis 17.00 Uhr. | Working hours at our business are 7:30 am to 5:00 pm.

Belastung [bəˈlastuŋ] *f*, -, -en | **strain** *n*

Nachtdienst ist eine große Belastung für die Arbeiter. | The night shift is a serious strain on the workers.

Belegschaft [bəˈleːkʃaft] *f*, -, -en | **staff** *n*

Die Belegschaft ist mit den neuen Urlaubsterminen einverstanden. | The staff has agreed to the new vacation schedule.

Beratung [bəˈraːtuŋ] *f*, -, -en | **advice** *n*

Bernd weiß noch nicht, welchen Beruf er lernen möchte. Er hat sich deshalb bei der Berufsberatung des Arbeitsamtes informiert. | Bernd doesn't know yet what he wants to be. So he has gotten advice and information from the employment office.

Beschäftigte [bəˈʃɛftigtə] *m/f*, -n, -n | **employees** *n*

Fast alle Beschäftigten haben am Betriebsausflug teilgenommen. | Almost all of the employees participated in the company trip.

Daten [ˈdaːt(ə)n] *nur Pl.* | **data** *n*

Sie arbeitet am Computer und gibt Daten ein. | She works with a computer, entering data.

Diktat [dikˈtaːt] *n*, -s, -e | **dictation** *n*

Die Chefin spricht ihre Diktate auf Kassette. | The boss records her dictations on a cassette.

Direktor [di'rɛktɔr] *m,* -s, -en **director** *n*
Direktorin [dirɛk'to:rin] *f,* -, -nen
Die Firma wird von zwei Direkto- The company is led by two direc-
ren geleitet. tors.

entlassen [ɛnt'las(ə)n] *V/t.,* ent- **let go, dismiss, fire** *v*
ließ, hat entlassen
Warum der Kollege Scholz ent- No one knows why our colleague
lassen wurde, weiß niemand. Scholz was fired.

Feierabend ['faiə*a:b(ə)nt] *m,* -s, **closing time** *n*
-e
Freitags haben wir schon um Fridays we close early, at 1 pm.
13.00 Uhr Feierabend.

Gewerkschaft [gə'vɛrkʃaft] *f,* -, **(trade) union** *n*
-en
Die Gewerkschaften kämpfen seit The unions have been fighting for
Jahren für eine Arbeitszeitverkür- years for shorter hours.
zung.

Handwerk ['hantvɛrk] *n,* -s, *kein* **manual work, trade, craft** *n*
Pl.
Automechaniker ist seit Jahren Auto mechanics has for years
der beliebteste Handwerksberuf been the favorite career choice
bei Jungen. for young men learning a trade.

Kollege [kɔ'le:gə] *m,* -n, -n **colleague** *n*
Kollegin [kɔ'le:gin] *f,* -, -nen
In unserer Abteilung sagen alle In our department all colleagues
Kollegen ‚du' zueinander. are on a first-name basis.

Konferenz [kɔnfə'rɛnts] *f,* -, -en **conference, meeting** *n*
Auf der Vertreterkonferenz wurde At the sales meeting the new
der neue Verkaufsleiter vorge- sales director was introduced.
stellt.

Kongress [kɔn'grɛs] *m,* -es, -e **conference, meeting, conven-**
Dr. Matz habe ich auf einem **tion** *n*
Medizinerkongress in Düsseldorf I met Dr. Matz at a medical confe-
kennen gelernt. rence in Düsseldorf.

Leiter ['laitə*] *m,* -s, - **manager, head,** *n*
Leiterin ['laitərin] *f,* -, -nen
Vor sechs Jahren hat sie als Ver- She started out as a salesperson
käuferin bei uns angefangen, jetzt here six years ago; now she is
ist sie schon Leiterin des Super- already the manager of our supermarktes. market.

Mitarbeiter ['mitarbaitə*] *m, -s, -*
Mitarbeiterin ['mitarbaitərin] *f, -, -nen*
    worker, employee *n*

Alle Mitarbeiter sind zu einer Betriebsversammlung eingeladen worden.
    All employees were invited to a company meeting.

Mitbestimmung ['mitbəʃtimuŋ] *f, -, kein Pl.*
    worker participation *n*

Die Mitbestimmung der Arbeitnehmer in den Betrieben ist keine wichtige politische Streitfrage mehr.
    The participation of employees in management decisions of the company is no longer an important of political issue.

Misserfolg ['misɛə*fɔlk] *m, -s, -e*
    failure *n*

Für die jüngsten wirtschaftlichen Misserfolge wird der Verkaufschef verantwortlich gemacht.
    The sales manager will be held responsible for the latest economic failure.

Notizbuch [no'ti:tsbu:x] *n, -(e)s,* Notizbücher
    date book, notebook *n*

Mein Notizbuch ist mein ‚zweites Gedächtnis'.
    My notebook is my 'second memory.'

Praktikant [prakti'kant] *m, -en, -en*
Praktikantin [prakti'kantin] *f, -, -nen*
    trainee *n*

In den Semesterferien arbeitet sie als Praktikantin in einer Textilfabrik.
    During semester vacation she works as a trainee in a textile factory.

Projekt [pro'jɛkt] *n, -(e)s, -e*
    project *n*

Unsere Gruppe arbeitet an einem geheimen Projekt.
    Our group is working on a secret project.

Schreibmaschine ['ʃraipmaʃi:nə] *f, -, -n*
    typewriter *n*

Wie schnell kannst du Schreibmaschine schreiben?
    How fast can you type?

Sitzung ['zitsuŋ] *f, -, -en*
    meeting *n*

Auf der letzten Sitzung der Geschäftsleitung wurde eine neue Arbeitszeitregelung besprochen.
    At their last meeting the company executives discussed a new regulation of working hours.

Streik [ʃtraik] *m, -s, -s*
    strike *n*

Die Mehrheit der Beschäftigten stimmte für den Streik.
    The majority of employees voted for the strike.

streiken [ˈʃtraik(ə)n] *V/i.,* streikte, hat gestreikt
Die Kollegen streiken für kürzere Arbeitszeiten.

strike *v*
The workers are striking for shorter hours.

Tarif [taˈriːf] *m,* -s, -e
Die Gewerkschaften verhandeln mit den Arbeitgebern über neue Gehaltstarife.

salary *n*
The unions and employers are discussing new salaries.

Termin [tɛrˈmiːn] *m,* -s, -e
Montag ist der letzte Termin. Bis dahin muss die Ware beim Kunden sein.

(delivery) date *n*
Monday is the last date for delivery. The merchandise has to get to the client by then.

Unterschrift [ˈʊntəˈʃrift] *f,* -, -en
Der Vertrag ist ohne die Unterschrift von Frau Brand nicht gültig.

signature *n*
The contract isn't valid without the signature of Ms. Brand.

verpachten [fɛəˈpaxt(ə)n] *V/t.,* verpachtete, hat verpachtet
Er hat sein Geschäft verpachtet.

lease *v*
He leased his business.

Vertreter [fɛəˈtreːtə*] *m,* -s, -
Vertreterin [fɛəˈtreːtərin] *f,* -, -nen
Der Chef ist nicht da. Sie können aber mit seinem Vertreter sprechen.

representative *n*

The boss isn't here, but you can speak with his representative.

Vorgänger [ˈfoːə*gɛŋə*] *m,* -s, -
Vorgängerin [ˈfoːə*gɛŋərin] *f,* -, -nen
Der neue Abteilungsleiter ist ein ganz anderer Mensch als sein Vorgänger.

predecessor *n*

The new department head is very different from his predecessor.

Vorsitzende [ˈfoːə*zits(ə)ndə] *] m/f.,* -n, -n
Sie ist seit acht Jahren Vorsitzende des Betriebsrates.

chairman, chairwoman, chair *(o a meeting) n*
She's been chair of the local union chapter for eight years.

Zusammenarbeit [tsuˈzamənarbait] *f,* -, *kein Pl.*
Die Zusammenarbeit mit der neuen Kollegin klappt gut.

cooperation, collaboration, *n*

Collaboration with the new colleague is going well.

zusammenarbeiten
[tsu'zamənarbait(ə)n] *V/i., + Präp.*
(mit), arbeitete zusammen, hat
zusammengearbeitet
Edith ist sehr nervös. Mit ihr kann
man nicht gut zusammenarbeiten.

cooperate, collaborate, work with *v*

Edith is very nervous. It's hard to
collaborate with her.

zuständig ['tsu:ʃtɛndiçº] *Adj., keine Komp.*
Wer ist in Ihrer Firma für Reklama-
tionen zuständig?

responsible

Who in your business is responsible for handling complaints?

6.5 Post und Telefon | 1-2000

6.5 Post Office, Telephone

Adresse [a'drɛsə] *f, -, -n*
Wie ist seine neue Adresse?

address *n*
What's his new address?

Anruf ['anru:f] *m, -es, -e*
Gab es einen Anruf für mich?

call *n*
Was there a call for me?

anrufen ['anru:f(ə)n] *V/t.,* rief an,
hat angerufen
Ich werde Sie morgen bestimmt
anrufen.

call, telephone *v*

I will certainly call you tomorrow.

Anschrift ['anʃrift] *f, -, -en*
Die Anschrift war falsch. Deshalb
kam der Brief zurück.

address *n*
The address was wrong. That's
why the letter was returned.

besetzt [bə'zɛtst] *Adj., keine
Komp.*
Ich habe versucht, dich anzuru-
fen, aber es war dauernd besetzt.

busy

I tried to call you, but the line was
constantly busy.

Brief [bri:f] *m, -(e)s, -e*
Der Brief von Frau Klausen muss
schnell beantwortet werden.

letter *n*
The letter from Ms. Klausen has to
be answered right away.

Briefmarke ['briːfmarkə] *f, -, -n*
Hast du eine 55-cent-Briefmarke für mich?

postage stamp *n*
Do you have a 55 cent stamp for me?

Empfänger [ɛm'pfɛŋə*] *m, -s, -*
Empfängerin [ɛm'pfɛŋərin] *f, -, -nen*
,Empfänger unbekannt' stand auf dem Umschlag.

addressee *n*

The envelope was stamped "addressee unknown."

Gespräch [gə'ʃprɛːç] *n, -(e)s, -e*
Auf Apparat Nr. 7 ist ein Gespräch für Sie.

call *n*
There's a call for you on line 7.

Paket [pa'keːt] *n, -(e)s, -e*
Große Firmen schicken ihre Pakete nicht mehr mit der Post, sondern mit einem privaten Paketdienst.

package, parcel (BE) *n*
Large firms no longer use the post office to send their packages; they use private package delivery services.

Porto ['pɔrto] *n, -s, -s (Porti)*
Wie hoch ist das Porto für diesen Brief nach Kanada?

postage *n*
How much is the postage for this letter to Canada?

Post [pɔst] *f, -, kein Pl.*
Bring bitte Briefmarken von der Post mit.

post office *n*
Please bring some stamps from the post office.

Päckchen ['pɛkçən] *n, -s, -*
Es ist ein Päckchen für dich angekommen.

small package, parcel *(BE)* *n*
A small package arrived for you.

Telefon ['teːlefoːn] *n, -s, -e*
Man kann Petra jetzt anrufen. Sie hat ein Telefon.

telephone *n*
We can call Petra now. She has a telephone.

Telefonbuch [tele'foːnbuːx] *n, -(e)s, Telefonbücher*
Deinen Namen konnte ich im Telefonbuch nicht finden.

telephone book *n*

I couldn't find your name in the telephone book.

telefonieren [telefo'niːrən] *V/i.,*
telefonierte, hat telefoniert
Ich habe ihn lange nicht gesehen, aber wir telefonieren jede Woche miteinander.

call, talk on the telephone *v*
I haven't seen him for a long time, but we talk on the telephone every week.

Telefonzelle [tele'fo:ntsɛlə] *f,* -, -n
Sie hat mich aus einer Telefonzelle angerufen.

public telephone, telephone booth *n*
She called me from a public telephone.

Telegramm [tele'gram] *n,* -s, -e
Dein Telegramm habe ich bekommen.

telegram *n*
I got your telegram.

2001-4000

Absender ['apzɛndə*] *m,* -s, -

Den Absender des Briefes kenne ich nicht.

sender, return address, person who sends (a letter) *n*
I don't know the person who sent this letter.

Anschluss ['anʃlus] *m,* -es, Anschlüsse
Ich konnte nicht telefonieren. Mein Anschluss war gestört.

connection *n*

I couldn't make the call. My connection was poor.

Briefkasten ['bri:fkast(ə)n] *m,* -s, Briefkästen
Der Briefkasten wird dreimal täglich geleert.

mailbox *n*

There are three pickups a day at this mailbox.

Briefträger ['bri:ftrɛ:gə*] *m,* -s, -
Briefträgerin ['bri:ftrɛ:gərin] *f,* -, -nen
Bei uns kommt der Briefträger erst mittags.

letter carrier, mailman, postman *(BE) n*

Our letter carrier doesn't come until around noon.

Briefumschlag ['bri:fumʃla:k] *m,* -s, Briefumschläge
Auf dem Briefumschlag stand kein Absender.

envelope *n*

There was no return address on the envelope.

Drucksache ['drukzaxə] *f,* -, -n
Diese Papiere kannst du als Drucksache schicken. Das ist billiger. (Im Inland: Infopost)

printed matter *n*
You can send these papers as printed matter; that's cheaper.

Einschreiben ['ainʃraib(ə)n] *n*, -s, -
Schick den Brief bitte als Einschreiben!

certified mail, recorded delivery *(BE) n*
Please send this letter as certified mail.

Ferngespräch ['fɛə*ngəʃprɛːç] *n*, -s, -e
Die Gebühren für Ferngespräche werden billiger.

long distance call *n*
The price of long distance calls is going down.

Kabine [ka'biːnə] *f*, -, -n
In der Kabine können Sie auch angerufen werden.

telephone booth, public telephone *n*
You can also receive calls at a public telephone booth.

Luftpost ['luftpɔst] *f*, -, *kein Pl.*
Trotz Luftpost war der Brief eine Woche unterwegs.

airmail *n*
The letter took a week, even by airmail.

Ortsgespräch ['ɔrtsgeʃprɛç] *n*, -s, -e
Das Gespräch kostet nicht viel, es ist ein Ortsgespräch.

local call *n*
The call won't cost much; it's a local call.

Postamt ['pɔstamt] *n*, -(e)s, Postämter
Das Postamt ist morgens von 9.00 Uhr bis 12.00 Uhr geöffnet.

post office *n*
The post office is open in the morning from 9:00 until 12:00.

Postanweisung ['pɔstanvaizuŋ] *f*, -, -en
Bitte schick mir das Geld mit einer Postanweisung.

postal, money order *n*
Please send me a money order.

Postkarte ['pɔstkartə] *f*, -, -n
Wir schicken Ihnen eine Postkarte, wenn die Ware angekommen ist.

postcard *n*
We'll send you a postcard when the goods have arrived.

postlagernd ['pɔstlaːgə*nt] *Adj.*, *keine Komp.*
Bitte schicke die Briefe postlagernd!

general delivery *n*
Please send the letters to general delivery.

Postleitzahl ['pɔstlait-tsaːl] *f*, -, -en
Kennst du die Postleitzahl von Hannover?

postal code, postcode, ZIP code *[USA] n*
Do you know the postal code for Hannover?

telegrafieren [telegra'fiːrən] *V/i.,*
telegrafierte, hat telegrafiert
Ich telegrafiere euch, wann ich
zurückkomme.

send a telegraph *v*

I'll send you a telegraph to let you
know when I'll be coming back.

6.6 Behörden, Polizei | 1-2000

Amt [amt] *n,* -(e)s, Ämter
Das Einwohnermeldeamt ist im
1. Stock, Zimmer 112.

bureau, office *n*
The bureau where you register is
in room 112, upstairs.

Ausweis ['ausvais] *m,* -(e)s,-e

Für den Ausweis brauchen Sie ein
neues Foto.

identification *(documents, papers),* **ID** *n*
You need a new photo for your ID.

Behörde [bə'høːə*də] *f,* -, -n
Er arbeitet als Beamter in der Ver-
kehrsbehörde.

authority, department *n*
He works in the office of the traffic
authority.

Feuerwehr ['fɔiə*veːə*] *f,* -, -en
Der Motorbrand wurde von der
Feuerwehr gelöscht.

fire department, fire brigade *n*
The fire in the motor was extin-
guished by the fire department.

Formular [fɔrmu'laː*] *n,* -s, -e
Für die Anmeldung müssen Sie
dieses Formular ausfüllen.

form *n*
For registration you have to fill out
this form.

Gebühr [gə'byːə*] *f,* -, -en
Der Reisepass kostet 20,- Euro
Gebühr.

fee *n*
There's a 20 euro fee for issuing
the passport.

Genehmigung [gə'neːmiguŋ] *f,*
-, -en
Auch für den Bau der Garage
brauchst du eine Baugenehmi-
gung.

permit *n*

You also need a permit to build
the garage.

gültig ['gyltiç°] *Adj., keine Komp.*
Der Ausweis ist fünf Jahre gültig.

good, in effect
The ID is good for five years.

Maßnahme ['maːsnaːmə] *f,* -, -n
Die Maßnahmen der Polizei hatten keinen Erfolg.

measures *n*
The measures the police took were unsuccessful.

öffentlich ['œf(ə)ntlɪç] *Adj.*
Dieser Gerichtsprozess ist nicht öffentlich.

public, open to the public
This trial is not public.

Polizei [poli'tsai] *f,* -, *kein Pl.*
Die Parkuhren werden selten von der Polizei kontrolliert.

police *n*
Parking meters are seldom controlled by the police.

Polizist [poli'tsist] *m,* -en, -en
Polizistin [poli'tsistin] *f,* -, -nen
Fragen Sie den Verkehrspolizisten dort. Er weiß sicher, wo die Uhlandstraße ist.

policeman, policewoman, police officer *n*
Ask that policeman. He certainly knows where Uhland Street is.

Unterlage ['untə*laːgə] *f,* -e, -en *(meist Pl.)*
Für Ihren Antrag fehlen noch wichtige Unterlagen.

document *n*
Some important documents are still missing in your application.

unterschreiben [untə*'ʃraib(ə)n] *V/t.,* unterschrieb, hat unterschrieben
Sie müssen Ihren Antrag noch unterschreiben.

sign *v*
You still have to sign your application.

Urkunde ['uːə*kundə] *f,* -, -n
Die Geburtsurkunde Ihres Kindes können Sie morgen abholen.

document, certificate *n*
You can pick up your child's birth certificate tomorrow.

verhaften [vɛə*'haft(ə)n] *V/t.,* verhaftete, hat verhaftet
Wegen Fluchtgefahr ist der Täter verhaftet worden.

arrest *v*
The suspect was arrested because they were afraid he would flee.

verlängern [fɛə*'lɛŋə*n] *V/t.,* verlängerte, hat verlängert
Der Ausweis kann verlängert werden.

renew, extend *v*
The ID can be renewed.

Verwaltung [fɛə*'valtuŋ] *f,* -, -en
Du musst deinen neuen Wohnsitz bei der Stadtverwaltung anmelden.

administration *n*
You have to inform the city administration about your new address.

Vorschrift ['foː*ʃrift] *f, -, -en*
Der Plan für das neue Haus entspricht in einigen Punkten nicht den Bauvorschriften.

instruction, regulation, code *n*
The plan for the new house does not follow the official codes in every detail.

2001-4000

abmelden ['apmɛld(ə)n] *V/t., refl.,*
meldete ab, hat abgemeldet
Hast du dich in deinem alten Wohnort schon abgemeldet?

leave *(officially) v*

Have you officially left your former place of residence?

Akte ['aktə] *f, -, -n*
Der Rechtsanwalt hat sich die Gerichtsakten angesehen.

file *n*
The lawyer looked over the court files.

anmelden ['anmɛld(ə)n] *V/t., refl.,*
+ Präp. (für), meldete an, hat angemeldet
Das Auto wird morgen angemeldet.
Ich habe mich für die Prüfung angemeldet.

register, sign up for *v*

The car will be registered tomorrow.
I've signed up for the test.

Antrag ['antraːk] *m, -(e)s, Anträge*
Über den Antrag hat man noch nicht entschieden.

application *n*
Nothing has yet been decided about the application.

ausfüllen ['ausfyl(ə)n] *V/t., füllte*
aus, hat ausgefüllt
Für den Antrag muss dieses Formular ausgefüllt werden.

fill out, complete *v*

For the application, this form must be filled out.

beantragen [bə'antraːg(ə)n] *V/t.,*
beantragte, hat beantragt
Wegen eines schweren Berufsunfalls hat er die Rente beantragt.

apply for *v*

He has applied for workmen's compensation because of a bad accident.

Bestimmung [bə'ʃtimuŋ] *f, -, -en*
In unserer Gemeinde gibt es die Bestimmung, dass Neubauten nicht mehr als zwei Stockwerke haben dürfen.

regulation *n*
In our town there is a regulation that new buildings not be higher than three stories.

eintragen [ˈaintraːg(ə)n] *V/t.,* trug ein, hat eingetragen
Sie müssen Ihren Namen in die Liste eintragen.

register *v*

You have to register your name in this list.

Papiere [paˈpiːrə] *nur Pl.*
Der Polizist bat den Autofahrer um die Wagenpapiere.

papers, documents *n*
The policeman asked the driver for the car's documents.

Paragraph [paraˈgraːf] *m,* -en, -en
Sie hat Paragraph 4 der Straßenverkehrsordnung verletzt.

section, part *n*

She violated section 4 of the traffic rules.

Regelung [ˈreːgəluŋ] *f,* -, -en
Bei uns im Büro gibt es die Regelung, dass nur während der Pausen geraucht werden darf.

rule *n*
In our office there is a rule that no smoking is allowed except during breaks.

Schalter [ˈʃaltəˀ] *m,* -s, -
Briefmarken gibt es am Schalter 3.

window *n*
You can buy stamps at window 3.

Stempel [ˈʃtɛmp(ə)l] *m,* -s, -
Ohne Behördenstempel ist die Genehmigung ungültig.

stamp *n*
The permit isn't good without an official stamp.

Zoll [tsɔl] *m,* -s, *kein Pl.*
Der Zoll hat uns an der Grenze nicht kontrolliert.

customs *n*
Customs didn't check us at the border.

6.7 Rechtswesen | 1-2000

6.7 Law

bestrafen [bəˈʃtraːf(ə)n] *V/t.,* bestrafte, hat bestraft
Der Dieb ist mit vier Monaten Gefängnis bestraft worden.

sentence, punish *v*

The thief was sentenced to four months in prison.

betrügen [bəˈtryːg(ə)n] *V/t.,* betrog, hat betrogen
Sie hat ihre Geschäftspartner betrogen.

cheat, deceive *v*

She deceived her business partners.

Beweis [bə'vais] *m*, -es, -e
Sie ist verdächtig, aber es gibt noch keinen Beweis für ihre Schuld.

evidence, proof *n*
She is under suspicion, but there's no proof of her guilt.

---

beweisen [bə'vaiz(ə)n] *V/i.*, bewies, hat bewiesen
Die Polizei hat ihm bewiesen, dass er am Tatort war.

prove *n*

The police proved he was at the site of the crime.

Dieb [di:p] *m*, -(e)s, -e
Diebin ['di:bin] *f*, -, -nen
Der Dieb war der Polizei bekannt.

thief, robber *n*

The police knew the thief.

Gefängnis [gə'fɛŋnis] *n*, -ses, -se
Sie wurde zu einer Gefängnisstrafe verurteilt.

prison *n*
She was given a sentence in prison.

Gericht [gə'riçt] *n*, -(e)s, -e
Das Gericht sprach ihn schuldig.

court *n*
The court found him guilty.

Gesetz [gə'zɛts] *n*, -es, -e
Manche Leute finden, dass die Gesetze nicht hart genug sind.

law *n*
Some people think the laws aren't strict enough.

Gewalt [gə'valt] *f*, -, *kein Pl.*
Nur mit Gewalt konnte er gestoppt werden.

force *n*
It took force to stop him.

Mord [mɔrt] *m*, -es, -e
Er steht wegen Mordes vor Gericht.

murder *n*
He's on trial for murder.

Prozess [pro'tsɛs] *m*, -es, -e
Den Prozess haben wir leider verloren.

case, trial *n*

Unfortunately, we lost the case.

Recht [rɛçt] *n*, -s, -e
Warum verteidigt ihr eure Rechte nicht?

right *n*
Why aren't you defending your rights?

Recht *n*, -s, *kein Pl.*
Das Recht ist auf eurer Seite.

right *n*
Right is on your side.

Rechtsanwalt ['rɛçtsanvalt] *m*,-s, Rechtsanwälte, **Rechtsanwältin** [-anvɛltin] *f*, -, nen
Rechtsanwalt Dr. Sauer ist Spezialist für Steuerrecht.

attorney, lawyer *n*

Mr. Sauer, the lawyer, is a specialist in tax law.

Richter [ˈrɪçtə*] *m*, -s, -
Richterin [ˈrɪçtərin] *f*, -, -nen
Die Richterin war sehr hart.

judge *n*

The judge was very hard.

Schuld [ʃult] *f*, -, *kein Pl.*
Er leugnet seine Schuld.

guilt *n*

He denies his guilt.

schuldig [ˈʃuldiç°] *Adj.*
Der Dieb wurde schuldig gesprochen.

guilty

The thief was found guilty.

stehlen [ˈʃteːl(ə)n] *V/t.*, stahl, hat gestohlen
Mein Fahrrad ist gestohlen worden.

steal *v*

My bicycle was stolen.

Strafe [ˈʃtraːfə] *f*, -, -n
Sie bekam eine Geldstrafe.

punishment, fine, sentence *n*

She had to pay a fine.

Urteil [ˈurtail] *n*, -s, -e
Auch der Rechtsanwalt fand das Urteil gerecht.

sentence, judgement *n*

Even the lawyer thought the sentence was just.

Verbot [fɛə*ˈboːt] *n*, -(e)s, -e
Dieses Verbot kannte ich nicht.

prohibition, ban *n*

I didn't know about this ban.

Verbrecher [fɛə*ˈbrɛçə*] *m*, -s, -
Verbrecherin [fɛə*ˈbrɛçərin] *f*, -, -nen
Der Verbrecher wurde zum zweiten Mal wegen einer ähnlichen Tat verurteilt.

criminal *n*

The criminal was sentenced for the second time for a similar crime.

Verdacht [fɛə*ˈdaxt] *m*, -(e)s, *kein Pl.*
Die Polizei hatte einen Verdacht, konnte ihn aber nicht beweisen.

suspicion *n*

The police had a suspicion but couldn't prove it.

verdächtig [fɛə*ˈdɛçtiç°] *Adj.*
Er hat sich verdächtig verhalten, aber er hat das Geld nicht gestohlen.

suspicious

He acted suspicious but he hadn't stolen the money.

Verteidiger [fɛə*ˈtaidigə*] *m*, -s, -
Verteidigerin [fɛə*ˈtaidigərin] *f*, -, -nen
Der Verteidiger überzeugte den Richter von der Unschuld der Angeklagten.

attorney for the defense, defense lawyer *n*

The attorney for the defense convinced the judge of his client's innocence.

verurteilen [fɛə*'urtail(ə)n] *V/t.,*
veruteilte, hat verurteilt
Er wurde zu einer Gefängnisstrafe
verurteilt.

sentence *v*

He was sentenced to prison.

Zeuge ['tsɔigə] *m,* -n, -n
Zeugin ['tsɔigin] *f,* -, -nen
Die Zeugin konnte sich genau an
die Tatzeit erinnern.

witness *n*

The witness could remember pre-
cisely the time of the crime.

| 2001-4000 |

Angeklagte ['angəklaːktə] *m/f,*
-n, -n
Die Angeklagte leugnete ihre
Schuld.

defendant *n*

The defendant denied her guilt.

anklagen ['ankla:g(ə)n] *V/t., +*
Präp. (wegen), klagte an, hat an-
geklagt
Er wurde wegen Mordes ange-
klagt.

accuse, charge *(with a crime) v*

He was charged with murder.

Anzeige ['antsaigə] *f,* -, -n
Die Anzeige gegen ihn wurde zurückgenommen.

report *n*
The report against him was re-
tracted.

anzeigen ['antsaig(ə)n] *V/t., +*
Präp. (wegen), zeigte an, hat an-
gezeigt
Er wurde wegen Raubs ange-
zeigt.

report *v*

He was reported for theft.

Berufung [bə'ru:fuŋ] *f,* -, -en
Gegen das Urteil legte die
Rechtsanwältin Berufung ein.

appeal *n*
The lawyer has filed an appeal
against the sentence.

beschuldigen [bə'ʃuldig(ə)n] *V/t.,*
beschuldigte, hat beschuldigt
Er wird beschuldigt, seine Kunden betrogen zu haben.

accuse, charge *v*

He's accused of cheating his
clients.

Betrüger [bə'try:gə*] *m,* -s, -
Betrügerin [bə'try:gərin] *f,* -, -nen
Pass auf! Er ist ein Betrüger.

swindler *n*

Watch out! He's a swindler.

Beute ['bɔitə] *f, -, kein Pl.*
Die Polizei konnte die Beute bis heute nicht finden.

loot *n*
The police still haven't found the loot.

Einbrecher ['ainbrɛçə*] *m, -s, -*
Einbrecherin ['ainbrɛçərin] *f, -, -nen*
Die Einbrecher waren genau informiert, wann niemand im Haus war.

robber *n*

The robbers knew exactly when no one would be home.

ermorden [ɛə*'mɔrd(ə)n] *V/t.*, ermordete, hat ermordet
Das Opfer wurde ermordet.

murder *v*

The victim was murdered.

erschießen [ɛə*'ʃiːs(ə)n] *V/t.*, erschoss, hat erschossen
Einer der Täter wurde von der Polizei erschossen.

shoot *v*

One of the perpetrators was shot by the police.

Fall [fal] *m, -(e)s, Fälle*
Die Zeitungen berichten täglich über den Mordfall.

case *n*
The newspapers report about the murder case every day.

fliehen ['fliː(ə)n] *V/i.*, floh, ist geflohen
Der Angeklagte ist während seines Prozesses geflohen.

flee, escape *v*

The accused fled during his trial.

Häftling ['hɛftliŋ] *m, -s, -e*
Einige Häftlinge lernen im Gefängnis einen Beruf.

prisoner *n*
Some prisoners learn a trade while in prison.

Justiz [jus'tiːts] *f, -, kein Pl.*
In der Presse wird die Justiz wegen der langen Dauer der Verfahren kritisiert.

justice *n*
In the press, justice is criticized for its long procedures.

Klage ['klaːgə] *f, -, -n*
Der Prozessgegner hat seine Klage zurückgezogen.

suit, complaint *n*
The opposing party has withdrawn his suit.

Kommissar [kɔmi'saː*] *m, -s, -e*
Kommissarin [kɔmi'saːrin] *f, -, -nen*
Er hat als Verkehrspolizist angefangen, jetzt ist er Kommissar geworden.

inspector, commissioner *n*

He began as a traffic policeman; now he is an inspector.

Motiv [mo'ti:f] *n*, -s, -e
Die Kommissarin sucht immer noch ein Motiv für die Tat.

motive *n*
The inspector is still looking for a motive for the crime.

Mörder ['mœrdə*] *m*, -s, -
Mörderin ['mœrdərin] *f*, -, -nen
Die Mörderin hat den Mord zugegeben.

murderer *n*

The murderer has pled guilty.

Raub [raup] *m*, -(e)s, *kein Pl.*
Raub muss mit Gefängnis bestraft werden.

robbery *n*
Robbery must be punished with a prison sentence.

---

schwören ['ʃvø:rən] *V/i.*, schwor, hat geschworen
Er schwor, die Wahrheit gesagt zu haben.

swear *v*

He swore he told the truth.

Staatsanwalt ['ʃta:tsanvalt] *m*, -(e)s, Staatsanwälte
Staatsanwältin ['ʃta:tsanvɛltin] *f*, -, -nen
Der Staatsanwalt konnte dem Angeklagten seine Schuld nicht beweisen.

district attorney,
public prosecutor *(BE)* *n*

The district attorney couldn't prove the defendant was guilty.

Täter ['tɛ:tə*] *m*, -s, -
Täterin ['tɛ:tərin] *f*, -, -nen
Die Zeugin konnte den Täter nicht wiedererkennen.

perpetrator *n*

The witness couldn't identify the perpetrator.

---

töten ['tø:t(ə)n] *V/t.*, tötete, hat getötet
Bei dem Verkehrsunfall wurde eine Person getötet.

kill *v*

One person was killed in the traffic accident.

Verfahren [fɛə*'fa:rən] *n*, -s, -
Das Gerichtsverfahren wird bei diesem schwierigen Fall sicher sehr lange dauern.

proceedings *n*
The court proceedings will certainly last a long time in this difficult case.

Verhandlung [fɛə*'handluŋ] *f*, -, -en
Die Verhandlung wurde unterbrochen.

trial, hearing *n*

The trial was interrupted.

Vernehmung [fɛə*'neːmuŋ] *f*, -, -en

Die Vernehmung der Zeugen brachte die Polizei keinen Schritt weiter.

examination, questioning *n*

Questioning the witnesses didn't help the police at all.

verstoßen [fɛə*'ʃtoːs(ə)n] *V/i.*, + *Präp.* (gegen), verstieß, hat verstoßen

Dem Firmeninhaber wird vorgeworfen, gegen das Arbeitsschutzgesetz verstoßen zu haben.

offend, violate *v*

The firm owner is accused of having violated the law that protects workers.

7.1 Theater, Film, bildende Kunst | 1-2000

bekannt [bə'kant] *Adj.,* -er, am -esten
Der Schauspieler ist bisher nur durch seine Theaterrollen bekannt geworden.

well known, famous
Up to now the actor is only well known for his theater roles.

berühmt [bə'ry:mt] *Adj.,* -er, am -esten
Sie ist durch den Film ‚Das Tal' berühmt geworden.

famous
She became famous for her film role in "The Valley."

Bühne ['by:nə] *f,* -, -n
Die Bühne im großen Theatersaal ist für dieses Stück nicht geeignet.

stage *n*
The stage in the large theater is not appropriate for this play.

Eintritt ['aintrit] *m,* -(e)s, *kein Pl.*
Der Eintritt kostet zwischen 8,- und 12,- Euro.

admission *(ticket) n*
Admission costs between 8.– and 12.– euros.

Film [film] *m,* -(e)s, -e
In diesem Kino werden recht gute Filme gezeigt.

film, movie *n*
This (film) theater shows very good films.

Instrument [instru'mɛnt] *n,* -s, -e
Spielst du ein Musikinstrument?

instrument *n*
Do you play a musical instrument?

Kapitel [ka'pit(ə)l] *n,* -s, -
Der Roman hat sechs Kapitel.

chapter *n*
The novel has six chapters.

Kino ['ki:no] *n,* -s, -s
Dieses Kino zeigt nachmittags Kinderfilme.

film theater, movie theater, cinema (BE) *n*
This movie theater shows children's movies in the afternoon.

Kultur [kul'tu:ə*] *f,* -, -en
In unserer Stadt gibt es jeden Sommer ein spezielles Kulturprogramm.

culture, civilization, fine arts *n*
In our city every summer there is a special program of cultural events.

Kunst [kunst] *f, -,* Künste
Der Musikabend wurde vom Kunstverein organisiert.

art *n*
The evening of music was organized by the art society.

Künstler [ˈkynstlə*] *m, -s, -*
Künstlerin [ˈkynstlərin] *f, -, -nen*
Einige Bilder des Künstlers sind in der Hamburger Kunsthalle zu sehen.

artist *n*

Some of the artist's pictures are on view at the Hamburg Art Museum.

Literatur [litəraˈtuːə*] *f, -, -en*
Afrikanische Literatur ist in Europa nicht sehr bekannt.

literature *n*
African literature is not well known in Europe.

malen [ˈmaːl(ə)n] *V/t.,* malte, hat gemalt
Wer hat dieses Bild gemalt?

paint *v*

Who painted this picture?

Maler [ˈmaːlə*] *m, -s, -*
Malerin [ˈmaːlərin] *f, -, -nen*
Die Arbeiten dieser Malerin sind sehr bekannt.

painter *n*

The works of this painter are very well-known.

Museum [muˈzeːum] *n, -s,* Museen
Das Museum ist auch am Sonntag geöffnet.

museum *n*

The museum is also open on Sunday.

Publikum [ˈpuːblikum] *n, -s, kein Pl.*
Das Publikum des Stadttheaters ist sehr kritisch.

audience, public *n*

The audience at the city theater is very critical.

Rolle [ˈrɔlə] *f, -, -n*
Diese Rolle ist besonders schwierig zu spielen.

role, part *n*
This role is especially difficult to act.

Schauspieler [ˈʃauʃpiːlə*] *m, -s, -,*
Schauspielerin *f, -, -nen*
Die Schauspieler des Stücks wurden von allen gelobt.

actor *n*

The actors in the play were praised by everyone.

spielen [ˈʃpiːl(ə)n] *V/t.,* spielte, hat gespielt
Sie hat schon als Schülerin Theater gespielt.

act, play a part *v*

She has acted in the theater since she was in school.

Theater [te'a:tə*] *n*, -s, -
Das Stadttheater hat ein treues Publikum.

theater (*BE:* theatre) *n*
The city theater has a loyal audience.

Theaterstück [te'a:tə*ʃtyk] *n*, -(e)s, -e
Das Theaterstück hatte großen Erfolg.

play *n*

The play was a great success.

Titel ['ti:t(ə)l] *m*, -s, -
Den Titel ihres neuesten Buches kenne ich nicht.

title *n*
I don't know the title of her most recent book.

Vorstellung ['fo:ə*ʃtɛluŋ] *f*, -, -en
Die Vorstellungen sind gut besucht.

performance *n*
The performances are well attended.

---

zeichnen ['tsaiçnən] *V/t.*, zeichnete, hat gezeichnet
Zeichnen ist mein Hobby.

draw *v*

Drawing is my hobby.

Zuschauer ['tsu:ʃauə*] *m*, -s, -
Zuschauerin [-ʃauərin] *f*, -, -nen
Die modernen Theaterstücke haben wenig Zuschauer.

spectator *n*

Modern plays have few spectators.

2001-4000

Akt [akt] *m*, -(e)s, -e
Nach dem 3. Akt gibt es eine Pause.

act *n*
There's an intermission after the third act.

Aufführung ['auffy:ruŋ] *f*, -, -en
Seit Monaten sind die Aufführungen ausverkauft.

performance *n*
The performances have been sold out for months.

Ausstellung ['ausʃtɛluŋ] *f*, -, -en
Die Ausstellung des berühmten Malers war gut besucht.

exhibition *n*
The exhibition of the famous painter was well attended.

Autor ['autɔr] *m*, -s, -en
Autorin [au'to:rin] *f*, -, -nen
Der Autor des Romans ist nicht sehr bekannt.

author *n*

The author of the novel isn't well known.

beliebt [bə'li:pt] *Adj.,* -er, am -esten
Der Schauspieler ist beim Publikum sehr beliebt.

popular
The actor is very popular with the audience.

Drama ['dra:ma] *n,* -s, Dramen
Komödien sind beim Publikum beliebter als Dramen.

drama *n*
The public prefers comedies to dramas.

Galerie [galə'ri:] *f,* -, -n
Die Galerie veranstaltet regelmäßig Ausstellungen junger Künstler.

gallery *n*
The gallery regularly organizes exhibitions of younger artists' work.

Gedicht [gə'diçt] *n,* -(e)s, -e
Der Autor las aus seinem neuesten Gedichtband vor.

poem *n*
The author read from his latest volume of poems.

Geschichte [gə'ʃiçtə] *f,* -, -n
Ich lese gerne Kurzgeschichten.

story *n*
I like to read short stories.

Komödie [ko'mø:diə] *f,* -, -n
Es gibt heute wenige Autoren, die Komödien schreiben.

comedy *n*
There are few authors today who write comedies.

Leser ['le:zə*] *m,* -s, -
Leserin ['le:zərin] *f,* -, -nen
Für den normalen Leser ist der Roman schwer zu verstehen.

reader *n*

This novel is too difficult for the normal reader to understand.

Lyrik ['ly:rik] *f,* -, *kein Pl.*
Moderne Lyrik findet großes Interesse.

lyric poetry *n*
Many are interested in modern lyric poetry.

Motiv [mo'ti:f] *n,* -s, -e
Die Motive des Malers sind in allen Bildern ähnlich.

theme, motif *n*
The themes are similar in all the pictures by this artist.

Pinsel ['pinz(ə)l] *m,* -s, -
Der Pinsel ist zu dick.

brush *n*
This brush is too thick.

Plakat [pla'ka:t] *n,* -(e)s, -e
Das Plakat finde ich zu bunt.

poster *n*
I think the poster is too colorful.

Regisseur [reʒi'sø'ə*] *m,* -s, -e
Regisseurin *f,* -, -nen
Eigentlich ist er Theaterregisseur, aber er macht auch Filme.

director *n*

He is a director in theater, but he also makes films.

Roman [ro'ma:n] *m,* -s, -e
In den Zeitungskritiken wurde der
Roman gelobt.

novel *n*
The novel was praised by newspaper critics.

Schriftsteller ['ʃriftʃtɛlə*] *m,*
-s, -
Schriftstellerin ['ʃriftʃtɛlərin]
f, -, -nen
Das neue Buch der Schriftstellerin erscheint im Herbst.

writer, author *n*

The author's new book will come
out this autumn.

Szene ['stse:nə] *f,* -, -n
Der Regisseur ließ die Szene
noch einmal spielen.

scene *n*
The director had the scenes
played again.

Zeichnung ['tsaiçnuŋ] *f,* -, -en
Die frühen Zeichnungen des Malers sind wenig bekannt.

drawing, sketch *n*
The painter's early drawings are
not well known.

7.2 Musik | 1-2000

7.2 Music

Beifall ['baifal] *m,* -s, *kein Pl.*
Das Orchester bekam viel Beifall.

applause *n*
The orchestra got a lot of applause.

Klavier [kla'vi:ə*] *n,* -s, -e
Als Kind habe ich Klavierunter-
richt gehabt.

piano *n*
I had piano lessons when I was a
child.

klingen ['kliŋən] *V/i.,* klang, hat
geklungen
Die Melodie klingt gut.

sound *v*

The melody sounds good.

Konzert [kɔn'tsɛrt] *n,* -(e)s, -e
Im 3. Programm hören Sie um
19.30 Uhr ein Konzert mit Werken
von Bach und Händel.

concert *n*
At 7:30pm there is a radio concert
on the third program with works
by Bach and Händel.

Lied [li:t] *n,* -(e)s, -er
Das Lied hat einen einfachen
Text.

song *n*
The song has a simple text.

Melodie [melo'diː] *f, -, -n*
Es wurden berühmte Melodien gespielt.

melody *n*
Famous melodies were played.

Musik [mu'ziːk] *f, -, kein Pl.*
Arabische Musik klingt für Europäer sehr fremd.

music *n*
Arabian music sounds very foreign to western ears.

Oper ['oːpə*] *f, -, -n*
In dieser Oper wird der italienische Originaltext gesungen.

opera *n*
In this opera the original Italian text will be sung.

Orchester [ɔr'kɛstə*] *n, -s, -*
Sie spielt Klavier in einem Rundfunkorchester.

orchestra *n*
She plays piano for a radio orchestra.

Schallplatte ['ʃalplatə] *f, -, -n*
Sie sammelt Schallplatten mit alten Opernarien.

record *n*
She collects records with old opera arias.

singen ['ziŋən] *V/t., i.,* sang, hat gesungen
Die Kinder sangen ihr ein Geburtstagslied.

sing *v*

The children sang "Happy Birthday" to her.

2001-4000

Chor [koːə*] *m, -(e)s, Chöre*
Auf der Schulfeier sang der Schulchor drei Lieder.

choir *n*
The school choir sang three songs at the school celebration.

Geige ['gaigə] *f, -, -n*
Geige spielen ist schwer zu lernen.

violin *n*
Learning to play the violin is difficult.

Kapelle [ka'pɛlə] *f, -, -n*
Auf der Hochzeitsfeier spielte eine kleine Tanzkapelle.

band *n*
A small dance band played at the wedding reception.

klassisch ['klasiʃ] *Adj.*
In der Stadthalle gibt es ein Gastkonzert mit klassischer Musik.

classical *n*
At the city hall there's a guest concert of classical music.

Komponist [kɔmpo'nist] *m, -en, -en,* **Komponistin** *f, -, -nen*
Welcher Komponist hat die Melodie geschrieben?

composer *n*

Which composer wrote the melody?

Plattenspieler ['plat(ə)nʃpiːlə*] *m*, -s, -	**record player** *n*
Der Plattenspieler muss repariert werden.	The record player needs to be repaired.
Rhythmus ['rytmus] *m*, -, Rhythmen	**rhythm** *n*
Nach dem Rhythmus dieser Musik kann man nicht gut tanzen.	You can't dance well to the rhythm of this music.
Sänger ['zɛŋə*] *m*, -s, - **Sängerin** ['zɛŋərin] *f*, -, -nen	**singer** *n*
Die Sängerin begeisterte das Publikum.	The singer charmed the audience.
Schlager ['ʃlaːgə*] *m*, -s, -	**hit** *n*
Man hört diesen Schlager überall.	You hear this hit everywhere.

7.3 Medien | 1-2000

7.3 Media

Fernsehapparat ['fɛə*nzeːapaːraːt] *m*, -s, -e	**television set** *n*
Vergiss nicht, den Fernsehapparat auszumachen!	Don't forget to turn off the television (set)!
fernsehen ['fɛə*nzeː(ə)n] *V/i*, sah fern, hat ferngesehen	**watch television** *v*
Gestern Abend habe ich ferngesehen.	Last evening I watched television.
Fernsehen *n*, -s, *kein Pl.*	**television** *n*
Das Programm des Fernsehens ist heute langweilig.	Today's television line-up is boring.
Fernseher ['fɛə*nzeːə*] *m*, -s, -	**television set** *n*
Wir haben uns einen Farb-Fernseher gekauft.	We bought a new color television set.
Illustrierte [ilusˈtriːə*tə] *f*, -n, -n	**magazine** *n*
In dieser Illustrierten gibt es jede Woche interessante Reiseberichte.	In this magazine every week there are interesting articles on travel.

Nachrichten ['na:xrɪçt(ə)n] *nur Pl.*
In den Fernsehnachrichten wurde gemeldet, dass der Innenminister entlassen worden ist.

news *n*
It was announced on the television news that the Secretary of the Interior has been dismissed.

Presse ['prɛsə] *f, -, kein Pl.*
Das Programm der Regierung wurde in der ganzen Presse kritisiert.

press *n*
The government's plans were criticized by all the press.

Programm [pro'gram] *n, -s, -e*
Wir können 14 Fernsehprogramme empfangen.

channel *(television, radio) n*
We can receive 14 television channels.

Radio ['ra:djo] *n, -s, -s*
Auch bei der Arbeit höre ich Radio.

radio *n*
I also listen to the radio while working.

Rundfunk ['rʊntfʊŋk] *m, -s, kein Pl.*
Hast du den Wetterbericht im Rundfunk gehört?

radio, broadcasting *n*
Did you hear the weather report on the radio?

---

senden ['zɛnd(ə)n] *V/t., sendete, hat gesendet*
Im 3. Programm wird viel klassische Musik gesendet.

broadcast *v*
A lot of classical music is broadcast on channel three.

Sendung ['zɛndʊŋ] *f, -, -en*
Sonntags gibt es viele Sportsendungen.

programme *(BE)*, **broadcast** *n*
There are a lot of sports programs on Sundays.

Sprecher ['ʃprɛçə*] *m, -s, -*
Sprecherin ['ʃprɛçərin] *f, -, -nen*
Die Nachrichtensprecherin ist beim Publikum beliebt.

announcer *n*

The news announcer is very popular with the audience.

Unterhaltung [ʊntə*'haltʊŋ] *f, -, kein Pl.*
Die Unterhaltungssendungen haben die besten Sendezeiten.

entertainment *n*

The entertainment programs have the best broadcast times.

Verlag [fɛə*'la:k] *m, -(e)s, -e*
Das Buch erscheint im Verlag Karl Sommer.

publisher *n*
The publisher of the book is Karl Sommer.

Zeitung ['tsaitʊŋ] *f,* -, -en
Die Wohnung haben wir durch eine Anzeige in der Zeitung gefunden.

newspaper *n*
We found the apartment through an ad in the newspaper.

2001-4000

Anzeige ['antsaigə] *f,* -, -n
Durch eine Zeitungsanzeige hat sie einen Käufer für ihr Auto gefunden.

advertisement, ad *n*
She found a buyer for her car through a newspaper ad.

Auflage ['aufla:gə] *f,* -, -n
Die Auflage der Zeitung ist samstags am größten.

circulation *n*
The newspaper circulation is highest on Saturdays.

drucken ['druk(ə)n] *V/t.,* druckte, hat gedruckt
Der Verlag lässt die Bücher bei verschiedenen Firmen drucken.

print *v*

The publishing house has its books printed by different firms.

Empfang [ɛm'pfaŋ] *m,* -s, *kein Pl.*
Weil wir in einem Tal wohnen, ist der Fernsehempfang nicht besonders gut.

reception *n*
Because we live in a valley, television reception is not especially good.

Hörer [hø:rə*] *m,* -s, -
Hörerin [hø:rərin] *f,* -, -nen
Bei dieser Sendung können die Hörer im Studio anrufen und sich einen Musiktitel wünschen.

listener *n*

During this program listeners can call the studio and request their favorite music title.

Interview ['intə*vju:] *n,* -s, -s
In den Nachrichten wurde ein Interview mit dem Präsidenten gesendet.

interview *n*
During the news they broadcast an interview with the president.

Redaktion [redak'tsjo:n] *f,* -, -en
In der Redaktion der Zeitung arbeiten 14 Journalisten.

editorial office *n*
Fourteen journalists work in the editorial office of the newspaper.

Schlagzeile ['ʃla:ktsailə] *f,* -, -n
Die Hauptschlagzeile wurde kurz vor Redaktionsschluss noch geändert.

headline *n*
The main headline was changed shortly before the paper went to press.

Störung ['ʃtøːruŋ] *f, -, -en*
Die Sprecherin entschuldigte sich
für die Programmstörung.

interruption *n*
The announcer apologized for the
interruption in the program(me).

Überschrift ['yːbə*ʃrift] *f, -, -en*
Die Überschrift des Berichts war
gut gewählt.

title *n*
The title of the report was well
chosen.

übertragen [yːbə*'traːg(ə)n] *V/t.,*
übertrug, hat übertragen
Die Tennisspiele werden täglich
direkt übertragen.

broadcast, transmit *v*

The tennis matches are broadcast live every day.

Übertragung [yːbə*'traːguŋ] *f,*
-, -en
Die Übertragung des Fußball-
spiels begann 10 Minuten später
als geplant.

broadcast, transmission *n*

The transmission of the football
game began 10 minutes later than
planned.

veröffentlichen
[fɛə*'œf(ə)ntliç(ə)n] *V/t.,* veröffent-
lichte, hat veröffentlicht
Die Zeitungen veröffentlichten
Teile der Geheimpapiere.

publish *v*

The newspapers published ex-
tracts of the secret papers.

Veröffentlichung
[fɛə*'œf(ə)ntliçuŋ] *f, -, -en*
Die Veröffentlichung des Briefes
bewies, dass die Politikerin gelogen hatte.

publication *n*

The publication of the letter
proved that the politician had lied.

Wetterbericht ['vɛtə*bəriçt] *m,*
-(e)s, -e
Der Wetterbericht hat für Diens-
tag schlechtes Wetter angekündigt.

**weather report, weather fore-
cast** *n*
The weather report predicted bad
weather for Tuesday.

Zeitschrift ['tsaitʃrift] *f, -, -en*
Sie ist Fotografin bei einer Mode-
zeitschrift.

magazine, periodical *n*
She is a photographer for a fashion magazine.

Zuschrift ['tsuːʃrift] *f, -, -en*
Ein Teil der Leserzuschriften wird
veröffentlicht.

address, letter to the editor *n*
Some of the reader's addresses
are published.

7.4 Freizeitbeschäftigungen | 1-2000

7.4 Leisure Activities

Bild [bilt] *n,* -(e)s, -er
Die Bilder, die sie malt, gefallen mir.
Das Bild ist unscharf.

picture *n*
I like the pictures she paints.
The picture is not in focus.

Eintrittskarte ['aintritskartə] *f,* -, -n
Im Vorverkauf sind die Eintrittskarten billiger.

ticket *n*
The tickets are cheaper if bought in advance.

erholen [ɛə*'ho:l(ə)n] *V/refl.* erholte, hat erholt
Wir haben uns im Urlaub gut erholt.

relax, rest *n*
On vacation we really relaxed.

Foto ['fo:to] *n,* -s, -s
Diese Fotos habe ich noch nie gesehen.

photo, photograph *n*
I've still never seen those photos.

fotografieren [fotogra'fi:rən] *V/ t., i.,* fotografierte, hat fotografiert
Bei diesem Licht kann man nicht fotografieren.

take a picture *v*
You can't take a picture in this light.

Freizeit ['fraitsait] *f,* -, *kein Pl.*
In ihrer Freizeit spielt sie Tennis.

free time, leisure time, time off *n*
She plays tennis in her free time.

tanzen ['tants(ə)n] *V/i.,* tanzte, hat getanzt.
Nach dieser Musik lässt sich gut tanzen.

dance *v*
This is good music to dance to.

2001-4000

amüsieren [amy'zi:rən] *V/refl.,* amüsierte, hat amüsiert
Wir haben uns auf der Feier gut amüsiert.

have fun *v*
We had a lot of fun at the celebration.

ausgehen ['ausge:(ə)n] *V/i.*, ging
aus, ist ausgegangen
Wir gehen abends selten aus.

go out *v*

We rarely go out in the evening.

Bummel ['bum(ə)l] *m*, -s, -
Lass uns noch einen Bummel
durch die Stadt machen.

stroll *n*
Let's take a stroll through the
town.

Dia ['di:a] *n*, -s, -s
Sie zeigte uns Dias von ihrer letzten Urlaubsreise.

(photographic) **slide** *n*
She showed us slides from her
last trip.

Fotoapparat ['fo:toapara:t] *m*,
-(e)s, -e
Der Fotoapparat ist vollautoma-
tisch.

camera *n*

The camera is completely automatic.

Hobby ['hɔbi] *n*, -s, -s
Für Hobbys hat sie keine Zeit.

hobby *n*
She has no time for hobbies.

Kamera ['kamərə] *f*, -, -s
Ohne Batterien funktioniert diese
Kamera nicht.

camera *n*
Without batteries this camera
won't work.

Rätsel ['rɛːts(ə)l] *n*, -s, -
Die Lösung des Rätsels war einfach.

puzzle, riddle *n*
The solution to the puzzle was
simple.

spazieren gehen
[ʃpaˈtsiːrən geː(ə)n] *V/i.*, ging spazieren, ist spazieren gegangen
Wir sind am Fluss entlang spazieren gegangen.

take a walk *v*

We took a walk along the river.

stricken ['ʃtrik(ə)n] *V/t.*, strickte,
hat gestrickt
Pullover strickt sie selbst.

knit *v*

She knits sweaters herself.

Tanz [tants] *m*, -es, Tänze
Darf ich Sie um diesen Tanz
bitten?

dance *n*
May I have this dance?

wandern ['vandə*n] *V/i.*, wander-
te, ist gewandert
Heute sind wir über 30 km gewandert.

hike *v*

Today we hiked over 30 kilometers.

7.5 Sport | 1-2000

7.5 Sports

Ball [bal] *m, -(e)s, Bälle*
Der Ball ist zu weich. Damit kann man nicht spielen.

ball *n*
The ball is too soft. We can't play with it.

Fußball ['fu:sbal] *m, -(e)s, kein Pl.*
Fußball ist bei uns die beliebteste Sportart.

football, soccer *n*
Football is the most popular sport in our country.

Fußball *m, -(e)s, Fußbälle*
Die Fußbälle sind aus Leder.

football, soccer ball *n*
Footballs are made of leather.

Kabine [ka'bi:nə] *f, -, -n*
Alle Kabinen sind zzt. besetzt.

cabin, booth *n*
All the booths are occupied at the moment.

Mannschaft ['manʃaft] *f, -, -en*
Die Mannschaft hat die beiden letzten Spiele gewonnen.

team *n*
The team won the last two games.

schwimmen ['ʃvimən] *V/i.,*
schwamm, ist geschwommen
Auch mit 79 Jahren schwimmt er jeden Tag eine halbe Stunde.

swim *v*

Even at 79 he swims every day for half an hour.

Spiel [ʃpi:l] *n, -(e)s, -e*
Das nächste Spiel wird schwer werden.

game, match *n*
The next game will be difficult.

spielen ['ʃpi:l(ə)n] *V/t., i.,* spielte,
hat gespielt
Fußballspielen ist sein Hobby.
Die Kinder spielen draußen.

play *v*

Playing football is his hobby.
The children are playing outside.

Sport [ʃpɔrt] *m, -s, kein Pl.*
Der Sportverein hat über 2000 Mitglieder.

sports *n*
The sports club has over 2000 members.

sportlich ['ʃpɔrtliç] *Adj.*
Bernd ist sehr sportlich.

sporty, interested in sports
Bernd is very sporty.

Stadion ['ʃta:djɔn] *n, -s, Stadien*
Das Stadion hat 25000 Plätze.

stadium *n*
The stadium has 25,000 seats.

Tor [toːə*] *n, -(e)s, -e*
Klaus hat bis jetzt die meisten Tore für die Mannschaft geschossen.

goal *n*
Klaus has shot most of the goals for the team this season.

Training [ˈtrɛːnɪŋ] *n, -s, kein Pl.*
Zweimal pro Woche ist Training.

practice, training *n*
There's practice twice a week.

Ziel [tsiːl] *n, -(e)s, -e*
Fast alle Radfahrer haben das Ziel erreicht.

finish line *n*
Almost all the cyclists have crossed the finish line.

2000-4000

Golf [gɔlf] *n, -s, kein Pl.*
Beim Golfspielen muss man viel laufen.

golf *n*
You have to walk a lot when playing golf.

jagen [ˈjaːg(ə)n] *V/t., i., jagte, hat gejagt*
Jagen ist in einigen Monaten des Jahres verboten.

hunt *v*

It's against the law to hunt in some months of the year.

Rad fahren [ˈraːt faːrən] *V/i., fuhr Rad, ist Rad gefahren*
Er fährt mit Freunden jeden Sonntag 3 Stunden Rad.

ride a bicycle, bike

Every Sunday he and his friends ride their bikes for 3 hours.

reiten [ˈraɪt(ə)n] *V/t., i., ritt, hat (ist) geritten*
Sie hat im Urlaub reiten gelernt.

ride (on horseback) *v*

While on vacation she learned how to ride.

Rekord [reˈkɔrt] *m, -(e)s, -e*
Ihre Rekordzeit aus dem letzten Jahr hat sie noch nicht wieder erreicht.

record *n*
This year she still hasn't repeated her record time of last year.

rennen [ˈrɛnən] *V/i., rannte, gerannt*
Warum rennst du so schnell? Wir haben doch Zeit.

run, race, hurry, go fast *v*

Why are you running so fast? We have plenty of time.

Rennen *n, -s, -*
Das Autorennen war bis zum Schluss spannend.

race *n*
The car race was exciting to the very end.

rudern ['ru:də*n] *V/t., i.*, ruderte, hat (ist) gerudert
Er rudert das Boot geschickt in den Hafen.

row *v*

He rows the boat very carefully in the harbor.

Schiedsrichter ['ʃi:tsriçtə*] *m, -s, -*
Schiedsrichterin *f, -, -nen*
Der Schiedsrichter leitete das Spiel sehr gut.

referee, umpire *n*

The referee led the game very well.

---

schießen ['ʃi:s(ə)n] *V/t.*, schoss, hat geschossen
Sie schießt sehr sicher, weil sie eine vollkommen ruhige Hand hat.

shoot *v*

She shoots very well because she has a very steady hand.

Schwimmbad ['ʃvimba:t] *n, -(e)s, Schwimmbäder*
Das Wasser in diesem Schwimmbad ist geheizt.

swimming pool *n*

The water in this swimming pool is heated.

---

segeln ['ze:g(ə)ln] *V/i.*, segelte, hat (ist) gesegelt
Bei diesem starken Wind ist es zu gefährlich zu segeln.

sail *n*

It's too dangerous to sail in this strong wind.

Ski [ʃi:] *m, -s, -er*
Kannst du Skilaufen?

ski *n*
Do you know how to ski?

Spieler ['ʃpi:lə*] *m, -s, -*
Spielerin ['ʃpi:lərin] *f, -, -nen*
Eine Spielerin ist verletzt worden.

player *n*

One player was hurt.

Sportart ['ʃportart] *f, -, -en*
Wasserball ist eine unbekannte Sportart.

kind of sport *n*

Waterball is an unknown kind of sport.

Sportler ['ʃportlə*] *m, -s, -*
Sportlerin ['ʃportlərin] *f, -, -nen*
Fast jeder Sportler ist Mitglied in einem Verein.

sportsman, sportswoman *n*

Almost every sportsman belongs to a club.

Sportplatz ['ʃportplats] *m, -es, Sportplätze*
Der Sportplatz ist gut gepflegt.

sports field, playing field *n*

The sports field is well taken care of.

Start [ʃtart] *m*, -s, -s
Der Start des Radrennens ist in einem Stadion.

starting point *n*
The starting point of the bicycle race is at a stadium.

tauchen ['taux(ə)n] *V/i.*, tauchte, hat (ist) getaucht
Sie kann fünf Minuten ohne Atemhilfe tauchen.

dive *v*

She can dive for five minutes without breathing equipment.

Tennis ['tɛnis] *n*, -, *kein Pl.*
Durch häufiges Tennisspielen ist mein rechter Arm viel dicker als mein linker.

tennis *n*
My right arm is much stronger then my left after playing lots of tennis.

Trainer ['trɛːnə*] *m*, -s, -
Trainerin ['trɛːnərin] *f*, -, -nen
Die Mannschaft bekommt für die nächste Saison einen neuen Trainer.

coach *n*

The team is getting a new coach for next season.

trainieren ['trɛniːrən] *V/t., i.*, trainierte, hat trainiert
Er hat die Mannschaft drei Jahre trainiert.
Kurz vor Wettbewerben trainiere ich weniger als normal.

train, practice, practise *(BE)* *v*

He trained the team for three years.
Just before the competition I train less than usual.

turnen ['turnən] *V/i.*, turnte, hat geturnt
Turnen verlangt viel Kraft und Mut.

do gymnastics *v*

Doing gymnastics takes a lot of strength and courage.

Wettkampf ['vɛtkampf] *m*, -(e)s, Wettkämpfe
Sie gewann in diesem Jahr fast alle wichtigen Wettkämpfe.

competition *n*

This year she won nearly all the important competitions.

wetten ['vɛt(ə)n] *V/i., + Präp.* (um), wettete, hat gewettet
Wettest du um Geld beim Pferderennen?

bet *v*

Do you bet money on horse races?

8.1 Staat und Politik | 1-2000

Ausländer ['auslɛndə*] *m*, -s, - **Ausländerin** *f*, -, -nen   **foreigner** *n*

Sie ist Ausländerin, aber sie spricht sehr gut Deutsch.

She is a foreigner, but she speaks German very well.

ausländisch ['auslɛndiʃ] *Adj., keine Komp.*   **foreign**

Ausländische Restaurants sind in der Bundesrepublik sehr beliebt.

Foreign restaurants are very popular in the Federal Republic.

Bürger ['byrgə*] *m*, -s, - **Bürgerin** ['byrgərin] *f*, -, -nen   **citizen** *n*

Die Bürger sind von der Stadt eingeladen worden, die Straßenbaupläne zu diskutieren.

The city invited the citizens to discuss the plans for road construction.

Bürgermeister ['byrgə*maistə*] *m*, -s, -, **Bürgermeisterin** *f*, -, -nen   **mayor** *n*

Der Bürgermeister wurde schon dreimal wiedergewählt.

The mayor has already been re-elected to three terms.

Demokratie [demokra'tiː] *f*, -, -n   **democracy** *n*

Von 1918 bis 1933 gab es in Deutschland zum ersten Mal eine Demokratie.

From 1918 to 1933 there was a democracy for the first time in Germany.

demokratisch [demo'kraːtiʃ] *Adj.*   **democratic**

Es wird bezweifelt, dass die Wahlen demokratisch waren.

It's doubtful that the election was democratic.

frei [frai] *Adj.*, -er, am -esten   **free, liberal**

Die politischen Häftlinge sind immer noch nicht frei.

The political prisoners are still not free.

In diesem Land kann ich frei meine Meinung sagen.

In this country I can freely express my opinion.

246

Freiheit ['fraihait] *f, -, -en*
Das Volk kämpft seit Jahren für seine Freiheit.

freedom *n*
The people have been fighting for their freedom for years.

Grenze ['grɛntsə] *f, -, -n*
Die Grenze zwischen den beiden Ländern wurde geschlossen.

border *n*
The border between the two countries was closed.

Heimat ['haima:t] *f, -, kein Pl.*
Die Flüchtlinge dürfen nicht in ihre Heimat zurück.

home country *n*
The refugees may not return to their home country.

international [intɛɐ*natsjo'na:l] *Adj.*
Auf der internationalen Währungskonferenz wurde die Dollarkrise diskutiert.

international

At the international currency conference the dollar crisis was discussed.

Kanzler ['kantslɐ*] *m, -s, -*
Kanzlerin ['kantslərin] *f, -, nen*
Der Kanzler ist der Chef der Regierung.

chancellor *n*

The chancellor is head of the government.

Land [lant] *n, -(e)s, Länder*
Das Land braucht eine neue Regierung.

country *n*
The country needs a new government.

Macht [maxt] *f, -, (kein Pl.)*
Das Militär ist in dem Land seit Jahren an der Macht.

power *n*
The military has been in power for years in that country.

Macht *f, -, Mächte*
Die beiden Großmächte USA und Russland verhandeln über eine Lösung des Konflikts.

power *n*
Two major powers, the USA and Russia, are discussing a solution for the conflict.

Minister [mi'nistɐ*] *m, -s, -*
Ministerin [mi'nistərin] *f, -, -nen*
Die Ministerin wurde für den Misserfolg verantwortlich gemacht.

(cabinet) minister, cabinet secretary *n*
The minister was held responsible for the failure.

Öffentlichkeit ['œf(ə)ntliçkait] *f, -, kein Pl.*
In der Öffentlichkeit wird die Außenpolitik der Regierung gelobt.

public *n*

The government's foreign policy is praised publically.

offiziell [ɔfi'tsjɛl] *Adj.*
Eine offizielle Äußerung der Regierung zu diesem Problem gibt es bis jetzt nicht.

official
There's still no official government statement about this problem.

Parlament [parla'mɛnt] *n, -(e)s, -e*
Die Regierungsparteien haben im Parlament eine große Mehrheit.

parliament *n*
The government parties have a large majority in parliament.

Partei [par'tai] *f, -, -en*
Das neue Programm wird in der Partei seit Monaten diskutiert.

party *n*
The party has been discussing the new program for months.

Politik [poli'ti:k] *f, -, kein Pl.*
In der Finanzpolitik der Regierung ist keine klare Linie zu erkennen.

policy *n*
There's no clear line in the government's financial policy.

---

politisch [po'li:tiʃ] *Adj.*
Das ist eine wichtige politische Frage.

political *n*
That is an important political question.

Präsident [prɛzi'dɛnt] *m, -en, -en*
Präsidentin *f, -, -nen*
Nächstes Jahr wird ein neuer Präsident gewählt.

president *n*

A new president will be elected next year.

---

regieren [re'gi:rən] *V/t., i.,* regierte, hat regiert
Das Land wird von fremden Mächten regiert.

rule *v*
The country is ruled by foreign powers.

Regierung [re'gi:ruŋ] *f, -, -en*
Die Regierung ist seit zwei Jahren im Amt.

government *n*
The government has been in power for two years.

Republik [repu'bli:k] *f, -, -en*
1918 wurde Deutschland Republik.

republic *n*
Germany became a republic in 1918.

Staat [ʃta:t] *m, -(e)s, -en*

Der Staat hat sehr viel Einfluss auf das Leben der Bürger.

country, nation, government, state *n*
The government has much influence on the life of its citizens.

---

staatlich ['ʃta:tliç] *Adj., keine Komp.*
Die Eisenbahn ist staatlich.

public

The railroad system is public.

Tradition [tradi'tsjo:n] *f, -, -en*
Es ist Tradition, dass der Parlamentspräsident Mitglied der stärksten Partei ist.

tradition *n*
Tradition is that the president of the parliament belongs to the party in power.

Verfassung [fɛə*'fasuŋ] *f, -, -en*
Die Verfassung der Bundesrepublik ist noch sehr jung.

constitution *n*
The constitution of Germany is still young.

verhandeln [fɛə*'hand(ə)ln] *V/t., i.,* verhandelte, hat verhandelt
Die beiden Länder verhandeln über einen Friedensvertrag.

negotiate *v*

The two countries are negotiating a peace treaty.

Verhandlung [fɛə*'handluŋ] *f, -, -en*
Die Verhandlungen sind bis jetzt ohne Ergebnis geblieben.

negotiations *n*

The negotiations still have had no results.

Volk [fɔlk] *n, -(e)s,* Völker
Im Volk ist man mit der wirtschaftlichen Situation sehr unzufrieden.

people *n*
The people are very dissatisfied with the economic situation.

Wahl [vaːl] *f, -, -en*
Es ist offen, wer die nächste Wahl gewinnt.

election *n*
No one knows who will win the next election.

wählen ['vɛːl(ə)n] *V/t.,* wählte, hat gewählt
Im August wird ein neues Parlament gewählt.

elect *v*

A new parliament will be elected in August.

2001-4000

Abgeordnete ['apgəɔrdnətə] *m/f, -n, -n*
Auch einige Abgeordnete der Regierungsparteien stimmten gegen den Ministerpräsidenten.

representative *n*

Even some of the representatives of the government parties voted against the president.

Abkommen ['apkɔmən] *n, -s, -*
Die beiden Staaten verhandeln über ein neues Handelsabkommen.

agreement *n*
The two countries are discussing a new trade agreement.

Außenminister ['aus(ə)nministə*] *m, -s, -*

Die Konferenz der Außenminister blieb ohne Ergebnis.

foreign minister, secretary of state *[AE],* **foreign secretary** *(BE) n*
The secretaries of state conference had no results.

Außenpolitik ['aus(ə)npɔliti:k] *f,* **foreign policy** *n*
-, *kein Pl.*
Im Parlament gab es Streit über
die Außenpolitik.

In parliament there was disagree-
ment about foreign policy.

Botschaft ['bo:tʃaft] *f, -, -en* **embassy** *n*
Die Visaabteilung der Botschaft
ist nur morgens geöffnet.

The visa office of the embassy is
only open in the morning.

bürgerlich ['byrgə*liç] *Adj.* **civil**
Das Bürgerliche Gesetzbuch trat
im Jahr 1900 in Kraft.

The civil code came into force in
1900.

Demonstration *f* **demonstration** *n*
[demɔnstra'tsjo:n] *f, -, -en*
Im ganzen Land gab es Demonst-
rationen gegen die Schulreform.

All over the country there were
demonstrations against the
school reform.

Diplomat [diplo'ma:t] *m, -en, -en* **diplomat** *n*
Diplomatin [diplo'ma:tin] *f, -, -nen*
Der Diplomat wird verdächtigt,
ein Spion zu sein.

The diplomat is suspected of
being a spy.

diplomatisch [diplo'ma:tiʃ] **diplomatic**
Adj.
Zwischen den beiden Ländern
gibt es gute diplomatische Bezie-
hungen.

There are good diplomatic relations between the two countries.

einheimisch ['ainhaimiʃ] *Adj.,* **local, native**
keine Komp.
Die Bevölkerung wird aufgefordert, nur einheimische Produkte
zu kaufen.

People are advised to buy only
local products.

Fahne ['fa:nə] *f, -, -n* **flag** *n*
Die französische Trikolore war
Vorbild für viele europäische Na-
tionalfahnen.

The French tricolor flag was the
model for many European national flags.

Finanzminister **finance minister, secretary of**
[fi'nantsministə*] *m, -s, -* **the treasury** *n*
Der Finanzminister fordert eine
Erhöhung der Umsatzsteuer.

The finance minister is recommending a raise in sales taxes.

gesetzlich [gə'zɛtsliç] *Adj., keine Komp.*
Bei dem Bau der Fabrik sind gesetzliche Vorschriften verletzt worden.

legal
Legal regulations were violated when the factory was built.

Gleichberechtigung ['glaiçbərɛçtiguŋ] *f, -, kein Pl.*
Die Gewerkschaft fordert die volle Gleichberechtigung von Mann und Frau.

equality, equal rights *n*
The union is recommending complete equality between men and women.

Grundgesetz ['gruntgəzɛts] *n, -es, kein Pl.*
Das Grundgesetz ist die Verfassung der Bundesrepublik.

basic law *n*
The Basic Law is the constitution of the Federal Republic of Germany.

herrschen ['hɛrʃ(ə)n] *V/i., + Präp.* (über), herrschte, hat geherrscht
In dem Land herrscht seit Jahren eine Militärregierung.

rule *v*

For years the military has ruled in that country.

Ideologie [ideolo'gi:] *f, -, -n*
Es ist schwer, mit Leuten zu diskutieren, die fest an ihre Ideologie glauben.

ideology *n*
It is hard to have a discussion with people who strongly believe in their ideology.

inländisch ['inlɛndiʃ] *Adj., keine Komp.*
Die inländische Industrie klagt über die niedrigen Preise der ausländischen Konkurrenz.

national, domestic, home *n*

National industries complain about the low prices of foreign competition.

Innenminister ['inənministə*] *m, -s, -*

Der Innenminister verteidigte die Maßnahmen der Polizei.

minister of the interior, home secretary *[GB]*, **secretary of state** *(AE) n*

The minister of the interior defended the police actions.

Innenpolitik ['inənpoliti:k] *f, -, kein Pl.*
In der Innenpolitik gibt es einen heftigen Streit um die Krankenversicherung.

domestic policy *n*

In domestic policy there is a big debate about health insurance.

Kabinett [kabi'nɛt] *n*, -s, -e
Das Kabinett beschließt heute die
Vorschläge des Innenministers.

cabinet *n*
Today the cabinet will vote on the
secretary of the interior's plans.

Kaiser ['kaizə*] *m*, -s, -
Kaiserin ['kaizərin] *f*, -, -nen
Bis 1918 hatte Deutschland einen
Kaiser.

emperor *n*
empress *n*
Germany had an emperor until
1918.

Kapitalismus [kapita'lismus] *m*,
-, *kein Pl.*
Für den Politiker sind Kapitalismus und soziale Gerechtigkeit
keine Gegensätze.

capitalism *n*

For the politician, capitalism and
civil rights are not opposites.

kapitalistisch [kapita'listiʃ] *Adj.*
Es wird kritisiert, dass im kapita-
listischen Wirtschaftssystem der
Unterschied zwischen Armen und
Reichen zu groß sei.

capitalist
Capitalist economies are criticized because the difference between rich and poor is supposedly
too great.

Koalition [koali'tsjo:n] *f*, -, -en
Die Koalition hat sich auf ein Re-
gierungsprogramm geeinigt.

coalition *n*
The coalition has agreed on a
government program.

Kommunismus [komu'nismus]
m, -, *kein Pl.*
Der Streit zwischen Kapitalismus
und Kommunismus war früher
härter als heute.

communism *n*

There used to be more difference
of opinion between capitalism
and communism than there is
today.

kommunistisch[komu'nistiʃ]*Adj.*
Der Handel zwischen den kom-
munistischen und den kapitalisti-
schen Ländern ist stärker geworden.

communist

Trade between communist and
capitalist countries has grown.

konservativ [konzɛrva'ti:f] *Adj.*
Die konservativen Parteien sind
gegen die Schulreform.

conservative
The conservative parties are
against school reform.

Kundgebung ['kuntge:buŋ] *f*, -,
-en
Die Kundgebung der Gewerkschaft war nur schwach besucht.

rally, assembly *n*

Not many came to the union rally.

König ['køːnɪçʰ] *m*, -s, -e
Königin ['køːnɪgɪn] *f*, -, -nen
Der schwedische König hat keine
große politische Macht.

king *n*
queen *n*
The Swedish king hasn't much political power.

Königreich ['køːnɪçʁaɪç] *n*, -(e)s,
-e
Es gibt nur noch wenige Königrei-
che, die meisten Länder sind Re-
publiken.

kingdom *n*

There are very few kingdoms today; most countries are repub-
lics.

liberal [libeˈraːl] *Adj.*
Die liberale und die konservative
Partei haben eine Koalition ver-
einbart.

liberal, middle-of-the-road
The liberal and conservative parties have joined in a coalition.

Mehrheit ['meːɐ*haɪt] *f*, -, -en
Für ein solches Gesetz gibt es im
Parlament keine Mehrheit.

majority *n*
There's no majority in parliament
for such a law.

Ministerpräsident
[miˈnɪstɐ*pʁɛzidɛnt] *m*, -en, -en
Ministerpräsidentin *f*, -, -nen
Die Ministerpräsidentin ist im
Volk beliebt.

prime minister *n*

The prime minister is very popular
with the people.

Nachfolger ['naːxfɔlgɐ*] *m*, -s, -
Nachfolgerin [-fɔlgərɪn] *f*, -, -nen
Der Nachfolger des gestorbenen
Innenministers ist noch nicht be-
kannt.

successor *n*

The successor to the late Minister
of the Interior is still unknown.

Nation [naˈtsjoːn] *f*, -, -en
Die ganze Nation wünscht ein Ende des langen Krieges.

nation *n*
The whole nation would like an
end to the long war.

national [natsjoˈnaːl] *Adj.*
Die nationalen Gesetze in West-
europa sollen einheitlicher werden.

national
National laws in western Europe
are supposed to become more
unified.

Opposition [ɔpoziˈtsjoːn] *f*, -, *kein
Pl.*
Die Oppositionsparteien kritisier-
ten die Regierung.

opposition *n*

The opposition parties criticized
the government.

Propaganda [propa'ganda] *f, -,*
kein Pl.
Die Regierung bezeichnet die Kritik der Opposition als Propaganda.

propaganda *n*

The government calls the opposition's criticism propaganda.

Provinz [pro'vints] *f, -, -en*
Während des Wahlkampfes besuchte der Präsident alle Provinzen.

province *n*
During the campaign the president visited every province.

Provinz *f, -, kein Pl.*

In der Provinz gibt es nur wenige Theater.

the provinces *n*
(area outside the main cities)
There are not many theaters in the provinces.

Rede ['re:də] *f, -, -n*
Die Rede des Politikers bekam viel Beifall.

speech, talk *n*
The politician's speech got a lot of applause.

Redner ['re:dnə*] *m, -s, -*
Rednerin ['re:dnərin] *f, -, -nen*
Die Redner auf der Kundgebung mussten von der Polizei geschützt werden.

speaker *n*

The speaker at the rally had to have police protection.

Reform [re'fɔrm] *f, -, -en*
Seit Monaten gibt es heftigen Streit um die Reform der Steuergesetze.

reform *n*
For months there has been conflict over the reform in the tax laws.

Regierungschef [re'gi:ruŋsʃɛf] *m, -s, -s,* **Regierungschefin** *f, -, -nen*
Die Regierungschefin ist auf einer Auslandsreise.

head of the government *n*

The head of the government has gone on a foreign trip.

Revolution [revolu'tsjo:n] *f, -, -en*
Wenn die soziale Lage nicht besser wird, besteht die Gefahr einer Revolution.

revolution *n*
If the social condition doesn't get better, there's a danger of revolution.

Rücktritt ['ryktrit] *m, -s, -e*
Der Regierungschef nahm den Rücktritt des Finanzministers an.

resignation *n*
The head of the government accepted the resignation of the finance minister.

sozial [zo'tsja:l] *Adj.*
Die alten Steuergesetze sind unsozial.

social
The old tax laws are anti-social.

Sozialismus [zotsja'lismus] *m, -, kein Pl.*
Der Sozialismus kam am Ende der 80er Jahre in eine große Krise.

socialism *n*

At the end of the eighties socialism entered a time of great crisis.

sozialistisch [zotsja'listiʃ] *Adj.*
Die sozialistische Partei wählte einen neuen Parteivorsitzenden.

socialist
The Socialist Party elected a new party chair.

Spion [ʃpi'o:n] *m, -s, -e*
Spionin [ʃpi'o:nin] *f, -nen*
Der Spion wurde verhaftet.

spy *n*

The spy was arrested.

Stellvertreter ['ʃtɛlfɛɐ*tre:tə*] *m, -s, -*, **Stellvertreterin** *f, -, -nen*
Der Stellvertreter des Bürgermeisters leitet die Sitzung.

deputy, representative *n*

The deputy of the mayor took charge of the meeting.

stimmen ['ʃtimən] *V/i., + Präp.* (für, gegen), stimmte, hat gestimmt
52,5 % der Wähler stimmten für die Regierungsparteien.

vote *v*

52.5% voted for the government parties.

unabhängig ['unaphɛniç°] *Adj.*
Das Land muss von Importen unabhängiger werden.

independent
The country must become more independent of imports.

Unabhängigkeit
['unaphɛniçkait] *f, -, kein Pl.*
Unabhängigkeit von den Großmächten ist das wichtigste Ziel der Regierungspolitik.

independence *n*

Independence from the great powers is the most important goal of the government policy.

Unruhe ['unru:ə] *f, -, -n*
Bei dieser Unruhe kann man nicht arbeiten.
In den westlichen Provinzen des Landes gibt es politische Unruhen.

disturbance *n*
You can't work with this disturbance!
In the western provinces of the country there are political disturbances.

Unterdrückung [untə*'drykuŋ] *f,* -, *kein Pl.*
Nur durch harte Unterdrückung der Opposition kann die Regierung an der Macht bleiben.

suppression *n*

The government can stay in power only with strong suppression of the opposition.

Wahlkampf ['va:lkampf] *m,* -(e)s, Wahlkämpfe
Es ist noch nicht klar, wer im Wahlkampf die besseren Argumente hat.

election campaign *n*

It's not clear yet who has the better arguments in the election campaign.

8.2 Krieg und Frieden | 1-2000

8.2 War and Peace

Armee [ar'me:] *f,* -, -n
In der Armee sind nur Berufssoldaten.

army *n*

There are only professional soldiers in the army.

Feind [faint] *m,* -(e)s, -e
Feindin ['faindin] *f,* -, -nen
Die Feinde wurden besiegt.

enemy *n*

The enemies were defeated.

Friede(n) ['fri:d(ə)n] *m,* -ns (-s), *kein Pl.*
Auch nach vier Jahren Krieg gibt es keine Hoffnung auf Frieden.

peace *n*

Even after four years of war there is no hope for peace.

---

friedlich ['fri:tlɪç] *Adj.*
Nach den Kämpfen in der letzten Woche ist die Situation an der Grenze friedlich.

peaceful

After the battles of last week the situation on the border is peaceful.

Gegner ['ge:gnə*] *m,* -s, -
Gegnerin ['ge:gnərin] *f,* -, -nen
Die früheren Kriegsgegner verhandeln über einen Friedensvertrag.

enemy *n*

The former war enemies are negotiating a peace treaty.

Kampf [kampf] *m, -(e)s, Kämpfe*
Die Kämpfe in den Bergen werden immer härter.

fight *n*
The fights in the mountains are getting harder and harder.

kämpfen [ˈkɛmpf(ə)n] *V/i., + Präp.* (um, für, gegen), kämpfte, hat gekämpft
Sein ganzes Leben kämpfte er für die Freiheit.

fight *v*
He spent his whole life fighting for freedom.

Krieg [kriːk] *m, -(e)s, -e*
Im letzten Krieg zwischen den beiden Ländern starben über 300000 Menschen.

war *n*
Over 300,000 died in the last war between the two countries.

Militär [miliˈtɛːə*] *n, -s, kein Pl.*
Das Militär fordert von der Regierung mehr Geld für neue Waffen.

military, armed forces *n*
The armed forces want more money from the government for new weapons.

siegen [ˈziːg(ə)n] *V/i., + Präp.* (in, über), siegte, hat gesiegt
In einem Atomkrieg wird niemand siegen.

win *v*
No one will win an atomic war.

Sieger [ˈziːgə*] *m, -s, -*
Siegerin [ˈziːgərin] *f, -, -nen*
Der Sieger verlangt, dass der Gegner alle Waffen abgibt.

winner, victor *n*
The victor demands that the enemy give up all weapons.

Soldat [zɔlˈdaːt] *m, -en, -en*
Soldatin [zɔlˈdaːtin] *f, -, -nen*
Die Armee hat über 250000 Soldaten.

soldier *n*
The army has over 250,000 soldiers.

verteidigen [fɛə*ˈtaidig(ə)n] *V/t., refl., + Präp.* (gegen), verteidigte, hat verteidigt
Mit dieser kleinen Armee kann das Land nicht verteidigt werden.
Sie konnten sich gegen die Feinde verteidigen.

defend *v*
The country cannot be defended with this small army.
They could defend themselves against the enemy.

Waffe [ˈvafə] *f, -, -n*
Die Polizei hat die Waffe gefunden, mit der die Frau erschossen wurde.

weapon *n*
The police has found the weapon the woman was shot with.

Widerstand [ˈviːdɐˌʃtant] *m*, -(e)s, Widerstände
Schon nach der ersten Niederlage gab die Armee den Widerstand auf.

resistance *n*

The army gave up its resistance after its first defeat.

zerstören [tsɛɐˈʃtøːrən] *V/t.*, zerstörte, hat zerstört
Im letzten Weltkrieg wurden in Deutschland viele alte Städte zerstört.

destroy *v*

In World War II many old cities in Germany were destroyed.

$$\boxed{2001\text{-}4000}$$

Abrüstung [ˈapryːstʊŋ] *f*, -, *kein Pl.*
Seit Jahren verhandeln die Großmächte über eine militärische Abrüstung.

disarmament *n*

The major powers have been negotiating disarmament for years.

Alarm [aˈlarm] *m*, -(e)s, -e
Man gab Alarm, weil man einen Angriff des Feindes befürchtete.

alarm *n*
There was an alarm because there was fear of an attack by the enemy.

angreifen [ˈangraɪf(ə)n] *V/t.*, griff an, hat angegriffen
Das Schiff wurde aus der Luft angegriffen.

attack *v*

The ship was attacked from the air.

Angriff [ˈangrɪf] *m*, -s, -e
Die Stadt konnte gegen starke Angriffe verteidigt werden.

attack *n*
The city could be defended against strong attacks.

Atombombe [aˈtoːmbɔmbə] *f*, -, -n
Die Staaten einigten sich darauf, in Zukunft keine neuen Atombomben zu produzieren.

atom bomb *n*

The countries agreed to produce no new atom bombs in the future.

besetzen [bəˈzɛts(ə)n] *V/t.*, besetzte, hat besetzt
Die Grenzgebiete sind vom Feind besetzt worden.

occupy *v*

The border areas were occupied by the enemy.

258

besiegen [bə'ziːg(ə)n] *V/t.,* besiegte, hat besiegt
Nach vier Tagen Kampf wurde der Gegner besiegt.

defeat *v*

After four days of fighting the enemy was defeated.

Bundeswehr ['bundəsveːəˑ] *f, -, kein Pl.*
Der Verteidigungsminister der Bundesrepublik hat in Friedenszeiten das Oberkommando über die Bundeswehr.

armed forces *(of the Federal Republic of Germany) n*

In peace time the German defense minister is chief of the armed forces.

erobern [ɛəˑ'oːbəˑn] *V/t.,* eroberte, hat erobert
Der Feind brauchte sieben Monate, um die Hauptstadt zu erobern.

defeat *v*

The enemy needed seven months to defeat the capital city.

Flucht [fluxt] *f, -, kein Pl.*
Tausende von Menschen sind auf der Flucht vor den feindlichen Truppen.

flight *n*

Thousands are in flight from enemy troops.

Flüchtling ['flʏçtlɪŋ] *m, -s, -e*
Die Flüchtlinge wohnen seit Monaten in Zelten.

refugee *n*

The refugees have been living in tents for months.

General [genəˑ'raːl] *m, -s,* Generäle
Die Generäle sind überzeugt, dass ihre Armee den Krieg gewinnen wird.

general *n*

The generals are convinced their army will win the war.

Gewehr [gəˑ'veːəˑ] *n, -s, -e*
Das Gewehr funktioniert nicht, weil es nass ist.

rifle *n*

The rifle doesn't work because it's wet.

grausam ['grauzaːm] *Adj.*
Die jungen Soldaten wussten nicht, dass der Krieg so grausam ist.

awful, cruel

The young soldiers didn't know war is so cruel.

Großmacht ['groːsmaxt] *f, -,* Großmächte
Nach langer Pause verhandeln die Großmächte wieder über eine Raketenabrüstung.

major power *n*

After a long pause the major powers are again negotiating a rocket disarmament plan.

Heer [he:ə*] *n*, -(e)s, -e
Die meisten Soldaten sind beim Heer.

army *n*
Most of the soldiers are in the army.

Held [hɛlt] *m*, -en, -en
Heldin ['hɛldin] *f*, -, -nen
Einige Kriegshelden wurden durch Presse und Rundfunk berühmt.

hero, heroine *n*

Some war heroes got famous from media reports.

Kanone [ka'no:nə] *f*, -, -n
Das Schiff verteidigte sich mit Kanonen gegen die Flugzeuge.

cannon, gun *n*
The ship defended itself with guns against the planes.

Kommando [kɔ'mando] *n*, -s, -s,
Alle Soldaten gehorchten den Kommandos.

command, order *n*
All soldiers obeyed the commands.

Kommando *n*, *kein Pl.*
Nach der Niederlage verlor der General das Kommando über seine Truppen.

command *n*
After the defeat the general lost command over his troops.

Konflikt [kɔn'flikt] *m*, -(e)s, -e
Der Krieg begann wegen eines Grenzkonflikts.

conflict *n*
The war began over a border conflict.

Kugel ['ku:g(ə)l] *f*, -, -n
Der Soldat wurde von einer Kugel getroffen.

bullet *n*
The soldier was hit by a bullet.

Luftwaffe ['luftvafə] *f*, -, -n
Die Luftwaffe verlor bei dem Angriff drei Kampfflugzeuge.

air force *n*
In the attack the air force lost three fighter planes.

Marine [ma'ri:nə] *f*, -, *kein Pl.*
Die Marine hat nicht genug Schiffe, um die ganze Küste verteidigen zu können.

navy *n*
The navy doesn't have enough ships to defend the whole coast.

marschieren [mar'ʃi:rən] *V/i.*,
marschierte, ist marschiert
Die Soldaten mussten eine lange Strecke zu Fuß marschieren.

march *v*

The soldiers had to march a long way on foot.

Niederlage ['ni:də*la:gə] *f*, -, -n
Nach der Kriegsniederlage trat die ganze Regierung zurück.

defeat *n*
After the defeat in the war the whole government resigned.

Offizier [ɔfiˈtsiːə*] *m*, -s, -e
Die Offiziere sind alle Berufssoldaten.

officer *n*
The officers are all career soldiers.

Pistole [pisˈtoːlə] *f*, -, -n
Für diese Pistole passen die Kugeln nicht.

pistol *n*
The bullets don't fit this pistol.

Rakete [raˈkeːtə] *f*, -, -n
Die Rakete kann über 7000 km weit fliegen.

rocket, missile *n*
The missile can fly over 7000 km.

Schlacht [ʃlaxt] *f*, -, -en
In dieser Schlacht gab es sehr viele Tote und Verwundete.

battle *n*
There were many dead and wounded in that battle.

Streitkräfte [ˈʃtraitkrɛftə] *nur Pl.*
Für die Streitkräfte werden jährlich über 30 % des Staatshaushaltes ausgegeben.

armed forces *n*
Over 30% of the national budget goes to the armed forces.

Truppe [ˈtrupə] *f*, -, -n
Die Truppen des Feindes marschierten gestern über die Grenze.

troops *n*
Yesterday enemy troops marched over the border.

Verbündete [fɛə*ˈbyndətə] *m/f*, -n, -n
Mit der Hilfe der Verbündeten konnte unser Land sich verteidigen.

ally *n*
Our country could defend itself with the help of its allies.

Weltkrieg [ˈvɛltkriːk] *m*, -(e)s, -e
Nach dem 2. Weltkrieg wurde Europa politisch geteilt.

world war *n*
After the Second World War Europe was politically divided.

8.3 Kirche und Religion | 1-2000

8.3 Church and Religion

beten [ˈbeːt(ə)n] *V/i.*, + *Präp.* (für, um), betete, hat gebetet
Früher wurde bei uns vor dem Essen gebetet.

pray *v*
We used to pray before a meal.

Bibel ['bi:b(ə)l] *f, -, -n*
Ich habe meiner Tochter eine Bibel gekauft.

Bible *n*
I bought a Bible for my daughter.

Christ [krist] *m, -en, -en*
Christin ['kristin] *f, -, -nen*
Die Christen fordern Hilfe für die armen Völker der Welt.

Christian *n*

Christians ask for help for the poor of the world.

christlich ['kristliç] *Adj., keine Komp.*
Ihr Mann kommt aus einer sehr christlichen Familie.

Christian

Her husband comes from a very Christian family.

Gebet [gə'be:t] *n, -(e)s, -e*
Meine Mutter spricht morgens immer ein Gebet.

prayer *n*
My mother says a prayer every morning.

Gewissen [gə'vis(ə)n] *n, -s, kein Pl.*
Ich habe nichts falsch gemacht. Ich habe ein gutes Gewissen.

conscience *n*

I didn't do anything wrong. My conscience is clear.

Glaube ['glaubə] *m, -ns, kein Pl.*
Welchen Glauben hat sie?

belief *n*
What beliefs does she have?

glauben ['glaub(ə)n] *V/i., + Präp. (an), glaubte, hat geglaubt*
Er glaubt an die Wiedergeburt nach dem Tod.

believe *v*

He believes in reincarnation.

Gott [gɔt] *m, -es, Götter*
Glaubst du an die Existenz eines Gottes?

God *n*
Do you believe there is a God?

Gottesdienst ['gɔtəsdi:nst] *m, -(e)s, -e*
Jeden Sonntag um 11.00 Uhr ist Gottesdienst.

religious (church) service *n*

Every Sunday there is a church service at 11 o'clock.

Kirche ['kirçə] *f, -, -n*
In unserer Stadt ist eine neue Kirche gebaut worden.
Es gibt viele verschiedene christliche Kirchen.

church *n*
A new church was built in our town.
There are many denominations of the Christian church.

Priester ['pri:stə*] *m, -s, -*
Priesterin ['pri:stərin] *f, -, -nen*
Er will Priester werden.

priest *n*

He wants to become a priest.

Religion [reli'gjo:n] *f, -, -en*
○ Welche Religion hat sie?
□ Ich glaube, sie ist Jüdin.

religion *n*
○ What is her religion?
□ I think she is Jewish.

Seele ['ze:lə] *f, -, -n*
Der Leib stirbt, aber nicht die Seele.

soul *n*
The body dies, but not the soul.

Sünde ['zyndə] *f, -, -n*
Im Gebet bat er Gott um Verzeihung für seine Sünden.

sin *n*
In prayer he asked God to forgive his sins.

Weihnachten ['vainaxt(ə)n] *n, (Sg. u. Pl.)*
Ich wünsche Ihnen fröhliche Weihnachten.

Christmas *n*

I wish you a merry Christmas.

2001-4000

Bischof ['biʃo:f] *m, -s,* Bischöfe
Die Bischöfe kritisierten die nach ihrer Meinung unchristlichen Scheidungsgesetze.

bishop *n*
The bishops criticised what was, in their opinion, unchristian divorce laws.

evangelisch [evaŋ'ge:liʃ] *Adj., keine Komp.*
Mein Mann ist katholisch, ich bin evangelisch.

(German) Lutheran, Protestant

My husband is Catholic; I'm Lutheran.

fromm [frɔm] *Adj.*
Er führt ein sehr frommes Leben.

religious, devout, pious
He leads a very religious life.

heilig ['hailiç°] *Adj.*
Paulus wurde von der katholischen Kirche heiliggesprochen.

holy, saint(ly)
The Catholic church recognized Paul as a saint.

Himmel ['him(ə)l] *m, -s, -*
„Die guten Menschen kommen in den Himmel", erzählte der Pfarrer den Kindern.

heaven *n*
"Good people go to Heaven," the minister told the children.

Hölle ['hœlə] *f, -, kein Pl.*
Ändere dein Leben, sonst wirst du für deine Taten in der Hölle bestraft.

hell *n*
Change your life or you will be punished in hell for what you've done.

Islam [isˈlaːm] *auch* [ˈislam] *m, -s, kein Pl.*

In vielen Ländern Afrikas und Asiens ist der Islam die Hauptreligion.

Islam *n*

In many countries of Africa and Asia Islam is the principal religion.

Jude [ˈjuːdə] *m, -n, -n*
Jüdin [ˈjyːdin] *f, -, -nen*

Nach ihrer Heirat ist sie Jüdin geworden.

Jew *n*

After her marriage, she became a Jew.

katholisch [kaˈtoːliʃ] *Adj., keine Komp.*

Unser Kind wird katholisch erzogen.

Catholic

Our child will be raised Catholic.

Ostern [ˈoːstəˀn] *n, -, -*

An Ostern machen wir immer einen Kurzurlaub.

Easter *n*

At Easter we always take a short vacation.

Papst [ˈpaːpst] *m, -es, Päpste*

Der Papst forderte die Kriegsgegner auf, Frieden zu schließen.

pope *n*

The pope urged the war enemies to make peace.

Pfarrer [ˈpfarəˀ] *m, -s, -*
Pfarrerin [ˈpfarərin] *f, -, -nen*

Unsere Kirchengemeinde bekommt einen neuen Pfarrer.

(Protestant) **minister** *n*

Our parish is getting a new minister.

religiös [reliˈgjøːs] *Adj., -er, am -esten*

Er ist sehr religiös und geht regelmäßig zum Gottesdienst.

religious

He is very religious and goes to services regularly.

Teufel [ˈtɔif(ə)l] *m, -s, -*

Hast du Angst vor dem Teufel?

devil *n*

Are you afraid of the devil?

8.4 Schule und Ausbildung　　1-2000

aufmerksam ['aufmɛrkzaːm] *Adj.*
Die Schüler hören dem Lehrer aufmerksam zu.

attentive
The school children listen to the teacher attentively.

Aufmerksamkeit
['aufmɛrkzaːmkait] *f, -, kein Pl.*
In den ersten Schulstunden ist die Aufmerksamkeit der Schüler am größten.

attention *n*

Children's attention is best in the early hours of the school day.

Ausbildung ['ausbilduŋ] *f, -, -en*
Die Ausbildungszeit für die meisten Berufe dauert drei Jahre.

education, training *n*
Most trades require three years of vocational training.

auswendig ['ausvɛndiç°] *Adj., keine Komp.*
Die Adresse von Sonja weiß ich auswendig.

by heart

I know Sonja's address by heart.

bestehen [bəˈʃteː(ə)n] *V/t.*, bestand, hat bestanden
Fast alle Teilnehmer des Kurses haben die Prüfung bestanden.

pass *v*

Nearly all the course participants passed the exam.

Fehler ['feːlə*] *m, -s, -*
In dem Text, den ich übersetzt habe, waren einige Fehler.

error, mistake *n*
There were some errors in the text I translated.

Ferien ['feːriən] *nur Pl.*
Nicht alle Schüler verreisen. Einige bleiben in den Ferien zu Hause.

vacation, time off *n*
Not all the students go away. Some stay at home during vacation.

Heft [hɛft] *n, -(e)s, -e*
Für jedes Schulfach hat Jörn ein eigenes Heft.

notebook *n*
Jörn has a separate notebook for each school subject.

Klasse ['klasə] *f, -, -n*
Knut ist in der 2. Klasse der Grundschule.

grade *n*
Knut is in the second grade in elementary school.

Kugelschreiber [ˈkuːg(ə)lʃraibə*]
m, -s, -
Ich schreibe lieber mit einem Bleistift als mit einem Kugelschreiber.

ball-point pen *n*

I prefer a pencil to a ball-point pen for writing.

Kurs [kurs] *m*, -es, -e
In unserem Italienisch-Kurs sind nur fünf Teilnehmer.

course *n*

There are only five students in our Italian course.

leicht [laiçt] *Adj.*, -er, am -esten
Am Anfang war der Kurs leicht, später wurde er immer schwerer.

easy

The class was easy at the beginning, but then it got harder and harder.

Lösung [ˈløːzuŋ] *f*, -, -en
Acht von zehn Lösungen in meiner schriftlichen Prüfung waren richtig.

answer *n*

Eight of the ten answers on my written exam were correct.

Note [ˈnoːtə] *f*, -, -n
Unser Lehrer gibt recht gute Noten.

grade *n*

Our teacher gives really good grades.

Pause [ˈpauzə] *f*, -, -n
Die Pausen zwischen den Unterrichtsstunden sind verschieden lang.

break *n*

Breaks between classes are of different lengths.

Prüfung [ˈpryːfuŋ] *f*, -, -en
Die schriftliche Prüfung war schwieriger als die mündliche.

exam *n*

The written exam was harder than the oral exam.

Schule [ˈʃuːlə] *f*, -, -n
Udo muss noch vier Jahre zur Schule gehen.
Ich fahre morgens mit dem Bus zur Schule.

school *n*

Udo still has four years of school.

In the morning I go to school by bus.

Schüler [ˈʃyːlə*] *m*, -s, -
Schülerin [ˈʃyːlərin] *f*, -, -nen
An unserer Schule sind über 1000 Schüler und Schülerinnen.

pupil, school child, student *n*

There are over 1000 pupils at our school.

Student [ʃtuˈdɛnt] *m*, -en, -en
Studentin [ʃtuˈdɛntin] *f*, -, -nen
Für Studenten ist es in unserer Stadt schwer, eine Wohnung zu finden.

(university) **student** *n*

In our town it's hard for students to find an apartment.

studieren [ʃtu'diːrən] *V/t., i.,* studierte, hat studiert
Wo hast du studiert?
Sigrid studiert Geschichte.

study, go to university, major in *(an academic subject) v*
Where did you go to college?
Sigrid is studying history.

Studium ['ʃtuːdjum] *n, -s,* Studien
Mein Studium hat fünf Jahre gedauert.

studies *n*
My studies lasted five years.

Test [tɛst] *m, -(e)s, -s*
Mit kurzen Tests wurden wir auf die Prüfung vorbereitet.

test *n*
Short tests prepared us for the exam.

Text [tɛkst] *m, -es, -e*
Bitte übersetzen Sie diesen Text ins Französische!

text *n*
Please translate this text into French.

Thema ['teːma] *n, -s,* Themen
Für die Prüfung können wir uns drei Themen aussuchen.

theme, subject, topic *n*
For the exam we can choose three topics.

Übung ['yːbuŋ] *f, -, -en*
In unserem Buch gibt es sehr viele Grammatikübungen.

exercise *n*
There are a lot of grammar exercises in our book.

Unterricht [untə*'riçt] *m, -s, kein Pl.*
Samstags haben wir keinen Unterricht.

classes, lessons *n*

We have no classes on Saturday.

unterrichten ['untə*riçt(ə)n] *V/t., i.,* unterrichtete, hat unterrichtet
Unsere Lehrerin unterrichtet neben Italienisch auch Spanisch.
Er unterrichtet an einer Grundschule.

teach *v*

Our instructor teaches Spanish as well as Italian.
He teaches at an elementary school.

Wörterbuch ['vœrtə*buːx] *n, -(e)s,* Wörterbücher
○ Wie heißt das Wort auf deutsch?
□ Das weiß ich nicht. Sieh doch im Wörterbuch nach!

dictionary *n*
○ How do you say this in German?
□ I don't know. Look it up in the dictionary.

vorbereiten ['foːə*bərait(ə)n] *V/t. refl.,* bereitete vor, hat vorbereitet
Die Studenten haben sich ein Jahr für die Prüfungen vorbereitet.

prepare *v*

The students prepared for the exam for a year.

Zeugnis ['tsɔiknis] *n,* -ses, -se
Ich bin mit den Noten in meinem
Zeugnis sehr zufrieden.

grades, report card *n*
I'm happy with my grades.

$$2001\text{-}4000$$

Aufgabe ['aufga:bə] *f,* -, -n
Die Aufgaben im Test waren zu
schwierig.

exercise *n*
The exercises on the exam were
too difficult.

Examen [ɛ'ksa:mən] *n,* -s, - (Ex-
amina)
Der wichtigste Teil des Examens
ist eine schriftliche Hausarbeit.

exam *n*

The most important part of the
exam is a written part to do at
home.

Fremdsprache ['frɛmtʃpra:xə] *f,*
-, -n
Welche Fremdsprachen sprechen Sie?

foreign language *n*

Which foreign languages do you
speak?

Füller ['fylə*] *m,* -s, -
Ich schreibe nur private Briefe mit
dem Füller.

fountain pen *n*
I only write personal letters with a
fountain pen.

Gymnasium [gym'na:zjum] *n,* -s,
Gymnasien
An unseren Gymnasien ist Fran-
zösisch die erste Fremdsprache.

college preparatory high school
n
At our college preparatory high
schools French is the first foreign
language.

Hausaufgabe ['hausaufga:bə] *f,*
-, -n
Oberschüler müssen täglich viele
Hausaufgaben machen.

homework *n*

High school students have a lot of
homework every day.

Hochschule ['ho:xʃu:lə] *f,* -, -n
Sonja zeichnet sehr gut und
möchte später an einer Kunst-
hochschule studieren.

college, university *n*
Sonja draws very well and later
would like to study art at an art
college.

Institut [insti'tu:t] *n,* -s, -e
Das Institut für Germanistik ist
das größte an unserer Universität.

department *n*
The German department is the
largest in our university.

Kindergarten [ˈkində*gart(ə)n] *m*, -s, Kindergärten
Unser Kind geht nachmittags in den Kindergarten.

kindergarten *n*
Our child goes to kindergarten in the afternoon.

Lehre [ˈleːrə] *f*, -, *kein Pl.*
Kurt macht eine Lehre als Elektriker.

apprenticeship *n*
Kurt is doing his apprenticeship as an electrician.

lösen [ˈløːz(ə)n] *V/t.*, löste, hat gelöst
Seit drei Stunden versuche ich diese Aufgabe zu lösen.

solve, figure out *v*
I've been trying to solve this problem for three hours.

Professor [proˈfɛsɔr] *m*, -s, -en
Professorin [profɛˈsoːrin] *f*, -, -nen
Meine Prüfung mache ich bei Frau Professor Meile.

professor *n*
Professor Melle is in charge of my exam.

Semester [zeˈmɛstə*] *n*, -s, -
Ich studiere jetzt im 5. Semester Tiermedizin.

semester, term *(BE)* *n*
This is my fifth semester of veterinary school.

Stundenplan [ˈʃtund(ə)nplan] *m*, -(e)s, Stundenpläne
Im Fach Medizin ist der Stundenplan genau festgelegt.

schedule *n*
In medical school the schedule is exactly planned out.

Tinte [ˈtintə] *f*, -, *kein Pl.*
Im Füller fehlt Tinte.

ink *n*
The pen is out of ink.

Tafel [ˈtaːf(ə)l] *f*, -, -n
Der Lehrer schreibt die Aufgabe an die Tafel.

board *n*
The teacher writes the question on the board.

Unterrichtsstunde [ˈuntə*riçtsʃtundə] *f*, -, -n
Wir haben täglich fünf Unterrichtsstunden.

class hour, period, lesson *n*
We have five class hours every day.

Bevölkerung [bə'fœlkəruŋ] *f, -, kein Pl.*
Die Bevölkerung ist gegen die neue Straße.

population *n*
The population is against the new road.

Dorf [dɔrf] *n, -(e)s, Dörfer*
Das Dorf hat 263 Einwohner.

village *n*
The population of the village is 263.

Gebäude [gə'bɔidə] *n, -s, -*
Das Bürogebäude hat 16 Stockwerke.

building *n*
The office building has 16 floors.

Gemeinde [gə'maində] *f, -, -n*
Die Gemeinde hat viel Geld für den Straßenbau ausgegeben.

community *n*
The community has spent a lot for street construction.

Halle ['halə] *f, -, -n*
Die Ware liegt in Halle 3.

hall *n*
The merchandise is in warehouse (hall) 3.

Hof [ho:f] *m, -(e)s, Höfe*
In diesem Hof darf nicht geparkt werden.

(court) yard *n*
There's no parking in this yard.

Ort [ɔrt] *m, -(e)s, -e*
In unserem Ort gibt es keine Post.

place, town *n*
There's no post office in our town.

Platz [plats] *m, -es, Plätze*
Der Platz ist mittwochs wegen des Wochenmarktes für Autos gesperrt.

town square *n*
On Wednesday the town square is closed to traffic because of the market.

Siedlung ['zi:dluŋ] *f, -, -en*
Die Häuser in der Siedlung sehen alle sehr ähnlich aus.

subdivision, development *n*
The houses in the subdivision are all similar.

Stadt [ʃtat] *f, -, Städte*
Das Zentrum der Stadt ist sehr alt.

city, town *n*
The central part of the city is very old.

Straße ['ʃtraːsə] *f,* -, -n
In welcher Straße ist das Geschäft?

street *n*
On what street is the store?

2001-4000

Bauernhof ['bauə*nhoːf] *m,* -(e)s,
Bauernhöfe
Zu dem Bauernhof gehören über
60 Hektar Land.

farm *n*

The farm has over 60 hectares.

Bewohner [bə'voːnə*] *m,* -s, -
Bewohnerin *f,* -, -nen
Fast alle Dorfbewohner haben an
dem Fest teilgenommen.

resident *n*

Almost all the residents of the
town took part in the celebration.

Bezirk [bə'tsirk] *m,* -s, -e
Die Stadtbezirke in Wien haben
Nummern.

district *n*
The city districts of Vienna have
numbers.

Brunnen ['brunən] *m,* -s, -
An der Seite des Brunnens ist ein
Wasserhahn.

well, fountain *n*
There is a water faucet by the
well.

Denkmal ['dɛŋkmaːl] *n,* -s, Denkmäler
Das Denkmal wird von vielen Touristen besucht.

monument *n*

Many tourists visit the monument.

Großstadt ['groːsʃtat] *f,* -, Großstädte
Die nächste Großstadt ist 40 km
von unserem Dorf entfernt.

large city *n*

The nearest large city is 40 km
from our town.

Grundstück ['gruntʃtyk] *n,* -(e)s,
-e
Das Grundstück ist ca. 900 m^2
groß.

lot, piece of land, estate *n*

The lot is about 900 square meters.

Hauptstadt ['hauptʃtat] *f,* -,
Hauptstädte
Die Hauptstadt der Niederlande
ist Den Haag, nicht Amsterdam.

capital *n*

The capital of the Netherlands is
The Hague, not Amsterdam.

Rathaus ['ra:thaus] *n*, -es, Rat-häuser | **city hall** *n*
Die Stadt will ein neues Rathaus bauen lassen. | The city wants to build a new city hall.

Schloss [ʃlɔs] *n*, -es, Schlösser | **castle** *n*
Das Schloss kann nur morgens besichtigt werden. | The castle can only be visited in the morning.

Stall [ʃtal] *m*, -(e)s, Ställe | **barn, stable, cowshed** *(BE) n*
In diesem Stall stehen 45 Kühe. | There are 45 cows in that barn.

Turm [turm] *m*, -(e)s, Türme | **tower** *n*
Der Turm ist 68 m hoch. | The tower is 68 meters high.

Umgebung [um'ge:buŋ] *f*, -, -en | **area around, surrounding area, environs** *n*
Die Umgebung der Stadt ist sehr schön. | The area around the city is very pretty.

Vorort ['fo:ə*ɔrt] *m*, -(e)s, -e | **suburb** *n*
Wir wohnen in einem Vorort von Köln. | We live in a suburb of Cologne.

Zoo [tso:] *m*, -s, -s | **zoo** *n*
Der Zoo hat auch im Winter ge-öffnet. | The zoo is also open in winter.

9.2 Landschaft | 1-2000

9.2 Landscape

Aussicht ['auszɪçt] *f*, -, *kein Pl.* | **view** *n*
Die Aussicht von dem Berg ist herrlich. | The view from the mountain is wonderful.

Berg [bɛrk] *m*, -(e)s, -e | **mountain** *n*
In den Bergen gibt es jetzt schon Schnee. | In the mountains there is already snow.

Brücke ['brykə] *f, -, -n*
Über diese Brücke dürfen nur
Wagen mit weniger als 4 t Ge-
wicht fahren.

bridge *n*
Only vehicles that weigh less than
4 tons may use this bridge.

Feld [fɛlt] *n, -(e)s, -er*
Das Getreide steht noch auf den
Feldern.

field *n*
The grain is still in the fields.

Felsen ['fɛlz(ə)n] *m, -s, -*
Am Strand liegen viele dicke
Felsen.

rock *n*
There are a lot of big rocks on the
beach.

Fluss [flus] *m, -es, Flüsse*
Wir sind mit einer Fähre über den
Fluss gefahren.

river *n*
We crossed the river on a ferry.

Gebirge [gə'birgə] *n, -s, -*
Die Berge in diesem Gebirge sind
nicht sehr hoch.

mountains *n*
The peaks in these mountains are
not very high.

Gegend ['ge:g(ə)nt] *f, -, -en*
In unserer Gegend gibt es viele
Industrieunternehmen.

region *n*
There is a lot of industry in our
region.

Hügel ['hy:g(ə)l] *m, -s, -*
Wegen ihrer vielen kleinen Hügel
ist die Landschaft sehr schön.

hill *n*
The landscape is very beautiful
because of its small hills.

Insel ['inz(ə)l] *f, -, -n*
Auf der Insel dürfen keine Autos
fahren.

island *n*
No car traffic is allowed on the
island.

Küste ['kystə] *f, -, -n*
Die Bewohner der Küste wurden
vor Hochwasser gewarnt.

coast *n*
Residents on the coast were
warned about high water.

Land [lant] *n, -(e)s, kein Pl.*
Die meisten Bauern in dieser Gegend haben wenig Land.

land *n*
Most farmers in this area have
very little land.

Landschaft ['lantʃaft] *f, -, -en*
Im Frühjahr ist die Landschaft auf
der Insel am schönsten.

landscape, countryside *n*
The landscape on this island is at
its most beautiful in the spring.

Landstraße ['lantʃtra:sə] *f, -, -n*
Die Strecke über die Landstraße
ist kürzer.

secondary road, country road *n*
The route over the secondary
road is shorter.

Park [park] *m,* -s, -s
Im Stadtpark gibt es ein gemütliches Café.

park *n*
There is a nice café in the city park.

See [ze:] *m,* -s, -n
An Wochenenden ist der See voller Boote.

lake *n*
The lake is full of boats on the weekends.

See *f,* -, *kein Pl.*
Nach einem Sturm hat die (Nord-)See hohe Wellen.

sea *n*
After a storm the (North)Sea shows high waves.

Tal [ta:l] *n,* -(e)s, Täler
Das Tal ist mit dem Auto schwer zu erreichen.

valley *n*
The valley is hard to drive to.

Ufer ['u:fə*] *n,* -s, -
Das ganze Ufer des Sees ist Naturschutzgebiet.

shore *n*
The entire lake shore is a nature reserve.

Wald [valt] *m,* -es, Wälder
In unserer Gegend gibt es nur wenige Wälder.

woods *n*
There are only a few woods in our area.

Weg [ve:k] *m,* -es, -e
Dieser Weg führt ins Tal.

way, path *n*
This path leads to the valley.

Wiese ['vi:zə] *f,* -, -n
Hinter dem Haus ist eine große Wiese.

meadow *n*
There is a big meadow behind the house.

2001-4000

Bach [bax] *m,* -(e)s, Bäche
In dem Bach sind keine Fische.

creek, brook *n*
There are no fish in the creek.

Boden ['bo:d(ə)n] *m,* -s, Böden
Für die Gemüsepflanzen ist der Boden im Garten zu trocken.

ground, soil *n*
The soil in the garden is too dry for the vegetables.

gebirgig [gə'birgiç°] *Adj.*
Die Gegend ist gebirgig.

mountainous
The region is mountainous.

Graben ['gra:b(ə)n] *m,* -s, Gräben
Im Sommer ist dieser Graben trocken.

ditch *n*
In the summer this ditch is dry.

Hang [haŋ] *m*, -(e)s, Hänge
Der Skihang ist für Anfänger zu steil.

slope *n*
The ski slope is too steep for beginners.

Horizont [hori'tsɔnt] *m*, -(e)s, -e
Am Horizont kann man ein Schiff erkennen.

horizon *n*
On the horizon you can see a ship.

Kanal [ka'naːl] *m*, -s, Kanäle
Durch den Kanal werden zwei Flüsse miteinander verbunden.

canal *n*
Two rivers are connected by the canal.

Sand [zant] *m*, -(e)s, *kein Pl.*
Der Sand am Flussufer ist sehr fein.

sand *n*
The sand on the river bank is very fine.

Teich [taiç] *m*, -(e)s, -e
In dem Teich sind viele Wasserpflanzen.

pond *n*
There are many aquatic plants in the pond.

Wüste ['vyːstə] *f*, -, -n
Viele junge Wüstenbewohner ziehen in die Städte im Norden des Landes.

desert *n*
Many young people who live in the desert move to the cities in the north of the country.

9.3 Natur: Allgemeines 1-2000

9.3 Nature: General

dunkel ['duŋk(ə)l] *Adj.*, dunkler, am dunkelsten
Die Wolken sind ganz dunkel.

dark

The clouds are very dark.

Dunkelheit ['duŋk(ə)lhait] *f*, -, *kein Pl.*
In der Dunkelheit ist das Haus schwer zu finden.

dark, darkness *n*

The house is hard to find in the dark.

Erde ['ɛə*də] *f*, -, *kein Pl.*
Auf der Erde wohnen bald über 6 Milliarden Menschen.
Die Erde in dieser Gegend ist braun-rot.

earth, ground, soil *n*
Soon over 6 billion people will be living on the earth.
In this area the soil is reddish-brown.

Gipfel ['gipf(ə)l] *m, -s, -*
Auf dem Gipfel des Berges ist eine kleine Hütte.

peak *n*
There's a little hut on the mountain peak.

---

hell [hɛl] *Adj.*
Das Sonnenlicht macht den Raum sehr hell.

bright
The sun light makes the room very bright.

Himmel ['him(ə)l] *m, -s, kein Pl.*
Am Himmel ist keine Wolke zu sehen.

sky *n*
There's not a cloud in the sky.

Karte ['kartə] *f, -, -n*
Ohne Wanderkarte hätten wir den Weg nicht gefunden.

map *n*
Without a hiking map we wouldn't have found the path.

Luft [luft] *f, -, kein Pl.*
Die Luft in den Bergen ist angenehm frisch.

air *n*
The air in the mountains is quite cool.

Meer [me:ə*] *n, -es, -e*
Die Stadt liegt nur 10 km vom Meer entfernt.

sea, ocean *n*
The city is only 10 km from the sea.

Mond [mo:nt] *m, -(e)s, -e*
Heute Nacht ist Vollmond.

moon *n*
There is a full moon tonight.

Natur [na'tu:ə*] *f, -, kein Pl.*
Die Natur muss stärker vor den Menschen geschützt werden.

nature *n*
Nature must be more strongly protected from people.

Norden ['nɔrd(ə)n] *m, -s, kein Pl.*
Im Norden des Landes gab es gestern den ersten Schnee.

north *n*
Yesterday the north of the country had its first snow.

---

nördlich ['nœrtliç] *Adj.*
Wir wohnen in einem Dorf 20 km nördlich von Frankfurt.

north
We live in a small town 20 km north of Frankfurt.

Osten ['ɔst(ə)n] *m, -s, kein Pl.*
Im Osten des Landes gibt es viele Seen.

east *n*
In the east of the country there are many lakes.

östlich ['œstliç] *Adj.*
Wolfsburg liegt östlich von Hannover.

east
Wolfsburg is east of Hannover.

Ozean ['o:tsea:n] *m, -s, -e*
Er ist mit einem kleinen Segelboot über den Indischen Ozean gefahren.

ocean *n*
He crossed the Indian Ocean in a small sail boat.

Rauch [raux] *m, -(e)s, kein Pl.*
Durch den Rauch bekamen wir Tränen in den Augen.

smoke *n*
We got tears in our eyes from the smoke.

Schatten ['ʃat(ə)n] *m, -s, -*
Sogar im Schatten war es über 30 °C heiß.

shade *n*
Even in the shade it was hot – over 30 °C.

Sonne ['zɔnə] *f, -, kein Pl.*
Diese Pflanze darf nicht direkt im Sonnenlicht stehen.

sun *n*
This plant must not be in direct sun light.

Stein [ʃtain] *m, -(e)s, -e*
In der Erde in unserem Garten sind leider viele Steine.

stone, rock *n*
Unfortunately the soil in our yard is full of stones.

Stern [ʃtɛrn] *m, -s, -e*
Der Nachthimmel ist so klar, dass man alle Sternbilder deutlich erkennt.

star *n*
The night sky is so clear you can see all the constellations of stars.

Süden ['zy:d(ə)n] *m, -s, kein Pl.*
Im Süden des Landes gab es gestern schwere Gewitter.

south *n*
Yesterday there were strong storms in the South.

südlich ['zy:tlɪç] *Adj.*
Italien liegt südlich der Alpen.

south
Italy is south of the Alps.

Temperatur [tɛmpəra'tu:ə*] *f, -, -en*
Die Temperaturen werden diese Nacht auf unter 0 °C sinken.

temperature *n*

Tonight the temperature will go down below freezing.

Umwelt ['umvɛlt] *f, -, kein Pl.*
Der Schutz der Umwelt ist ein wichtiges politisches Thema geworden.

environment *n*
Protection of the environment has become an important political theme.

wachsen ['vaks(ə)n] *V/i., wuchs, ist gewachsen*
In diesem Boden wachsen Kartoffeln besonders gut.

grow *v*

Potatoes grow especially well in this soil.

Wasser ['vasə*] *n, -s, kein Pl.*
Vorsicht, das ist kein Trinkwasser!

water *n*
Be careful, it's not safe to drink that water.

Welt [vɛlt] *f, -, kein Pl.*
Die Sahara ist die größte Wüste der Welt.

world *n*
The Sahara is the largest desert in the world.

Westen ['vɛst(ə)n] *m, -s, kein Pl.*
Der Wind kommt von Westen.

west *n*
The wind is coming from the west.

westlich ['vɛstliç] *Adj.*
Am westlichen Seeufer ist ein Sandstrand.

western
There's a sandy beach on the western shore of the sea.

2001-4000

Ebbe ['ɛbə] *f, -, kein Pl.*
Am Nachmittag fährt kein Schiff zur Insel. Es ist Ebbe.

low tide *n*
No one is sailing to the island this afternoon. It's low tide.

Festland ['fɛstlant] *n, -(e)s, kein Pl.*
Sie arbeitet auf dem Festland, aber sie wohnt auf der Insel.

mainland *n*

She works on the mainland, but she lives on the island.

Flachland ['flaxlant] *n, -(e)s, kein Pl.*
Ich finde das Flachland langweilig.

lowland *n*

I think the lowland is boring.

fließen ['fli:s(ə)n] *V/i.,* floss, ist geflossen
Der Bach fließt sehr langsam.

flow *v*

The stream flows very slowly.

Flut [flu:t] *f, -, kein Pl.*
Wir können am Nachmittag im Meer schwimmen. Dann ist Flut.

high tide *n*
We could swim in the ocean this afternoon. It's high tide then.

frieren ['fri:rən] *V/i.,* fror, hat (ist) gefroren
Diese Nacht soll es frieren.

freeze, go down to freezing *v*

It's supposed to freeze tonight.

Kontinent ['kɔntinɛnt] *m, -s, -e*
Europa wird auch der ‚alte Kontinent' genannt.

continent *n*
Europe is also called the "old continent."

Planet [pla'ne:t] *m, -en, -en*
Der Planet Mars hat zwei Monde.

planet *n*
The planet Mars has two moons.

Pol [po:l] *m, -s, -e*
Vom 21. März bis zum 23. September scheint am Nordpol Tag und Nacht die Sonne.

pole *n*
From March 21 to September 23 the sun shines day and night at the North Pole.

Schlamm [ʃlam] *m*, -s, *kein Pl.*
Nach dem Hochwasser blieb am
Ufer sehr viel Schlamm liegen.

mud *n*
After the flood there was a lot of
mud on the bank.

Strand [ʃtrant] *m*, -(e)s, Strände
Das Hotel hat einen eigenen
Strand.

beach *n*
The hotel has its own beach.

Weltall [ˈvɛltal] *n*, -s, *kein Pl.*
Es wurde ein neuer Fernsehsatel-
lit ins Weltall geschossen.

(outer) space, universe *n*
A new television satellite was shot
into space.

9.4 Tiere

1-2000

9.4 Animals

Fisch [fiʃ] *m*, -(e)s, -e
In diesem See gibt es viele
Fische.

fish *n*
There are many fish in that lake.

Geflügel [gəˈflyːg(ə)l] *n*, -s, *kein
Pl.*
Isst du gerne Geflügel?

poultry *n*

Do you like to eat poultry?

Hund [hunt] *m*, -(e)s, -e
Er hat Angst vor Hunden.

dog *n*
He is afraid of dogs.

Insekt [inˈzɛkt] *n*, -s, -en
Unsere Obstbäume sind krank,
weil Insekten die Blätter auf-
fressen.

insect *n*
Our fruit trees are sick because
insects are eating up the leaves.

Kalb [kalp] *n*, -(e)s, Kälber
Für dieses Gericht kann man nur
zartes Kalbfleisch nehmen.

calf *[the animal]*, **veal** *[the meat] n*
For this dish you can only use
tender veal.

Katze [ˈkatsə] *f*, -, -n
Unsere Katze und unser Hund
verstehen sich gut.

cat *n*
Our cat and our dog get along
well.

Kuh [kuː] *f*, -, Kühe
Frische Kuhmilch hat ca. 3,7 %
Fett.

cow *n*
Fresh cow's milk has about 3.7 %
fat.

Lebewesen ['le:bəve:z(ə)n] *n,*
-s, -
Auf dem Mond hat man noch keine Lebewesen entdeckt.

living thing *n*

Not a living thing has been found
on the moon.

Pferd [pfe:ə*t] *n,* -(e)s, -e
Auf diesem Pferd können auch
Kinder reiten. Es ist sehr ruhig.

horse *n*

Even children can ride this horse.
He is very calm.

Rind [rint] *n,* -(e)s, -er
In diesem Stall sind über 200
Rinder.

(beef) **cattle, beef** *[the meat] n*

There are over 200 head of cattle
in that barn.

Schwein [ʃvain] *n,* -(e)s, -e

Ich esse lieber Schweinefleisch
als Rindfleisch.

pig *[the animal],* **pork** *[the meat],*
hog, *n*

I prefer pork to beef.

Tier [ti:ə*] *n,* -(e)s, -e
In dieser Wohnung darf man keine Haustiere haben.

animal, *(house)* **pet** *n*

We are not allowed to have pets in
this apartment.

Vieh [fi:] *n,* -s, *kein Pl.*
Der Bauer Janßen hat über 250
Stück Vieh in seinen Ställen.

livestock *n*

Farmer Janßen has over 250 head
of livestock in his barns.

Vogel ['fo:g(ə)l] *m,* -s, Vögel
Im Winter füttern wir draußen die
Vögel.

bird *n*

In the winter we feed the birds
outside.

Wild [vilt] *n,* -(e)s, *kein Pl.*
In diesem Tierschutzgebiet darf
kein Wild geschossen werden.

game *n*

No game may be shot in this nature reserve.

2001-4000

Affe ['afə] *m,* -n, -n
Linda hat einen kleinen Affen als
Haustier.

monkey *n*

Linda has a little monkey as a pet.

bellen ['bɛl(ə)n] *V/i.,* bellte, hat ge-
bellt
Wenn fremde Leute kommen,
bellt unser Hund sofort.

bark *v*

Our dog barks right away when a
stranger comes by.

Biene ['bi:nə] *f,* -, -n
Unser Nachbar hat vier Bienen-
häuser.

bee *n*

Our neighbor has four bee hives.

Elefant [ele'fant] *m, -en, -en*
In Indien werden Elefanten als Arbeitstiere verwendet.

elephant *n*
In India elephants are used as work animals.

Ente ['ɛntə] *f, -, -n*
Zum Mittagessen gibt es einen Entenbraten.

duck *n*
There's roast duck for dinner.

Feder ['fe:də*] *f, -, -n*
Unser Vogel verliert Federn. Er ist sicher krank.

feather *n*
Our bird is losing feathers. He is certainly sick.

Fliege ['fli:gə] *f, -, -n*
Die Küche ist voller Fliegen.

fly *n*
The kitchen is full of flies.

fressen ['frɛs(ə)n] *V/t.,* fraß, hat gefressen
Unsere Katze frisst gerne Fisch.

eat *n*

Our cat likes to eat fish.

füttern ['fytə*n] *V/t.,* fütterte, hat gefüttert
Unser Hund wird nur einmal am Tag gefüttert.

feed *v*

We feed our dog only once a day.

Gans [gans] *f, -,* Gänse
Bernd kann Gänse und Enten nicht unterscheiden.

goose *n*
Bernd can't tell the difference between ducks and geese.

Hahn [ha:n] *m, -(e)s,* Hähne
Wir haben 12 Hühner und einen Hahn.

rooster, cock *n*
We have twelve hens and one rooster.

Haustier ['hausti:ə*] *n, -(e)s, -e*
○ Hast du ein Haustier?
□ Ja, einen Hund.

pet *n*
○ Do you have a pet?
□ Yes, a dog.

Henne ['hɛnə] *f, -, -n*
Die alten Hennen legen weniger Eier als die jungen.

hen *n*
The old hens lay fewer eggs than the young ones.

Kaninchen [ka'ni:nçən] *n, -s, -*
Das Gemüse in unserem Garten müssen wir vor den Kaninchen schützen.

rabbit *n*
We have to protect the vegetables in our garden from the rabbits.

Lamm [lam] *n*, -(e)s, Lämmer
In den meisten Metzgereien in unserer Stadt kann man kein Lammfleisch kaufen.

lamb *n*
In most butcher shops in our city you can't buy lamb.

Löwe ['lø:və] *m*, -n, -n
In diesem kleinen Zoo gibt es keine Löwen.

lion *n*
There are no lions in this small zoo.

Maus [maus] *f*, -, Mäuse
Im Keller in unserem Haus sind Mäuse.

mouse *n*
There are mice in the basement in our house.

Ochse ['ɔksə] *m*, -n, -n
Ich kenne einen Bauern, der noch Ochsen als Arbeitstiere hat.

ox *n*
I know a farmer who still uses oxen as work animals.

Pelz [pɛlts] *m*, -es, -e
Diese Pelzjacke ist sehr warm.

fur *n*
This fur jacket is very warm.

Rasse ['rasə] *f*, -, -n
Wie heißt diese Hunderasse?

breed *n*
What breed is that dog?

Ratte ['ratə] *f*, -, -n
Im Hühnerstall habe ich eine Ratte gesehen.

rat *n*
I saw a rat in the chicken coop.

Schaf [ʃaːf] *n*, -(e)s, -e
Der Pullover ist aus Schafswolle.

sheep *n*
The sweater is made of sheep's wool.

Schlange ['ʃlaŋə] *f*, -, -n
Diese Schlange ist ungefährlich.

snake *n*
That snake is not dangerous.

Schmetterling ['ʃmɛtəˈlɪŋ] *m*, -s, -e
Erika sammelt Schmetterlinge.

butterfly *n*
Erika collects butterflies.

Schwanz [ʃvants] *m*, -es, Schwänze
Hunde dieser Rasse haben einen sehr kurzen Schwanz.

tail *n*
Dogs of that breed have a very short tail.

Taube ['taubə] *f*, -, -n
Es gibt zu viele Tauben in unserer Stadt.

pigeon *n*
There are too many pigeons in our city.

Wolf [vɔlf] *m*, -(e)s, Wölfe
In Mitteleuropa gibt es fast keine Wölfe mehr.

wolf *n*
There are almost no more wolves in central Europe.

Wurm [vurm] *m,* -(e)s, Würmer
Er fängt Fische mit lebenden Würmern.

worm *n*
He fishes with live worms.

zahm [tsa:m] *Adj.*
Ist der Vogel zahm?

tame
Is the bird tame?

Ziege ['tsi:gə] *f,* -, -n
Ich esse gerne Ziegenkäse.

goat *n*
I like to eat goat cheese.

züchten ['tsyçt(ə)n] *V/t.,* züchtete,
hat gezüchtet
Peter züchtet seltene Fische.

breed *v*

Peter breeds a rare type of fish.

9.5 Pflanzen | 1-2000

9.5 Plants

Baum [baum] *m,* -(e)s, Bäume
Der Baum ist über 80 Jahre alt.

tree *n*
The tree is over 80 years old.

Blatt [blat] *n,* -(e)s, Blätter
In diesem Jahr sind die Blätter
sehr früh von den Bäumen gefallen.

leaf *n*
This year the leaves fell off the
trees early.

Blume ['blu:mə] *f,* -, -n
Welche Blume magst du am
liebsten?

flower *n*
What flower do you like best?

Blüte ['bly:tə] *f,* -, -n
Diese Blume hat blaue Blüten.

blossom *n*
This flower has blue blossoms.

Ernte ['ɛrntə] *f,* -, -n
Die Ernte des letzten Jahres war
schlechter als dieses Jahr.

harvest *n*
Last year's harvest was worse
than this year's.

Getreide [gə'traidə] *n,* -s, *kein Pl.*
Wegen des feuchten Sommers
war die Getreideernte nicht sehr
gut.

grain, corn *(BE) n*
The grain harvest wasn't good
because of the rainy summer.

Gras [gra:s] *n,* -es, *kein Pl.*
Weil es wenig geregnet hat, ist
das Gras gelb geworden.

grass *n*
The grass turned yellow because
of the lack of rain.

Pflanze ['pflantsə] *f,* -, -n
Für trockenes Klima ist die Pflanze nicht geeignet.

plant *n*
This plant isn't good for a dry climate.

pflanzen ['pflants(ə)n] *V/t.,*
pflanzte, hat gepflanzt
Die Bäume müssen im Herbst gepflanzt werden.

plant *v*

The trees must be planted in the fall.

Wurzel ['vurts(ə)l] *f,* -, -n
Die Wurzeln dieser Pflanze sind über einen Meter tief in der Erde.

root *n*
The roots of this plant are over a meter/metre deep in the earth.

Zweig [tsvaik] *m,* -(e)s, -e
Durch den Sturm hat der Baum einige Zweige verloren.

branch, twig *n*
The tree lost several branches in the storm.

2001-4000

Ast [ast] *m,* -(e)s, Äste
Im Herbst sollte man die Äste der Obstbäume schneiden.

branch *(large) n*
In autumn you should trim the branches of the fruit trees.

blühen ['bly:(ə)n] *V/i.,* blühte, hat geblüht
Diese Blume blüht im Herbst.

blossom, bloom *v*

This flower blooms in autumn.

Rose ['ro:zə] *f,* -, -n
Fast alle Rosen sind durch den starken Frost kaputtgegangen.

rose *n*
Almost all roses were destroyed by the hard frost.

säen ['zɛ:(ə)n] *V/t.,* säte, hat gesät
Der Weizen wird schon im März gesät.

sow *v*

Wheat is sown in March.

Samen ['za:mən] *m,* -s, -
Es gibt verschiedene Sorten von Grassamen.

seed *n*
There are different kinds of grass seed.

Stamm [ʃtam] *m,* -(e)s, Stämme
Der Stamm des Baumes ist innen faul.

trunk (of a tree) *n*
The trunk of the tree is rotten inside.

Stiel [ʃti:l] *m,* -(e)s, -e
Vorsicht, die Stiele der Blumen sind sehr zart!

stem *n*
Careful, the stems of the flowers are very tender.

Strauß [ʃtraus] *m,* -es, Sträuße
Der Blumenstrauß ist wirklich sehr schön.

bouquet *n*
The flower bouquet is really very pretty.

Tomate [toˈmaːtə] *f,* -, -n
Für den Salat brauchen wir Tomaten.

tomato *n*
We need tomatoes for the salad.

Traube [ˈtraubə] *f,* -, -n
Die Trauben schmecken sauer.

grape *n*
The grapes taste sour.

9.6 Wetter und Klima | 1-2000

9.6 Weather and Climate

Frost [frɔst] *m,* -es, *kein Pl.*
Die Pflanze muss vor Frost geschützt werden.

frost *n*
The plant has to be protected from frost.

Gewitter [gəˈvitə*] *n,* -s, -
Mach alle Fenster zu! Es gibt gleich ein Gewitter.

thunder storm *n*
Close all the windows! A thunder storm is on the way.

Hitze [ˈhitsə] *f,* -, *kein Pl.*
Andreas kann große Hitze nicht vertragen.

heat *n*
Andreas cannot stand high temperatures/heat.

kalt [kalt] *Adj.,* kälter, am kältesten
Zieh dich warm an! Draußen ist es kalt.

cold
Dress warmly! It is cold outside.

Kälte [ˈkɛltə] *f,* -, *kein Pl.*
Die Kälte ist ungewöhnlich für die Jahreszeit.

cold *n*
The cold is unusual for the season.

Klima [ˈkliːma] *n,* -s, Klimata (Klimate)
Im Norden des Landes ist das Klima feucht und kalt.

climate *n*

In the northern part of the country the climate is humid and cold.

kühl [kyːl] *Adj.*
Das Wasser ist zu kühl zum Baden.

cool
The water is too cool to swim in.

Nebel ['ne:b(ə)l] *m*, -s, *kein Pl.*
Der Nebel ist so dicht, dass man kaum 20 Meter weit sehen kann.

fog *n*
The fog is so thick, that you can't see 20 meters/metres in front of you.

Regen ['re:g(ə)n] *m*, -s, *kein Pl.*
Der Wetterbericht hat für morgen Regen gemeldet.

rain *n*
The weather report for tomorrow is rain.

---

regnen ['re:gnən] *V/i.*, regnete, hat geregnet
Es hat schon seit Wochen nicht geregnet.

rain *v*

It has not rained for weeks.

---

scheinen ['ʃainən] *V/i.*, schien, hat geschienen
Wir hatten im Urlaub gutes Wetter. Jeden Tag schien die Sonne.

shine *v*

We had good weather on vacation. Every day the sun shone.

Schnee [ʃne:] *m*, -s, *kein Pl.*
Zum Skifahren gibt es leider nicht genug Schnee.

snow *n*
Unfortunately, there is not enough snow for skiing.

---

schneien ['ʃnai(ə)n] *V/i.*, schneite, hat geschneit
Seit zwei Stunden schneit es.

snow *v*

It has been snowing for two hours.

---

sonnig ['zɔniç°] *Adj.*
In den letzten Tagen war das Wetter meistens sonnig.

sunny
The weather has been mostly sunny in the last few days.

Sturm [ʃturm] *m*, -(e)s, Stürme
Der Sturm hat schwere Schäden verursacht.

storm *n*
The storm caused severe damages.

---

stürmen ['ʃtyrmən] *V/i.*, stürmte, hat gestürmt
Draußen stürmt und schneit es.

storm *v*

Outside it is storming and snowing.

Tropfen ['trɔpf(ə)n] *m*, -s, -
Es gibt Regen. Die ersten Tropfen fallen schon.

drop *n*
It's raining. The first drops are already falling.

---

warm [varm] *Adj.*, wärmer, am wärmsten
Du brauchst keine Jacke. Es ist warm draußen.

warm

You don't need a jacket. It is warm outside.

Wärme ['vɛrmə] *f, -, kein Pl.*
Der Ofen macht eine angenehme
Wärme.

warmth *n*
The oven produces a pleasant
warmth.

wehen [veː(ə)n] *V/i.,* wehte, hat
geweht
Seit Stunden weht ein starker
Wind.

blow *(wind) v*

A strong wind has been blowing
for hours.

Wetter ['vɛtə*] *n, -s, kein Pl.*
Wie wird das Wetter morgen?

weather *n*
What is the weather going to be
tomorrow?

Wind [vɪnt] *m, -(e)s, -e*
Der Wind kommt von Westen.

wind *n*
The wind is coming from the west.

Wolke ['vɔlkə] *f, -, -n*
Die Wolken wurden immer
dunkler.

cloud *n*
The clouds got darker and darker.

2001-4000

Blitz [blɪts] *m, -es, -e*
Hast du den Blitz gesehen?

lightning *n*
Did you see the lightning?

Donner ['dɔnə*] *m, -s, kein Pl.*
Hast du den Donner gehört? Es
gibt gleich ein Gewitter.

thunder *n*
Did you hear the thunder? There's
a storm coming soon.

Eis [ais] *n, -es, kein Pl.*
Das Eis trägt. Man kann darauf
laufen.

ice *n*
The ice is solid. You can walk on
it.

Hochwasser ['hoːxvasə*] *n, -s,
kein Pl.*
Wegen des Hochwassers müssen die Küstenbewohner ihre
Häuser verlassen.

high water, flood *n*

Because of the high water the
coastal residents have to leave
their houses.

Katastrophe [katasˈtroːfə] *f, -, -n*
Die Flutkatastrophe forderte viele
Opfer.

catastrophe, disaster *n*
The flood disaster claimed many
victims.

mild [mɪlt] *Adj., -er, am -esten*
Typisch für die Gegend ist das
milde Winterklima.

mild
Mild winters are typical for the
area.

neblig ['ne:blɪç°] *Adj.*
Fahr langsamer, es ist neblig!

foggy
Drive more slowly, it is foggy!

regnerisch ['re:gnərɪʃ] *Adj.*
Das Wetter ist seit Tagen kalt und regnerisch.

rainy
The weather has been cold and rainy for days.

Schauer ['ʃauə*] *m,* -s, -
Nach dem kurzen Schauer schien wieder die Sonne.

shower *n*
After the brief shower the sun shone again.

Sonnenschein ['zɔnənʃain] *m,* -s, *kein Pl.*
Ich wünsche euch für euren Urlaub viel Sonnenschein.

sunshine *n*
I hope you have lots of sunshine for your vacation.

10.1 Technik	**1-2000**

10.1 Technology

anmachen ['anmax(ə)n] *V/t.,*
machte an, hat angemacht
Mach bitte den Fernsehapparat an!

turn on *v*

Please turn on the television.

---

an sein ['an zain] *V/i.,* war an, ist
an gewesen
Warum ist in der Garage das Licht an?

be (turned) on *v*

Why is the garage light on?

Apparat [apa'ra:t] *m,* -s, -e
Der Fernsehapparat steht im Wohnzimmer.

set *n*

The television set is in the living room.

---

ausmachen ['ausmax(ə)n] *V/t.,*
machte aus, hat ausgemacht
Vergiss nicht, das Radio auszumachen!

turn off *v*

Don't forget to turn off the radio.

---

aus sein ['aus zain] *V/i.,* war aus,
ist aus gewesen
Es ist kalt hier. Ist die Heizung aus?

be off *v*

It's cold in here! Is the heat turned off?

Automat [auto'ma:t] *m,* -en, -en
Wo gibt es hier einen Zigarettenautomaten?

vending machine *n*

Where is there a cigarette vending machine?

---

automatisch [auto'ma:tiʃ] *Adj.*
Das Licht geht automatisch an.

automatic

The light turns on automatically.

Computer [kɔm'pju:tə*] *m,* -s, -
Unsere Rechnungen werden alle von einem Computer geschrieben.

computer *n*

All our invoices are written by a computer.

Dampf [dampf] *m,* -(e)s, Dämpfe
Diese Maschine funktioniert noch mit Dampfkraft.

steam *n*

This engine is still driven by steam.

dicht [dɪçt] *Adj.*, -er, am -esten
Die Gasleitung ist nicht dicht.

tight
The gas pipe isn't tight.

Draht [draːt] *m*, -(e)s, Drähte
Die Leitungen kannst du mit Draht zusammenbinden.

wire *n*
You can connect the pipes with wire.

elektrisch [e'lɛktrɪʃ] *Adj., keine Komp.*
Er benutzt einen elektrischen Rasierapparat.

electric
He uses an electric razor.

Energie [enɛr'giː] *f*, -, -n
Die Kosten für Heizenergie sind gesunken.

energy *n*
The price of energy for heat has gone down.

Funk [fʊŋk] *m*, -s, *kein Pl.*
Die Polizei hat über Funk einen Krankenwagen gerufen.

radio *n*
The police called an ambulance by radio.

funktionieren [fʊŋktsjo'niːrən] *V/i.*, funktionierte, hat funktioniert
Die Waschmaschine funktioniert nicht.

work *v*
The washing machine doesn't work.

Gas [gaːs] *n*, -es, -e
Wir haben einen Gasherd.

gas
We have a gas stove.

Glas [glaːs] *n*, -es, *kein Pl.*
Auf der Kiste steht: ‚Vorsicht Glas!'

glass *n*
There's a sign on the crate: "Attention! Glass!"

Kabel ['kaːb(ə)l] *n*, -s, -
Für diese Stromstärke ist das Kabel nicht stark genug.

wire, cord *n*
This wire isn't strong enough for this strength of the electric current.

Lärm [lɛrm] *m*, -s, *kein Pl.*
Leider macht die Maschine sehr viel Lärm.

noise *n*
Unfortunately the machine makes a lot of noise.

Leitung ['laitʊŋ] *f*, -, -en
Im letzten Winter ist unsere Wasserleitung eingefroren.

pipe *n*
Last winter our water pipe froze.

leuchten ['lɔiçt(ə)n] *V/i.*, leuchtete, hat geleuchtet
Die Lampe leuchtet sehr stark.

shine *v*
The lamp shines very brightly.

Licht [liçt] *n, -(e)s, -er*
Mach bitte das Licht aus!

light *n*
Please turn off the light.

Maschine [maˈʃiːnə] *f, -, -n*
Diese Maschine ist sehr teuer.

machine *n*
This machine is very expensive.

Motor [ˈmoːtɔr] *m, -s, -en*
Der Motor der Maschine macht
ein komisches Geräusch.

motor *n*
The machine's motor is making a
funny sound.

Pumpe [ˈpumpə] *f, -, -n*
Die Pumpe der Waschmaschine
ist kaputt.

pump *n*
The pump for the washing machine is broken.

Rohr [roː*] *n, -(e)s, -e*
Das Rohr hat ein Loch.

pipe *n*
The pipe has a hole.

Schalter [ˈʃaltə*] *m, -s, -*
Der Lichtschalter ist links neben
der Tür.

switch *n*
The light switch is left of the door.

Strom [ʃtroːm] *m, -s, kein Pl.*
Die neue Waschmaschine
braucht weniger Strom als die
alte.

power, energy *n*
The new washing machine uses
less power than the old one.

Technik [ˈtɛçnik] *f, -, -en*

Die Technik moderner Automotoren wird immer komplizierter.

**technology, engineering,
mechanics** *n*
The technology of newer car motors is getting more and more
complicated.

technisch [ˈtɛçniʃ] *Adj.*
Diese Maschine ist eine technische Sensation.

technical
This machine is a technical sensation.

2001-4000

Atomenergie [aˈtoːmenɛrgiː] *f, -,
kein Pl.*
Ein großer Teil des Stroms in der
Bundesrepublik wird aus Atomenergie gewonnen.

atomic energy *n*

A great deal of the electric power
in the Federal Republic of Germany comes from atomic energy.

bedienen [bəˈdiːnən] *V/t.,* bediente, hat bedient
Die Maschine darf nur von einem
Fachmann bedient werden.

operate *v*

Only an expert may operate the
machine.

Brett [brɛt] *n*, -(e)s, -er
Die Bretter sind 22 mm stark.

board *n*
The boards are 22 mm thick.

Dichtung ['dɪçtuŋ] *f*, -, -en
Die Dichtung des Wasserhahns ist kaputt.

seal *n*
The seal on the faucet is broken.

Elektrizität [elɛktritsi'tɛ:t] *f*, -, *kein Pl.*
Elektrizität ist die sauberste Energieart.

electricity *n*
Electricity is the cleanest kind of energy.

Feder ['fe:dǝ*] *f*, -, -n
Durch eine Feder wird die Tür automatisch zugezogen.

spring *n*
A spring closes the door automatically.

Gebrauchsanweisung
[gǝ'brauxsanvaizuŋ] *f*, -, -en
Bitte lesen Sie die Gebrauchsanweisung genau durch!

user's instructions *n*

Please read the user's instructions carefully.

Instrument [instru'mɛnt] *n*, -s, -e
Mein Arzt hat in seiner Praxis alle wichtigen medizinischen Instrumente.

instrument *n*
My doctor has all the important medical instruments he needs in his office.

Kapazität [kapatsi'tɛ:t] *f*, -, -en
Die Fabrik hat keine Produktionskapazität mehr frei.

capacity *n*
The factory has no more production capacity.

Konstruktion [kɔnstruk'tsjo:n] *f*, -, -en
Wegen ihrer einfachen technischen Konstruktion ist die Maschine leicht zu reparieren.

construction *n*
The machine is easy to repair because of its simple technical construction.

Lautsprecher ['lautʃprɛçǝ*] *m*, -s, -
Für dieses Radio sind die Lautsprecher zu klein.

loud-speaker *n*
The loud-speakers are too small for this radio.

Modell [mo'dɛl] *n*, -s, -e
Für dieses alte Modell gibt es keine Ersatzteile mehr.

model *n*
There are no more parts for this old model.

Rost [rɔst] *m*, -(e)s, *kein Pl.*
Die Eisentür muss vor Rost geschützt werden.

rust *n*
The iron door has to be protected from rust.

Skala ['ska:la] *f, -, Skalen*
Laut Skala ist der Öltank voll.

scale *n*
According to the scale, the oil tank is full.

Spannung ['ʃpanuŋ] *f, -, -en*
In unserem Land ist die Stromspannung niedriger.

voltage *n*
In our country the electrical voltage is lower.

Struktur [ʃtruk'tu:ɐ*] *f, -, -en*
Die Verkehrsstruktur in unserem Gebiet soll verbessert werden.

pattern, structure *n*
The traffic pattern in our area should be improved.

Verfahren [fɛɐ*'fa:rən] *n, -s, -*
Das neue Herstellungsverfahren ist wirtschaftlicher.

procedure *n*
The new production procedure is more economical.

10.2 Materialien | 1-2000

10.2 Materials

Asche ['aʃə] *f, -, -en*
Der Ofen ist voll Asche.

ash *n*
The furnace is full of ashes.

Blech [blɛç] *n, -s, -e*
Das Blech ist zu dick, um es zu schneiden.

metal *n*
The metal is too thick to cut.

Eisen ['aiz(ə)n] *n, -s, -*
Die Leiter ist aus Eisen.

iron *n*
The ladder is made of iron.

Erdöl ['e:ɐ*tø:l] *n, -s, kein Pl.*
Die Preise für Erdöl sind wieder gestiegen.

petroleum *n*
The price of petroleum has gone up again.

fein [fain] *Adj.*
Der Wollstoff ist sehr fein.

fine, good
The wool fabric is very good.

fest [fɛst] *Adj., -er, am -esten*
Die Schraube sitzt ziemlich fest.

tight
The screw is in really tight.

flüssig ['flysiçº] *Adj.*
Das Öl sollte warm und sehr flüssig sein.

liquid
The oil should be warm and very liquid.

Flüssigkeit ['flysiçkait] *f*, -, -en
Vorsicht! Diese Flüssigkeit ist giftig.

liquid *n*
Watch out! This liquid is poisonous.

Gold [gɔlt] *n*, -(e)s, *kein Pl.*
Das Armband ist aus Gold.

gold *n*
The bracelet is made of gold.

---

grob ['grɔp] *Adj.*, gröber, am gröbsten
Der Sand ist zu grob.

coarse
The sand is too coarse.

Gummi ['gumi] *n*, -s, *kein Pl.*
Die Schuhe sind aus Gummi.

rubber *n*
These shoes are made of rubber.

---

hart [hart] *Adj.*, härter, am härtesten
Für Treppen verwendet man hartes Holz.

hard

Hard wood is used for steps.

---

heiß [hais] *Adj.*, -er, am -esten
Das Öl ist heiß. Pass auf!

hot
Be careful! The oil is hot!

---

hohl [hoːl] *Adj.*
Die Tür ist innen hohl.

hollow
The door is hollow.

Holz [hɔlts] *n*, -es, Hölzer
In der Wohnung ist ein Holzfußboden.

wood *n*
There's a wood floor in the apartment.

---

klar [klaː*] *Adj.*
Das Wasser in dem See ist klar und sauber.

clear
The water in the lake is clear and clean.

Kohle [koːlə] *f*, -, -n
Wir haben einen Kohleofen in der Küche.

coal
We have a coal stove in the kitchen.

Kunststoff ['kunstʃtɔf] *m*, -(e)s, -e
Das Fenster ist aus Kunststoff.

synthetic material, plastic *n*
The window is made of synthetic material.

---

leicht [laiçt] *Adj.*, -er, am -esten
Die neuen Autos sind viel leichter als die alten.

light, lightweight
The new cars are much lighter than the old ones.

Material [mateˈrjaːl] *n,* -s, Materialien
Aus was für einem Material ist die Tasche?

material *n*

What kind of material is the bag made of?

Metall [me'tal] *n*, -s, -e
Das Tor ist aus Metall.

metal *n*
The gate is made of metal.

Mischung ['miʃuŋ] *f*, -, -en
Der Motor läuft mit einer Mischung aus Benzin und Öl.

mix, mixture *n*
The motor runs on a mix of gas and oil.

nass [nas] *Adj.*, nässer, am nässesten (nassesten)
Das Holz ist nass.

wet

The wood is wet.

neu [nɔi] *Adj.*, -er, am -esten
Der neue Apparat funktioniert besser.

new
The new machine works better.

Öl [øːl] *n*, -(e)s, -e
Das Motoröl muss gewechselt werden.

oil *n*
The motor oil has to be changed.

Papier [pa'piːə*] *n*, -s, -e
Gib mir bitte ein Blatt Papier!

paper *n*
Please give me a sheet of paper.

Plastik ['plastik] *n*, -s, *kein Pl.*
Beim Camping verwenden wir Plastikgeschirr.

plastic
When camping we use plastic dishes.

Pulver ['pulfə*] *n*, -s, -
Der Schnee ist fein wie Pulver.

powder *n*
The snow is as fine as powder.

schwer [ʃveːə*] *Adj.*
Dieser Stoff ist warm, aber sehr schwer.

heavy
This fabric is warm but very heavy.

Silber ['zilbə*] *n*, -s, *kein Pl.*
Deine Silberkette gefällt mir gut.

silver *n*
I really like your silver chain.

Stahl ['ʃtaːl] *m*, -s, Stähle
Er arbeitet in der Stahlindustrie.

steel *n*
He works in the steel industry.

Stoff [ʃtɔf] *m*, -(e)s, -e
Die Verwendung gefährlicher chemischer Stoffe soll besser kontrolliert werden.

material, substance *n*
The use of dangerous chemical substances should be better controlled.

trocken ['trɔk(ə)n] *Adj.*
Ist die Wäsche schon trocken?

dry
Is the wash already dry?

weich [vaiç] *Adj.*, -er, am -(e)sten
Der Teppich ist angenehm weich.

soft
The carpet is nice and soft.

Wolle ['vɔlə] *f, -, kein Pl.*
Der Mantel ist aus reiner Wolle.

wool *n*
The coat is made of pure wool.

Ziegel ['tsi:g(ə)l] *m, -s, -*
Das Haus ist aus roten Ziegeln gebaut.

brick *n*
The house is made of red brick.

2001-4000

Aluminium [alu'mi:njum] *n, -s, kein Pl.*
Das Fahrrad ist aus Aluminium. Es ist leicht und rostet nicht.

aluminum *n*
The bicycle is aluminum. It is lightweight and doesn't rust.

auflösen ['aʊflø:z(ə)n] *V/t.,* löste auf, hat aufgelöst
Das Pulver muss in Wasser aufgelöst werden.

dissolve *v*
The powder must be dissolved in water.

Baumwolle ['baʊmvɔlə] *f, -, kein Pl.*
Der Pullover ist aus Baumwolle.

cotton *n*
The sweater is made of cotton.

Blei [blaɪ] *n, -(e)s, kein Pl.*
Der Automotor läuft auch mit bleifreiem Benzin.

lead *n*
The car motor also runs on lead-free gas.

Kupfer ['kʊpfə*] *n, -s, kein Pl.*
Die Kanne ist aus Kupfer.

copper *n*
The pot is made of copper.

locker ['lɔkə*] *Adj.*
Die Schraube sitzt locker.

loose
The screw is loose.

lose ['lo:zə] *Adj.*
Ein Knopf an der Jacke ist lose.

loose
A button on the jacket is loose.

rein [raɪn] *Adj.*
Ist die Hose aus reiner Baumwolle?

pure
Are the trousers pure cotton?

stabil [ʃta'bi:l] *Adj.*
Das Regal ist sehr stabil.

sturdy
The shelves are very sturdy.

11.1 Reise | 1-2000

abfahren ['apfa:rən] *V/i.,* fuhr ab, ist abgefahren
Der Zug fährt um 19.12 Uhr ab.

leave *v*
The train leaves at 19:12.

Abfahrt ['apfa:*t] *f, -, -en*
Abfahrt ist um 7.00 Uhr.

departure *n*
Departure is at 7 a.m.

Abreise ['apraizə] *f, -, -n*
Die Abreise ist nach dem Frühstück.

departure *n*
Departure is after breakfast.

abreisen ['apraiz(ə)n] *V/i.,* reiste ab, ist abgereist
Frau Pauls ist schon gestern abgereist.

leave, depart *v*
Ms. Pauls left yesterday.

ankommen ['ankɔmən] *V/i.,* kam an, ist angekommen
Das Gepäck kommt erst morgen an.

arrive *v*
The luggage won't arrive until tomorrow.

Ankunft ['ankunft] *f, -, kein Pl.*
Die genaue Ankunftszeit des Zuges kenne ich nicht.

arrival *n*
I don't know the exact time of arrival of the train.

Aufenthalt ['aufənthalt] *m, -(e)s, -e*
In Hannover haben Sie 40 Minuten Aufenthalt.

stop, stay *n*
You have a 40-minute stop in Hannover.

Ausland ['auslant] *n, -s, kein Pl.*
Sie hat drei Jahre im Ausland gelebt.

foreign country *n*
She lived in a foreign country for three years.

Gepäck [gə'pɛk] *n, -s, kein Pl.*
Sie dürfen nur 20 kg Gepäck mitnehmen.

luggage *n*
You may take only 20 kg of luggage.

Hotel [ho'tɛl] *n, -s, -s*
Das Hotel hat nur Doppelzimmer.

hotel *n*
The hotel only has double rooms.

Koffer ['kɔfə*] *m*, -s, -
Trägst du bitte den Koffer?

suitcase *n*
Would you please carry the suitcase?

Landkarte ['lantkartə] *f*, -, -n
Diesen kleinen Ort kann ich auf der Landkarte nicht finden.

map *n*
I can't find that little place on the map.

packen ['pak(ə)n] *V/t.*, packte, hat gepackt
Ich habe schon meine Koffer gepackt.

pack *v*

I've already packed my suitcase.

Passagier [pasa'ʒiːə*] *m*, -s, -e
Passagierin [pasa'ʒiːrin] *f*, -, -nen
Das Flugzeug hat Platz für 250 Passagiere.

passenger *n*

The plane has room for 250 passengers.

Pass [pas] *m*, -es, Pässe
Der Pass ist noch zwei Jahre gültig.

passport *n*
The passport is good for two more years.

Rast [rast] *f*, -, *kein Pl.*
Während der Autofahrt haben wir zweimal Rast gemacht.

rest *n*
During the auto trip we stopped twice for a rest.

Reise ['raizə] *f*, -, -n
Die Reise dauert 10 Tage.

trip, journey *n*
The trip lasts 10 days.

reisen ['raiz(ə)n] *V/i.*, reiste, ist gereist
Wir sind vier Wochen durch Schweden gereist.

travel *v*

We spent four weeks traveling through Sweden.

Stadtplan ['ʃtatplaːn] *m*, -(e)s, Stadtpläne
Dieser Stadtplan ist nur für die Innenstadt.

city map *n*

This city map is only for the central part.

Ticket ['tikət] *n*, -s, -s
Das Ticket ist ein Jahr gültig.

ticket *n*
The ticket is good for a year.

Tourist [tu'rist] *m*, -en, -en
Touristin [tu'ristin] *f*, -, -nen
Im Sommer gibt es in München viele Touristen.

tourist *n*

In the summer there are many tourists in Munich.

übernachten [yːbə*'naxt(ə)n] *V/i.*
übernachtete, hat übernachtet
Du kannst bei mir übernachten.

spend the night *v*

You can spend the night at my place.

Unterkunft [ˈʊntəˈkʊnft] *f,* -, Unterkünfte
Ich suche eine Unterkunft für vier Tage.

lodging, place to stay, accommodation *n*
I'm looking for a place to stay for four days.

---

unterwegs [ʊntəˈveːks] *Adv.*
Das Wetter unterwegs war gut.

on the way
The weather on the way was good.

---

verpassen [fɛəˈpas(ə)n] *V/t.,* verpasste, hat verpasst
Du musst gehen, sonst verpasst du den Zug.

miss *v*
You must leave or you'll miss the train.

Verpflegung [fɛəˈpfleːgʊŋ] *f,* -, *kein Pl.*
Die Verpflegung in dem Gasthaus war gut.

food service, meals, catering *n*
The meals at the restaurant were very good.

---

verreisen [fɛəˈraiz(ə)n] *V/i.,* verreiste, ist verreist
Zu Ostern verreisen wir immer.

leave, go away *v*
We always go away at Easter.

2001-4000

Abflug [ˈapfluːk] *m,* -(e)s, Abflüge
Man muss 40 Minuten vor dem Abflug am Flughafen sein.

departure *n*
You have to be at the airport 40 minutes before departure.

---

auspacken [ˈauspak(ə)n] *V/t.,* packte aus, hat ausgepackt
Soll ich den Koffer auspacken?

unpack *v*
Should I unpack the suitcase?

Ausreise [ˈausraizə] *f,* -, -n
Bei der Ausreise gab es keine Zollkontrolle.

departure *n*
There was no customs check at departure.

Besichtigung [bəˈzɪçtigʊŋ] *f,* -, -en
Eine Besichtigung des Schlosses ist leider nicht möglich.

sightseeing, visit *n*
Unfortunately, the castle is not open for sightseeing.

---

buchen [ˈbuːx(ə)n] *V/t.,* buchte, hat gebucht
Unsere Urlaubsreise haben wir schon fest gebucht.

reserve, make reservations *v*
We've already made reservations for our vacation trip.

Camping ['kɛmpiŋ] *n, -s, kein Pl.*
Ich mache gerne Campingurlaub.

camping *n*
I really like to spend my vacation camping.

Campingplatz ['kɛmpiŋplats] *m, -es, Campingplätze*
Im Sommer sind die Campingplätze an der Küste alle besetzt.

campground, camping site *n*
In the summer all the campgrounds by the coast are full.

---

einpacken ['ainpak(ə)n] *V/t., packte ein, hat eingepackt*
Ich habe vergessen, Strümpfe einzupacken.

pack *v*
I forgot to pack stockings.

Einreise ['ainraizə] *f, -, -n*
Das Visum ist für mehrere Einreisen gültig.

entry *n*
The visa is good for more than one entry.

---

erreichen [ɛə*'raiç(ə)n] *V/t., erreichte, hat erreicht*
Kann man den Ort mit dem Zug erreichen?

reach, get to *v*
Can you get there by train?

Führer ['fy:rə*] *m, -s, -*
Führerin ['fy:rərin] *f, -, -nen*
Im Sommer arbeitet sie als Touristenführerin.

guide *n*
In the summer she works as a tour guide.

Hinfahrt ['hinfa:*t] *f, -, -en*
Bei der Hinfahrt sind wir über Frankfurt gefahren.

the way there *n*
On the way there we went via Frankfurt.

Pension [pã'zjo:n] *f, -, -en*
Die Pension liegt ruhig.

boarding house, guest house *n*
The guest house is in a quiet location.

Reisebüro ['raizəbyro:] *n, -s, -s*
Zugfahrkarten können Sie auch im Reisebüro kaufen.

travel bureau/agency *n*
You can also buy train tickets in the travel bureau.

---

reservieren [rezɛr'vi:rən] *V/t., reservierte, hat reserviert*
Für uns sind drei Plätze reserviert worden.

reserve *v*
There are three seats reserved for us.

Rückfahrkarte ['rykfa:*kartə] *f, -, -n*
Die Rückfahrkarte ist billiger.

return ticket, round-trip ticket *n*
The return ticket is cheaper.

Rückfahrt ['rykfa:*t] *f, -, -en*
Bei der Rückfahrt hält der Zug auch in Würzburg.

return journey, way back *n*
On the way back the train stops also in Würzburg.

Rückkehr ['rykke:ə*] *f, -, kein Pl.*
Einen Tag nach der Rückkehr fängt die Arbeit wieder an.

return *n*
One day after our return work starts up again.

Saison [zɛ'zõ:] *f, -, kein Pl.*
In der Hochsaison ist es hier schwierig, ein Hotelzimmer zu finden.

season *n*
During the high season it is difficult to find a hotel room here.

Sehenswürdigkeit
['ze:ənsvyrdiçkait] *f, -, -en*
Wien ist eine Stadt voll Sehenswürdigkeiten.

(tourist) sight *n*

Vienna is a city full of sights.

Station [ʃta'tsjo:n] *f, -, -en*
Bei der nächsten Station müssen wir aussteigen.

station, stop *n*
At the next station we have to get off.

umsteigen ['umʃtaig(ə)n] *V/i.*,
stieg um, ist umgestiegen
In Köln müssen Sie umsteigen.

change *(trains, buses, planes, etc.) v*
You have to change trains in Cologne.

verzollen [fɛə*'tsɔl(ə)n] *V/t.*, verzollte, hat verzollt
Das Gepäck muss nicht verzollt werden.

pay (customs) duty *v*

There is no duty to pay on the luggage.

Visum ['vi:zum] *n, -s, Visa*
Ich habe ein Visum für vier Wochen beantragt.

visa *n*
I applied for a visa for four weeks.

Zelt [tsɛlt] *n, -(e)s, -e*
Das Zelt hat Platz für vier Personen.

tent *n*
The tent has room for four people.

Zimmervermittlung
['tsimə*fɛə*mitluŋ] *f, -, -en*
Die Zimmervermittlung ist mittags geschlossen.

room reservation *n*

The room reservation office is closed in the afternoon.

11.2 Straßenverkehr | 1-2000

11.2 Street Traffic

abbiegen ['apbi:g(ə)n] *V/i.,* bog ab, ist abgebogen

An der Kreuzung darf man nicht links abbiegen.

turn *v*

You may not turn left at the intersection.

Ampel ['amp(ə)l] *f, -, -n*

Die Ampel ist nachts ausgeschaltet.

traffic light *n*

The traffic light is turned off at night.

anhalten ['anhalt(ə)n] *V/t., i.,* hielt an, hat angehalten

Die Taxis können Sie an der Straße anhalten.

Würden Sie bitte anhalten? Ich möchte aussteigen.

stop *v*

You can get a taxi on the street.

Would you please stop here? I'd like to get out.

Ausfahrt ['ausfa:*t] *f, -, -en*

Vor der Ausfahrt kannst du nicht parken.

exit *n*

You can't park in front of the exit.

Autobahn ['autoba:n] *f, -, -en*

Nach Bremen fährst du am besten über die Autobahn.

freeway, motorway, interstate highway *[USA] n*

The best way you can take from Bremen is the freeway.

Fahrer ['fa:rə*] *m, -s, -*
FahrerIn ['fa:rərin] *f, -, -nen*

Die Busfahrerin war schuld an dem Unfall.

driver *n*

The accident was the bus driver's fault.

Fahrplan ['fa:*pla:n] *m, -(e)s,* Fahrpläne

Der Fahrplan ist geändert worden.

route, travel plan *n*

The travel plan was changed.

Fahrrad ['fa:*rat] *n, -(e)s, -räder*

Er fährt mit dem Fahrrad zur Arbeit.

bicycle *n*

He rides his bicycle to work.

Fahrt [fa:*t] *f, -, -en*

Die Fahrt dauert 3 Stunden.

trip, voyage *n*

The trip takes three hours.

Fußgänger ['fu:sgɛŋə*] *m*, -s, -
Fußgängerin *f*, -, -nen
Diese Straße ist für Fußgänger sehr gefährlich.

pedestrian *n*

This street is very dangerous for pedestrians.

Geschwindigkeit [gə'ʃvindiçkait] *f*, -, -en
Der Unfall geschah wegen zu hoher Geschwindigkeit.

speed *n*

The accident was caused by excessive speed.

halten ['halt(ə)n] *V/t., i.*, hielt, hat gehalten
Halt! Von rechts kommt ein Auto.

stop *v*

Stop! There's a car on the right.

Kreuzung ['krɔitsuŋ] *f*, -, -en
An dieser Kreuzung ist viel Verkehr.

intersection, crossroad *n*
There's a lot of traffic at this intersection.

Kurve ['kurvə] *f*, -, -n
Vorsicht, die Kurve ist scharf!

curve *n*
Careful! That's a sharp curve!

langsam ['laŋza:m] *Adj.*
Fahr bitte langsamer!

slow
Please drive more slowly!

parken ['park(ə)n] *V/t., i.*, parkte, hat geparkt
Auf der Straße kannst du hier nicht parken.

park *v*

You can't park on the street here.

Rad [ra:t] *n*, -(e)s, Räder
Ein Rad am Kinderwagen ist locker.

wheel *n*
A wheel on the baby carriage is loose.

Schild [ʃilt] *n*, -(e)s, -er
Sie hat das Stopp-Schild nicht beachtet.

sign *n*
She didn't pay attention to the stop sign.

schnell [ʃnɛl] *Adj.*
Ich fahre gerne schnell Auto.

fast
I like to drive a car fast.

stoppen ['ʃtɔp(ə)n] *V/t., i.*, stoppte, hat gestoppt
Das Auto wurde von der Polizei gestoppt.
Das Auto stoppte plötzlich.

stop *v*

The car was stopped by the police.
The car stopped suddenly.

Taxi ['taksi] *n*, -s, -s
Würden Sie mir bitte ein Taxi rufen?

taxi *n*
Would you please call a taxi for me?

Umleitung ['umlaitʊŋ] *f,* -, -en
Bei einer Umleitung sind wir in die falsche Richtung gefahren.

detour, diversion *n*
On a detour we went in the wrong direction.

Unfall ['unfal] *m,* -s, Unfälle
Die Zahl der Verkehrsunfälle steigt wieder.

accident *n*
The number of automobile accidents is increasing.

Verkehr [fɛə*'ke:ə*] *m,* -s, *kein Pl.*
Am Wochenende wird auf den Autobahnen starker Verkehr erwartet.

traffic *n*
Heavy traffic on the freeway is expected on the weekend.

2001-4000

Einfahrt ['ainfa:*t] *f,* -, -en
Das Tor der Einfahrt ist geschlossen.

entrance, entry, way in *n*
The door to the entrance is closed.

Fahrgast ['fa:*gast] *m,* -(e)s, Fahrgäste
Der Kapitän begrüßte die Fahrgäste.

passenger *n*
The captain greeted the passengers.

Fahrkarte ['fa:*kartə] *f,* -, -n
Fahrkarten gibt es aus dem Automaten.

ticket *n*
Tickets can be bought at the vending machine.

Fahrschein ['fa:*ʃain] *m,* -(e)s, -e
Mit diesem Fahrschein können Sie auch die U-Bahn benutzen.

ticket *n*
With this ticket you can also take the subway.

Geschwindigkeitsbegrenzung [gə'ʃvindiçkaitsbəgrɛntsuŋ] *f,* -, -en
Die Geschwindigkeitsbegrenzung wird kaum beachtet.

speed limit *n*

Very few people observed the speed limit.

Haltestelle ['haltəʃtɛlə] *f,* -, -n
Die Bushaltestelle ist 300 m weiter links, vor der Post.

stop *n*
The bus stop is 300 m to the left, in front of the Post Office.

Höchstgeschwindigkeit ['hø:çstgəʃvindiçkait] *f,* -, -en
Das Auto hat eine Höchstgeschwindigkeit von 160 km/h.

top/maximum speed *n*

The top speed of the car is 160 km an hour.

Spur [ʃpuːɐ̯] *f, -, -en*
Um links abzubiegen, musst du die Fahrspur wechseln.

lane *n*
To turn left you have to change lanes.

Tempo ['tɛmpo] *n, -s, kein Pl.*
Die Lastwagen fahren oft mit sehr hohem Tempo.

speed *n*
Trucks often drive at a very high speed.

überholen [yːbɐˈhoːl(ə)n] *V/t.,*
überholte, hat überholt
Warum überholst du das Auto nicht?

pass, overtake *v*

Why don't you pass the car?

Verkehrszeichen
[fɛɐ̯ˈkeːɐ̯stsaiç(ə)n] *n, -s, -*
Weißt du, was dieses Verkehrszeichen bedeutet?

traffic sign *n*

Do you know what that traffic sign means?

vorbeifahren [foɐ̯ˈbaifaːrən] *V/i.,* fuhr vorbei, ist vorbeigefahren
Der Bus fuhr an der Haltestelle vorbei, ohne anzuhalten.
Fahr bitte beim Bäcker vorbei und hol Brot!

drive by, pass *v*

The bus drove right by the stop.

Please drive by the bakery and pick up some bread.

Vorfahrt ['foɐ̯faːɐ̯t] *f, -, kein Pl.*
Das Taxi hatte Vorfahrt.

right of way *n*
The taxi had the right of way.

Zusammenstoß [tsuˈzamənʃtoːs] *m, -es, Zusammenstöße*
Hatten Sie Schuld an dem Zusammenstoß?

crash *n*

Was the crash your fault?

11.3 Kraftfahrzeuge | 1-2000

11.3 Vehicles

Auto ['auto] *n, -s, -s*
Das Auto muss dringend gewaschen werden.

car, auto, automobile *n*
The car really needs to be washed.

Benzin [bɛnˈtsiːn] *n, -s, kein Pl.*
Der Motor verbraucht wenig Benzin.

gasoline, petrol *(BE) n*
The car doesn't use much gasoline.

Bus [bus] *m*, -ses, -se
Wann fährt der Bus?

bus *n*
When does the bus leave?

Diesel ['di:z(ə)l] *m*, -s, *kein Pl.*
Das Auto hat einen Dieselmotor.

diesel *n*
The car has a diesel engine.

Lastwagen ['lastva:g(ə)n] *m*, -s, -
(-wägen), (Lastkraftwagen = LKW)
Dieser Lastkraftwagen hat über
45 Tonnen Gesamtgewicht.

truck, lorry *(BE) n*

This truck weighs over 45 tons.

Motorrad ['mo:tɔə*ra:t] *n*, -(e)s,
Motorräder
Im Sommer fahre ich gerne Mo-
torrad.

motorcycle, motorbike *n*

In the summer I like to ride a motorcycle.

Panne ['panə] *f*, -, -n
Wir sind später gekommen, weil
wir eine Reifenpanne hatten.

puncture, flat, breakdown *n*
We came late because we had a
flat tire.

Parkplatz ['parkplats] *m*, -es,
Parkplätze
Der Parkplatz ist besetzt.

parking place *n*

The parking place is occupied.

Reifen ['raif(ə)n] *m*, -s, -
Hast du Winterreifen an deinem
Auto?

tire *n*
Do you have snow tires on your
car?

Reparatur [repara'tu:ə*] *f*, -, -en
Kleine Reparaturen mache ich
selbst.

repair *n*
I do simple repairs myself.

reparieren [repa'ri:rən] *V/t*, re-
parierte, hat repariert
Das Türschloss muss repariert
werden.

repair *v*

The door lock has to be repaired.

Straßenbahn ['ʃtra:s(ə)nba:n] *f*, -,
-en
Die Straßenbahn Nr. 8 fährt zum
Meisterplatz.

streetcar *n*

Streetcar no. 8 is headed toward
Meisterplatz.

tanken ['taŋk(ə)n] *V/t., i.*, tankte,
hat getankt
Bitte tanken Sie das Auto voll!
Ich muss noch tanken.

get gas, fill the tank, tank up *v*

Please fill the tank!
I still have to get some gas.

Tankstelle ['taŋkʃtɛlə] *f*, -, -n
An dieser Tankstelle gibt es kein
Diesel.

(gas) station, petrol station *n*
There's no diesel at that station.

U-Bahn ['uːbaːn] *f,* -, -en
Mit der U-Bahn sind Sie am
schnellsten in der Stadt.

subway, underground *(BE) n*
The subway is the fastest way to
get to town.

Wagen ['vaːg(ə)n] *m,* -s, -
Der Wagen ist 12 Jahre alt, ist
aber nur 60000 km gelaufen.

car, auto, automobile *n*
The car is 12 years old but has
only 60,000 km on it.

2001-4000

---

abschleppen ['apʃlɛp(ə)n] *V/t.,*
schleppte ab, hat abgeschleppt
Der Wagen musste abgeschleppt
werden.

tow *v*

The car had to be towed.

Anhänger ['anhɛŋə*] *m,* -s, -
Mit dem Wagen darf man Anhänger bis 600 kg ziehen.

trailer *n*
With this car you can have a trailer
of up to 600 kg.

Autofahrer ['autofaːrə*] *m,* -s, -
Autofahrerin [-faːrərin] *f,* -, -nen
Bei dem Autofahrer wurde ein Al-
koholtest gemacht.

car driver *n*

The car driver was given an alcohol test.

Baujahr ['baujaː*] *n,* -(e)s, -e
Das Auto ist Baujahr 1989.

model year *n*
The car is from model year 1989.

Bremse ['brɛmzə] *f,* -, -n
Die Bremsen ziehen nicht gleichmäßig.

brake *n*
The brakes aren't coordinated.

bremsen ['brɛmz(ə)n] *V/i.,* bremste, hat gebremst
Der Fahrer konnte nicht mehr
bremsen und fuhr gegen das Ver-
kehrsschild.

brake, step on the brakes *v*

The driver couldn't brake any
more and ran into the traffic sign.

Führerschein ['fyːrə*ʃain] *m,* -s,
-e
Sigrid hat endlich ihren Führerschein bekommen.

driver's license *n*

Sigrid finally got her driver's license.

hupen ['huːp(ə)n] *V/i.,* hupte, hat
gehupt
Der Fahrer hupt ohne Grund.

sound, blow the horn, honk *v*

The driver is blowing his horn for
no reason.

Kofferraum ['kɔfə*raum] *m*, -(e)s, Kofferräume
Der Kofferraum des neuen Modells ist größer.

trunk *n*
The trunk on the new model is bigger.

Moped ['mo:pɛt] *n*, -s, -s
Jens fährt mit dem Moped zur Schule.

motor bike, moped *n*
Jens drives to school on his moped.

Parkuhr ['parku:ə*] *f*, -, -en
Vergiss nicht, Geld in die Parkuhr zu stecken.

parking meter *n*
Don't forget to put money in the parking meter.

Rücklicht ['ryklçt] *n*, -(e)s, -er
Das rechte Rücklicht funktioniert nicht.

back-up light *n*
The right back-up light isn't working.

Scheinwerfer ['ʃainvɛrfə*] *m*, -s, -
Im linken Scheinwerfer ist die Birne kaputt.

headlight *n*
The bulb in the left headlight is burnt out.

Sitzplatz ['zitsplats] *m*, -es, Sitzplätze
Der Bus hat 55 Sitzplätze.

seat *n*
The bus has 55 seats.

Traktor ['traktɔr] *m*, -s, -en
Mit dem neuen Traktor geht die Feldarbeit schneller.

tractor *n*
Field work goes faster with the new tractor.

11.4 Eisenbahn, Flugzeug, Schiff | 1-2000

11.4 Rail, Plane, Ship

aussteigen ['ausʃtaig(ə)n] *V/i.*, stieg aus, ist ausgestiegen
An welcher Station muss ich aussteigen?

get off *v*
At which station do I have to get off?

Bahn [ba:n] *f*, -, -en
Ich fahre gerne mit der Bahn.

train *n*
I like to travel on the train.

Bahnhof ['ba:nho:f] *m*, -(e)s, Bahnhöfe
In diesem Ort gibt es keinen Bahnhof.

train station *n*
There's no train station in this town.

Boot [bo:t] *n*, -(e)s, -e
Zu dieser Insel fährt ein Linienboot.

boat *n*
There's a regular boat to the island.

einsteigen ['ainʃtaig(ə)n] *V/i.*,
stieg ein, ist eingestiegen
Steig ein! Wir wollen losfahren.

get in *v*

Get in! We want to get going.

Eisenbahn ['aiz(ə)nba:n] *f*, -, -en
Nach der Eisenbahnbrücke müssen Sie rechts abbiegen.

railroad *n*
After the railroad bridge you have to turn right.

fliegen ['fli:g(ə)n] *V/i.*, flog, ist geflogen
Fliegen Sie, oder fahren Sie mit der Bahn?

fly *v*

Are you flying, or are you going by train?

Flug [flu:k] *m*, -(e)s, Flüge
Wegen Nebels wurde der Flug gestrichen.

flight *n*
The flight was canceled because of fog.

Flughafen ['flu:kha:f(ə)n] *m*, -s, Flughäfen
Ich bringe dich zum Flughafen.

airport *n*

I'll take you to the airport.

Flugplatz ['flu:kplats] *m*, -es, Flugplätze
Der Flugplatz liegt 30 km vor der Stadt.

air field, airport *n*

The airport is 30 km from the city.

Flugzeug ['flu:ktsɔik] *n*, -s, -e

Das Flugzeug hat Verspätung.

airplane, aeroplane *(BE)*, **aircraft** *n*
The airplane is late.

Hafen ['ha:f(ə)n] *m*, -s, Häfen
Das Schiff bleibt nur einen Tag im Hafen.

harbor, port *n*
The ship will spend only one day in that port.

Kapitän [kapi'tɛ:n] *m*, -s, -e
Kapitänin [kapi'tɛ:nin] *f*, -, -nen
Er ist Kapitän eines Flussschiffes.

captain *n*

He is captain of a river boat.

landen ['land(ə)n] *V/i.*, landete, ist gelandet
Das Flugzeug ist noch nicht gelandet.

land *v*

The airplane hasn't landed yet.

Lokomotive [lɔkomo'ti:və] *f*, -, -n
Im Frankfurter Bahnhof wurde die Lokomotive gewechselt.

engine, locomotive *n*
The engine was changed at the Frankfurt station.

Mannschaft ['manʃaft] *f, -, -en*
In Hamburg übernahm eine andere Mannschaft das Schiff.

crew *n*
In Hamburg another crew took
over the ship.

Pilot [pi'lo:t] *m, -en, -en*
Pilotin [pi'lo:tin] *f, -, -nen*
Die Pilotin begrüßte die Flug-
gäste.

pilot *n*

The pilot greeted the passengers.

Schiff [ʃif] *n, -(e)s, -e*
Das Schiff fährt regelmäßig von
Hamburg nach Nordamerika.

ship *n*
The ship sails regularly from
Hamburg to North America.

starten ['ʃtart(ə)n] *V/t., i.,* startete,
ist gestartet
Sie konnte den Motor nicht
starten.
Das Flugzeug soll um 8.15 Uhr
starten.

start, leave *v*

She couldn't start the engine.

The plane is supposed to leave at
8:15 a.m.

Untergrundbahn, U-Bahn
['untə*gruntba:n] *f, -, -en*
Es soll eine neue Untergrundbahn
gebaut werden.

subway, underground *(BE) n*

A new subway is supposed to be
built.

Zug [tsu:k] *m, -(e)s, Züge*
Wir fahren mit dem Zug, nicht mit
dem Auto.

train *n*
We're going on the train; we're
not driving.

2001-4000

abfliegen ['apfli:g(ə)n] *V/i.,* flog
ab, ist abgeflogen
Das Flugzeug ist schon abgeflogen.

take off, leave *v*

The plane has already left.

ablegen ['aple:g(ə)n] *V/i.,* legte
ab, hat abgelegt
Pünktlich um 16.00 Uhr legte das
Schiff ab.

cast off, leave, depart *(ships) v*

The ship leaves at exactly 4:00
p.m.

abstürzen ['apʃtyrts(ə)n] *V/i.,*
stürzte ab, ist abgestürzt
Kurz nach dem Start stürzte das
Flugzeug ab.

crash *v*

The plane crashed right after
taking off.

anlegen ['anle:g(ə)n] *V/i.,* legte
an, hat angelegt
Das Schiff legt im Osthafen an.

come in, arrive *(ships)* v

The ship is coming in to the east
port.

auslaufen ['auslauf(ə)n] *V/i.,* lief
aus, ist ausgelaufen
Das Schiff läuft morgen aus.

leave *(ships)* v

The ship is leaving tomorrow.

Bahnsteig ['ba:nʃtaik] *m,* -(e)s, -e
Der Zug fährt von Bahnsteig 6 ab.

track n
The train leaves from track 6.

Besatzung [bə'zatsuŋ] *f,* -, -en
Moderne Schiffe fahren nur mit
einer kleinen Besatzung.

crew n
Modern ships sail with only a
small crew.

ertrinken [ɛə*'triŋk(ə)n] *V/i.,* er-
trank, ist ertrunken
Drei Matrosen sind bei dem
Schiffsunglück ertrunken.

drown v

Three sailors drowned in the
ship's accident.

Fluglinie ['flu:kli:njə] *f,* -, -n
Diese Fluglinie ist sehr pünktlich.

airline n
This airline is very punctual.

Gleis [glais] *n,* -es, -e
Der Zug kommt auf Gleis 3 an.

track, line n
The train arrives on track 3.

Schiene ['ʃi:nə] *f,* -, -n
Das Schienennetz der Bahn soll
modernisiert werden.

rail n
The train rails are to be modern-
ized.

Matrose [ma'tro:zə] *m,* -n, -n
Matrosin [ma'tro:zin] *f,* -, -nen
Die meisten Matrosen des Schif-
fes kommen aus asiatischen Ländern.

sailor n

Most of the sailors on the ship
come from Asian countries.

Seereise ['ze:raizə] *f,* -, -n
In meinem nächsten Urlaub mache ich eine Seereise.

ocean trip, cruise, voyage n
I will take a cruise for my next
vacation.

untergehen ['untə*ge:(ə)n] *V/i.,*
ging unter, ist untergegangen
Nach dem Zusammenstoß ging
das kleinere Schiff langsam unter.

sink v

After the collision the smaller ship
slowly sank.

Wrack [vrak] *n,* -s, -s
Das Wrack soll gehoben werden.

wreck n
The wreck is to be brought to the
surface.

12.1 Geographische Namen | 1-2000

12.1 Geographical Names

Afrika ['aːfrika] *n*	**Africa**
Amerika [a'meːrika] *n*	**America**
Argentinien [argən'tinjən] *n*	**Argentina**
Asien ['aːzjən] *n*	**Asia**
Australien [aus'traːljən] *n*	**Australia**
Belgien ['bɛlgjən] *n*	**Belgium**
Brasilien [bra'siljən] *n*	**Brazil**
BRD [beːɛr'deː] = Bundesrepublik Deutschland, (die)	**Federal Republic of Germany**
Bundesrepublik ['bundəsrepubliːk] *f*	**Federal Republic**
Chile ['tʃiːlə] *n*	**Chile**
China ['çiːna] *n*	**China**
Dänemark ['dɛːnəmark] *n*	**Denmark**
Deutschland ['dɔitʃlant] *n*	**Germany**
England ['ɛŋlant] *n*	**England**
Estland ['eːstlant] *n*	**Estonia**
Europa [ɔi'roːpa] *n*	**Europe**
Finnland ['finlant] *n*	**Finland**
Frankreich ['fraŋkraiç] *n*	**France**
Griechenland ['griːç(ə)nlant] *n*	**Greece**
Großbritannien [groːsbri'tanjən] *n*	**Great Britain**
Indien ['indjən] *n*	**India**
Irland ['irlant] *n*	**Ireland**
Italien [i'taːljən] *n*	**Italy**

2001-4000

Japan ['ja:pan] *n*	**Japan**
Jugoslawien [jugo'sla:vjən] *n*	**Yugoslavia**
Kanada ['kanada] *n*	**Canada**
Kroatien [kro'atjən] *n*	**Croatia**
Lettland ['lɛtlant] *n*	**Latvia**
Litauen ['litauən] *n*	**Lithuania**
Mexiko ['meksiko] *n*	**Mexico**
Niederlande ['ni:də*landə] (die), *Pl.*	**Netherlands**
Norwegen ['nɔrve:g(ə)n] *n*	**Norway**
Österreich ['ø:stəraiç] *n*	**Austria**
Polen ['po:l(ə)n] *n*	**Poland**
Portugal ['pɔrtugal] *n*	**Portugal**
Russland ['ruslant] *n*	**Russia**
Schweden ['ʃve:d(ə)n] *n*	**Sweden**
Schweiz [ʃvaits] (die), *f*	**Switzerland**
Slowakei [slova'kai] (die), *f*	**Slovakia**
Spanien ['ʃpa:njən] *n*	**Spain**
Tschechien ['tʃɛxjən]	**Czechia**
Türkei [tyr'kai] (die), *f*	**Turkey**
Ungarn ['uŋgarn] *n*	**Hungary**
USA [u:ɛs'a:] (die), *Pl.*	**USA**

12.2 Nationalitäten, Bewohner, Sprachen | 1-2000

12.2 Nationalities, Inhabitants, Languages

Amerikaner [ameriˈkaːnə*] *m* **Amerikanerin** [ameriˈkaːnərin] *f, -, -nen*	**American** *n*
amerikanisch [ameriˈkaːniʃ] *Adj.*	**American**
arabisch [aˈraːbiʃ] *Adj.*	**Arab**
britisch [ˈbritiʃ, ˈbriːtiʃ] *Adj.*	**British**
deutsch [ˈdɔitʃ] *Adj.* Er hat einen deutschen Pass.	**German** He has a German passport.
Deutsch(e) [ˈdɔitʃ(ə)] *n, -n, kein Pl.* Ihr Deutsch ist ausgezeichnet. Das Deutsche gilt als schwierige Sprache.	**German** *(language) n* Your German is excellent. German has a reputation of being hard to learn.
Deutsche [ˈdɔitʃə] *m/f, -n, -n*	**German** *(people) n*
englisch [ˈɛŋliʃ] *Adj.*	**English**
Englisch(e) [ˈɛŋliʃ(ə)] *n, -n, kein Pl.*	**English** *(language) n*
Engländer [ˈɛŋlɛndə*] *m, -s, -* **Engländerin** [ˈɛŋlɛndərin] *f, -, -nen*	**Englishman, Englishwoman** *n*
Europäer [ɔiroˈpɛːə*] *m, -s, -* **Europäerin** [ɔiroˈpɛːərin] *f, -, -nen*	**European** *n (person)*
europäisch [ɔiroˈpɛːiʃ] *Adj.*	**European**
Franzose [franˈtsoːzə] *m, -n, -n* **Französin** [franˈtsøːzin] *f, -, -nen*	**French** *n (person)*
Französisch(e) [franˈtsøːziʃ] *n, -n, kein Pl.*	**French** *(language) n*
französisch [franˈtsøːziʃ] *Adj.*	**French**

Österreicher [ˈøːstəraiçə*] m, -s, -, **Österreicherin** [ˈøːstə-raiçərin] f, -, -nen | **Austrian** n (person)

österreichisch [ˈøːstəraiçiʃ] Adj. | **Austrian**

Schweizer [ˈʃvaitsə*] m, -s, - **Schweizerin** [ˈʃvaitsərin] f, -, -nen | **Swiss** n (person)

2001-4000

Afrikaner [afriˈkaːnə*] m, -s, - **Afrikanerin** [afriˈkaːnərin] f, -, -nen | **African** n (person)

afrikanisch [afriˈkaːniʃ] Adj. | **African**

Chinese [çiˈneːzə] m, -n, -n **Chinesin** [çiˈneːzin] f, -, -nen | **Chinese** n (person)

Chinesisch(e) [çiˈneːziʃ(ə)] n, -n, kein Pl. | **Chinese** (language) n

chinesisch [çiˈneːziʃ] Adj. | **Chinese**

Grieche [ˈgriːçə] m, -n, -n **Griechin** [ˈgriːçin] f, -, -nen | **Greek person** n

Griechisch(e) [ˈgriːçiʃ(ə)] n, -n, kein Pl. | **Greek** (language)

Holländer [ˈhɔlɛndə*] m, -s, - **Holländerin** [ˈhɔlɛndərin] f, -, -nen | **Dutch person** n

Holländisch(e) [ˈhɔlɛndiʃə] n, -n, kein Pl. | **Dutch** (language) n

holländisch [ˈhɔlɛndiʃ] Adj. | **Dutch**

Inder [ˈində*] m, -s, - **Inderin** [ˈindərin] f, -, -nen | **person from India,** (Asian) **Indian** n

indisch [ˈindiʃ] Adj. | **Indian**

Ire [ˈiːrə] m, -n, -n **Irin** [ˈiːrin] f, -, -nen | **Irish** n (person)

irisch [ˈiːriʃ] Adj. | **Irish**

Italiener [ita'lje:nə*] *m*, -s, - **Italienerin** [ita'lje:nərin] *f*, -, -nen	**Italian** *(person) n*
Italienisch(e) [ita'lje:niʃ(ə)] *n*, -n, *kein Pl.*	**Italian** *(language) n*
italienisch [ita'lje:niʃ] *Adj.*	**Italian**
Japaner [ja'pa:nə*] *m*, -s, - **Japanerin** [ja'pa:nərin] *f*, -, -nen	**Japanese person** *n*
Japanisch(e) [ja'pa:niʃ(ə)] *n*, -n, *kein Pl.*	**Japanese** *(language) n*
japanisch [ja'pa:niʃ] *Adj.*	**Japanese**
Pole ['po:lə] *m*, -n, -n **Polin** ['po:lin] *f*, -, -nen	**Pole, Polish person** *n*
Polnisch(e) ['pɔlniʃ(ə)] *n*, -n, *kein Pl.*	**Polish** *(language) n*
polnisch ['pɔlniʃ] *Adj.*	**Polish**
Russe ['rusə] *m*, -n, -n **Russin** ['rusin] *f*, -, -nen	**Russian** *(person) n*
Russisch(e) ['rusiʃ(ə)] *n*, -n, *kein Pl.*	**Russian** *(language) n*
russisch ['rusiʃ] *Adj.*	**Russian**
Spanier ['ʃpa:njə*] *m*, -s, - **Spanierin** ['ʃpa:njərin] *f*, -, -nen	**Spaniard, Spanish person** *n*
Spanisch(e) ['ʃpa:niʃ(ə)] *n*, -n, *kein Pl.*	**Spanish** *(language) n*
spanisch ['ʃpa:niʃ] *Adj.*	**Spanish**

13 Zeit

13 Time

13.1 Jahreseinteilung 　　　1-2000

13.1 Divisions of the Year

Feiertag ['faiə*ta:k] *m*, -es, -e
Morgen ist ein Feiertag. Dann muss ich nicht arbeiten.

holiday *n*
Tomorrow is a holiday. I don't have to work.

Frühjahr ['fry:ja:*] *n*, -es, -e
Im Frühjahr ist das Wasser im Meer noch zu kalt zum Baden.

spring *n*
In the spring the water is still too cold to swim in the ocean.

Frühling ['fry:liŋ] *m*, -s, -e
Diese Blumen blühen schon im Frühling.

spring *n*
These flowers bloom early in the spring.

Herbst [hɛrpst] *m*, -es, -e
Dieses Jahr hat es schon im Herbst geschneit.

fall, autumn *(BE) n*
This year it already snowed in the fall.

Jahr [ja:*] *n*, -es, -e
Im nächsten Jahr werden wir euch bestimmt besuchen.

year *n*
Next year we'll visit you for sure.

Jahreszeit ['ja:rəstsait] *f*, -, -en
Für mich ist der Sommer die schönste Jahreszeit.

season, time of year *n*
For me, summer is the nicest time of year.

Monat ['mo:nat] *m*, -s, -e
Ich habe im nächsten Monat Geburtstag.

month *n*
My birthday is next month.

Sommer ['zomə*] *m*, -s, -
Der letzte Sommer war heiß und trocken.

summer *n*
Last summer was hot and dry.

Tag [ta:k] *m*, -(e)s, -e
Sie steht jeden Tag zur gleichen Zeit auf.

day *n*
She gets up the same time every day.

Winter ['vintə*] *m*, -s, -
Sie fährt jeden Winter in die Alpen zum Skifahren.

winter *n*
Every winter she goes to the Alps to ski.

Woche ['vɔxə] *f*, -, -n
Bis Weihnachten sind es nur noch drei Wochen.

week *n*
There are only three weeks until Christmas.

Halbjahr ['halpja:*] *n*, -(e)s, -e
Im letzten Halbjahr lief das Geschäft sehr gut.

half year *n*
Business was very good in the last half year.

jährlich ['jɛ:ə*liç] *Adj., keine Komp.*
Die Gebühren werden jährlich bezahlt.

annual

The fees are paid annually.

monatlich ['mo:natliç] *Adj., keine Komp.*
Unser Gehalt bekommen wir monatlich.

monthly

We get paid monthly.

täglich ['tɛ:kliç] *Adj., keine Komp.*
Die Tabletten müssen Sie dreimal täglich nehmen.

daily, a day
You must take these pills three times daily.

Vorjahr ['fo:ə*ja:*] *n*, -(e)s, -e
Die Ernte des Vorjahres war besser.

last year, year before, previous year *n*
The harvest of the previous year was better.

Wochenende ['vɔx(ə)nɛndə] *n*, -s, -n
Am Wochenende sind wir selten zu Hause.

weekend *n*
We're seldom at home during the weekend.

Wochentag ['vɔx(ə)nta:k] *m*, -(e)s, -e
Das Geschäft ist an allen Wochentagen vormittags geöffnet.

weekday *n*
The business is open every weekday in the morning.

wöchentlich ['vœç(ə)ntliç] *Adj., keine Komp.*
Ich gehe wöchentlich einmal ins Hallenbad zum Schwimmen.

weekly, a week
I go swimming at the indoor pool once a week.

13.2 Monatsnamen

13.2 The Names of the Months

Januar ['janua:*] *m*, -(s), -e Wir heiraten im Januar.	**January** *n* We are getting married in January.
Februar ['fe:brua:*] *m*, -(s), -e	**February** *n*
März [mɛrts] *m*, -, -e	**March** *n*
April [a'pril] *m*, -(s), -e	**April** *n*
Mai [mai] *m*, -(s), -e(n)	**May** *n*
Juni ['ju:ni] *m*, -(s), -s	**June** *n*
Juli ['ju:li] *m*, -(s), -s	**July** *n*
August [au'gust] *m*, -(s), -e	**August** *n*
September [zɛp'tɛmbə*] *m*, -(s), -	**September** *n*
Oktober [ɔk'to:bə*] *m*, -(s), -	**October** *n*
November [no'vɛmbə*] *m*, -(s), -	**November** *n*
Dezember [de'tsɛmbə*] *m*, -(s), -	**December** *n*

13.3 Wochentage

13.3 Weekdays

Montag ['mo:nta:k] *m*, -s, -e (Am) Montag muss ich nicht arbeiten.	**Monday** *n* (On) Monday I do not have to work.
Dienstag ['di:nsta:k] *m*, -s, -e	**Tuesday** *n*
Mittwoch ['mitvɔx] *m*, -s, -e	**Wednesday** *n*
Donnerstag ['dɔnə*sta:k] *m*, -s, -e	**Thursday** *n*
Freitag ['fraita:k] *m*, -s, -e	**Friday** *n*
Samstag ['zamsta:k] *m*, -s, -e	**Saturday** *n*
Sonnabend ['zɔna:b(ə)nt] *m*, -s, -e	**Saturday** *n*
Sonntag ['zɔnta:k] *m*, -s, -e	**Sunday** *n*

13.4 Tageszeit

13.4 Times of Day

Abend ['a:b(ə)nt] *m*, -s, -e
Ich rufe dich am Abend an.
Mittwochabend sind wir bei Jochen eingeladen.

evening *s*
I'll call you in the evening.
Wednesday evening we have been invited to Jochen's house.

abends ['a:b(ə)nts] *Adv.*
Abends bin ich meistens zu Hause.

in the evening
In the evening I am usually (at) home.

Mittag ['mita:k] *m*, -s, -e
Er ist bis Mittag im Büro.

noon *n*
He is in the office until noon.

mittags ['mita:ks] *Adv.*
Mittags esse ich in der Kantine.

at noon, at lunchtime
At noon I eat in the cafeteria.

Mitternacht ['mitə*naxt] *f*, -, *kein Pl.*
Um Mitternacht war die Feier zu Ende.

midnight *n*

At midnight the party ended.

Morgen ['mɔrg(ə)n] *m*, -s, -
Ich stehe jeden Morgen um 7.00 Uhr auf.
Donnerstagmorgen habe ich einen Termin beim Arzt.

morning *n*
I get up every morning at 7.00 a.m.
Thursday morning I have an appointment at the doctor's.

morgens ['mɔrg(ə)ns] *Adv.*
Morgens habe ich keinen Hunger.

in the morning, every morning
I am not hungry in the morning.

Nachmittag ['na:xmita:k] *m*, -s, -e
Ines war bis zum Nachmittag bei uns.

afternoon *n*
Ines was with us until the afternoon.

Nacht [naxt] *f*, -, Nächte
Letzte Nacht habe ich gut geschlafen.

night *n*
Last night I slept well.

nachts [naxts] *Adv.*
Um 1.00 Uhr nachts hat er mich
geweckt.

at night, in the morning
At one o'clock in the morning he
woke me.

Vormittag ['fo:ə*mita:k] *m, -s, -e*
Sie arbeitet nur am Vormittag.

morning *n*
She only works in the morning.

13.5 Uhrzeit

13.5 Clock Time

Uhr [u:ə*] *f, -, -en*
Der Film fängt um 19.00 Uhr an.

o'clock *n*
The film begins at 7 o'clock.

halb [halp] *Adj., keine Komp.*
Ich bin um halb fünf zurück.

half-past
I'll be back at half-past four.

Minute [mi'nu:tə] *f, -, -n*
Es ist zwei Minuten vor zehn.

minute *n*
It's two minutes before ten.

Sekunde [ze'kundə] *f, -, -n*
Er ist 100 Meter in 10,8 Sekunden
gelaufen.

second *n*
He ran 100 meters in 10.8 sec-
onds.

Stunde ['ʃtundə] *f, -, -n*
Bitte kommen Sie in zwei
Stunden.

hour *n*
Please come (by) in two hours.

um [um] *Präp.*
Herr Funke kommt um 15.00 Uhr.

at
Mr. Funke is coming at 3 p.m.

Viertel ['firt(ə)l] *n, -s, -*
Es ist Viertel nach sieben.

quarter *n*
It is a quarter past seven.

Viertelstunde [firt(ə)l'ʃtundə] *f, -,
-n*
Wir sind eine Viertelstunde zu
spät gekommen.

quarter hour *n*

We came a quarter hour too late.

13.6 Sonstige Zeitbegriffe
13.6 Other Concepts of Time

13.6.1 Substantive | 1-2000
13.6.1 Nouns

Anfang ['anfaŋ] m, -s, Anfänge Am Anfang des Spiels war er besser.	**beginning** n He played better at the beginning of the game.
Augenblick ['aug(ə)nblik] m, -s, -e Warten Sie bitte einen Augenblick!	**moment** n Please wait a moment.
Beginn [bə'gin] m, -s, kein Pl. Am Beginn war der Film langweilig.	**beginning** n The beginning of the film was boring.
Datum ['da:tum] n, -s, Daten Welches Datum steht in dem Brief?	**date** n What's the date on the letter?
Ende ['ɛndə] n, -s, kein Pl. Am Ende des Gesprächs fand man doch noch eine Lösung.	**end** n At the end of the talks they came to an agreement.
Jahrhundert [ja:*'hundə*t] n, -s, -e Die Brücke wurde im letzten Jahrhundert gebaut.	**century** n The bridge was built in the last century.
Jahrzehnt [ja:*'tse:nt] n, -s, -e In den letzten Jahrzehnten gab es in Europa keine Kriege.	**decade** n In the last decades there have been no wars in Europe.
Mal [ma:l] n, -(e)s, -e Das nächste Mal müssen die Arbeiten besser geplant werden.	**time** n The work has to be better planned the next time.
Moment [mo'mɛnt] m, -s, -e Bitte haben Sie einen Moment Geduld!	**moment, minute** n Please be patient for a moment!

Schluss [ʃlus] *m, -es, kein Pl.*
Einige Zuschauer gingen schon vor dem Schluss der Veranstaltung nach Hause.

end, conclusion *n*

Some of the spectators went home before the end of the performance.

Vergangenheit [fɛɐ̯'gaŋənhait] *f, -, kein Pl.*
In der Vergangenheit gab es solche Maschinen nicht.

past *n*

In the past there were no such machines.

Zeit [tsait] *f, -, -en*
In der letzten Zeit habe ich ihn nicht gesehen.

time *n*

Recently (*lit.:* In recent times) I have not seen him.

Zeitpunkt ['tsaitpuŋkt] *m, -(e)s, -e*
Zum Zeitpunkt der Tat war er bei Freunden.

(point in) time *n*

At the time of the deed he was with friends.

Zukunft ['tsu:kunft] *f, -, kein Pl.*
Du musst auch an die Zukunft denken.

future *n*

You must also think of the future.

2001-4000

Frist [frist] *f, -, -en*

Der Einspruch kommt zu spät. Die Frist ist um 2 Tage überschritten.

time period, deadline, grace period *n*

The protest comes too late. The deadline was exceeded by two days.

Gegenwart ['ge:g(ə)nvart] *f, -, kein Pl.*
Sie lebt nur in der Gegenwart, an die Zukunft denkt sie nicht.

present *n*

She only lives in the present; she does not think of the future.

Höhepunkt ['hø:əpuŋkt] *m, -s, -e*
Dieser Film war der Höhepunkt der Münchener Filmtage.

pinnacle, high point, climax *n*

This film was the high point of the Munich Film Festival.

Jahresende ['ja:rəsɛndə] *n, -s, kein Pl.*
Am Jahresende gibt es in unserer Firma immer eine Feier.

end of the year *n*

At the end of the year there is always a party in our office.

Mittelalter ['mit(ə)laltə*] *n, -s, kein Pl.*
Über die Geschichte des Mittelalters weiß ich wenig.

the Middle Ages *n*
I know very little about the history of the Middle Ages.

Verspätung [fɛə*'ʃpɛːtuŋ] *f, -, -en*
Der Zug hatte 12 Minuten Verspätung.

delay *n*
The train had a delay of 12 minutes.

Verzögerung [fɛə*'tsøːgəruŋ] *f, -, -en*
Wegen des schlechten Wetters gab es Verzögerungen beim Bau des Hauses.

delay *n*
Because of the bad weather there were delays in the construction of the house.

Weile ['vailə] *f, -, kein Pl.*
Es dauert nur noch eine Weile, dann bin ich fertig.

(a) while, *n*
It will take a while longer, then I'll be finished.

Zeitalter ['tsaitaltə*] *n, -s, -*
Ich hätte gerne im Zeitalter der Renaissance gelebt.

age, historical period *n*
I would have loved to have lived in the Age of the Renaissance.

Zeitraum ['tsaitraum] *m, -(e)s, Zeiträume*
Dieser Plan soll in einem Zeitraum von drei Jahren verwirklicht werden.

(period of) time *n*
This plan should be completed in (*lit.:* the period of time of) three years.

13.6.2 Verben

13.6.2 Verbs

anfangen ['anfaŋən] *V/i., fing an, hat angefangen*
Wann fängt das Konzert an?

begin *v*
When does the concert begin?

andauern ['andauə*n] *V/i., dauerte an, hat angedauert*
Der Sturm dauerte die ganze Nacht an.

last, continue *v*
The storm lasted all night.

beenden [bə'ɛnd(ə)n] *V/t.,* beendete, hat beendet

end *v*

Wir haben unseren Streit beendet.

We have ended our fight.

beginnen [bə'gin(ə)n] *V/t., i.,* begann, hat begonnen

begin, start *v*

Die Arbeiten sind sofort begonnen worden.

The work began immediately.

Die Schulferien beginnen morgen.

The school holidays begin tomorrow.

dauern ['dauə*n] *V/i.,* dauerte, hat gedauert

last *v*

Das Gespräch wird nicht lange dauern.

The conversation won't last long.

enden ['ɛnd(ə)n] *V/i.,* endete, hat geendet

end *v*

Das Fußballspiel endet um 10.00 Uhr.

The football game ends at 10 o'clock.

fortsetzen ['fɔrtzɛts(ə)n] *V/t.,* setzte fort, hat fortgesetzt

continue *v*

Nach einer Pause setzten wir die Fahrt fort.

After a break we continued the trip.

verkürzen [fɛə*'kyrts(ə)n] *V/t.,* verkürzte, hat verkürzt

shorten *v*

Die Arbeitszeit wird verkürzt.

The work time is being shortened.

verschieben [fɛə*'ʃiːb(ə)n] *V/t., refl.,* verschob, hat verschoben

postpone *v*

Der Termin wurde um eine Woche verschoben.

The appointment was postponed for a week.

verspäten [fɛə*'ʃpɛːt(ə)n] *V/refl.,* verspätete, hat verspätet

be late *v*

Warum hast du dich so lange verspätet?

Why were you so late?

13.6.3 Adjektive | 1-2000

13.6.3 Adjectives

---

dauernd ['dauə*nt] *Adj., keine Komp.*

continual, constant

Ich werde dauernd gestört.

I am constantly being disturbed.

endgültig ['ɛntgyltiç°] *Adj., keine Komp.*

once and for all

Du musst dich jetzt endgültig entscheiden.

You must decide once and for all.

früh [fry:] *Adj., früher, am frühesten*

early, former

Wir sind am frühen Abend fertig gewesen.

We were ready in the early evening.

Er ist ein früherer Kollege von mir.

He is a former colleague of mine.

gleichzeitig ['glaiçtsaitiç°] *Adj., keine Komp.*

at the same time, simultaneous

Ich kann nicht beide Arbeiten gleichzeitig machen.

I cannot do both jobs at the same time.

häufig ['hɔifiç°] *Adj.*

often, frequent

Das ist schon häufiger passiert.

This has already happened often.

heutig ['hɔitiç°] *Adj., keine Komp.*

today's, of today

Die Meldung stand in der heutigen Zeitung.

The report was in today's newspaper.

kurz [kurts] *Adj., kürzer, am kürzesten*

short

Wir haben eine kurze Pause gemacht.

We took a short break.

lang [laŋ] *Adj., länger, am längsten*

long

Er war lange Zeit krank.

He was sick for a long time.

modern [mo'dɛrn] *Adj.*

modern

Die Wohnung ist modern möbliert.

The apartment has modern furniture.

nächste ['nɛ:çstə] *Adj., keine Komp.*

next

Nächstes Jahr wird er Rentner.

Next year he will retire.

plötzlich ['plœtsliç] *Adj., keine Komp.*
Sie ist ganz plötzlich gestorben.

sudden
She died suddenly.

pünktlich ['pyŋktliç] *Adj.*
Bitte sei morgen pünktlich um 19.00 Uhr da.

on time
Please be there on time tomorrow at 7 p.m.

rechtzeitig ['reçt-tsaitiç°] *Adj.*
Den Verletzten konnte rechtzeitig geholfen werden.

in time
The injured could be helped in time.

regelmäßig ['re:g(ə)lmɛ:siç°] *Adj.*
Gehst du regelmäßig zum Zahnarzt?

regular
Do you go to the dentist regularly?

spät [ʃpɛ:t] *Adj., -er, am -esten*
Sie können auch am späten Abend anrufen.

late
You can also call late in the evening.

ständig ['ʃtɛndiç°] *Adj., keine Komp.*
Sie ist ständig am Rauchen.

continual, constant
She is constantly smoking.

vorig ['fo:riç°] *Adj., keine Komp.*
Voriges Jahr hat er seine Prüfung gemacht.

previous, last
Last year he took his exam.

vorläufig ['fo:ə*rlɔifiç°] *Adj., keine Komp.*
Das ist nur eine vorläufige Lösung.

temporary
That is only a temporary solution.

2001-4000

bisherig [bis'he:riç°] *Adj., keine Komp.*
Mit der bisherigen Regelung sind wir zufrieden.

up to now, to date, previous
We are satisfied with the arrangement(s) to date.

damalig ['da:ma:liç°] *Adj., keine Komp.*
Dafür war der damalige Chef verantwortlich.

at that time
The boss at that time was responsible for it.

dauerhaft ['dauə*haft] *Adj.,* -er, am -esten | **lasting, durable**

Der neue Kunststoff ist dauerhafter und trotzdem billiger. | The new synthetic is longer lasting but nevertheless cheaper.

gegenwärtig ['ge:g(ə)nvɛrtiç°] *Adj., keine Komp.* | **present, current**

Es gibt viel Kritik an der gegenwärtigen Regierung. | There is considerable criticism of the current government.

gelegentlich [gə'le:g(ə)ntliç] *Adj., keine Komp.* | **occasional**

Ich besuche Petra gelegentlich. | I visit Petra occasionally.

jahrelang ['ja:rəlaŋ] *Adj., keine Komp.* | **for years**

Sie wohnt schon jahrelang in dieser Wohnung. | She has lived for years in this apartment.

künftig ['kynftiç°] *Adj., keine Komp.* | **future**

Wir müssen auch an die Folgen für künftige Generationen denken. | We also have to think about the results for future generations.

kurzfristig ['kurtsfristiç°] *Adj.* | **on short notice, short-term**

Der Plan ist kurzfristig geändert worden. | The plan was changed on short notice.

langfristig ['laŋfristiç°] *Adj.* | **long-term**

Das Problem muss langfristig gelöst werden. | The problem has to be solved on a long-term basis.

rasch [raʃ] *Adj.,* -er, am -esten | **quick**

Wir werden uns rasch entscheiden. | We will decide quickly.

unregelmäßig ['unre:g(ə)lmɛ:siç°] *Adj.* | **irregular**

Sie hat eine unregelmäßige Arbeitszeit. | She has an irregular work time.

vorübergehend [fo'ry:bə*ge:ənt] *Adj., keine Komp.* | **temporary**

Herr Behrens arbeitet vorübergehend in einer anderen Abteilung. | Mr. Behrens is working temporarily in another department.

13.6.4 Adverbien | 1-2000

bald [balt] *Adv.*
Bald ist Feierabend.

soon
Soon we can go home.

bereits [bə'raits] *Adv.*
Das ist bereits erledigt.

already
This has already been taken care of.

bisher [bis'he:ə*] *Adv.*
Das neue Modell habe ich bisher noch nicht gesehen.

until now, up to now
I have not yet seen the new model.

damals ['da:ma:ls] *Adv.*
Damals gab es noch keine Computer.

then, at that time, back then
At that time there was still no computer.

danach [da'na:x] *Adv.*
Erst war ich beim Arzt. Danach habe ich eingekauft.

after that, then
First I went to the doctor. After that I did the shopping.

dann [dan] *Adv.*
Erst das Programm wählen und dann einschalten.
Ich brauche noch eine Woche Zeit. Dann ist die Zeichnung bestimmt fertig.

then
First choose the program, and then turn on the electricity.
I still need a week. Then the drawing will certainly be finished.

diesmal ['di:sma:l] *Adv.*
Bitte sei diesmal pünktlich!

this time
Please be on time this time!

eben ['e:b(ə)n] *Adv.*
Die Post ist eben gekommen.

just
The mail just came.

eher ['e:ə*] *Adv.*
Warum haben Sie uns nicht eher informiert?

earlier, sooner
Why didn't you inform us earlier?

endlich ['ɛntliç] *Adv.*
Wann kommt das Taxi endlich?

finally, at last
When is that taxi finally coming?

erst [ɛə*st] *Adv.*
Ich gehe erst nach dem Fernsehfilm schlafen.

right (now), just (now)
I'll go to bed right after the TV film.

früher ['fry:ə*] *Adv.*
Wir essen heute eine Stunde früher.

earlier, previous
Today we're eating an hour earlier.

---

gestern ['gɛstə*n] *Adv.*
Gestern hatte ich noch kein Fieber.

yesterday
Yesterday I still didn't have a fever.

---

gleich [glaiç] *Adv.*
Einen Moment, ich komme gleich.

right away
Just a moment; I'm coming right away.

---

heute ['hɔitə] *Adv.*
Heute soll es regnen.

today
It's supposed to rain today.

---

immer ['imə*] *Adv.*
Er ist immer nett und höflich.

always,
He is always pleasant and polite.

---

inzwischen [in'tsviʃ(ə)n] *Adv.*
Während ich spüle, kannst du inzwischen die Küche aufräumen.

in the meantime
While I'm washing the dishes you can straighten up the kitchen.

---

jemals ['je:ma:ls] *Adv.*
Ich bezweifle, dass er jemals Erfolg haben wird.

ever
I doubt he will ever be successful.

---

jetzt [jɛtst] *Adv.*
Jetzt oder nie! Du musst dich entscheiden.

now
Now or never! You have to make up your mind.

---

kaum [kaum] *Adv.*
Er lacht kaum.

hardly, scarcely
He hardly ever laughs.

---

lange ['laŋə] *Adv.*
Ihre Gespräche dauern immer lange.

a long time
Her conversations always last a long time.

---

längst ['lɛŋst] *Adv.*
Du hättest das längst erledigen müssen.

a long time ago
You should have taken care of that a long time ago.

---

manchmal ['mançma:l] *Adv.*
Er kann manchmal sehr unfreundlich sein.

sometimes
Sometimes he can be very unfriendly.

---

mehrmals ['me:ə*ma:ls] *Adv.*
Ich habe wegen der Sache mehrmals mit ihr gesprochen.

several times
I've talked to her several times about this.

---

meistens ['maistəns] *Adv.*
Morgens trinke ich meistens nur einen Kaffee.

mostly, most of the time, usually
Most of the time I just drink coffee in the morning.

nachher [naːxˈheːə*] *Adv.*
Gehen wir nachher noch etwas essen?

afterwards
Are we still going to eat something afterwards?

neulich [ˈnɔɪlɪç] *Adv.*
Wir haben neulich einen Brief von Gunter bekommen.

recently
We recently got a letter from Gunter.

nie [niː] *Adv.*
Ich habe noch nie geraucht.

never
I have never smoked.

niemals [ˈniːmaːls] *Adv.*
Ohne deine Hilfe hätte ich das niemals geschafft.

never
I would have never finished that without your help.

noch [nɔx] *Adv.*
Arbeitest du noch als Verkäuferin?
Wie lange müssen wir noch warten?

still, yet
Are you still working as a saleswoman?
How much longer do we still have to wait?

nochmals [ˈnɔxmaːls] *Adv.*
Sie muss nochmals zum Arzt.

again, once more
She has to go to the doctor again.

nun [nuːn] *Adv.*
Du hast gekündigt. Was machst du nun?

now
You resigned. What are you going to do now?

oft [ɔft] *Adv.*
Wir gehen oft zusammen aus.

often
We go out together often.

schließlich [ˈʃliːslɪç] *Adv.*
Schließlich hat es doch noch geklappt.

finally, eventually, after all
Eventually things worked out.

schon [ʃoːn] *Adv.*
Kann das Kind schon laufen?

already
Can the child walk already?

selten [ˈzɛlt(ə)n] *Adv.*
Wir gehen selten ins Kino.

seldom
We seldom go to the movies.

soeben [zoˈeːb(ə)n] *Adv.*
Sie ist soeben nach Hause gekommen.

just now
She just now got home.

sofort [zoˈfɔrt] *Adv.*
Ich komme sofort.

right away, now, immediately
I'm coming right away.

später [ˈʃpɛːtə*] *Adv.*
Lass uns später essen, nicht jetzt.

later
Let's eat later, not now.

spätestens ['ʃpɛ:təstəns] *Adv.*
Spätestens um 9.00 Uhr muss ich im Büro sein.

at the latest
I have to be in the office at 9 a.m. at the latest.

übermorgen ['y:bə*mɔrg(ə)n] *Adv.*
Übermorgen ist ein Feiertag.

the day after tomorrow
The day after tomorrow is a holiday.

vor kurzem [fo:ə*'kurtsəm] *Adv.*
Ich habe vor kurzem noch mit ihr gesprochen.

recently
I spoke to her again recently.

vorbei [fo:ə*'bai] *Adv.*
Hoffentlich ist das schlechte Wetter bald vorbei.

past, over
We hope the bad weather will be over soon.

vorgestern ['fo:e*gɛstə*n] *Adv.*
Der Unfall ist vorgestern passiert.

the day before yesterday
The accident happened the day before yesterday.

vorher ['fo:ə*he:ə*] *Adv.*
Warum haben Sie mir das nicht vorher gesagt?

before
Why didn't you tell me that before?

vorhin [fo:ə*'hin] *Adv.*
○ Haben Sie Frau Pauls gesehen?
□ Ja, vorhin war sie noch in ihrem Zimmer.

before that, just a moment ago
○ Have you seen Ms. Pauls?
□ Yes. Just a moment ago she was still in her room.

wann [van] *Adv.*
Wann wollen wir uns treffen?

when?
When shall we meet?

wieder ['vi:də*] *Adv.*
Du musst ihn daran erinnern, sonst vergisst er es wieder.

again
You have to remind him of it or he'll forget it again.

zuerst [tsu'e:ə*st] *Adv.*
Was soll zuerst gemacht werden?

first (of all)
What's supposed to be done first?

zuletzt [tsu'lɛtst] *Adv.*
Vorige Woche habe ich ihn zuletzt gesehen.

finally, last
The last time I saw him was last week.

zunächst [tsu'nɛ:çst] *Adv.*
Zunächst habe ich es nicht verstanden, aber man hat es mir dann erklärt.

first (of all), at first
At first I didn't understand, but then they explained it to me.

bislang [bis'laŋ] *Adv.*
Bislang bin ich mit diesem Auto sehr zufrieden.

so far, until now
So far I'm very satisfied with this car.

daraufhin [darauf'hin] *Adv.*
Petra ging zuerst. Daraufhin sind wir auch gegangen.

after that, following that
Petra went first. After that we also went.

dazwischen [da'tsviʃ(ə)n] *Adv.*
Ich habe um 14.00 und 16.00 Uhr eine Verabredung. Dazwischen habe ich keine Zeit.

in the meantime, in between
I have appointments at 2 and 4. I don't have time in between.

demnächst [de:m'nɛ:çst] *Adv.*
Mein Bruder heiratet demnächst.

soon, in the near future
My brother is getting married soon.

heutzutage ['hɔit-tsuta:gə] *Adv.*
Heutzutage leben die Menschen länger als früher.

today, nowadays, these days
Today people live longer than they used to.

jedes Mal ['je:dəs 'ma:l] *Adv.*
Wir freuen uns jedes Mal über deinen Besuch.

every time, each time
We're happy every time to have your visit.

kürzlich ['kyrtsliç] *Adv.*
Ich habe ihn kürzlich getroffen.

recently
I ran into him recently.

neuerdings ['nɔiə*'diŋs] *Adv.*
Ralf raucht neuerdings nicht mehr.

recently
Ralf recently stopped smoking.

zeitweise ['tsaitvaizə] *Adv.*
Sie arbeitet zeitweise in einem Cafe.

at times, sometimes
Sometimes she works in a café.

zuweilen [tsu'vail(ə)n] *Adv.*
Zuweilen lese ich gerne einen Kriminalroman.

from time to time, now and then
From time to time I like to read a detective novel.

13.6.5 Präpositionen

13.6.5 Prepositions

ab [ap] *Präp.*
Das Geschäft ist ab 9.00 Uhr geöffnet.

from, starting at
The business is open starting at 9 a.m.

bis [bis] *Präp.*
Die Veranstaltung dauert bis Mitternacht.

until
The performance lasts until midnight.

in [in] *Präp.*
Er ruft in einer Stunde wieder an.

in
He'll call back in an hour.

innerhalb ['inə*halp] *Präp.*
Sie kommen innerhalb der nächsten Woche zurück.

within
They'll be back within the next week.

nach [na:x] *Präp.*
Sie war nach einer Woche wieder gesund.

after
She got well after a week.

seit [zait] *Präp.*
Ich habe seit vier Wochen nichts von ihm gehört.

for, since
I haven't heard anything from him for four weeks.

um [um] *Präp.*
Sie ist um 19.00 Uhr gegangen.

around, about, at *(clock time)*
She left at 7 p.m.

vor [fo:ə*] *Präp.*
Vor Weihnachten habe ich wenig Zeit.

before
I don't have much time before Christmas.

während ['vɛ:rənt] *Präp.*
Während der Ferien ist die Bibliothek geschlossen.

during
During vacation the library is closed.

zwischen ['tsviʃ(ə)n] *Präp.*
Sie wollen uns zwischen Weihnachten und Neujahr besuchen.

between
They want to visit us between Christmas and New Years.

13.6.6 Konjunktionen

als [als] *Konj.*
Sie bremste sofort, als sie den Radfahrer sah.

when *(in the past)*
She stepped on the brakes the moment when she saw the cyclist.

---

bevor [bə'fo:ə*] *Konj.*
Ich möchte zu Hause sein, bevor es dunkel ist.

before
I'd like to get home before it gets dark.

---

ehe ['e:ə] *Konj.*
Sie lief weg, ehe ich etwas sagen konnte.

before
She ran away before I could say anything.

---

nachdem [na:x'de:m] *Konj.*
Nachdem er gegessen hatte, trank er eine Tasse Kaffee.

after
After he had eaten, he drank a cup of coffee.

---

seitdem [zait'de:m] *Konj.*
Ina hatte mit 25 Jahren einen Unfall. Seitdem ist sie blind.

since then
Ina had an accident when she was 25. Since then she's been blind.

---

sobald [zo'balt] *Konj.*
Ich rufe Sie an, sobald ich etwas Neues weiß.

as soon as
I'll call you as soon as I have some news.

---

solange [zo'laŋə] *Konj.*
Solange mein Wagen in der Werkstatt ist, fahre ich mit dem Bus zur Arbeit.

as long as
As long as my car is being repaired, I'll take the bus to work.

---

wenn [vɛn] *Konj.*
Wenn ich ihn sehe, frage ich ihn.

if, whenever, when
I'll ask him if I see him.

14.1 Substantive | 1-2000

14.1 Nouns

Abstand ['apʃtant] *m*, -(e)s, Abstände
Der Ofen muss 40 cm Abstand zur Wand haben.

distance *n*
The stove has to be at a distance of 40 cm from the wall.

Breite ['braitə] *f*, -, -n
Der Tisch hat eine Breite von 80 cm.

width *n*
The width of the table is 80 cm.

Ende ['ɛndə] *n*, -s, -n
Der Speisewagen ist am Ende des Zuges.

end *n*
The dining car is at the end of the train.

Entfernung [ɛnt'fɛrnuŋ] *f*, -, -en
Wegen der großen Entfernung konnte ich ihn nicht erkennen.

distance *n*
I couldn't recognize him from that distance.

Größe ['grø:sə] *f*, -, -n
Die genaue Größe der Wohnung kenne ich nicht.
Was ist Ihre Schuhgröße?

size *n*
I don't know the exact size of the apartment.
What is your shoe size?

Höhe ['hø:ə] *f*, -, -n
Hast du die Höhe des Raums gemessen?

height *n*
Did you measure the room's height?

Lage ['la:gə] *f*, -, -n
Die Lage des Hauses ist phantastisch.

position, situation, site, location *n*
The house site is fantastic!

Länge ['lɛŋə] *f*, -, -n
Das Bett gibt es in drei verschiedenen Längen.

length *n*
The bed is available in three lengths.

Lücke ['lykə] *f*, -, -n
Zwischen ihren Häusern ist nur eine schmale Lücke.

space *n*
There's only a small space between their houses.

Mitte ['mitə] *f, -, -n*
In der Mitte des Raums steht ein großer Tisch.

middle *n*
There's a big table in the middle of the room.

Nähe ['nɛːə] *f, -, kein Pl.*
Sie wohnt in der Nähe des Bahnhofs.

area near(by), neighborhood *n*
She lives in the area near the train station.

Ort [ɔrt] *m, -(e)s, -e*
Ort und Zeit des Treffens müssen noch verabredet werden.

place *n*
The time and place of the meeting still have to be arranged.

Platz [plats] *m, -es, Plätze*
In meinem Auto ist noch Platz.
An diesem Platz im Garten gibt es viel Sonne.

place, room, square *(in a town) n*
There's still room in my car.
This place in the garden is very sunny.

Punkt [puŋkt] *m, -(e)s, -e*
Hast du einen Treffpunkt verabredet?

point, place *n*
Have you arranged a place to meet?

Rand [rant] *m, -(e)s, Ränder*
Der Weg führt am Rand des Waldes entlang.

edge *n*
The path goes along the edge of the woods.

Raum [raum] *m, -(e)s, Räume*
Der Raum zwischen den Häusern ist sehr eng.

room, space *n*
The space between the houses is very narrow.

Richtung ['riçtuŋ] *f, -, -en*
Ich glaube, wir fahren in die falsche Richtung.

direction *n*
I think we're driving in the wrong direction.

Seite ['zaitə] *f, -, -n*
Auf beiden Seiten der Straße stehen Bäume.

side *n*
There are trees on both sides of the street.

Spitze ['ʃpitsə] *f, -, -n*
Wegen des Schnees konnten wir die Spitze des Berges nicht erreichen.

top, peak *n*
We couldn't get to the mountain peak because of the snow.

Stelle ['ʃtɛlə] *f, -, -n*
Diese Stelle am Fuß tut weh.

place, spot, area *n*
This place on my foot hurts.

Strecke ['ʃtrɛkə] *f, -, -n*
Wir haben die Strecke in zwei Tagen zurückgelegt.

distance *n*
We covered the distance within two days.

Tiefe ['ti:fə] *f,* -, -n
Der Schrank hat eine Tiefe von
60 cm.

depth *n*
The cabinet is 60 centimeters in
depth.

$$\boxed{2001\text{-}4000}$$

Außenseite ['aus(ə)nzaitə] *f,* -, -n
Die Außenseite der Haustür ist
dreckig.

outside, exterior *n*
The outside of the front door is
dirty.

Hintergrund ['hintə*grunt] *m,*
-(e)s, Hintergründe
Im Hintergrund der Bühne waren
Häuser auf Pappe gemalt.

background *n*

For the stage background houses
were painted on cardboard.

Innenseite ['inənzaitə] *f,* -, -n
Die Innenseite des Koffers ist aus
Kunststoff.

inside *n*
The inside of the trunk is made of
plastic.

Oberfläche ['o:bə*flɛçə] *f,* -, -n
Die Oberfläche des Tisches ist
sehr glatt.

surface *n*
The table surface is very smooth.

Position [pozi'tsjo:n] *f,* -, -en
Seit Tagen gibt es von dem Schiff
keine Positionsmeldung.

position *n*
There hasn't been a position report from the ship for days.

Vordergrund ['fɔrdə*grunt] *m,*
-(e)s, Vordergründe
Das kleine Mädchen im Vordergrund des Fotos bin ich.

foreground *n*

The little girl in the foreground of
the photo is me.

Vorderseite ['fɔrdə*zaitə] *f,* -, -n
Die Vorderseite des Hauses soll
gestrichen werden.

front *n*
The front of the house needs
paint.

Zentrum ['tsɛntrum] *n,* -s, Zent-
ren
Die Straßen im Stadtzentrum sind
sehr eng.

center *n*

The streets in the city center are
very narrow.

14.2 Adjektive | 1-2000

14.2 Adjectives

breit [brait] *Adj.*, -er, am -esten
Der Rhein wird in Holland sehr breit.

wide
The Rhine becomes very wide in Holland.

eng [ɛŋ] *Adj.*
Die Hose ist mir zu eng.
Der Raum ist eng.
Die Blumen sind eng nebeneinandergepflanzt.

narrow, close together, tight
The trousers are too tight for me.
The room is narrow.
The flowers are planted close together.

entfernt [ɛntˈfɛəˀnt] *Adj.*, -er, am -esten
Wie weit ist Mainz von Frankfurt entfernt?

distant, far

How far is Mainz from Frankfurt?

hoch [hoːx] *Adj.*, höher, am höchsten
Wie hoch ist der Raum?

high

How high is the room?

kurz [kurts] *Adj.*, kürzer, am kürzesten
Die Hose ist zu kurz.

short

The trousers are too short.

lang [laŋ] *Adj.*, länger, am längsten
Die Brücke ist über 2 km lang.

long

The bridge is over 2 km. long.

linke [ˈlɪŋkə] *Adj.*, *keine Komp.*
Der Eingang ist an der linken Seite des Hauses.

left
The entrance is on the left side of the house.

nah(e) [naː(ə)] *Adj.*, näher, am nächsten
Wo ist die nächste Bushaltestelle?

near, close

Where is the nearest bus stop?

ober(e) [ˈoːbəˀ(ˈoːbərə)] *Adj.*
Die Strümpfe liegen in der obersten Schublade.

upper, top
The stockings are in the top drawer.

offen [ˈɔf(ə)n] *Adj.*, *keine Komp.*
Ich schlafe bei offenem Fenster.

open
I sleep with the window(s) open.

rechte ['rɛçtə] *Adj., keine Komp.*
Die Apotheke ist von hier aus das fünfte Haus auf der rechten Straßenseite.

right
The drug store is the fifth house on the right side of the street.

schief [ʃiːf] *Adj.*
Der Tisch steht schief.

crooked, lopsided
The table is crooked.

tief [tiːf] *Adj.*
Wie tief ist das Regal?
Ist das Wasser des Sees sehr tief?

deep
How deep is the bookcase?
Is the water in the lake very deep?

unter(e) ['untə*('untərə)] *Adj.*
Das Buch steht im untersten Fach des Regals.

lower, bottom
The book is on the lowest shelf of the bookcase.

weit [vait] *Adj., -er, am -esten*
Sie trägt gern weite Röcke.
Er wohnt nicht weit von hier.

far, wide
She likes to wear wide skirts.
He does not live far from here.

2001-4000

aufrecht ['aufrɛçt] *Adj., keine Komp.*
Der Behälter muss immer aufrecht stehen.

upright
The container must always be kept upright.

senkrecht ['zɛŋkrɛçt] *Adj., keine Komp.*
Das Flugzeug stürzte fast senkrecht ab.

vertical
The plane went down almost vertically.

umgeben [um'geːb(ə)n] *Part. II* von ,umgeben'
Der See ist von Felswänden umgeben.

surrounded
The lake is surrounded by rock walls.

waag(e)recht ['vaːkrɛçt('vaːgərɛçt] *Adj., keine Komp.*
Der Kühlschrank muss waag(e)recht stehen.

horizontal
The refrigerator has to stand level (lit. horizontally).

zentral [tsɛn'traːl] *Adj.*
Die Wohnung liegt sehr zentral.

central
The apartment/flat has a very central location.

14.3 Adverbien

14.3 Adverbs

abwärts [ˈapvɛrts] *Adv.*
Der Fahrstuhl fährt abwärts.

down
The elevator is going down.

aufwärts [ˈaufvɛrts] *Adv.*
Der Weg führt steil aufwärts.

up
The path climbs up steeply.

auseinander [ausaiˈnandə*] *Adv.*
Die Häuser stehen weit auseinander.

apart
The houses are far apart.

außen [ˈaus(ə)n] *Adv.*
Das Auto sah außen gut aus.

on the outside
The car looked good on the outside.

da [daː] *Adv.*
Wer ist da an der Tür?
Setz dich da auf den Stuhl.

there
Who's there at the door?
Sit down there on the chair.

dahin [ˈdaːhin] *Adv.*
Stell die Kiste dahin!

there
Put the crate there!

daneben [daˈneːb(ə)n] *Adv.*
Siehst du den großen Sessel dort? Die Frau daneben ist Frau Patzke.

next to
Do you see that big arm chair? The woman next to it is Ms Patzke.

daran [ˈdaːran] *Adv.*
Die Wand ist zu dünn. Daran kann man das Regal nicht befestigen.

there on it
The wall is too thin. You can' fasten the shelves there on it.

darauf [ˈdaːrauf] *Adv.*
Siehst du den Tisch dort? Darauf kannst du die Bücher legen.

on it
See that table? You can lay the books on it.

darin [ˈdaːrin] *Adv.*
Du hast gestern ein Paket bekommen. Was war darin?

in it
You got a package yesterday. What was in it?

darunter [daˈruntə*] *Adv.*
Die Wohnung im 3. Stock links ist vermietet. Die Wohnung darunter ist noch frei.

below
The apartment on the third floo left is rented. The apartment be low it is still available.

davor ['da:fo:ə*] *Adv.*
Das ist eine Einfahrt. Davor darfst du nicht parken.

in front
That's a driveway. You can't park in front of it.

dazwischen [da:'tsviʃən] *Adv.*
Siehst du den blauen BMW und den gelben Ford dort? Das Auto dazwischen ist meins.

between
Do you see the blue BMW and the yellow Ford? The car between them is mine.

dort [dɔrt] *Adv.*
Dort möchte ich gerne wohnen.

there
I'd really like to live there.

draußen ['draus(ə)n] *Adv.*
Warst du heute schon draußen?

outside
Have you been outside yet today?

drinnen ['drinən] *Adv.*
Komm rein! Drinnen ist es schön warm.

inside
Come in! It's nice and warm inside.

entlang [ɛnt'laŋ] *Adv.*
Der Zug ist lange direkt am Rhein entlang gefahren.

along
The train went directly along the Rhine for a long time.

geradeaus [gə'ra:dəaus] *Adv.*
Gehen Sie geradeaus und dann die zweite Straße links rein.

straight ahead
Go straight ahead and then turn left at the second street.

heraus [hɛ'raus] *Adv.*
Bitte kommen Sie heraus!

out (of there)
Please come out of there!

herein [hɛ'rain] *Adv.*
Herein bitte! Die Tür ist offen.

in here
In here please! The door is open.

herum [hɛ'rum] *Adv.*
Um den ganzen See herum gibt es einen Wanderweg.

around
There's a hiking path all around the lake.

herunter [hɛ'runtə*] *Adv.*
Herunter vom Baum! Du kannst dir wehtun.

down
Get down from the tree! You could hurt yourself!

hier [hi:ə*] *Adv.*
Der Schlüssel muss hier in diesem Zimmer sein.

here
The key must be here in this room.

hierher ['hi:ə*'hɛə*] *Adv.*
Setz dich hierher! Der Sessel ist bequemer.
Bitte legen Sie die Zeitung hierher!

over here
Sit down over here. This chair is more comfortable.
Please put the newspaper right here!

hinauf [hi'nauf] *Adv.*
Bis zum Gipfel hinauf braucht man mindestens drei Stunden.

up to the top
It takes at least three hours to get up to the peak.

---

hinaus [hi'naus] *Adv.*
Hinaus mit dir!

out
Get out!

---

hinein [hi'nain] *Adv.*
Bitte gehen Sie schon hinein. Ich komme gleich.

in
Please go on in. I'll be right along.

---

hinten ['hint(ə)n] *Adv.*
Im Auto sitze ich am liebsten hinten.

in the back
In the car I prefer to sit in the back.

---

hinüber [hi'ny:bə*] *Adv.*
Die Ampel ist grün. Wir können hinübergehen.

across
The light is green. We can go a-cross.

---

innen ['inən] *Adv.*
Das Haus ist aus dem 19. Jahrhundert, aber innen ist alles neu.

inside
The house was built in the 19th century, but inside everything is new.

---

irgendwo ['irgəntvo:] *Adv.*
Irgendwo habe ich meine Brieftasche verloren.

somewhere
I lost my briefcase somewhere.

---

links [liŋks] *Adv.*
Vorsicht! Links kommt ein Auto.

from the left, on the left
Watch out! There's a car coming from the left.

---

mitten ['mit(ə)n] *Adv.*
Das Geschäft ist mitten in der Stadt.

in the middle
The store is in the middle of town.

---

nirgends ['nirg(ə)nts] *Adv.*
Ich habe die Tasche nirgends gefunden.

nowhere, not anywhere
I didn't find the bag. Nowhere!

---

nirgendwo ['nirg(ə)ntvo:] *Adv.*
Ich habe ihn nirgendwo getroffen.

nowhere, not anywhere
I didn't meet him anywhere.

---

oben ['o:b(ə)n] *Adv.*
Die Katze sitzt oben im Baum.

up, up there
The cat is sitting up there in the tree.

---

quer [kve:ə*] *Adv.*
Der Bus stand quer auf der Straße.

crosswise
The bus was standing crosswise on the street.

rechts [rɛçts] *Adv.*
Die Drogerie ist rechts neben dem Rathaus.

on the right
The drugstore is on the right, next to the city hall.

rückwärts ['rykvɛrts] *Adv.*
Man muss rückwärts aus der Einfahrt rausfahren.

backwards, (in) reverse
You have to drive out of the driveway in reverse.

überall ['y:bə*al] *Adv.*
Ich habe überall gesucht.

everywhere
I've looked everywhere.

unten ['unt(ə)n] *Adv.*
Das Fahrrad steht unten im Keller.

downstairs, below
The bicycle is downstairs in the basement.

voraus [fo'raus] *Adv.*
Ich kenne den Weg nicht. Fahr du deshalb voraus.

ahead
I don't know the way. You drive ahead of me.

vorbei [fo:ə*'bai] *Adv.*
Sie ist an mir vorbeigegangen, ohne zu grüßen.

past
She went past me without saying hello.

vorn(e) [fɔrn(ə)] *Adv.*
Vorn(e) am Haus ist die Lampe kaputt.

in front
The lamp at the front of the house is burnt out.

vorwärts ['fo:ə*vɛrts] *Adv.*
Fahren Sie bitte noch einen Meter vorwärts!

forward
Please drive another meter forward.

weg [vɛk] *Adv.*
Ist das weit weg?
Meine Handschuhe sind weg.

away, gone
Is that far away?
My gloves are gone.

wo [vo:] *Adv.*
Wo liegt der Ort?

where
Where is that place?

woher [vo'he:ə*] *Adv.*
Woher kommen Sie?

from where
Where do you come from?

wohin [vo'hin] *Adv.*
Wohin hast du die Tageszeitung gelegt?

where
Where did you put today's newspaper?

zurück [tsu'ryk] *Adv.*
Herr Kammer kommt morgen zurück.

back
Mr. Kammer is coming back tomorrow.

dahinter [da'hɪntɐ*] *Adv.*
Das Haus ist direkt an einer lauten Straße, aber im Garten dahinter ist es ruhig.

behind, in the back
The house is on a busy street, but in the garden in the back it's very peaceful.

dorthin ['dɔrthɪn] *Adv.*
Bitte leg die Post dorthin.

over there, to that place
Please put the mail over there.

drüben ['dry:b(ə)n] *Adv.*
Mannheim liegt drüben auf der anderen Seite des Flusses.

over there
Mannheim is over there on the other side of the river.

herab [hɛ'rap] *Adv.*
Steig bitte von der Leiter herab!

down
Climb down from the ladder!

heran [hɛ'ran] *Adv.*
Stell doch den Stuhl näher an den Tisch heran!

close, near
Put the chair closer to the table.

herauf [hɛ'rauf] *Adv.*
Das Mädchen ist allein den Baum heraufgeklettert.

up
The girl climbed up the tree by herself.

hindurch [hɪn'durç] *Adv.*
Ich habe Angst, durch diesen engen Tunnel hindurchzufahren.

through
I'm afraid of driving through this narrow tunnel.

hinterher [hɪntɐ*'he:ɐ*] *Adv.*
Fahr du voraus, ich fahre hinterher.

behind
Drive on out; I'll drive behind you.

hinunter [hɪ'nʊntɐ*] *Adv.*
Diesen Berg kann man nur langsam hinunterfahren.

down
You have to drive slowly down this mountain.

14.4 Präpositionen

14.4 Prepositions

an [an] *Präp. (+ Dat., Akk.)*
Dein Mantel hängt an der Garderobe.
Bitte häng den Mantel an die Garderobe.

on, [here] in
Your coat is in the closet.

Please hang your coat in the closet.

auf [auf] *Präp. (+ Dat., Akk.)*
Sie sitzt auf dem Balkon.
Setz dich doch auf den Balkon!

on
She's sitting on the balcony.
Sit out on the balcony.

aus [aus] *Präp. (+ Dat.)*
Er ist gerade aus dem Haus gegangen.
Sie kommt aus Brasilien.

out, from
He just went out of the house.

She comes from Brazil.

außerhalb ['ausə*halp] *Präp. (+ Gen.)*
Wir wohnen außerhalb der Stadt.

outside

We live outside the city.

bei [bai] *Präp. (+ Dat.)*
Du kannst bei mir übernachten.

with *(=at the residence, home of)*
You can spend the night with me.

bis [bis] *Präp. (+ Akk.)*
Am ersten Tag sind wir bis Freiburg gefahren.

up to, as far as
The first day we drove as far as Freiburg.

durch [durç] *Präp. (+ Akk.)*
Wir können durch den Park gehen.

through
We can go through the park.

gegenüber [ge:g(ə)n'y:bə*] *Präp. (+ Dat.)*
Das Haus liegt gegenüber der Bank.

opposite, across from

The house is across from the bank.

hinter ['hintə*] *Präp. (+ Dat., Akk.)*
Hinter dem Haus kann man parken.

behind
You can park behind the building.

in [in] *Präp. (+ Dat., Akk.)*
In diesem Restaurant kann man gut essen.
Lass uns in dieses Restaurant gehen und etwas essen.

in
In this restaurant they serve very good food.
Let's go in this restaurant and get something to eat.

innerhalb ['inə*halp] *Präp. (+ Gen.)*
Innerhalb des Stadtzentrums ist es schwer, einen Parkplatz zu finden.

within
It's hard to find a place to park within the central part of the city.

neben ['ne:b(ə)n] *Präp. (+ Dat., Akk.)*
Ich habe neben ihr gesessen.
Ich habe mich neben sie gesetzt.

next to, beside
I was sitting beside her.
I sat down next to her.

oberhalb ['o:bə*halp] *Präp. (+ Gen.)*
Oberhalb der Berghütte führt der Weg weiter.

above
The path continues above the mountain cabin.

über ['y:bə*] *Präp. (+ Dat., Akk.)*
Die Klingel ist über der Eingangstür.
Wir sind mit einer Fähre über den Fluss gefahren.

over
The bell is over the front door.
We went over the river on a ferry.

um [um] *Präp. (+ Akk.)*
Er trägt immer einen Schal um den Hals.

around
He always wears a scarf around his neck.

unter ['untə*] *Präp. (+ Dat., Akk.)*
Die Tasche liegt unter deiner Jacke.
Wer hat die Tasche unter die Jacke gelegt?

under
The bag is under your jacket.
Who put the bag under the jacket?

von [fɔn] *Präp. (+ Dat.)*
Sie ist vom Büro direkt nach Hause gegangen.

from
She went straight home from the office.

vor [fo:ə*] *Präp. (+ Dat., Akk.)*
Vor dem Bahnhof stehen immer Taxis.
Stell die dreckigen Stiefel bitte vor die Tür.

in front of, outside
There are always taxis in front of the train station.
Please put the dirty boots outside the door.

zu [tsu:] *Präp. (+ Dat.)*

Gehst du zum Bäcker und holst Brot?

to

Are you going to the bakery to get bread?

zwischen ['tsviʃ(ə)n] *Präp. (+ Dat., Akk.)*

Zwischen den beiden Häusern ist ein Tor.

Stell die Stehlampe zwischen die beiden Sessel.

between

There's a gate between the two houses.

Put the floor lamp between the two chairs.

15.1 Mengenbegriffe | 1–2000

15.1 Concepts of Quantity

alle [ˈalə] *Pron.*
Wo sind die Zigaretten? Hast du alle allein geraucht?

all, everyone
Where are the cigarettes? Did you smoke all of them?

Anzahl [ˈantsaːl] *f, -, kein Pl.*
Eine kleine Anzahl von Kollegen ist gegen die Lösung.

number *n*
A small number of colleagues are against the settlement.

bisschen [ˈbɪsçən] *Pron.*
Es hat nur ein bisschen geregnet.

a little, a bit
It only rained a little.

bloß [bloːs] *Adv.*
Wir haben bloß wenig Zeit.

really, only
We really have only a little time.

doppelt [ˈdɔp(ə)lt] *Adj., keine Komp.*
Es kamen doppelt so viele Gäste wie erwartet.

twice, double

Twice as many guests came as expected.

Drittel [ˈdrɪt(ə)l] *n, -s, -*
Ein Drittel des Grundstücks wurde verkauft.

third *n*
A third of the land was sold.

Dutzend [ˈdʊts(ə)nt] *n, -s, -*
In der Packung sind ein Dutzend Eier.

dozen *n*
There are a dozen eggs in the package.

einmal [ˈainmaːl] *Adv.*
Nehmen Sie einmal täglich drei Tabletten.

once
Take three tablets once a day.

einzige [ˈaintsigə] *Adj., keine Komp.*
Sie war die einzige Zeugin.

only

She was the only witness.

etwa [ˈɛtva] *Adv.*
Die Fahrt dauert etwa zwei Stunden.

about, around, approximately
The drive takes about two hours.

etwas ['ɛtvas] *Pron.*
Möchtest du etwas zu essen?
Der Kuchen ist etwas zu süß.
Kannst du mir etwas Geld geben?

some, something, somewhat
Would you like something to eat?
The cake is somewhat too sweet.
Can you give me some money?

fast [fast] *Adv.*
Wir haben es fast geschafft.

almost
We've almost got it done.

ganz [gants] *Adj., keine Komp.*
Ich habe den ganzen Abend gelesen.
Er ist ein ganz guter Handwerker.
Habt ihr das ganze Obst gegessen?

whole, all, entire, very
I spent the whole evening reading.
He is a very good craftsman.
Did you eat all the fruit?

genug [gə'nu:k] *Adv.*
Haben wir genug Getränke für die Gäste?

enough
Do we have enough drinks for the guests?

genügen [gə'ny:g(ə)n] *V/i.*, genügte, hat genügt
Die Getränke genügen für alle.

be enough, suffice *v*

There are enough drinks for everyone.

gering [gə'riŋ] *Adj.*
Es gab nur geringe Schwierigkeiten.

minimal, a little, a few
There were only a few difficulties.

gesamt [gə'zamt] *Adj., keine Komp.*
Das gesamte Gebäude wurde durch das Feuer zerstört.

whole

The whole building was destroyed in the fire.

Gruppe ['grupə] *f, -, -n*
Nur als Gruppe kann man das Schloss besichtigen.

group *n*
You can only visit the castle as part of a group.

halb [halp] *Adj., keine Komp.*
Das Stadion war nur halb gefüllt.

half
The stadium was only half full.

Hälfte ['hɛlftə] *f, -, -n*
Die Hälfte des Gartens gehört uns.

half *n*
Half of the garden belongs to us.

höchstens ['hø:çstəns] *Adv.*
Die Fahrt von München nach Hamburg dauert höchstens zehn Stunden.

at most
Traveling from Munich to Hamburg takes at most ten hours.

Inhalt ['inhalt] *m*, -(e)s, -e
Die Flasche hat 1,5 l Inhalt.

contents, volume *n*
The bottle has a volume of 1.5 liters.

---

knapp [knap] *Adj.*, -er, am -esten
Das Benzin wird knapp, ich muss tanken.

scarce, low
The gas is getting low; I have to fill up.

---

leer [le:ə*] *Adj.*
Die Flasche ist leer.

empty
The bottle is empty.

Masse ['masə] *f*, -, -n
Wir haben eine Masse Blumen verkauft.

a lot, a great deal *n*
We sold a lot of flowers.

---

mehrere ['me:rərə] *Pron.*
Sie hat mehrere Kleider probiert, aber keines gefiel ihr.

several
She tried on several dresses, but none pleased her.

---

mehrfach ['me:ə*'fax] *Adj. keine Komp.*
Ich habe ihr mehrfach geschrieben.

several times, repeatedly
I wrote her several times.

---

meiste ['maistə] *Adj. Superlativ*
Die meisten Bücher sind heute Taschenbücher.

most
Most books now are paperbacks.

Menge ['mɛŋə] *f*, -, -n
Für die Gardinen brauchst du eine große Menge Stoff.

quantity *n*
You need a large quantity of fabric for the curtains.

---

messen ['mɛs(ə)n] *V/t.*, maß, hat gemessen
Ich messe regelmäßig den Benzinverbrauch des Autos.

measure *v*
I regularly measure my car's gas mileage.

---

mindestens ['mindəstəns] *Adv.*
Eine Kinokarte kostet mindestens 9,- Euro.

at least
A movie ticket costs at least 9 euros.

Nummer ['numə*] *f*, -, -n
Er hat eine neue Telefonnummer bekommen.

number *n*
He got a new telephone number.

---

paar [pa:*] *Indefinitpronomen*
Bitte warten Sie ein paar Minuten!

a few
Please wait a few minutes.

Prozent [pro'tsɛnt] *n*, -(e)s, -e
Wir bekommen 4,5 % mehr Lohn.

percent *n*
We're getting a 4.5% pay raise.

Rest [rɛst] *m*, -(e)s, -e
Bitte iss den Rest auch noch!

rest, what's left *n*
Please eat the rest!

schätzen ['ʃɛts(ə)n] *V/t.*, schätzte, hat geschätzt
Sein Alter kann man schlecht schätzen.

estimate *v*
It's hard to estimate his age.

Stück [ʃtyk] *n*, -(e)s, -e
Ich habe acht Stück Kuchen gekauft.

piece *n*
I bought eight pieces of cake.

Summe ['zumə] *f*, -, -n
Die Summe der Rechnung stimmt nicht.
Ich habe die Summe schon bezahlt.

sum, total *n*
The total on the check is wrong.

I already paid the sum.

Teil [tail] *m*, -s, -e
Der letzte Teil des Buches ist besonders spannend.

part *n*
The last part of the book is especially thrilling.

übrig ['y:briç] *Adj., keine Komp.*
Ist noch Kaffee übrig?

left
Is there any coffee left?

Umfang ['umfaŋ] *m*, -s, Umfänge
Wie groß ist der Umfang des Brunnens?

circumference *n*
How big is the circumference of the well?

viel [fi:l] *Adj.*, mehr, am meisten
Die Arbeit im Garten kostet viel Zeit.

a lot, much
Working in the garden takes a lot of time.

Viertel ['fi:ə*t(ə)l] *n*, -s, -
Im ersten Viertel des Jahres haben wir gute Geschäfte gemacht.

quarter *n*
We had really good business in the first quarter of the year.

voll [fɔl] *Adj.*
Danke, keinen Wein mehr! Mein Glas ist noch halb voll.

full
Thanks, but no more wine. My glass is still half full.

wenig ['ve:niç] *Adj.*
Er soll weniger essen.

less
He should eat less.

wenigstens ['ve:niçst(ə)ns] *Adv.*
Du hättest mich wenigstens informieren können, dass du wegfährst.

at least
You could have at least let me know you were going away.

wie viel ['vi: fi:l] *Adv.*
Wie viel Gäste hast du eingeladen?

how many, how much
How many guests did you invite?

Zahl [tsa:l] *f, -, -en*
Die Zahl der Verletzten ist noch unbekannt.

number *n*
The number of injured is still unknown.

zählen ['tsɛ:l(ə)n] *V/t.,* zählte, hat gezählt
Hast du das Geld gezählt?

count *v*

Did you count the money?

zunehmen ['tsu:ne:mən] *V/i.,* nahm zu, hat zugenommen
Die Zahl der Autos hat stark zugenommen.

increase, go up *v*

The number of cars has gone up a lot.

zusätzlich ['tsu:zɛtsliç] *Adj., keine Komp.*
Zusätzlich muss noch eine Gebühr bezahlt werden.

another, additional

An additional fee must still be paid.

zu viel [tsu 'fi:l] *Pron.*
Du hast zu viel Salz in die Suppe getan.

too much
You put too much salt in the soup.

2001-4000

Achtel ['axt(ə)l] *n, -s, -*
Etwa ein Achtel aller Pflanzen ist im Winter erfroren.

eighth *n*
About an eighth of all the plants froze during the winter.

allermeisten ['alə*maist(ə)n] *Adj., keine Komp.*
Die allermeisten Pflanzen haben den Winter gut überstanden.

most, the majority

The majority of the plants made it through the winter.

ausreichen ['ausraiç(ə)n] *V/i.,* reichte aus, hat ausgereicht
Die Zahl der Sitzplätze im Saal reichte nicht aus.

be enough *v*

There weren't enough places to sit in the room.

Betrag [bə'tra:k] *m, -(e)s, Beträge*
Wie ist der Betrag?

amount
How much is the amount?

betragen [bə'tra:g(ə)n] *V/i.,* betrug, hat betragen
Die Strecke beträgt ungefähr 25 Kilometer.

be *v*

The distance is about 25 km.

Durchschnitt [ˈdurçʃnit] *m*, -s, -e
Wir verbrauchen im Durchschnitt 4000 Liter Heizöl im Jahr.

average *n*
We use an average of about 4000 liters of heating oil a year.

durchschnittlich [ˈdurçʃnitlɪç] *Adj., keine Komp.*
Der Zug hat eine durchschnittliche Geschwindigkeit von 100 km/h erreicht.

average

The train has reached an average speed of 100 km an hour.

Höhe [ˈhøːə] *f*, -, -n
Die Höhe des Schadens wird circa 6000 DM betragen.

[here] **amount** *n*
The amount of damage will be about 6000 DM.

insgesamt [ɪnsgəˈzamt] *Adv.*
Insgesamt fahren 42 Personen mit.

altogether
Altogether 42 people are going along.

keinerlei [ˈkainɐˈlai] *Adj., indekl.*
An der Grenze gab es keinerlei Kontrolle.

none (at all)
There were no checks at all at the border.

lediglich [ˈleːdɪklɪç] *Adv.*
Die Versicherung zahlt lediglich 60 % der Kosten.

only
The insurance pays only 60% of the costs.

Paar [paː*] *n*, -(e)s, -e
Ich habe ihr ein Paar Ohrringe gekauft.

a pair *n*
I bought her a pair of earrings.

pro [proː] *Präp. (+ Akk.)*
Pro Kilogramm Mehl muss man drei Eier nehmen.

per *prep*
You need three eggs per kilogram(me) of flour.

reichlich [ˈraiçlɪç] *Adj.*
Es wurde reichlich getrunken.

quite a lot, more than sufficient
There was quite a lot of drinking.

sämtlich [ˈzɛmtlɪç] *Adj., keine Komp.*
Wegen des Streiks sind sämtliche Tageszeitungen mit Verspätung erschienen.

all, every single one

Because of the strike not a single daily newspaper appeared on time.

teilweise [ˈtailvaizə] *Adj., keine Komp.*
Du hast teilweise recht, aber nicht ganz.

partly, partially, in parts

You are partially right, but not completely.

umfangreich [ˈumfaŋraiç] *Adj.*
Ihr Wissen ist sehr umfangreich.

extensive
Her knowledge is very extensive.

354

ungefähr ['ʊngəfɛːɐ*] *Adj., keine Komp.*   **approximate**
Ich wiege ungefähr 70 Kilo.   I weigh approximately 70 kg.

vergrößern [fɛɐ*'grøːsə*n] *V/t.,* vergrößerte, hat vergrößert   **increase, enlarge** *v*
Das Foto ist stark vergrößert worden.   The photo was enlarged considerably.

Zunahme ['tsuːnaːmə] *f, -, -n*   **increase** *n*
Eine so starke Zunahme des Luftverkehrs wurde nicht erwartet.   Such a large increase in air traffic was not expected.

15.2 Grundzahlen

15.2 Cardinal Numbers

null [nʊl]	zero
eins [aɪns]	one
zwei [tsvaɪ]	two
drei [draɪ]	three
vier [fiːɐ*]	four
fünf [fʏnf]	five
sechs [zɛks]	six
sieben ['ziːb(ə)n]	seven
acht [axt]	eight
neun [nɔɪn]	nine
zehn [tseːn]	ten
elf [ɛlf]	eleven
zwölf [tsvœlf]	twelve
dreizehn ['draɪtseːn]	thirteen
vierzehn ['fɪrtseːn]	fourteen
fünfzehn ['fʏnftseːn]	fifteen
sechzehn ['zɛçtseːn]	sixteen

siebzehn ['ziːptseːn]	**seventeen**
achtzehn ['axtseːn]	**eighteen**
neunzehn ['nɔintseːn]	**nineteen**
zwanzig ['tsvantsiç]	**twenty**
einundzwanzig ['ainʊntˈtsvantsiç°]	**twenty-one**
zweiundzwanzig ['tsvaiʊntˈtsvantsiç°]	**twenty-two**
dreißig ['draisiç°]	**thirty**
vierzig ['firtsiç°]	**forty**
fünfzig ['fynftsiç°]	**fifty**
sechzig ['zɛçtsiç°]	**sixty**
siebzig ['ziːptsiç°]	**seventy**
achtzig ['axtsiç°]	**eighty**
neunzig ['nɔintsiç°]	**ninety**
hundert ['hʊndɐt°]	**hundred**
tausend ['tauz(ə)nt°]	**thousand**
Million [mɪlˈjoːn] f, -, -en	**million**
Milliarde [mɪlˈjardə] f, -, -n	**billion, thousand millions** *(BE)*

15.3 Maße und Gewichte

15.3 Measurements and Weights

Durchmesser ['dʊrçmɛsɐ*] m, -s, -
Die Rohre haben verschiedene Durchmesser.

diameter *(BE:* **diametre**) n
The pipes have different diameters.

Gewicht [gəˈviçt] n, -(e)s, -e
Postpakete dürfen bis zu 20 kg Gewicht haben.

weight n
Postal packages can weigh up to 20 kg.

Grad [gra:t] *m* -(e)s, -e, (°)
Es ist draußen 2 Grad unter 0.

degree *n*
Outside it is two degrees below zero.

Gramm [gram] *n*, -s, -e, (g)
200 Gramm Schinken bitte!

gram (*BE:* gramme) *n*
Two hundred gram(me)s of ham, please!

Hektar ['hɛkta:*] *m*, -s, -, (ha)
Der Bauer hat über 40 Hektar Land.

hectare *n*
The farmer has over 40 hectares of land.

Kilo(-gramm) ['ki:lo(gram)] *n*, -s, -(e), (kg)
Wie viel Kilo(-gramm) Kartoffeln hast du gekauft?

kilo(gram) (*BE:* kilo(gramme) *n*
How many kilos of potatoes did you buy?

Kilometer [kilo'me:tə*] *m*, -s, -, (km)
Wir müssen noch etwa 100 Kilometer fahren.

kilometer (*BE:* kilometre) *n*
We still have approximately 100 kilometers to go.

Liter ['li:tə*] *m*, -s, -, (l)
In der Flasche sind 1,5 Liter Milch.

liter (*BE:* litre) *n*
There are 1.5 liters of milk in the bottle.

Maß [ma:s] *n*, -es, -e
Die Maße der Möbel habe ich auf einen Zettel geschrieben.

measurement *n*
I wrote down the measurements of the furniture on a piece of paper.

Maßstab ['ma:sʃta:b] *m*, -(e)s, Maßstäbe
Kauf lieber eine Karte mit einem kleineren Maßstab.

scale *n*
It's better to buy a map with a smaller scale.

Meter ['me:tə*] *m* (auch *n*), -s, -, (m)
Das Zimmer ist über fünf Meter lang.

meter (*BE:* metre) *n*
The room is over five meters long.

Pfund [pfunt] *n*, -(e)s, -e (500 g)
Ich möchte zwei Pfund Tomaten.

pound *n*
I would like two pounds of tomatoes.

Quadratmeter [kva'dra:tme:tə*] *m*, -s, -, (m²)
Das Grundstück ist 950 Quadratmeter groß.

square meter, metre (*BE*) *n*
The parcel of land is 950 square meters big.

Tonne ['tɔnə] *f,* -, -n, (t)
Lastwagen mit über 12 Tonnen Gewicht dürfen nicht über die Brücke fahren.

ton *n*
Trucks that weigh over 12 tons are not allowed to drive over the bridge.

Zentimeter [tsɛnti'me:tə*] *m,* -s, -, (cm)
Bitte machen Sie die Hose um zwei Zentimeter kürzer!

centimeter (*BE:* centimetre) *n*

Please shorten the trousers (by) two centimeters.

16.1 Ordnung, Einteilung | 1-2000

16.1 Order, Division

allein [a'lain] *Adv., keine Komp.*
Die Arbeit schaffe ich allein.
Ich bin allein wegen dir gekommen.

alone, solely
I'll get the work done alone.
I came solely because of you.

andere ['andərə] *Pron., Adj.*
Alle anderen hatten frei, nur ich musste arbeiten.
Ich habe am anderen Tag mit ihr gesprochen.

other
All the others were off; I'm the only one who had to work.
I spoke with her the other day.

auch [aux] *Adv.*
Möchtest du auch ein Eis?

also, too
Would you like some ice cream too?

außer ['ausə*] *Präp. (+ Dat.)*
Außer dieser Karte kam keine Post.

besides, other than, apart from
There was no mail other than that card.

beide ['baidə] *Pron.*
Beide sind 32 Jahre alt.

both
Both are 32 years old.

Beziehung [bə'tsi:uŋ] *f, -, -en*
Zwischen den beiden Ereignissen besteht eine Beziehung.
Zu meinem Chef habe ich eine gute Beziehung.

relationship, connection *n*
There's a connection between these two events.
I have a good relationship with my boss.

eigentlich ['aig(ə)ntliç] *Adj., keine Komp.*
Ihre eigentlichen Interessen an der Sache kenne ich nicht.
Eigentlich wollten wir das Haus nicht kaufen, sondern nur mieten.

real, actual, true

I don't know her real interests in this.
We really didn't want to buy the house, just rent it.

einander [ai'nandə*] *Pron.*
Wir sind einander erst einmal begegnet.

each other
We've just met each other once.

einschließlich [ˈainʃliːsliç] *Präp. (+ Gen.)*

Einschließlich der Heizkosten kostet die Wohnung 860,- € Miete pro Monat.

including

The apartment rent is 860 € a month including heat.

einzeln [ˈaints(ə)ln] *Adj., keine Komp.*

Jedes einzelne Teil der Maschine wurde geprüft.

single

Every single part of the machine was tested.

entsprechend [ɛntˈʃprɛç(ə)nt] *Präp. (+ Gen.)*

Alle Angestellten werden entsprechend ihrer Leistung bezahlt.

according to

All employees will be paid according to their work.

fehlen [ˈfeːl(ə)n] *V/i., fehlte, hat gefehlt*

Es fehlen noch Steine. Diese hier reichen nicht für die ganze Mauer.

be missing *v*

There are still stones missing. There aren't enough here for the whole wall.

folgende [ˈfɔlg(ə)ndə] *Adj., keine Komp.*

Über folgende Punkte müssen wir noch sprechen.

(the) following

We still have to discuss the following points.

Gegensatz [ˈgeːg(ə)nzats] *m, -es, Gegensätze*

Trotz großer Gegensätze haben wir weiter verhandelt.

difference, conflict *n*

We continued to negotiate in spite of great differences.

Gegenteil [ˈgeːg(ə)ntail] *n, -s, -e*

Er macht genau das Gegenteil von meinem Rat.

opposite *n*

He's doing just the opposite of what I advised.

gehören [gəˈhøːr(ə)n] *V/i., gehörte, hat gehört*

Wem gehören diese Sachen?
Diese Sachen gehören in den Schrank.

belong *v*

To whom do these things belong?
These things belong in the closet.

gemeinsam [gəˈmainzaːm] *Adj., keine Komp.*

Lass uns gemeinsam ins Kino gehen.
Sie haben ein gemeinsames Geschäft.

together

Let's go to the movie together.

They have a business together.

jeweils ['je:vails] *Adv.*
Die Miete muss jeweils am ersten
Tag des Monats bezahlt werden.

each time
The rent has to be paid each time
on the first day of the month.

letzte ['lɛtstə] *Adj., keine Komp.*
Ich lese gerade die letzten Seiten
des Buches.

last
I'm just now reading the last
pages of the book.

mit [mit] *Präp. (+ Dat.)*
Ich bin mit ihm essen gegangen.

with
I went to eat with him.

miteinander [mitai'nandə*] *Adv.*
Wir spielen oft Schach miteinander.

with each other
We often play chess with each
other.

mittlere ['mitlərə] *Adj., keine
Komp.*
Die Fotos sind im mittleren Fach.

middle

The photos are in the middle
drawer.

nächste ['nɛ:çstə] *Adj., keine
Komp.*
An der nächsten Station müssen
wir aussteigen.

next

We have to get out at the next
station.

nebenbei [ne:b(ə)n'bai] *Adv.*
Beim Lesen kann ich nebenbei
keine Musik hören.

at the same time, simultaneous
When reading I can't listen to music at the same time.

nebeneinander
[ne:b(ə)nai'nandə*] *Adv.*
In der Schule haben wir nebeneinander gesessen.

next to each other

In school we sat next to each
other.

nur [nuə*] *Adv.*
Den Ort kann man nur zu Fuß
erreichen.

only
You can only get to that place on
foot.

ohne ['o:nə] *Präp. (+ Akk.)*
Ohne Wörterbuch kann ich den
Text nicht übersetzen.

without
I can't translate the text without a
dictionary.

ordnen ['ɔrdnən] *V/t.,* ordnete, hat
geordnet.
Die Bücher sind nach Themen
geordnet.

arrange *v*

The books are arranged according to subject matter.

Ordnung ['ɔrdnuŋ] *f, -, kein Pl.*
Er ist für die Ordnung im Lager
verantwortlich.

order, rules *n*
He's responsible for order in the
storage.

Regel ['re:g(ə)l] *f, -, -n*
Die Regel dieses Spiels kenne ich nicht.

rule *n*
I don't know the rules of this game.

Reihe ['raiə] *f, -, -n*
Wir haben die Plätze 24 und 25 in Reihe 12.

row *n*
We have seats 24 and 25 in row 12.

Reihenfolge ['raiənfɔlgə] *f, -, -n*
In welcher Reihenfolge sollen die Arbeiten gemacht werden?

order *(of presentation) n*
In what order should the work be done?

solcher ['zɔlçə*] (solche, solches) *Pron.*
Solche Blumen haben wir auch im Garten.

such, like this (that, these, those)

We have some flowers like those in our garden, too.

sonst [zɔnst] *Adv.*
Wer will sonst noch mitspielen?
Du musst gehen, sonst kommst du zu spät.
Ich habe lange nichts von ihm gehört. Wir haben uns sonst jede Woche getroffen.

else, otherwise
Who else wants to play?
You have to leave; otherwise you'll get there too late.
I haven't heard anything from him for a long time. Other than that we saw each other every week.

sonstige ['zɔnstigə] *Adj., keine Komp.*
In dem Geschäft kann man Geschirr und sonstige Haushaltswaren kaufen.

other

In the store you can buy dinnerware and other housewares.

statt [ʃtat] *Präp. (+ Gen.)*
Statt des Radios schenke ich ihr lieber eine Uhr.

instead of
Instead of the radio I'd rather give her a watch.

System [zys'te:m] *n, -s, -e*
Welches System hat dein Computer?

system *n*
What system does your computer use?

trotz [trɔts] *Präp. (+ Gen.)*
Trotz der Kälte haben sie draußen weitergearbeitet.

in spite of
They kept on working outside in spite of the cold weather.

Unordnung ['unɔrdnuŋ] *f, -, kein Pl.*
Auf seinem Schreibtisch ist eine große Unordnung.

disorder, mess *n*

Things are in a big mess on his desk.

unterscheiden [untə*'ʃaid(ə)n] *V/ t.*, unterschied, hat unterschieden
Die beiden Zwillinge kann ich nicht unterscheiden.

distinguish, tell the difference *v*
I can't tell the difference between the twins.

Unterschied ['untə*ʃiːt] *m, -(e)s, -e*
Bei den Geräten gibt es große Preis- und Qualitätsunterschiede.

difference *n*
There are great quality and price differences among the tools.

Verhältnis [fɛə*'hɛltnis] *n, -ses, -se*
Das Pulver muss mit Wasser im Verhältnis 3:1 gemischt werden.

proportion *n*
The powder must be mixed with water in a proportion of 3 to 1.

---

voneinander [fɔnai'nandə*] *Adv.*
Wir haben voneinander viel gelernt.

from each other
We learned a lot from each other.

---

zusammen [tsu'zamən] *Adv.*
Wir arbeiten seit acht Jahren zusammen.

together
We've been working together for eight years.

2001-4000

Abschnitt ['apʃnit] *m, -s, -e*
Hast du jeden Abschnitt des Textes genau gelesen?

part, section *n*
Have you read every part of the text carefully?

---

anstatt [an'ʃtat] *Präp. (+ Gen.)*
Anstatt einer Blume würde ich ihr lieber ein Buch schenken.

instead of
I'd rather give her a book instead of a plant as a gift.

Anteil ['antail] *m, -s, -e*
Der größte Anteil an dem Unternehmen gehört einer Bank.

share, interest *n*
A bank owns the greatest share of the business.

---

ausgenommen ['ausgənɔmən] *Konj.*
Der Arzt hat jeden Tag Sprechstunde, ausgenommen am Wochenende.

except
The doctor has office hours every day except on the weekend.

---

auslassen ['auslas(ə)n] *V/t.*, ließ aus, hat ausgelassen
In der Zeile ist ein Wort ausgelassen worden.

leave out *v*
A word was left out in that line.

Ausnahme ['ausnaːmə] *f, -, -n*
Sie können heute früher gehen,
aber das ist eine Ausnahme.

exception *n*
You can leave early today, but
that's an exception.

---

ausschließlich ['ausʃliːsliç] *Adv.,*
Präp. (+ Gen. o. Dat.)
Sie trinkt abends ausschließlich
schwarzen Tee.

only, without exception,
exclusively
In the evening she drinks only tea.

---

beispielsweise ['baiʃpiːlsvaizə]
Adv.
Alle Kopien sind schlecht, schau-
en Sie sich beispielsweise diese
hier an.

for, as an example

All the copies are bad; look at this
one as an example.

Bestandteil [bə'ʃtantail] *m, -s, -e*
Es gibt heute Farben ohne giftige
Bestandteile.

part, component, ingredient *n*
Today there are paints without
poisonous components.

---

betreffen [bə'trɛf(ə)n] *V/t.,* betraf,
hat betroffen
Ich bin von der neuen Regelung
nicht betroffen.

be related, concerned by, affect
v
I'm not affected by the new rule.

---

derartig ['deːɐʔaːˀtiç] *Adj., keine*
Komp.
Eine derartige Krankheit gibt es
selten.

such, like that

A disease like that is rare.

Detail [de'tai] *n, -s, -s*
Über einige Details des Vertrages
müssen wir noch sprechen.

detail *n*
We still have to discuss some details of the contract.

---

direkt [di'rɛkt] *Adj., -er, am -esten*
Das ist der direkteste Weg.
Direkt neben der Post ist ein Su-
permarkt.

direct, right
That is the most direct way.
There's a supermarket right next
to the post office.

---

einheitlich ['ainhaitliç] *Adj.*
Die Regelung ist in allen Firmen
einheitlich.

the same, uniform
The regulation is the same in all
firms.

Einzelheit ['aints(ə)lhait] *f, -, -en*
Die genauen Einzelheiten des
Plans kenne ich nicht.

detail *n*
I don't know the exact details of
the plan.

Element [ele'mɛnt] *n, -(e)s, -e*
Die Elemente des Systems passen alle zusammen.

element, part *n*
All the elements of the system fit
together.

entgegengesetzt [εnt'ge:g(ə)n-gəzεtst] *Adj., keine Komp.*
Es wurden zwei entgegengesetzte Vorschläge gemacht.

opposing, opposite
Two opposing suggestions were made.

erforderlich [εɐ*'fɔrdə*liç] *Adj.,*
Für diese Arbeit ist viel Erfahrung erforderlich.

required, necessary
For this work, much experience is required.

erfordern [εɐ*'fɔrdə*n] *V/t.,* erforderte, hat erfordert
Dieser Beruf erfordert Fremdsprachenkenntnisse.

require *v*
This profession requires the knowledge of foreign languages.

Ersatz [εɐ*'zats] *m, -es, kein Pl.*
Für den kranken Mitarbeiter wurde noch kein Ersatz gefunden.

substitute, replacement *n*
There was still no substitute for the sick worker.

folgen ['fɔlg(ə)n] *V/i.,* folgte, ist (hat) gefolgt
Wann folgt der 2. Teil des Berichts?
Ich zeige Ihnen den Weg. Bitte folgen Sie mir!

follow, continue *v*

When will the second part of the report be out?
I'll show you the way. Please follow me.

Gebiet [gə'bi:t] *n, -(e)s, -e*
Er ist Fachmann auf seinem Gebiet.

Große Gebiete des Landes sind Wüste.

field, area *n*
He is an expert in his field.

Large areas of the country are desert.

gegenseitig ['ge:g(ə)nzaitiç°] *Adj., keine Komp.*
Deutschland und die USA haben ein gegenseitiges Abkommen geschlossen.

mutual, bilateral

Germany and the USA made a bilateral arrangement.

Hauptsache ['hauptzaxə] *f, -, -n*
Gute Qualität des Materials ist die Hauptsache.

main thing, most important thing
The quality of the materials is the most important thing.

hierbei ['hi:ɐ*bai] *Adv.*
Hierbei kann ich dir nicht helfen.

with this, at this time
I can't help you with this.

hierfür ['hi:ɐ*fy:ɐ*] *Adv.*
Hierfür brauchst du Spezialwerkzeug.

for this
You need special tools for this.

Hinsicht ['hɪnzɪçt] *f*, -, -en
In dieser Hinsicht muss ich Ihnen Recht geben.

regard, respect *n*
In regards to this, I must say you're right.

hinsichtlich ['hɪnzɪçtlɪç] *Präp. (+ Gen.)*
Hinsichtlich dieses Punktes gab es verschiedene Meinungen.

concerning, in regards to
There were various opinions concerning this point.

Klasse ['klasə] *f*, -, -n
Sie ist erster Klasse gereist.
Das ist das beste Auto in dieser Preisklasse.

class *n*
She traveled in first class.
That is the best car in that price class.

Kombination [kɔmbina'tsjoːn] *f*, -, -en
Die Sendung war eine gelungene Kombination von Information und Unterhaltung.

combination *n*
The broadcast was a successful combination of news and entertainment.

Liste ['lɪstə] *f*, -, -n
Ihren Namen kann ich in der Liste nicht finden.

list *n*
I can't find your name in the list.

Niveau [ni'voː] *n*, -s, -s
Die Ausstellung hatte hohes Niveau.

level, class *n*
The exhibition was high class.

Original [ɔrigi'naːl] *n*, -s, -e
Wo ist das Original des Briefes? Ich habe nur eine Kopie.

original *n*
Where is the original of the letter? I only have a copy.

Schwerpunkt ['ʃveːɐ*puŋkt] *m*, -(e)s, -e
Kürzere Arbeitszeiten sind der Schwerpunkt der Forderungen.

most important point, main focus *n*
Shorter working hours are the most important point of the demands.

Serie ['zeːrjə] *f*, -, -n
Das ist der fünfte Band einer Serie von Abenteuerromanen.

series *n*
That is the fifth volume of a series of adventure novels.

Typ [tyːp] *m*, -s, -en
Die Maschinen des neuen Typs sind schneller und leiser.

type *n*
The new type machines are faster and quieter.

überflüssig ['yːbɐ*flysɪç°] *Adj.*
Mach dir keine überflüssigen Sorgen! Wir werden die Arbeit schon schaffen.

unnecessary, superfluous
Don't worry unnecessarily. We'll get the work done.

umgekehrt ['umgəke:ə*t] *Adj.*

Sie hat es umgekehrt gemacht, nicht wie ich es ihr geraten habe.

the opposite, the other way around, vice versa
She did it the other way around, not the way I advised her.

untereinander [untə*ai'nandə*] *Adv.*
Stell die Kisten untereinander.

Wir haben selten Streit untereinander.

on top of each other, with each other
Put the boxes on top of each other.
We seldom have arguments with each other.

ursprünglich ['u:ə*ʃpryŋliç] *Adj.*
Ursprünglich war die Reise anders geplant.

original, initial
Originally the trip was planned in a different way.

verschiedenartig
[fɛə*'ʃi:d(ə)nartiç°] *Adj.*
Trotz verschiedenartiger Meinungen verstehen wir uns gut.

different

We understand each other well in spite of differing opinions.

weiter ['vaitə*] *Adj.*,
Gibt es noch weitere Probleme als diese?
Wir sollen morgen Bescheid bekommen, man hat mir weiter nichts gesagt.

more, additional, further
Are there still more problems besides these?
We should find out tomorrow; no one has told me anything additional.

16.2 Ordnungszahlen

erste ['e:ə*stə]	**first**
zweite ['tsvaitə]	**second**
dritte ['dritə]	**third**
vierte ['fi:ə*tə]	**fourth**
fünfte ['fynftə]	**fifth**
sechste ['zɛkstə]	**sixth**

sieb(en)te ['zi:ptə, 'zi:b(ə)ntə]	seventh
achte ['axtə]	eighth
neunte ['nɔintə]	ninth
zehnte ['tse:ntə]	tenth
elfte ['ɛlftə]	eleventh
zwölfte ['tsvœlftə]	twelfth
dreizehnte ['draitse:ntə]	thirteenth
vierzehnte ['firtse:ntə]	fourteenth
fünfzehnte ['fynftse:ntə]	fifteenth
sechzehnte ['zɛçtse:ntə]	sixteenth
siebzehnte ['zi:ptse:ntə]	seventeenth
achtzehnte ['axtse:ntə]	eighteenth
neunzehnte ['nɔintse:ntə]	nineteenth
zwanzigste ['tsvantsiçstə]	twentieth
einundzwanzigste ['ainunt'tsvantsiçstə]	twenty-first
zweiundzwanzigste ['tsvaiunt'tsvantsiçstə]	twenty-second
dreißigste ['draisiçstə]	thirtieth
vierzigste ['firtsiçstə]	fortieth
fünfzigste ['fynftsiçstə]	fiftieth
sechzigste ['zɛçtsiçstə]	sixtieth
siebzigste ['zi:ptsiçstə]	seventieth
achtzigste ['axtsiçstə]	eightieth
neunzigste ['nɔintsiçstə]	ninetieth
hundertste ['hundə*tstə]	hundredth
tausendste ['tauz(ə)ntstə]	thousandth
millionste [mil'jo:nstə]	millionth
erstens ['ɛrst(ə)ns]	first (of all)
zweitens ['tsvait(ə)ns]	second (of all), secondly
drittens ['drit(ə)ns]	third (of all), thirdly
viertens ['fi:ə*t(ə)ns]	fourth (of all), fourthly

17.1 Art und Weise

1-2000

17.1 Ways and Methods

Art [a:*t] *f, -,* -en
Seine Art zu sprechen finde ich komisch.

way, method, kind, manner *n*
I find his way of speaking funny.

genau [gə'nau] *Adj.,* -er, am -esten
Hast du genau gemessen? Passt der Schrank in das Zimmer?

exact

Did you take exact measurements? Does the cabinet fit into the room?

gleichmäßig ['glaiçmɛ:siç°] *Adj.*
Die Geschenke für die Kinder sollen gleichmäßig verteilt werden.

equally, even, regular
The presents for the children should be distributed equally.

grundsätzlich ['gruntzɛtsliç] *Adj.*
Grundsätzlich bin ich für den Vorschlag.

basically, in principle
Basically, I'm in favor of the suggestion.

irgendwie ['iə*g(ə)ntvi:] *Adv.*
Irgendwie werden wir den richtigen Weg noch finden.

somehow
Somehow we will find the right way.

so [zo:] *Adv.*
So hat man mir das erklärt.
Das Auto startete nicht, weil es so kalt war.

so, like that, that way
They explained it to me that way.
The car didn't start because it was so cold.

sogar [zo'ga:*] *Adv.*
Er hat viele Talente, er kann sogar gut kochen.

even
He has lots of talents. He can even cook well.

Weise ['vaizə] *f, -,* -n
Auf diese Weise hat sie Erfolg gehabt.

way *n*
In that way, she was successful.

2001-4000

ausdrücklich ['ausdryklıç] *Adj.*
Ich habe ihn ausdrücklich gewarnt.

clear, explicit
I clearly warned him.

ausführlich ['ausfy:ə*lıç] *Adj.*
Er hat einen ausführlichen Bericht geschrieben.

thorough, detailed
He wrote a detailed report.

gründlich ['gryntlıç] *Adj.*
Sie arbeitet sehr gründlich.

thorough
She works very thoroughly.

hastig ['hastıç°] *Adj.*
Ich sah sie hastig zum Bus laufen.

hasty, in a hurry
I saw her running to the bus in a hurry.

konsequent [kɔnze'kvɛnt] *Adj.*,
-er, am -esten
Die Regierung bleibt konsequent und ändert ihre Politik nicht.

consistent

The government remains consistent and isn't changing its policy.

typisch ['ty:pɪʃ] *Adj.*
Das ist ein typisches Beispiel.

typical
That's a typical example.

üblich ['y:plıç] *Adj.*
Wie üblich bin ich um 17.00 Uhr zu Hause.

usual
As usual, I'll be home at 5 p.m.

unverändert ['unfɛə*'ɛndə*t] *Adj.*
Das Wetter ist seit Tagen unverändert.

unchanged, the same
The weather has been the same for days.

17.2 Grad, Vergleich | 1-2000
17.2 Degree, Comparison

allgemein ['algə'maın] *Adj.*
Das ist ein allgemeines Verbot.

general
That is a general prohibition.

als [als] *Konj.*
Seine Leistungen waren dieses Jahr besser als im letzten.

than
His accomplishments were better this year than last.

anders [ˈandəˀs] *Adv.*
So geht das nicht, das muss man anders machen.

different(ly)
That won't work, you have to do that differently.

äußerst [ˈɔisəˀst] *Adv.*
Der Preis ist äußerst günstig.

extremely
The price is extremely good.

bedeutend [bəˈdɔit(ə)nt] *Adj.*
Das war damals eine bedeutende Erfindung.
Die Arbeit dauerte bedeutend länger als geplant.

significant
That was at the time a significant invention.
The work took significantly longer than was planned.

beinah(e) [ˈbaina:(ə)] *Adv.*
Beinahe hätte ich den Termin vergessen.

almost
I almost forgot the appointment.

besonder- [bəˈzɔndər-] *Adj., keine Komp.*
Das ist ein ganz besonderes Essen.

special

That is a very special meal.

besonders [bəˈzɔndəˀs] *Adv.*
Dieser Auftrag muss besonders schnell erledigt werden.

especially
This assignment has to be taken care of especially fast.

dringend [ˈdriŋənt] *Adj.*
Ich habe eine dringende Bitte an dich. Leih mir 10,- Euro.

urgent
I have an urgent request. Lend me 10 euros.

ebenfalls [ˈe:b(ə)nfals] *Adv.*
Hast du das ebenfalls erst heute erfahren?

also
Did you also hear about that only today?

ebenso [ˈe:b(ə)nzo:] *Adv.*
Sie kann ebenso gut Englisch sprechen wie ich.

as well as
She can speak English just as well as I do.

erheblich [ɛəˀˈhe:pliç] *Adj.*
Die Stahlpreise sind erheblich gestiegen.

considerable
The prices of steel have risen considerably.

genauso [gəˈnauzo:] *Adv.*
Ich habe es genauso gemacht, wie du es mir erklärt hast.

exactly
I did it exactly as you explained it to me.

gerade [gəˈra:də] *Adv.*
Gerade dieser Punkt ist wichtig.

Er ist gerade weggegangen.

exactly, just
It is exactly this point that is important.
He just left.

hauptsächlich ['hauptzɛçliç]
Adj., keine Komp.
Hauptsächlich die Öltemperatur
muss kontrolliert werden.

main, primary

Primarily, the temperature of the
oil has to be checked.

heftig ['hɛftiçº] *Adj.*
Er hat heftig geschimpft.

violent, energetic
He cursed violently.

insbesondere [insbə'zɔndərə]
Adv.
Der Mantel gefällt mir, insbeson-
dere die Farbe.

especially

I like the coat, expecially the
color.

recht [rɛçt] *Adv.*
Ihr Schulzeugnis ist recht gut.

really, quite
Her report card is quite good.

sehr [ze:ə*] *Adv.*
Sie war sehr freundlich zu mir.

very
She was very friendly to me.

total [to'ta:l] *Adj., keine Komp.*
Die Stadt wurde im Krieg total
zerstört.

total, complete
The city was completely destroyed in the war.

unterschiedlich ['untə*ʃi:tliç] *Adj.*
Die beiden Schwestern haben
sehr unterschiedliche Meinungen.

different
The two sisters have very different opinions.

Vergleich [fɛə*'glaiç] *m, -s, -e*
Im Vergleich zu früher leben die
Menschen heute länger.

comparison *n*
In comparison to earlier times,
people today live longer.

vergleichen [fɛə*'glaiç(ə)n] *V/t.,*
verglich, hat verglichen
Er hat die verschiedenen Ange-
bote genau verglichen.

compare *v*

He carefully compared the various offers.

verschieden [fɛə*'ʃi:d(ə)n] *Adj.*
Die beiden Schwestern sehen
sehr verschieden aus.

different
The two sisters look very different.

vollkommen [fɔl'kɔmən] *Adj.*
Er ist vollkommen gesund.

complete
He is completely healthy.

vollständig ['fɔlʃtɛndiçº] *Adj.*
Er ist vollständig betrunken.

complete
He is completely drunk.

völlig ['fœliçº] *Adj., keine Komp.*
Dein Rat war völlig richtig.

complete
Your advice was completely right.

vor allem [foːəˈʔaləm]

Wir haben vor allem über Politik diskutiert.

first and foremost, primarily, most (of all)
We discussed mostly politics.

wenig [ˈveːnɪçº] *Adj.*
Ich habe wenig Lust zu tanzen.

very little, not much
I have very little desire to dance.

wie [viː] *Adv.*
Wie konnte das passieren?
Seine Füße waren kalt wie Eis.
Es war so, wie ich es vermutete.

how, as
How could that happen?
His feet were as cold as ice.
Things were as I imagined.

ziemlich [ˈtsiːmlɪç] *Adv.*
Er hat ziemlich lange Haare.

rather
He has rather long hair.

zu [tsuː] *Adv.*
Das dauert viel zu lange.

too
That's taking much too long.

zumindest [tsuˈmɪndəst] *Adv.*
Du hättest mich zumindest fragen können.

at least
You could have at least asked me.

2001-4000

absolut [apzoˈluːt] *Adj., keine Komp.*
Das ist das absolut beste Gerät.

Er will das Gerät absolut kaufen.

absolutely, definitely

That is absolutely the best appliance.
He will definitely buy the machine.

ähnlich [ˈɛːnlɪç] *Adj.*
Wir haben ähnliche Interessen.

similar
We have similar interests.

allermeist [aləˈmaist] *Adj., keine Komp.*
Der jüngste Kandidat bekam die allermeisten Stimmen.

the most, by far the most

The youngest candidate got by far the most votes.

Ausmaß [ˈausmaːs] *n, -es, -e*
Das Ausmaß der Wirtschaftskrise wird immer größer.

extent *n*
The extent of the economic crisis is becoming wider and wider.

außerordentlich
['ausə*'ɔrd(ə)ntliç] *Adj.*
Das war eine außerordentliche Leistung.
Über das Geschenk hat sie sich außerordentlich gefreut.

extraordinary, exceptional

That was an extraordinary achievement.
She was exceptionally pleased with the gift.

einigermaßen ['ainigə*'ma:-s(ə)n] *Adv.*
Mit dem Ergebnis war man einigermaßen zufrieden.

somewhat, to a certain extent

They were somewhat satisfied with the result.

relativ ['relati:f] *Adj., keine Komp.*
Er hat relativ viel Glück gehabt.

relatively
He had relatively a lot of luck.

überwiegend [y:bə*'vi:g(ə)nt] *Adj., keine Komp.*
In dem Betrieb arbeiten überwiegend Frauen.

mostly, predominately

Mostly women work in the business.

verhältnismäßig [fɛə*'hɛltnismɛ:siç°] *Adv.*
Es gab verhältnismäßig wenig Ärger.

relative, comparative

There was relatively little annoyance.

vorwiegend ['fo:ə*'vi:g(ə)nt] *Adj., keine Komp.*
Am Wochenende ist er vorwiegend bei seinen Eltern.

predominantly, mainly

On the weekend he is mainly at his parents' house.

weitgehend ['vaitge:ənt] *Adj.*
Wir sind uns weitgehend einig.

to a large extent
We agree to a large extent.

zumeist [tsu'maist] *Adv.*
Ich esse zumeist in der Kantine.

mostly
Mostly I eat in the cafeteria.

18 Farben

18 Colors

blau [blau] Adj.	**blue**
braun [braun] Adj.	**brown**
Farbe ['farbə] *f, -, -n* Die Farbe finde ich zu hell.	**color, colour** *(BE) n* I find the color too bright.
gelb [gɛlp] Adj.	**yellow**
grau [grau] Adj.	**gray**
grün [gryːn] Adj.	**green**
lila ['liːla] Adj., *indekl.*	**lilac** *(the color, not the flower)*
rosa ['roːza] Adj., *indekl.*	**pink, rose**
rot [roːt] Adj., röter, am rötesten	**red**
schwarz [ʃvarts] Adj., schwärzer, am schwärzesten	**black**
weiß [vais] Adj., weißer, am wei- ßesten	**white**

19 Formen

19 Forms

1-2000

Ecke ['ɛkə] *f,* -, -n Dort an der Straßenecke müssen Sie rechts fahren.	**corner** *n* There at the street corner you have to turn right.
flach [flax] *Adj.* Das Land ist flach.	**flat** The land is flat.
Fläche ['flɛçə] *f,* -, -n Die Fläche ist 350 m² groß.	**area** The area measures 350 square meters.
Form [fɔrm] *f,* -, -en Der Hut hat eine komische Form.	**form** *n* The hat has a funny shape.
gerade [gə'raːdə] *Adj., keine Komp.* Die Bäume stehen in einer geraden Linie.	**straight** *n* The trees are growing in a straight line.
glatt [glat] *Adj.,* -er, am -esten Kann man das Blech wieder glatt machen?	**smooth, flat** Is it possible to make the metal plate smooth again?
Kreis [krais] *m,* -es, -e Wir saßen in einem Kreis.	**circle** *n* We sat in a circle.
Kugel ['kuːg(ə)l] *f,* -, -n Der Käse hat die Form einer Kugel.	**ball** *n* This cheese is in the shape of a ball.
Linie ['liːnjə] *f,* -, -en Diese Linie ist die Grenze.	**line** *n* This line is the border.
niedrig ['niːdrɪç] *Adj.* Die Zimmer sind niedrig.	**low** The rooms have low ceilings.
rund [runt] *Adj.,* -er, am -esten Der Platz ist fast rund.	**round** The space is nearly round.
scharf [ʃarf] *Adj.,* schärfer, am schärfsten Vorsicht, der Kasten hat scharfe Ecken!	**sharp** Be careful! The box has sharp corners.

schmal [ʃmaːl] *Adj., (Komp. auch* schmäler, am schmälsten) Die Treppe ist schmal.

narrow
The stairway is narrow.

spitz [ʃpits] *Adj.,* -er, am -esten
Er hat eine spitze Nase.

pointed
He has a pointed nose.

steil [ʃtail] *Adj.*
Der Weg geht steil nach oben.

steep
The path climbs steeply.

stumpf [ʃtumpf] *Adj.*
Das Messer ist stumpf.

dull, blunt
The knife is dull.

2001-4000

Dicke ['dikə] *f,* -, -n
Die Dicke der Bretter ist verschieden.

thickness *n*
The boards are of various thickness.

Kante ['kantə] *f,* -, -n
Das Blech hat scharfe Kanten.

edge *n*
The piece of metal has sharp edges.

Knoten ['knoːt(ə)n] *m,* -s, -
Ich kann den Knoten nicht öffnen.

knot *n*
I can't untie the knot.

Kreuz [krɔits] *n,* -es, -e
Das Kreuz ist das Symbol für die Christen.

cross *n*
The cross is the Christian symbol.

Quadrat [kvaˈdraːt] *n,* -(e)s, -e
Die Fläche des Wohnzimmers ist fast ein Quadrat.

square *n*
The living room is nearly square.

riesig ['riːziç°] *Adj.*
In der Nähe des Flughafens wird ein riesiges Hotel gebaut.

gigantic, huge, very big
A huge hotel is being built near the airport.

Strich [ʃtriç] *m,* -(e)s, -e
Die Striche an der Wand hat unser Kind gemacht.

stroke, line *n*
Our child made the lines on the wall.

winzig ['vintsiç°] *Adj.*
Wo hast du diesen winzigen Fernsehapparat gekauft?

tiny
Where did you buy that tiny television?

20 Ursache und Wirkung | 1-2000

20 Cause and Effect

abhängig ['aphɛniç°] *Adj.*
Der Start der Rakete ist vom Wetter abhängig.

dependent
The missile launch is dependent on the weather.

Anlass ['anlas] *m*, -es, Anlässe
Was war der Anlass eures Streits?

cause *n*
What was the cause of your dispute?

Bedingung [bə'diŋuŋ] *f*, -, -en
Die Bedingungen für den Erfolg sind Ruhe und Geduld.

condition *n*
The conditions for success are calm and patience.

entstehen [ɛnt'ʃte:(ə)n] *V/i.*, entstand, ist entstanden
Wodurch ist der Schaden entstanden?

originate, arise, cause *v*
What caused that damage?

entwickeln [ɛnt'vik(ə)ln] *V/t., refl.*
Die Maschine wurde ganz neu entwickelt.
Die Pflanzen haben sich gut entwickelt.

develop, produce *v*
The machine was newly developed.
The plants developed well.

Entwicklung [ɛnt'vikluŋ] *f*, -, -en
Keiner weiß, wohin die politische Entwicklung geht.

development *n*
No one knows where the political development is going.

Ergebnis [ɛə*'ge:pnis] *n*, -ses, -se
Das Ergebnis der Wahlen ist noch nicht bekannt.

result *n*
The election result is still not known.

Folge ['fɔlgə] *f*, -, -n
Das Unglück wird Folgen haben.

consequence *n*
The accident will have consequences.

Grund [grunt] *m*, -(e)s, Gründe
Es gibt keinen Grund, sich darüber aufzuregen.

reason *n*
There's no reason to get excited about it.

Quelle [ˈkvɛlə] *f, -, -n*
Was ist die Quelle deiner Informationen?

source *n*
What's the source of your information?

Ursache [ˈuːɐ̯zaxə] *f, -, -n*
Die Ursache des Fehlers wurde gefunden.

cause *n*
The cause of the mistake was found.

Voraussetzung
[foˈrauszɛtsung] *f, -, -en*
Trockenes Wetter ist Voraussetzung für die Arbeiten.

prerequisite, qualification *n*

Dry weather is a prerequisite for the work.

warum [vaˈrum] *Adv.*
Warum ist das passiert?

why
Why did that happen?

wegen [ˈveːg(ə)n] *Präp. (+ Gen.)*
Wegen des starken Windes wurde das Feuer immer größer.

because of, on account of
The fire got bigger and bigger because of the strong wind.

Wirkung [ˈvirkuŋ] *f, -, -en*
Die Tabletten haben eine starke Wirkung.

effect *n*
The tablets have a strong effect.

Zusammenhang [tsuˈzamənhaŋ] *m, -s, Zusammenhänge*
Zwischen den beiden Ereignissen besteht ein Zusammenhang.

connection, context *n*

There's a connection between the two events.

Zweck [tsvɛk] *m, -(e)s, -e*
Welchen Zweck hat Ihre Frage?

purpose *n*
What's the purpose of your question?

2001-4000

abhängen [ˈaphɛŋən] *V/i., +Präp.*
(von), hing ab, hat abgehangen
Der Erfolg hängt von einer guten Organisation ab.

depend on *v*

Success depends on good organization.

anlässlich [ˈanlɛsliç] *Präp. (+ Gen.)*
Anlässlich der neuen Situation müssen wir noch einmal über die Sache reden.

because of, on the occasion of
We have to talk about it again because of the new situation.

Ausweitung [ˈausvaituŋ] *f, -, -en*
Die Länder drohten mit einer Ausweitung des Krieges.

expansion *n*
The countries are threatening an expansion of the war.

Auswirkung [ˈausvirkuŋ] *f, -, -en*
Die höheren Ölpreise werden wirtschaftliche Auswirkungen haben.

effect, consequence *n*
The higher oil prices will have an effect on the economy.

---

bedingen [bəˈdiŋən] *V/t.*, bedingte, hat bedingt
Die langen Lieferzeiten sind durch Streiks bedingt.

require, cause *v*
The long delivery time is caused by the strikes.

---

beruhen [bəˈruːən] *V/i.*, + *Präp.* (auf)
Sein Rat beruht auf langer Erfahrung.

be founded, based on *v*
His advice is founded on long experience.

---

dank [daŋk] *Präp. (+ Gen.)*
Dank ihrer Hilfe haben wir es geschafft.

thanks to
Thanks to your help we managed to do it.

---

ergeben [ɛəˈgeːb(ə)n] *V/t., refl.,* + *Präp.* (aus), ergab, hat ergeben
Die Untersuchung ergab, dass er schuldig ist.
Aus der Untersuchung ergab sich, dass er schuldig ist.

result in *v*

The investigation resulted in proving his guilt.
The investigation resulted in proving that he is guilty.

Faktor [ˈfaktɔr] *m, -s, -en*
Für diese Entwicklung sind mehrere Faktoren verantwortlich.

factor *n*
Several factors are responsible for this development.

Funktion [fuŋkˈtsjoːn] *f, -, -en*
Was ist die Funktion dieses Schalters?

function *n*
What is the function of this switch?

---

führen [ˈfyːrən] *V/i.,* + *Präp.* (zu), führte, hat geführt
Ein technischer Fehler führte zu dem Unfall.

lead to *v*

A technical error led to the accident.

Grundlage [ˈgruntlaːgə] *f, -, -en*
Für diesen Verdacht gibt es keine Grundlage.

foundation *n*
There's no foundation for this suspicion.

Herkunft [ˈheːəˈkunft] *f, -, kein Pl.*
Die Ware ist spanischer Herkunft.

origin *n*
The product is of Spanish origin.

Konsequenz [kɔnzeˈkvɛnts] *f, -, -en*
Der Fehler hatte schlimme Konsequenzen.

consequence *n*

The error had bad consequences.

Prinzip [prin'tsi:p] *n*, -s, Prinzipien
Die Bremsen funktionieren nach
einem neuen Prinzip.

principle *n*
The brakes work according to a
new principle.

Reaktion [reak'tsjo:n] *f*, -, -en
Die schnelle Reaktion der Fahrerin verhinderte einen Unfall.

reaction *n*
The driver's quick reaction pre-
vented an accident.

sofern [zo'fɛrn] *Konj.*
Sofern es keine besonderen Probleme gibt, ist der Wagen morgen
fertig.

as long as, provided (that)
As long as there are no special
problems, the car will be ready
tomorrow.

Ursprung ['u:ə*ʃpruŋ] *m*, -s, Ursprünge
Die Ursprünge dieser alten Kultur
sind unbekannt.

origin *n*

The origins of this old culture are
unknown.

verdanken [fɛə*'daŋk(ə)n] *V/t.*,
verdankte, hat verdankt
Das ist dem Zufall zu verdanken.

**be because of, be a result of,
result from**
That is a result of chance.

verursachen [fɛə*'u:ə*zax(ə)n]
V/t., verursachte, hat verursacht
Das Hochwasser verursachte ei-
ne Katastrophe.

cause *v*

The flood caused a catastrophe.

vorkommen ['fo:ə*kɔmən] *V/i.*,
kam vor, ist vorgekommen
Dieser Fehler darf nicht wieder
vorkommen.

occur *v*

This mistake may not happen
again.

wirksam ['virkza:m] *Adj.*
Die neuen Bestimmungen sind ab
1. Januar wirksam.

effective *n*
The new regulations are effective
as of January first.

Wirksamkeit ['virkza:mkait] *f*, -,
kein Pl.
Ich zweifle an der Wirksamkeit
des Medikaments.

effectiveness *n*

I doubt the effectiveness of the
medicine.

21 Zustand und Veränderung | 1-2000

21 Condition and Change

Ablauf ['aplauf] *m, -(e)s, Abläufe*

course of events, way of proceeding *n*

Es gab mehrere Vorschläge für den Ablauf des Programms.

There were several suggestions for the course of the program.

---

allmählich [al'mɛːliç] *Adj., keine Komp.*

gradual

Er beruhigte sich allmählich.

He gradually calmed down.

---

fertig ['fɛrtiçº] *Adj., keine Komp.*

ready, finished

Ist das Essen fertig?

Is dinner ready?

---

schmelzen ['ʃmɛlts(ə)n] *V/t., i.,* schmolz, hat (ist) geschmolzen

melt *v*

Das Metall hat man geschmolzen.

The metal was melted.

Veränderung [fɛəˈ*ɛndəruŋ] *f, -, -en*

change *n*

Jeder bemerkte die Veränderung ihres Verhaltens.

Everyone noticed the change in her behavior/behaviour (BE).

Wechsel ['vɛks(ə)l] *m, -s, kein Pl.*

change *n*

Es gab einen Wechsel in der Leitung des Unternehmens.

There was a change in company management.

---

zu sein ['tsuː zain]

be closed *v*

Der Kühlschrank ist nicht zu.

The refrigerator isn't closed.

Zustand ['tsuːʃtant] *m, -(e)s, Zustände*

condition *n*

Dieser Zustand muss verändert werden.

This condition will have to be changed.

2001-4000

ansteigen ['anʃtaig(ə)n] *V/i.,* stieg an, ist angestiegen

go up *v*

Die Temperatur steigt weiter an.

The temperature keeps going up.

Anzeichen ['antsaiç(ə)n] *n, -s, -*

sign *n*

Es gibt Anzeichen, dass sich die Situation verbessert.

There are signs that the situation is getting better.

ausbreiten [ˈausbrait(ə)n] *V/refl.,*
breitete aus, hat ausgebreitet
Die Krise breitet sich aus.

spread *v*

The crisis is spreading.

Ausgangspunkt
[ˈausgaŋspuŋkt] *m,* -(e)s, -e
Was war eigentlich der Ausgangspunkt unseres Gesprächs?

starting point *n*

What was really the starting point
of our discussion?

erweitern [ɛə*ˈvaitə*n] *V/t.,* er-
weiterte, hat erweitert
Die Firma hat ihr Produktpro-
gramm erweitert.

enlarge *v*

The company has enlarged its
product line.

Erweiterung [ɛə*ˈvaitəruŋ] *f,* -, -en
Man plant eine Erweiterung des
Stadtparkes.

enlargement, expansion *n*
An expansion of the city park is
being planned.

Gleichgewicht [ˈglaiçgəviçt] *n,*
-(e)s, *kein Pl.*
Bergsteiger brauchen ein gutes
Gefühl für das Gleichgewicht.

balance *n*

Mountain climbers need a good
sense of balance.

Phase [ˈfaːzə] *f,* -, -n
Die Entwicklung ist in einer
schwierigen Phase.

phase *n*
The development is in a difficult
phase.

Rückgang [ˈrykgaŋ] *m,* -(e)s,
Rückgänge
Der Rückgang der Verkaufszah-
len beunruhigt die Geschäftsleitung.

retreat, fall *n*

The business leaders are worried
about the fall in sales.

steigen [ˈʃtaig(ə)n] *V/i.,* stieg, ist
gestiegen
Die Flut steigt nicht mehr.

rise, go up *v*

The water isn't rising any more.

Verlauf [fɛə*ˈlauf] *m,* -(e)s, Ver-
läufe
Ich bin mit dem Verlauf der Verhandlung zufrieden.

development, course *n*

I'm satisfied with the course of the
negotiations.

verlaufen [fɛə*ˈlauf(ə)n] *V/i.,* ver-
lief, ist verlaufen
Die Krankheit ist normal verlaufen.

proceed, run *v*

The disease ran its course nor-
mally.

Vorgang [ˈfoːə*gaŋ] *m,* -(e)s, Vor-
gänge
Man hat mir von dem Vorgang
berichtet.

process, course of events *n*

I was informed of the course of
events.

22 Pronomen
22 Pronouns

22.1 Personalpronomen | 1-2000
22.1 Personal Pronouns

ich [iç] *1. P. Sg. Nom.* Ich verstehe das nicht.	**I** I don't understand that.
mir [miːɐ*] *1. P. Sg. Dat.* Gib mir bitte den Zucker!	**me** Please pass me the sugar!
mich [miç] *1. P. Sg. Akk.* Hast du mich gestern nicht gesehen?	**me** Didn't you see me yesterday?
du [duː] *2. P. Sg. Nom.* Was bist du von Beruf?	**you** *(informal, sing.)* What do you do for a living?
dir [diːɐ*] *2. P. Sg. Dat.* Kann ich dir etwas zeigen?	**you, to you** Can I show you something?
dich [diç] *2. P. Sg. Akk.* Ich liebe dich.	**you** I love you.
Sie [ziː] *2. P. Sg. Nom.* Frau Birner, haben Sie heute Abend Zeit?	**you** Ms. Birner, are you busy tonight?
Ihnen ['iːnən] *2. P. Sg. Dat.* Ich soll Ihnen diesen Brief geben, Frau Schulz.	**you, to you** *(formal, sing.)* I'm supposed to give you this letter, Ms. Schulz.
Sie *2. P. Sg. Akk.* Ja, ich rufe Sie morgen an, Herr Meier.	**you** *(formal, sing.)* Yes, I'll call you tomorrow, Mr. Meier.
er [eːɐ*] *3. P. Sg. Nom. m* Wann ist er gegangen? Der Wein schmeckt gut, er ist aus Norditalien.	**he, it** When did he leave? The wine is good; it's from northern Italy.
ihm [iːm] *3. P. Sg. Dat. m* Ich habe mit ihm gesprochen. Wenn der Computer dich etwas fragt, musst du ihm ,ja' oder ,nein' antworten.	**to him, to it** I spoke with him. When the computer asks you a question, you have to give it the answer "yes" or "no".

ihn [iːn] *3. P. Sg. Akk. m*
Der neue Kollege ist komisch, ich mag ihn nicht.
Den neuen Schrank, wie findest du ihn?

him, it
The new colleague is odd; I don't like him.
What do you think of this new cabinet?

---

sie [ziː] *3. P. Sg. Nom. f*
Petra ist in Köln. Dort studiert sie Physik.
Ich suche die Taschenlampe. Weißt du, wo sie ist?

she, it
Petra is in Cologne. She is studying physics there.
I'm looking for the flashlight. Do you know where it is?

---

ihr [iːə*] *3. P. Sg. Dat. f*
Ich habe ihr das versprochen.
Die Puppe ist schön, man kann ihr verschiedene Kleider anziehen.

to her, to it
I promised her that.
The doll is beautiful; you can dress it in different outfits.

---

sie [ziː] *3. P. Sg. Akk. f*
Ich habe sie zum Essen eingeladen.
Die Kaffeemaschine funktioniert nicht, hast du sie kaputtgemacht?

her, it
I invited her to dinner.
The coffee machine doesn't work; did you break it?

---

es [ɛs] *3. P. Sg. Nom. n*
Das Kind weint, weil es Bauchschmerzen hat.
Ich kenne das Haus, es liegt am Park.

it
The child is crying because he/she has a stomach ache.
I know that house; it's by the park.

---

ihm [iːm] *3. P. Sg. Dat. n*
Das Kind spielt mit der Schere. Du musst sie ihm wegnehmen.

Das neue Automodell gefällt mir ganz gut, aber es fehlt ihm ein starker Motor.

to him, to it, from him, from it
The child is playing with the shears. You'll have to take them away from him/her.
I like the new car model very much, but it needs a stronger motor.

---

es [ɛs] *3. P. Sg. Akk. n*
○ Wo ist das Kind?
□ Ich habe es im Garten gesehen.
Ich habe euch letzte Woche ein Paket geschickt, habt ihr es bekommen?

it
○ Where is the child?
□ I saw him/her outside in the yard.
I sent you a package last week. Did you get it?

---

wir [viːə*] *1. P. Pl. Nom.*
Wir haben uns noch nicht entschieden.

we
We haven't decided yet.

uns [uns] *1. P. Pl. Dat.*
Bitte sage uns früh genug Bescheid.

us, to us
Please let us know soon enough.

---

uns *1. P. Pl. Akk.*
Sie wird uns besuchen.

us
She will visit us.

---

ihr [iːə*] *2. P. Pl. Nom.*
Habt ihr Lust spazieren zu gehen?

you *(informal, plural)*
Would you like to go for a walk?

---

euch [ɔiç] *2. P. Pl. Dat.*
Wer hat euch das gesagt?

you, to you *(informal, plural)*
Who told you that?

---

euch *2. P. Pl. Akk.*
Ich möchte euch nicht stören.

you
I wouldn't want to disturb you.

Sie [ziː] *2. P. Pl. Nom.*
Kommen Sie bitte, meine Damen, hier ist die Modenschau!
Würden Sie bitte die Türen schließen, meine Herren!

you *(formal, plural)*
Would you please come this way, ladies; here's the fashion show.
Gentlemen, would you please close the doors!

Ihnen ['iːnən] *2. P. Pl. Dat.*
Sehr geehrte Damen! Ich danke Ihnen für den freundlichen Brief.

you, to you
Dear Ladies: I thank you for your friendly letter.

Sie [ziː] *2. P. Pl. Akk.*
Meine Herren, ich rufe Sie morgen an.

you *(formal, plural)*
Gentlemen, Im going to call you tomorrow.

---

sie *3. P. Pl. Nom*
Für dieses Ziel haben sie, die Franzosen und ihre Verbündeten, lange gekämpft.
Hier sind die Kartoffeln, sie müssen noch gekocht werden.

they
They, the French and their allies, have fought for a long time for this goal.
Here are the potatoes; they still have to be cooked.

---

ihnen ['iːnən] *3. P. Pl. Dat.*
○ Hast du den Pflanzen schon Wasser gegeben?
□ Nein, ich habe ihnen noch keins gegeben.

them, to them
○ Have you watered the plants yet?
□ No, I haven't watered them yet.

---

sie [ziː] *3. P. Pl. Akk.*
Warum grüßen die Nachbarn nicht mehr? Hast du sie geärgert?

Die Bücher kannst du haben, ich schenke sie dir.

them
Why don't the neighbors even say hello to us anymore? Did you make them angry?
You may have the books; I'm giving them to you.

22.2 Reflexivpronomen

22.2 Reflexive Pronouns

mir [miːɐ*] *1. P. Sg. Dat.*
Ich kann mir selbst helfen.

to me, to myself
I can help myself.

mich [miç] *1. P. Sg. Akk.*
Ich muss mich noch waschen.

me, myself
I still have to wash myself.

dir [diːɐ*] *2. P. Sg. Dat.*
Willst du dir wirklich selbst die Haare schneiden?

to you, to yourself
Do you really want to cut your own hair?

dich [diç] *2. P. Sg. Akk.*
Du musst dich auf einen Schock gefasst machen.

you, yourself
You'd better prepare yourself for a shock.

sich [ziç] *3. P. Sg. Dat.*
Er nimmt sich selbst immer das beste Stück.

for him, herself
He always takes the best piece for himself.

sich [ziç] *2. P., Sg. u. Pl., Akk.*
Haben Sie sich schon angemeldet?
Bitte bedienen Sie sich selbst!

yourself
Have you registered yet?

Please help yourself!

sich *3. P. Sg. Akk.*
Sie hat sich selbst bedient.

him, herself
She helped herself.

uns [uns] *1. P. Pl. Dat.*
Wir haben uns einen Kaffee gemacht.

ourselves, for ourselves
We made ourselves some coffee.

uns *1. P. Pl. Akk.*
Wir haben uns sehr über die Arbeitsbedingungen aufgeregt.

us, ourselves
We really worked ourselves up over the work conditions.

euch [ɔiç] *2. P. Pl. Dat.*
Wollt ihr euch eine Wohnung kaufen?

yourselves, for yourselves
Do you want to buy an apartment for yourselves?

euch *2. P. Pl. Akk.*
Ihr könnt euch hierhin setzen.

you, yourselves
You can sit down here.

22.3 Possessivpronomen | 1-2000

22.3 Possessive Adjectives

mein [main] *1. P. Sg.*
Das ist mein Mantel!

my
That is my coat!

dein [dain] *2. P. Sg.*
Sind das deine Zigaretten?

your
Are those your cigarettes?

Ihr [iːə*] *2. P., Sg. u. Pl.*
Ihr Telegramm habe ich noch nicht bekommen.

your *(formal, sing.)*
I have not yet received your telegram(me).

sein [zain] *3. P. Sg. n. + m.*
Ich habe an seine Tür geklopft.

his
I knocked at his door.

ihr [iːə*] *3. P., Sg. f. und Pl. m/f*
Sie hat mir ihre Skier geliehen.
Bernd und Klaus haben die Reisegruppe in ihren zwei Autos mitgenommen.

her, their
She leant me her skis.
Bernd and Klaus took the travel group in their two cars.

unser ['unzə*] *1. P. Pl.*
Wir haben unseren Arzt gefragt.

our
We asked our doctor.

euer ['ɔiə*] *2. P. Pl.*
Wer passt auf eure Kinder auf?

your
Who's watching your children?

22.4 Demonstrativpronomen | 1-2000

22.4 Demonstrative Adjectives

dieser ['diːzə*] (diese, dieses)
Dieses Kleid habe ich selbst genäht.

this
I made this dress myself.

jener ['jeːnə*] (jene, jenes)
Wer hat jenes Bild gemalt?

that
Who painted that picture?

selber ['zɛlbə*] (selbst)
Die Garage haben wir selber (selbst) gebaut.

-self
We built the garage ourselves.

derjenige ['deːə*jeːnigə] diejeni-
ge, dasjenige
Diejenigen, die für den Antrag
sind, sollen den Arm heben.

whoever

Whoever is for the contract
should raise his/her hand.

derselbe [deːə*'zɛlbə] dieselbe,
dasselbe
Ich stehe immer um dieselbe Zeit
auf.

the same

I always get up at the same time.

22.5 Frage-/Relativpronomen · 1-2000

22.5 Question Pronouns, Relative Pronouns

der, die, das [deːə*, diː, das] *For-
men wie Artikel, aber Gen.:* des-
sen, deren
Das Käsegeschäft, in dem du ein-
kaufst, ist wirklich gut.

which/who/whom/that

The cheese store where (in which)
you shop is really good.

was [vas]
Was hat sie dir erzählt?
Das, was sie dir erzählt hat,
stimmt.

what
What did she tell you?
What she told you is right.

was für ['vas fyːə*]
Aus was für einem Material ist die
Decke?

what kind of
What kind of material is the blanket made of?

welcher ['vɛlçə*] welche, welches
○ Welchen Wein sollen wir
nehmen?
□ Nimm denselben, den wir letzte Woche hatten.

which
○ Which wine should we take?
□ Take the same one we took
last week.

wer [veːəˀ], wessen, wem, wen
Ich weiß nicht, wer dafür verant-
wortlich ist.
Wessen Mantel ist das?
Wem gehört der Mantel?
Wen hast du getroffen?

who, whom, whose
I don't know who is responsible
for that.
Whose coat is that?
To whom does the coat belong?
Whom did you meet?

22.6 Indefinitpronomen | 1-2000

22.6 Indefinite Pronouns

alle [ˈalə] alles
Sie wünschte allen ein gutes neues Jahr.

everyone, all
She wished everyone a Happy
New Year.

einer [ˈainəˀ] eine, eins
○ Ist noch ein Stück Kuchen da?

□ Ja, im Kühlschrank steht noch
eins.

a, an
○ Is there still a piece of cake
left?
□ Yes, there's still one in the
refrigerator.

einige [ˈainigə]
Einigen hat das Spiel nicht gefallen.

some, some people
Some people didn't like the
game.

etwas [ˈɛtvas]
Da ist etwas nicht in Ordnung.

something
Something is wrong there.

irgendein(er) [ˈirg(ə)ntain(eˀ)] -ei-
ne, -ein(e)s, -welcher, -welche,
-welches
○ Welchen Tabak rauchst du?
□ Irgendeinen, der nicht zu teuer
ist.

any, anyone

○ What tobacco do you smoke?
□ Anyone that's not too expensive.

jeder [ˈjeːdəˀ] jede, jedes
Er kennt jede Straße in der Stadt.

every, everyone
He knows every street in the city.

jemand [ˈjeːmant]
Hast du jemanden gesehen?

someone, anyone
Did you see anyone?

keiner [ˈkainəˀ] keine, keines
Ich kenne keinen der Gäste.

none
I know none of the guests.

man [man]
Man sollte es zumindest versuchen, sie kennenzulernen.

one, they, you
One should at least try to get acquainted with her.

mancher ['mançə*] manche, manches
Manche (der) Gäste sind sehr interessant, manche weniger.

some
Some of the guests are very interesting, some less.

nichts [niçts]
Er hat noch nichts gegessen.

nothing, not anything
He still has not eaten anything.

niemand ['niːmant]
Du darfst niemandem darüber etwas erzählen.

no one, not anyone, nobody
You may not tell anyone anything about it.

welcher ['vɛlçə*] welche, welches
○ Ist noch Bier da?
□ Nein, aber ich kaufe welches.

some
○ Is there any beer left?
□ No, but I'll buy some.

23 Konjunktionen | 1-2000

21 Conjunctions

aber [ˈaːbə*]
Ich habe ihn eingeladen, aber er hat keine Zeit.

but
I invited him, but he has no time.

---

als ob [als ˈɔp]
Er tat so, als ob er nicht wüsste.

as if
He acted as if he knew nothing.

---

da [daː]
Wir mussten ein Taxi nehmen, da keine Busse mehr fuhren.

since, because
We had to take a taxi because there were no more busses.

---

damit [daˈmit]
Stell die Milch in den Kühlschrank, damit sie nicht sauer wird.

so, so that
Put the milk in the refrigerator so it won't get sour.

---

dass [das]
Ich habe gehört, dass Ulrike und Thomas sich scheiden lassen.

that
I've heard that Ulrike and Thomas are getting a divorce.

---

denn [dɛn]
Ich glaube ihr nicht, denn sie hat schon öfter gelogen.

because, for
I don't believe her because she has often lied.

---

deshalb [ˈdɛshalp]
Der Kühlschrank war zu teuer, deshalb haben wir ihn nicht gekauft.

so, because of that, therefore
The refrigerator was too expensive; so we didn't buy it.

---

deswegen [ˈdɛsveːg(ə)n]
Das Auto hatte kein Benzin mehr, deswegen konnten wir nicht weiterfahren.

so, because of that, therefore
The car ran out of gasoline, we couldn't drive any further.

---

falls [fals]
Falls du einkaufen gehst, bring bitte Butter mit.

if, in case
If you go shopping, please get butter.

---

indem [inˈdeːm]
Dein Spanisch kannst du am schnellsten verbessern, indem du ein paar Wochen in Spanien lebst.

if
You can improve your Spanish most if you spend a few weeks in Spain.

inzwischen [in'tsviʃ(ə)n]
Du kannst den Tisch decken, inzwischen koche ich einen Kaffee.

in the meantime, while
You can set the table while I make some coffee.

je ... desto [je: ... 'dɛsto]
Je reifer die Birnen sind, desto besser schmecken sie.

the more ... the more
The riper the pears are, the better they taste.

jedoch [je'dɔx]
Die Wohnung ist schön, jedoch die Lage ist schlecht.

but, however
The apartment is beautiful; however, the location is not good.

ob [ɔp]
Er fragte mich, ob ich ihm die Regel erklären könnte.

if, whether
He asked me whether I could explain the rule to him.

obgleich [ɔp'glaiç]
Obgleich ich vorsichtig war, ist der Film gerissen.

although
Although I was careful, the film tore.

obwohl [ɔp'vo:l]
Obwohl er starke Schmerzen hat, nimmt er nie ein Medikament.

although
Although he has strong pain, he never takes any medicine.

oder ['o:də*]
Gehst du auch schon oder bleibst du noch?

or
Are you leaving as well, or are you staying longer?

so dass [zo'das]
Sie sprach sehr leise, so dass wir nicht alles verstehen konnten.

so, so that
She spoke very quietly, so we couldn't understand everything.

sondern ['zɔndə*n]
Sie schreibt nie mit der Hand, sondern immer mit der Schreibmaschine.

but
She never writes longhand but always types.

soweit [zo'vait]
Soweit ich informiert bin, ist er morgen wieder da.

as far as
As far as I know, he'll be back tomorrow.

sowohl ... als auch [zo'vo:l ... als aux]
Ich mag sowohl moderne als auch klassische Musik.

as well as

I like modern as well as classical music.

um so ['umzo]
Je wütender er wurde, um so röter wurde sein Gesicht.

the more ... the more
The more he got angry, the more his face got red.

um ... zu [um ... tsu]
Wir gingen in ein Café, um uns zu unterhalten.

in order to
We went to a café in order to talk.

und [unt]
Er sah einen Film, und sie las die Zeitung.

and
He watched a film, and she read the newspaper.

während ['vɛ:rənt]
Während er einen Roman las, konnte er die Welt um sich vergessen.

while
While he was reading a novel he could forget the world around him.

weil [vail]
Weil es schneller geht, fahre ich lieber mit der U-Bahn.

because
Because it goes faster, I prefer to go by subway.

wenn [vɛn]
Wenn du sie bitten würdest, würde sie dir das Auto bestimmt leihen.

if, whenever
If you would ask her, she would surely lend the car to you.

zumal [tsu'ma:l]
Ich kann dir helfen, zumal ich Urlaub habe.

because, since
I can help you since I am on holiday.

zwar ... aber ['tsva:* ... 'a:bə*]
Wir sind zwar oft verschiedener Meinung, aber wir streiten uns selten.

be sure ... but
We often have different opinions, to be sure, but we rarely fight.

24 Adverbien | 1-2000

also ['alzo]
Sie ist also 1961 geboren, dann ist sie ja jünger als ich.

thus, therefore, so
So she was born in 1961; then she must be younger than I.

außerdem ['ausə*de:m]
Er ist intelligent und außerdem auch nett.

besides, in addition, as well
He is intelligent and nice as well.

dabei ['da:bai, da'bai]
Ich habe Fleisch geschnitten, dabei habe ich mich verletzt.

while, at that time
I was cutting meat and cut myself while doing that.

dadurch ['da:durç]

Er wurde schnell operiert und dadurch gerettet.

therefore, because of that, in that way
He was operated on quickly and therefore his life was saved.

dafür [da'fy:ə*]
○ Wie findest du die Idee?
□ Ich bin dafür!

for, in favor of it
○ What do you think of the idea?
□ I'm in favor of it!

dagegen [da'ge:g(ə)n]
Die Ursache der Krankheit ist zwar bekannt, aber man hat noch kein Mittel dagegen gefunden.

against it
The cause of the disease is known, but no medication against it has yet been found.

daher ['da:he:ə*, da'he:ə*]

○ Aus welcher Richtung kommt der Bus?
□ Von daher.
Das Licht am Auto war die ganze Nacht an. Daher ist die Batterie jetzt leer.

from there, because of that, from that, that's why
○ What direction does the bus come from?
□ From that way.
The car light was on all night. That's why the battery is dead now.

damit ['da:mit]
Das Messer ist stumpf. Damit kann man nicht mehr schneiden.

with it
The knife is dull. You can't cut anything with it anymore.

darum ['da:rum]
Das Gesetz ist ungerecht. Darum bin ich dagegen.

therefore, that's why
The law is unfair. That's why I'm against it.

davon ['da:fɔn]
○ Weißt du, dass Bernd nach Bochum ziehen wird?
□ Nein, davon hat er mir nichts gesagt.

about it
○ Do you know Bernd is moving to Bochum?
□ No; he hasn't said anything to me about it.

nämlich ['nɛ:mlɪç]
Ich muss noch ein Geschenk kaufen, Karin hat nämlich morgen Geburtstag.

because, you see
I still have to buy a gift because Karin's birthday is tomorrow.

teils ... teils [taıls ... taıls]
Die Ausstellung war teils interessant, teils langweilig.

partly ... partly
The exhibition was partly interesting, partly boring.

trotzdem ['trɔtsde:m]

Die Straße war schlecht. Sie fuhr trotzdem sehr schnell.

in spite of that, in spite of it, anyway
The road was in poor condition. She drove fast in spite of that.

weder ... noch ['ve:də* ... nox]
Weder den Brief noch das Telegramm habe ich bekommen.

neither ... nor
I received neither the letter nor the telegram.

weshalb [vɛs'halp]
Weshalb hat er schlechte Laune?

why, for what reason
Why is he in a bad mood?

wie [vi:]
Wie ist das passiert?

how
How did that happen?

wieso [vi'zo:]
Wieso haben Sie mir das nicht gesagt?

why
Why didn't you tell me that?

zudem [tsu'de:m]

Die Hose ist hässlich und zudem passt sie nicht.
Deutsch ist interessant und zudem nützlich.

moreover, what's more, as well, in addition
These slacks aren't good looking, and, moreover, they don't fit.
German is interesting, and useful as well.

Index

Pronunciation

To indicate how a word is pronounced, the following symbols from the IPA (International Phonetic Alphabet) appear in brackets after each word.

1. General Symbols

[']	appears before the stressed syllable: spielen ['ʃpiːl(ə)n].
[:]	indicates the length of the vowel: Nase ['naːzə].
[*]	indicates vocalized or silent final r *cf. also 4.*
[°]	points to the shift between [ç]/[k] and [g].
[(ə)]	indicates optional pronunciation: Kegel ['keːg(ə)l].

2. Vowels

2.1 Monophtongs

[i]	bitten, Mitte	[œ]	können, öffnen, Körper
[iː]	Miete, Drogerie	[ə]	Anfrage, erwähnen, Bekannte
[y]	glücklich, füllen, Physik	[ə*]	weakened a-sound, as for ex-
[yː]	fühlen, prüfen, Physiker		ample "-er" in Vater, international;
[u]	kurz, Kusine		the "r" is not pronounced.
[uː]	gut, Schuh	[ɔ]	Stock, Kontrolle
[e]	konsequent, Mechanik	[a]	Kaffee, Saft, warten
[eː]	geben, Zeh, Gelee	[aː]	nachdenken, Rad, fahren
[øː]	hören, gewöhnlich	[aː*]	can either be pronounced
[o]	probieren, Notiz, wohin		[aː] or [aːə*], i.e. with a short
[oː]	Bewohner, Zoo, Hof		a-sound following the long "a":
[ɛ]	echt, ändern, Camping		klar, Wahrheit.
[ɛː]	allmählich, bestätigen		The "r" is not pronounced.

Nasals

[ɛ̃ː]	Cousin	[ã]	Pension
[õː]	Saison	[ãː]	Chance, Restaurant

2.2 Diphtong and other vowel combinations

[iːə]	siehe	[uːə]	Ruhe
[iːə*]	Bier, Passagier	[uːə*]	Uhr, ursprünglich, beurlauben
[iə*]	irgendwie	[eːə]	Ehe, gehen
	(alternative ['irg(ə)ntviː])	[eːə*]	sehr, Beschwerde
[yːə]	Mühe	[ɛə*]	erkenntlich, vergessen,
[yːə*]	Tür		Erbse *(alternative ['ɛrpsə])*
[uə*]	Vorurteil *(alternative [-urtail])*	[ɛːə]	Krähe

[ɛ:ə*]	gefährlich, Sekretär	[ɔə]	Motorrad ['mo:tɔə*ra:t]
[ø:ə]	Höhe		(alternative ['mo:tɔra:t])
[ø:ə*]	höher	[ɔi*]	heute, Bäume
[o:ə]	frohe	[a:ə]	nahe
[o:ə*]	Ohr	[ai]	reinigen, Eile
		[au]	sauber, Haus

3. Consonants

[b]	Begriff, bleiben	[n]	nein, kennen, Konzert
[d]	Dame, reden	[ŋ]	empfangen, Verabredung,
[f]	Fest, Treffen		Bank
[g]	Gast, ausbaggern	[p]	Party, lieb, verabschieden
[ʒ]	Genie, Reportage,	[r]	regnen, zurück
	Journalist	[s]	Haus, essen, Fuß, mittags
[h]	halten, abholen	[z]	singen, Rose, Überweisung,
[ç]	ich, echt, durch, nächste,		Musik
	möchte, fürchten	[ʃ]	schwer, stellen, entstehen,
[x]	achten, doch, Buch		Wunsch
[j]	ja, Junge	[t]	Tag, Mitglied, Freundschaft,
[k]	Krise, Berg, beklagt, täglich		Wand
[l]	Leben, voll, Willi	[v]	Wasser, Winter, Feuerwehr,
[m]	mit, Kamm		Vase, Verb, Villa

4. Notes on final consonants

-(e)r: A final r, including r in the syllable "er" is either vocalized or completely silent:

Bier [bi:ə*]   **Ohr** [o:ə*]   **Masseur** [ma'seə*]   **Tür** [ty:ə*]
Bär [bɛ:ə*]   **Uhr** [u:ə*]   **Gehör** [gə'høə*]   **Vater** ['fa:tə*]

-ig: The suffix -ig is represented by [-iç] in the IPA. [-iç°] indicates the the basic form is pronounced differently in final position, either [-iç] in Northern Germany or [ik] in Southern Germany, while the inflected forms [-ig-] are pronounced with the intervocalic [-g-]:

selig ['ze:liç°] = North, ['ze:lik] = South, but generally: **selige, seliger, seliges** ['z:eligə, 'ze:ligə*, 'ze:ligəs] etc.

-b, -d, -g, -s: in final position are voiceless [-p, -t, -k, -s], but are voiced before a following vowel:

Kalb [kalp]   but: **Kälber** ['kɛlbə*]
Wald [valt]   **Wälder** ['vɛldə*]
Anzug ['antsuk]   **Anzüge** ['antsy:gə]
Haus [haus]   **Häuser** ['hɔizə*]